Your future is just four parts away.

Welcome to the Becker CPA Exam Review! Congratulations on taking the first step to becoming a CPA. As the industry's leading partner in CPA Exam preparation, we know you're not just studying for an exam – you are preparing for your future. To help you get there, Becker CPA Exam Review is as close as you can get to the real thing. So let's get started.

Access Becker's CPA Exam Review course

Log in to your CPA Exam Review course anytime at **cpa.becker.com**. Watch our orientation video and download the mobile app to access your studies on the go. Your progress will automatically sync among all your devices, so you can pick up where you left off. For more on getting started, visit **becker.com/cpa-review/getting-started**.

Utilize the Becker resources

Make studying more organized with our study planner. With interactive tools to help you determine your ideal study schedule and to recommend your ideal exam-taking time, it's easy to plan your preparation so you can become Exam Day Ready℠. Here are the added benefits of Becker:

- Take advantage of unlimited practice tests, personalized by Adapt2U Technology
- Access 1-on-1 academic support from our experienced CPA instructors
- Test your knowledge with our simulated exams – the closest thing you can get to the actual CPA Exam

You're not in it alone!

For tips, stories, and advice, visit our blog at **becker.com/blog**. You can also collaborate with other Becker students studying FAR on our Facebook study group at **facebook.com/groups/BeckerFARStudyGroup/**.

application

It takes time for your CPA Exam application to be approved – so don't wait until the last minute.

Once your CPA Exam application has been processed, your Notice to Schedule will give you a limited window of time to schedule your exam.

Your state board of accountancy sets the amount of time you have, so be sure to check your state's requirements.

Once you schedule your exam, add it to the study planner so we can share tips, strategies, and more as your test date approaches.

Becker.

Join the community!

Becker.

This textbook contains information that was current at the time of printing.
Your course software will be updated on a regular basis as the content
that is tested on the CPA Exam evolves and as we improve our materials.
Note the version reference below and select your replacement textbook
at **becker.com/cpa-replacements-upgrades** to learn if a newer version
of this book is available to be ordered.

CPA Exam Review

Financial Accounting and Reporting (FAR)

For Exams Scheduled
After June 30, 2025

V 1.3

COURSE DEVELOPMENT TEAM

Timothy F. Gearty, CPA, MBA, JD, CGMA . . . . .Editor in Chief, Financial/Regulation (Tax) National Editor

Angeline S. Brown, CPA, CGMA. . . . . Sr. Director, Product Development

Michael Potenza, CPA, JD, EA . . . . Sr. Director of Instruction, Curriculum

Lauren Chin, CPA . . . . Director, Curriculum

Nancy Gauldie, CPA . . . . .Senior Manager, Curriculum

Wanda Kaminski, CPA . . . . .Senior Manager, Curriculum

Angelle Cascio, CPA, CMA, EA . . . . .Manager, Curriculum

Stephen Bergens, CPA . . . . .Manager, Curriculum

Bill Karalius, CPA. . . . . .Sr. Specialist, Curriculum

Emily Krysl, CPA . . . . .Sr. Specialist, Curriculum

Savannah Hooper, CPA . . . . .Sr. Specialist, Curriculum

Anson Miyashiro. . . . . Manager, Course Development

Tim Munson . . . . Project Manager, Course Development

Joe Antonio . . . . Manager, Course Development

Shelly McCubbins, MBA. . . . . Project Manager, Course Development

CONTRIBUTING EDITORS

Heather Baiye, CPA, MBA

Michael Brown, CPA, CMA

Kelvin Chang, CFA, AWS-CSA, CPA (inactive)

Elliott G. Chester, CPA, CMA, CFE

Courtney Chianello, CPA

Zachariah M. Chism, CPA, CFE

Stephen Cochran, CPA

Tom Cox, CPA, CMA

Michael Deldon, CPA

R. Thomas Godwin, CPA, CGMA

Liliana Hickman-Riggs, CPA, CMA, CIA, CFE, CITP, CFF, CGMA, FCPA, MS

Christopher R. Issa, CPA

Steven J. Levin, JD

Stephanie Morris, CPA, MAcc

Michelle Moshe, CPA, DipIFR

Brittany Nance, CPA

Sandra Owen, JD, MBA, CPA

Jennifer J. Rivers, CPA

Josh Rosenberg, MBA, CPA, CFA, CFP

Jonathan R. Rubin, CPA, MBA

Susan M. Tillery, CPA/PFS

Thomas N. Tillery, MA Ed, MSFS, CFP, ChFC, CLU, CRPC

Permissions

Material from *Uniform CPA Examination Selected Questions and Unofficial Answers*, 1989–2025, copyright © by American Institute of Certified Public Accountants, Inc., is reprinted and/or adapted with permission.

Any knowing solicitation or disclosure of any questions or answers included on any CPA Examination is prohibited.

Financial Accounting and Reporting (FAR)

Table of Contents

FAR 5: *Investments, Statement of Cash Flows, and Income Taxes*

FAR 6: *NFP Accounting and Governmental Accounting*

Introduction

FAR

NOTES

Financial Accounting and Reporting (FAR) Overview

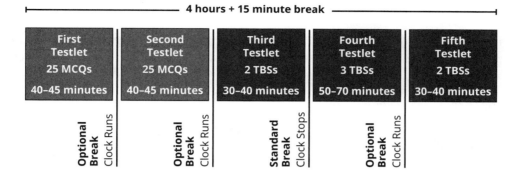

FAR Exam: Summary Blueprint

Content Area Allocation	Weight
Financial Reporting	30–40%
Select Balance Sheet Accounts	30–40%
Select Transactions	25–35%
Skill Allocation	**Weight**
Evaluation	—
Analysis	35–45%
Application	45–55%
Remembering and Understanding	5–15%

Becker's CPA Exam Review: Course Introduction

Becker Professional Education's CPA Exam Review products were developed with you, the candidate, in mind. To that end we have developed a series of tools designed to tap all of your learning and retention capabilities. The Becker lectures, comprehensive tests, and course software are designed to be fully integrated to give you the best chance of passing the CPA Exam.

Passing the CPA Exam is difficult, but the professional rewards a CPA enjoys make this a worthwhile challenge. We created our CPA Exam Review after evaluating the needs of CPA candidates and analyzing the CPA Exam over the years. Our course materials comprehensively present topics you must know to pass the examination, teaching you the most effective tactics for learning the material.

The Uniform CPA Exam: Overview

Exam Sections

The CPA Examination consists of three Core sections and three Discipline sections. You must pass all three Core sections and one of the Discipline sections to become a licensed CPA.

The three Core sections are:

Financial Accounting and Reporting (FAR)

The FAR section consists of a four-hour exam covering financial accounting and reporting for commercial entities under U.S. GAAP, not-for-profit accounting, and the basics of government accounting.

Auditing and Attestation (AUD)

The AUD section consists of a four-hour exam. This section covers all topics related to auditing, including audit reports and procedures, generally accepted auditing standards, attestation and other engagements, and government auditing.

Taxation and Regulation (REG)

The REG section consists of a four-hour exam, combining topics from business law and federal taxation, including the taxation of property transactions, individuals, and entities.

The three Discipline sections (you must pass one) are:

Business Analysis and Reporting (BAR)

The BAR section consists of a four-hour exam covering advanced financial accounting and reporting, government accounting, financial management, operations management, and managerial and cost accounting.

Information Systems and Controls (ISC)

The ISC section consists of a four-hour exam and includes topics related to information systems and data management, security, confidentiality and privacy, and system and organization controls (SOC) engagements.

Tax Compliance and Planning (TCP)

The TCP section consists of a four-hour exam and includes topics related to personal financial planning, entity tax compliance, entity tax planning, and property transactions.

Question Formats

The chart below illustrates the question format breakdown by exam section.

Section	Multiple-Choice Questions (MCQs) Percentage	Multiple-Choice Questions (MCQs) Number	Task-Based Simulations (TBSs) Percentage	Task-Based Simulations (TBSs) Number
FAR	50%	50	50%	7
AUD	50%	78	50%	7
REG	50%	72	50%	8
BAR	50%	50	50%	7
ISC	60%	82	40%	6
TCP	50%	68	50%	7

Each exam will contain testlets. A testlet is either a series of multiple-choice questions or a set of task-based simulations. For example, the Financial examination will contain five testlets. The first two testlets will be multiple-choice questions and the third, fourth, and fifth testlets will contain task-based simulations. Each testlet must be finished and submitted before continuing to the next testlet. Candidates cannot go back to view a previously completed testlet or go forward to view a subsequent testlet before closing and submitting the earlier testlet. Our simulated exams contain these types of restrictions so that you can familiarize yourself with the functionality of the CPA Exam.

Exam Schedule

Candidates can schedule an exam date directly with Prometric (www.prometric.com/cpa) after receiving a notice to schedule.

Eligibility and Application Requirements

Each state sets its own rules of eligibility for the examination. Please visit www.becker.com/cpa-review/requirements as soon as possible to determine your eligibility to sit for the exam.

Application Deadlines

With the computer-based exam format, set application deadlines generally do not exist. You should apply as early as possible to ensure that you are able to schedule your desired exam dates. Each state has different application requirements and procedures, so be sure to gain a thorough understanding of the application process for your state.

Grading System

You must pass all three Core exams and one of the Discipline exams to become a CPA. You must score 75 or better on a part to receive a passing grade.

Becker Customer and Academic Support

You can access Becker's Customer and Academic Support from within the course software by clicking Help Center at the top at:

cpa.becker.com

You can also access customer service and technical support by calling 1-877-CPA-EXAM (outside the U.S. +1-630-472-2213).

FAR
1

Financial Reporting

Module

NOTES

Balance Sheet, Income Statement, and Comprehensive Income

1 Balance Sheet

Under U.S. GAAP, general purpose financial reporting is defined as a full set of financial statements and notes to the financial statements. A full set of financial statements typically includes:

- Statement of financial position (balance sheet)
- Statement of earnings (income statement)
- Statement of comprehensive income
- Statement of cash flows
- Statement of owners' equity

Entities may present a classified balance sheet that distinguishes current and non-current assets and liabilities. When appropriate, a balance sheet presentation based on liquidity is also permissible. The following is an example of a classified balance sheet.

Company Name
Balance Sheet
As of December 31, Year 1

Assets	*Liabilities and Stockholders' Equity*
Current assets	**Current liabilities**
Cash and cash equivalents	Current portion of long-term debt
Trading securities, at fair value	Accounts payable
Accounts receivable, net of allowance	Notes payable
Notes receivable	Interest payable
Inventory	Salaries payable
Prepaid expenses	Unearned revenue
Investments	**Long-term liabilities**
Available-for-sale securities, at fair value	Bonds payable
Held-to-maturity securities	Deferred income tax liability
Investments in affiliates	Pension and other postretirement benefit liabilities

(continued)

(continued)

<table>
<tr><td colspan="2">Assets</td><td>Liabilities and Stockholders' Equity</td></tr>
</table>

Property, plant, and equipment
  Land
  Building
  Equipment
  Less: accumulated depreciation

Intangible assets
  Goodwill
  Patents, net of amortization

Other assets
  Pension and other postretirement
    benefit assets
  Deferred income tax asset

Total assets

Total liabilities

Stockholders' equity
  Capital stock
    Preferred stock, $10 par, 8% cumulative
      and nonparticipating, 10,000 shares
      authorized, 5,000 shares issued and
      outstanding
    Common stock, $0.01 par, 600,000,000
      shares authorized, 57,598,000
      shares issued and 57,178,485 shares
      outstanding
  Paid-in capital in excess of par
  Retained earnings
  Accumulated other comprehensive income
  (Treasury stock at cost) (419,515 shares)

Total stockholders' equity

Total liabilities and stockholders' equity

2 Uses of the Income Statement and Terminology

The purpose of the income statement is to provide information about the uses of funds in the income process (i.e., expenses), the uses of funds that will never be used to earn income (i.e., losses), the sources of funds created by those expenses (i.e., revenues), and the sources of funds not associated with the earnings process (i.e., gains).

2.1 Uses of the Income Statement

The income statement is useful in determining profitability, value for investment purposes, and creditworthiness. The income statement is also useful in predicting information about future cash flows (e.g., the amounts, timing, and uncertainty of cash flows) based on past performance.

2.2   Terminology

2.2.1   Cost and Unexpired Costs

- **Cost** is an amount (measured in money) expended for items such as capital assets, services (e.g., payroll), and merchandise received. Cost is the amount actually paid for something.

- **Unexpired costs** are costs that will expire in future periods and be charged (allocated in a systematic and rational manner or matched) against revenues from future periods.

Unexpired Costs (Asset)		Expired Costs (Expense)
1. Inventory	→	Cost of goods sold
2. Unexpired (prepaid) cost of insurance	→	Insurance expense
3. Net book value of fixed assets	→	Depreciation expense
4. Unexpired cost of patents	→	Patents expense (amortization)

2.2.2   Gross Concept (Revenues and Expenses)

- **Revenues** are reported in the gross amount of consideration to which the entity expects to be entitled in exchange for the specified goods or services transferred.

- **Expenses** (costs that benefit only the current period or the allocation of unexpired costs to the current period for the benefit received) are reported at their gross amounts.

2.2.3   Net Concept (Gains and Losses)

- **Gains** are reported at their net amounts (i.e., proceeds less net book value). A gain is the recognition of an asset either not in the ordinary course of business (e.g., gains on the sale of a fixed asset) or without the incurrence of an expense (e.g., finding gold on the company's property).

- **Losses** are reported at their net amounts (i.e., proceeds less net book value). A loss is cost expiration either not in the ordinary course of business (e.g., loss on the sale of investment assets) or without the generation of revenue (e.g., abandonment).

Note: Items of income or loss that are unusual or infrequent (or both) should be reported separately as part of income from continuing operations. The nature of the item and the financial statement effects should be disclosed on the face of the income statement or in the footnotes.

3 Income From Continuing Operations

3.1 Multiple-Step Income Statement

The multiple-step income statement reports operating revenues and expenses separately from nonoperating revenues and expenses and other gains and losses. The benefit of the multiple-step income statement is enhanced user information (because the line items presented often provide the user with readily available data with which to calculate various analytical ratios).

Example 1   Multiple-Step Income Statement

Facts: The following trial balance contains a list of income statement accounts for the year ended December 31, Year 1.

Trial Balance: Income Statement Accounts *Only*
For the Year Ended December 31, Year 1

4000	Sales revenue		$380
4050	Sales returns	$ 25	
4060	Sales discounts	5	
4100	Service revenue		200
4200	Rental revenue		100
5000	Cost of goods sold	200	
5100	Cost of services sold	150	
5200	Cost of rental income	60	
5250	Salaries expense*	70	
5300	Freight out	25	
5400	Commissions	40	
5500	Advertising	15	
5600	Insurance expense	20	
5800	Depreciation expense	80	
5900	Income tax expense	100	
6000	Interest revenue		170
6200	Other revenue		130
6500	Gain on sale of available-for-sale securities		50
7000	Interest expense	50	
7500	Loss on sale of fixed assets	40	
7550	Restructuring expense**	100	
8000	Loss on discontinued operations (net of tax)	25	

*Salaries expense: $20 relates to salaries for salespeople and $50 relates to salaries for officers of the company.
**Restructuring expense relates to an infrequent restructuring of service division.

(continued)

(continued)

Note: The trial balance does not balance, as the balance sheet accounts are excluded.

Required: Prepare a multiple-step income statement prepared from the trial balance information above.

Solution:

Radon Industries Inc.
Income Statement
For the Year Ended December 31, Year 1
(in thousands)

Net sales (including goods, services, and rentals), less discounts and returns		$650
Cost of sales (including goods, services, and rentals):		(410)
Gross margin		$240
Selling expenses	$100	
General and administrative expenses	70	
Depreciation expense	80	(250)
Income (loss) from operations		$ (10)
Other revenues and gains:		
Interest revenue	170	
Gain on sale of available-for-sale securities	50	
Other revenue	130	350
Other expenses and losses:		
Interest expense	50	
Loss on sale of fixed assets	40	
Restructuring expense	100	(190)
Income before income tax		150
Income tax expense		(100)
Income from continuing operations		$ 50
Discontinued operations (net of tax)		(25)
Net income		$ 25

Selling expenses include freight out, salaries for salespeople, commissions, and advertising. General and administrative expenses include officers' salaries and insurance. Nonoperating revenues and gains include auxiliary activities.

3.2   Single-Step Income Statement

In the single-step income statement presentation of income from continuing operations, total expenses (including income tax expense) are subtracted from total revenues; thus, the income statement has a single step. The benefits of a single-step income statement are its simple design and the fact that the presentation of types of revenues or expenses do not appear to the user to be classified as more important than others.

Example 2   Single-Step Income Statement

Facts: Same as Example 1.

Required: Using the trial balance from Example 1, prepare a single-step income statement.

Solution:

Radon Industries Inc.
Income Statement
For the Year Ended December 31, Year 1
(in thousands)

Revenues and other items:	
Sales revenue	$ 350
Service revenue	200
Interest revenue	170
Rental revenue	100
Gain on sale of available-for-sale securities	50
Other revenue	130
Total revenues and other items	**$1,000**
Expenses and other items:	
Cost of goods sold	$ 200
Cost of services sold	150
Cost of rental income	60
Selling expenses	100
General and administrative expenses	70
Interest expense	50
Depreciation expense	80
Loss on sale of fixed assets	40
Restructuring expense	100
Income tax expense	100
Total expenses and other items	**$ 950**
Income from continuing operations	$ 50
Discontinued operations (net of tax)	25
Net income	**$ 25**

---

4   Income From Discontinued Operations

Discontinued operations are reported separately from continuing operations in the income statement, net of tax. A discontinued operation may include a component of an entity, a group of components of an entity, or a business or nonprofit activity. Items reported within discontinued operations can consist of an impairment loss, a gain or loss from actual operations, and a gain or loss on disposal. All of these amounts are included in discontinued operations in the period in which they occur.

4.1   Types of Entities to Be Considered

The results of operations of a component of an entity or a group of components of an entity, or a business or nonprofit activity, will be reported in discontinued operations if it:

- has been disposed of; or
- is classified as held for sale.

4.2   Conditions That Must Be Present

All related costs shall be recognized when the obligations to others exist, not necessarily in the period of commitment to a plan. A disposal of a component or group of components is reported in discontinued operations if the disposal represents a strategic shift that has or will have a major effect on an entity's operations and financial results.

Examples of a strategic shift that could have a major effect on operations and financial results may include, among others:

- Disposal of a major geographical area
- Disposal of a major equity method investment
- Disposal of a major line of business

A business or nonprofit activity that, on acquisition, meets the criteria to be classified as held for sale is a discontinued operation.

Illustration 1   Discontinued Operation

Am-Serv Inc. is a food service company that delivers frozen food products to food service providers. Its clients include fast-food restaurants, high-end steak houses, home-delivery diet food companies, and institutions such as schools and hospitals. Historically, the fast-food restaurants have been the largest segment of Am-Serv's business in terms of revenue and operating profit. However, that division is now forecast to begin to decline in revenues because the public is looking for healthier options. Am-Serv has decided to sell its fast-food operation and, instead, focus on selling to locally operated restaurants offering a healthier fare. Such restaurants will generally show lower revenue per unit, but higher operating profit per unit. Because the fast-food division is the largest component in terms of revenue and operating profit, the disposal represents a major strategic shift, and will be reported as a discontinued operation.

4.3   Discontinued Operations Calculation

4.3.1   Types of Items Included in Results of Discontinued Operations

■ Results of operations of the component.

■ Gain or loss on disposal of the component.

■ Impairment loss (and subsequent increases in fair value) of the component.

- **Initial and Subsequent Impairment Losses**

    A loss is recognized for recording the impairment of the component (i.e., any initial or subsequent write-down to fair value less costs to sell).

- **Subsequent Increases in Fair Value**

    A gain is recognized for any subsequent increase in fair value minus the costs to sell (but not in excess of the previously recognized cumulative loss).

4.3.2   Report in the Period Disposed of or Held for Sale

The results of discontinued operations of a component are reported in discontinued operations (for the current period and for all prior periods presented) in the period the component is either disposed of or is held for sale. The results of subsequent operations of a component classified as held for sale are reported in discontinued operations in the period in which they occur.

4.3.3   Depreciation and Amortization

Once management decides to dispose of the component, assets within the component are no longer depreciated or amortized.

4.4   Measurement and Valuation

A component classified as held for sale is measured at the lower of its carrying amount or fair value less costs to sell. Costs to sell are the incremental direct costs to transact the sale.

4.5   Presentation and Disclosure

■ **Present as a Separate Component of Income:** The results of discontinued operations, net of tax, are reported as a separate component of income, below income from continuing operations.

■ **Disclose in Face or in Notes:** A gain or loss recognized on the disposal shall be disclosed either on the face of the income statement or in the notes to the financial statements.

Example 3	**Discontinued Operations Calculations and Income Statement Presentation**

Facts: The trial balance below presents the income statement accounts for Year 1 from All Sports Company's trial balance. The golf division of All Sports has been losing money on a monthly basis. The golf division's income statement accounts are also presented below. The board of directors decides on April 30, Year 1, to dispose of the golf division. The carrying value of the golf division on April 30, Year 1, is $4,000,000, and its fair value less costs to sell is $2,200,000. After months of negotiations, the division's net assets are sold on June 30, Year 2, for $2,000,000. The golf division has continuing losses in Year 2 of $200,000 per month. All Sports' income tax rate is 40 percent for Years 1 and 2. Assume that All Sports' income from continuing operations is $4,875,000 in Year 1 and $5,200,000 in Year 2.

All Sports Company Trial Balance
Year 1

		All Components	Golf Division
4000	Sales revenue	$21,000,000	$2,500,000
5000	Cost of goods sold	$9,500,000	1,850,000
5300	Freight out	155,000	135,000
5400	Commissions	900,000	220,000
5500	Advertising	1,200,000	600,000
5600	Insurance expense	1,400,000	750,000
5700	Salaries expense	2,500,000	850,000
5800	Depreciation expense	950,000	495,000
6000	Interest revenue	750,000	
6200	Other revenue	300,000	
6500	Gain on sale of assets	400,000	
7000	Interest expense	120,000	
7500	Impairment loss	1,800,000	1,800,000

Required: How should the disposal of the golf division be reported on All Sports Company's Year 1 and Year 2 financial statements?

(continued)

(continued)

Solution:

Reporting for Year 1:

The golf division was not disposed of until Year 2 and would be reported as held for sale in the Year 1 financial statements.

The continuing loss from the golf division would be included in discontinued operations in Year 1.

Loss from operations = $2,500,000 − ($1,850,000 + $135,000 + $220,000 + $600,000 + $750,000 + $850,000 + $495,000) = ($2,400,000).

Loss from operations, net of tax = ($2,400,000) × (1 − 40%) = ($1,440,000)

Impairment loss = $2,200,000 − $4,000,000 = ($1,800,000)

Impairment loss, net of tax = ($1,800,000) × (1 − 40%) = ($1,080,000)

Income Statement Presentation Year 1:

Income from continuing operations	$4,875,000
Discontinued operations	
Loss from operations of discontinued component, net of tax	(1,440,000)
Loss from impairment of discontinued operations, net of tax	(1,080,000)
Net income	$2,355,000

Reporting for Year 2:

In Year 2, discontinued operations would include the continuing losses incurred before the sale and the loss on disposal.

Loss from operations (Jan 1 − June 30) = ($200,000) × 6 = ($1,200,000)

Loss from operations, net of tax = ($1,200,000) × (1 − 40%) = ($720,000)

Loss on disposal = $2,000,000 − $2,200,000 = ($200,000)

Loss on disposal, net of tax = ($200,000) × (1 − 40%) = ($120,000)

Income Statement Presentation Year 2:

Income from continuing operations	$5,200,000
Discontinued operations	
Loss from operations of discontinued component, net of tax	(720,000)
Loss from sale (disposal) of discontinued operations, net of tax	(120,000)
Net income	$4,360,000

5   Foreign Currency Transactions

Foreign currency transaction gains and losses occur when a company buys from or sells to a foreign company with whom it has no ownership interest and agrees to pay or accept payment in a foreign currency. Transactions between subsidiary and parent of a permanent financing nature are not considered foreign currency transactions.

5.1   Foreign Currency Terminology

- **Exchange Rate:** Exchange rate is the price of one unit of a currency expressed in units of another currency; the rate at which two currencies will be exchanged at equal value. The exchange rate may be expressed as:

  - **Direct Method:** The direct method is the domestic price of one unit of another currency. For example, one euro costs $1.47.

  - **Indirect Method:** The indirect method is the foreign price of one unit of the domestic currency. For example, 0.68 euro buys $1.00.

- **Current Exchange Rate:** Current exchange rate is the exchange rate at the current date, or for immediate delivery of currency, often referred to as the spot rate.

- **Denominated or Fixed in a Currency:** A transaction is denominated or fixed in the currency used to negotiate and settle the transaction, either in U.S. dollars or a foreign currency.

5.2   Changes in Exchange Rate

A foreign exchange transaction gain or loss will result if the exchange rate changes between the time a purchase or sale in foreign currency is contracted for and the time actual payment is made.

5.3   Transaction Not Settled at Balance Sheet Date

A foreign exchange transaction gain or loss that is recognized in current net income must be computed at each balance sheet date on all recorded transactions denominated in foreign currencies that have not been settled. The difference between the exchange rate used in recording the transaction in dollars and the exchange rate at the balance sheet date (current exchange rate) is an unrealized gain or loss on the foreign currency transaction.

5.4   Valuation of Assets and Liabilities

The assets or liabilities resulting from foreign currency transactions should be recorded in the U.S. company's books using the exchange rate in effect at the date of the transaction.

Example 4   Foreign Currency Transaction

Facts: On 12/1/Yr 1, Olinto Company purchased goods on credit for 100,000 pesos. Olinto Company paid for the goods on 2/1/Yr 2. The exchange rates were:

Date	Rate
12/1/Yr 1	$0.10
12/31/Yr 1	$0.08
2/1/Yr 2	$0.09

Required: Prepare the journal entries related to this foreign currency transaction.

Solution:

12/1/Yr 1

DR	Purchases (100,000 pesos × $0.10 exchange rate)	$10,000	
CR	Accounts payable		$10,000

12/31/Yr 1

DR	Accounts payable [100,000 pesos × ($0.10 – $0.08)]	$2,000	
CR	Foreign exchange transaction gain		$2,000

100,000 pesos can be purchased for $8,000 at 12/31/Yr 1. The difference between the $8,000 and the original recorded liability of $10,000 is a foreign exchange transaction gain that increases net income for Year 1.

2/1/Yr 2

DR	Accounts payable	$8,000	
DR	Foreign exchange transaction loss [100,000 × ($0.08 – $0.09)]	1,000	
CR	Cash (100,000 pesos × $0.09)		$9,000

---

6   Statement of Comprehensive Income

6.1   Definitions

6.1.1   Comprehensive Income

Comprehensive income is the change in equity (net assets) of a business enterprise during a period from transactions and other events and circumstances from nonowner sources. It includes all changes in equity during a period except those resulting from investments by owners and distributions to owners.

> Net income
> +   Other comprehensive income
> _____
> Comprehensive income
> _____

6.1.2 Net Income

Net income includes the following items:

1. Income from continuing operations
2. Discontinued operations

6.1.3 Other Comprehensive Income

Other comprehensive income items are revenues, expenses, gains, and losses that are included in comprehensive income but excluded from net income under U.S. GAAP.

An entity must classify the specific items by their nature, such as:

■ **Pension Adjustments**

Under U.S. GAAP, certain gains and losses from defined benefit pension plan accounting must be recognized in other comprehensive income in the year the changes occur. These gains and losses are included in other comprehensive income until recognized as pension expense on the income statement.

Note: Defined benefit pension plan accounting is no longer tested on the CPA Exam.

■ **Unrealized Gains and Losses (Available-for-Sale Debt Securities and Hedges)**

The following types of unrealized gains and losses on certain investments in debt securities and hedges are reported as components of other comprehensive income until the securities are sold or until the cash flows associated with the hedged item are realized.

- Unrealized holding gains and losses on "available-for-sale debt securities."
- Unrealized holding gains and losses that result from a debt security being transferred into the "available-for-sale" category from "held to maturity."
- Subsequent decreases or increases in the fair value of "available-for-sale" debt securities previously written down as impaired.
- Gains or losses on derivative instruments that are designated as, and qualify as, cash flow hedges.
- For derivatives that are designated in qualifying hedging relationships (both fair value and cash flow) with an excluded component (a component excluded from the assessment of hedge effectiveness), an entity is permitted to recognize, as a component of other comprehensive income, differences between the changes in fair value of the excluded component and initial amounts recognized under a systematic and rational method in earnings.

■ **Foreign Currency Items**

Foreign currency translation adjustments and gains and losses on foreign currency transactions that are designated as (and are effective as) economic hedges of a net investment in a foreign entity are reported as a component of other comprehensive income. Foreign currency translation adjustments remain in other comprehensive income until the sale or liquidation of the investment in the foreign entity. Also, gains and losses on intra-entity foreign currency transactions that are of a long-term investment nature, when the entities to the transaction are consolidated, are combined or accounted for by the equity method.

■ **Instrument-Specific Credit Risk**

For liabilities for which the fair value option is elected, changes in fair value that are attributable to instrument-specific credit risk are included in comprehensive income.

6.1.4 Reclassification Adjustments

Reclassification adjustments move other comprehensive income items from accumulated other comprehensive income to the income statement.

6.1.5 Accumulated Other Comprehensive Income

Accumulated other comprehensive income is a component of equity that includes the total of other comprehensive income for the current period and all previous periods. Other comprehensive income for the current period is "closed" to this account, which is reconciled each period similar to the manner in which retained earnings are reconciled.

Pass Key

At the end of each accounting period, all components of comprehensive income are closed to the balance sheet. Net income is closed to retained earnings, and other comprehensive income is closed to accumulated other comprehensive income.

6.2 Financial Statement Reporting

Comprehensive income and its components shall be displayed in a financial statement that is presented with the same prominence as the other financial statements that constitute a full set of financial statements. The requirements to present comprehensive income do not apply to not-for-profit entities or to any company that does not have any item of other comprehensive income. Comprehensive income should not be reported on a per share basis.

Under U.S. GAAP, comprehensive income may be presented in:

- a single statement of comprehensive income (single-statement approach); or
- an income statement followed by a separate statement of comprehensive income that begins with net income (two-statement approach).

6.2.1 Single-Statement Approach

The single-statement approach displays other comprehensive income items individually and in total, below the net income amount, and totals them for comprehensive income.

Example 5	Single-Statement Approach

Facts: The following other comprehensive income items were noted in the Year 1 trial balance of Sydney Technologies Inc. The tax rate for other comprehensive income items is 25 percent for Year 1.

Unrealized holding gains	$400,000
Foreign currency translation gains	50,000
Unrealized holding losses	120,000
Foreign currency translation losses	120,000

Required: Compute the net of tax amounts to be reported in the statement of comprehensive income and complete the following statement of comprehensive income using the single-statement approach.

(continued)

(continued)

Solution:

The net of tax amounts to be reported in the statement of comprehensive income for each other comprehensive income item is as follows:

Unrealized holding net gains	$280,000 × (1 − 25%) = 210,000
Foreign currency items	$70,000 × (1 − 25%) = (52,500)

Sydney Technologies Inc.
Statement of Comprehensive Income
For the Year Ended December 31, Year 1

Revenues	$ 20,000,000
Expenses	(18,400,000)
Income before income taxes	$ 1,600,000
Income tax (25%)	(400,000)
Net income	$ 1,200,000
Other comprehensive income, net of income tax:	
Unrealized holding gains (available-for-sale securities)	$ 210,000
Foreign currency items	(52,500)
Other comprehensive income	157,500
Comprehensive income	$ 1,357,500

6.2.2 Two-Statement Approach

The two-statement approach displays comprehensive income as a separate statement that immediately follows the income statement.

Sydney Technologies Inc.
Statement of Comprehensive Income
For the Year Ended December 31, Year 1

Net income	$1,200,000
Other comprehensive income, net of income tax:	
Unrealized holding gains (available-for-sale securities)	$ 210,000
Foreign currency items	(52,500)
Other comprehensive income	157,500
Comprehensive income	$1,357,500

6.3   Other Reporting Issues

6.3.1   Other Comprehensive Income

Components of other comprehensive income may be reported either (i) net of tax; or (ii) before related tax effects, with one amount shown for the aggregate income tax expense or benefit related to the total of other comprehensive income items.

6.3.2   Income Tax Expense or Benefit

The amount of income tax expense or benefit allocated to each component of other comprehensive income is disclosed either on the face of the statement in which those components are displayed or in the notes to the financial statements.

6.3.3   Interim Period Reporting

A total for comprehensive income shall be reported in condensed financial statements of interim periods issued to shareholders.

6.3.4   Required Disclosures

All formats must disclose:

- The tax effects of each component included in (current) other comprehensive income, either as part of the statement presentation or in the notes to the financial statements.

- The changes in the accumulated balances of each component of other comprehensive income (e.g., pension adjustments, unrealized holding gains and losses on available-for-sale debt securities and hedges, foreign currency items, and interest-specific credit risk).

    - The changes in the accumulated balances by component may be shown on the face of the financial statements or in the notes to the financial statements.

- Total accumulated other comprehensive income in the balance sheet as an item of equity.

- The reclassification adjustments, which are made to avoid double counting in other comprehensive income items that are displayed in net income for the current year (e.g., previously reported unrealized gains on available-for-sale securities that were realized during the current year).

    - Disclosure is required for:

        —Changes in AOCI balances by component of other comprehensive income. The entity must separately disclose (i) reclassification adjustments; and (ii) current-period OCI.

        —Significant items reclassified out of AOCI must be disclosed either on the face of the statement where net income is presented, or as a separate disclosure in the notes to the financial statements.

    - Amounts by OCI component may be presented either before-tax or net-of-tax, as long as the tax effect is shown in either the financial statements or the notes.

1 SEC Reporting Requirements

The Securities and Exchange Commission (SEC) requires that more than 50 forms be filed to comply with reporting requirements. These forms are filed electronically through the *electronic data gathering, analysis, and retrieval system* (EDGAR) and are available online to the public.

1.1 Form 10-K

Form 10-K is the annual report that must be filed by U.S. registered companies (issuers). The report provides details to current and prospective investors about the business of a company and the relevant risk factors it faces, its financial and operating results for the year, and the perspective of its executive leadership. The filing deadlines relative to fiscal year-end are as follows:

- 60 days for large accelerated filers;
- 75 days for accelerated filers; and
- 90 days for all other registrants.

Pass Key

A large accelerated filer is defined by the SEC as an issuer with a worldwide market value of outstanding common equity held by nonaffiliates of $700 million or more as of the last business day of the issuer's most recently completed second fiscal quarter. An accelerated filer is defined as an issuer with a worldwide market value of outstanding common equity held by nonaffiliates of $75 million to less than $700 million and annual revenue of $100 million or more. Smaller reporting companies, which are entities with annual revenues of less than $100 million, are excluded from the definition of large accelerated filers or accelerated filers.

Specific items of importance contained in the 10-K report are as follows:

- **Part II, Item 7: "Management's Discussion and Analysis of Financial Condition and Results of Operations" (MD&A)**

  The objective of this section is to provide perspective on the business results of the company in management's own words. The MD&A will include the following components:

  - Material information that is relevant to an assessment of the financial condition and results of operations of the registrant, including information on liquidity and capital resources, as well as material impacts of cybersecurity incidents.

  - Summarized financial and operating results, trends, risks, and uncertainties.

  - Material changes and uncertainties relative to the prior period.

  - Critical accounting estimates and assumptions.

■ **Part II, Item 7A: "Quantitative and Qualitative Disclosures about Market Risk"**

Market risk includes the risk of potential loss in value of financial instruments due to changes in interest rates, exchange rates, cybersecurity threats, and other market-related factors. The disclosures required in this item include:

- Quantitative information as of the end of the latest fiscal year, presented in one of the following three disclosure alternatives:

  —Tabular presentation of information related to market risk sensitive instruments

  —Sensitivity analysis disclosures expressing potential loss in future earnings, fair value, or cash flows of market risk sensitive instruments

  —Value-at-risk disclosures expressing potential loss in future earnings, fair value, or cash flows or market risk sensitive instruments

- Qualitative information regarding primary market risk exposures, the management of these exposures, and changes relative to the most recently completed fiscal year and expectations for future periods.

■ **Part II, Item 8: "Financial Statements and Supplementary Data"**

- Audited financial statements (income statement, balance sheets, statement of cash flows, and statement of stockholders' equity) and accompanying notes presented using generally accepted accounting principles (GAAP). Time periods covered include the following:

  —Balance sheets for the two most recent fiscal years.

  —Income statements (and statement of comprehensive income) for each of the three fiscal years preceding the date of the most recent audited balance sheet.

  —Statement of cash flows for each of the three fiscal years preceding the date of the most recent audited balance sheet.

  —Changes in owners' equity for each of the three fiscal years preceding the date of the most recent audited balance sheet.

- The auditor's report.

- Certifications from the company's CEO and CFO regarding the accuracy and completeness of the 10-K.

1.2 Form 10-Q

Form 10-Q is the quarterly report that must be filed by U.S. registered companies for each of the first three quarters of every fiscal year. The report provides an overview of business operations, financial statements, nonfinancial information (e.g., legal items, risk factors, recent equity sales), and relevant disclosures. The filing deadlines relative to fiscal quarter-end are as follows:

■ 40 days for large accelerated and accelerated filers; and

■ 45 days for all other registrants.

Specific items of importance contained in the 10-Q report are as follows:

■ **Part I, Item 1: "Financial Statements"**

Requirements are similar to Form 10-K, Part II, Item 8, with the following notable differences:

- They are generally unaudited financial statements.

- They must be filed for each of the first three fiscal quarters of the entity's fiscal year.

- They may be presented in a condensed format and should reflect adjustments necessary to fairly state the results of the interim period, with a statement to that effect included in the notes to the financial statements. If all such adjustments are of a normal recurring nature, a statement should be made to that effect. The financial statements should include a detailed description of the nature and amounts of adjustments that are not normal recurring adjustments.

- Balance sheet presentations:

  — As of the end of the most recent fiscal quarter and as of the end of the preceding fiscal year.

  — May also include balance sheet as of the end of the corresponding fiscal quarter for the preceding fiscal year if necessary to understand the impact of seasonal fluctuations.

- Income statements and comprehensive income presentations:

  — For the most recent fiscal quarter, for the period between the end of the preceding fiscal year and the end of the most recent fiscal quarter, and for the corresponding periods of the preceding fiscal year.

  — May also include income statements for the cumulative 12-month period ended during the most recent fiscal quarter and for the corresponding preceding period.

- Statement of cash flows presentations:

  — For the period between the end of the preceding fiscal year and the end of the most recent fiscal quarter, and the corresponding period for the preceding fiscal year.

  — May also include statements of cash flows for the cumulative 12-month period ended during the most recent fiscal quarter and for the corresponding preceding period.

Part I, Item 2: "Management's Discussion and Analysis of Financial Condition and Results of Operations"

Requirements are similar to Form 10-K, Part II, Item 7, along with the following additional disclosures related to any material changes in:

- Financial condition from the end of the preceding fiscal year to the date of the most recent interim balance sheet. If an interim balance sheet as of the corresponding interim date of the preceding fiscal year is included, management should disclose any material changes in financial condition from that date to the date of the most recent interim balance sheet.

- Operational results with respect to the most recent fiscal year-to-date period where a statement of comprehensive income is provided, and the corresponding year-to-date period of the preceding fiscal year.

- Operational results with respect to the most recent quarter for which a statement of comprehensive income is provided and either the corresponding quarter for the preceding fiscal year or the immediately preceding sequential quarter.

Part I, Item 3: "Quantitative and Qualitative Disclosures About Market Risk"

Requirements are similar to Form 10-K, Part II, Item 7A. Discussion and analysis should help the reader understand changes in market risk from the end of the preceding fiscal year to the date of the most recent interim balance sheet.

1.3   Form 8-K

This form is filed by U.S. registered companies to disclose changes whenever a material event occurs. Examples of material events are as follows:

- Bankruptcy
- Acquisition or disposition of assets
- Material cybersecurity incidents
- New material financial obligations
- Costs associated with exit or disposal activities
- Material asset impairments
- Changes in the public accounting firm used to audit the company
- Changes in securities and trading markets
- Changes in or election of directors and officers
- Amendments to bylaws or articles of incorporation
- Changes in fiscal year
- Financial statement changes
- Material definitive agreements

Companies generally have four business days to file the form for any event that triggers a filing requirement.

2   Earnings per Share Overview

Under U.S. GAAP, all public entities (or entities that have made a filing for a public offering) are required to present earnings per share on the face of the income statement. An entity's capital structure determines the manner in which earnings per share are disclosed.

An entity has a simple capital structure if it has only common stock outstanding. The entity presents basic per-share amounts for income from continuing operations and for net income on the face of the income statement.

All other entities must present basic and diluted per-share amounts for income from continuing operations and for net income on the face of the income statement (or statement of income and comprehensive income if the entity is using the one-statement approach).

If the entity reports a discontinued operation, the entity must present the basic and diluted (if applicable) per-share amounts for that item either on the face of the income statement or in the notes to the financial statements.

3   Simple Capital Structure (Report Basic EPS Only)

An entity that issues only common stock (or no other securities that can become common stock, such as noncovertible preferred stock) is said to have a simple capital structure. This organization will present EPS for income from continuing operations and for net income on the face of the income statement. The number of common shares outstanding (the denominator) used in the EPS calculation is arrived at by the weighted average method.

3.1　Basic EPS Formula

For an organization with a simple capital structure, the formula for earnings per share is as follows:

$$\text{Basic EPS} = \frac{\text{Income available to common shareholders}}{\text{Weighted average number of common shares outstanding}}$$

3.2　Income Available to the Common Shareholders

Income available to common shareholders is determined by deducting from the line item income from continuing operations and net income (1) dividends declared in the period on noncumulative preferred stock (regardless of whether they have been paid) and (2) dividends accumulated in the period on cumulative preferred stock (regardless of whether they have been declared).

If there is a loss from continuing operations (or a net loss), the amount of the loss should be increased by the preferred shareholders' dividends or claims to determine income available to the common shareholders.

3.3　Weighted Average Number of Common Shares Outstanding

The weighted average number of common shares outstanding during the period is the mean (average) of shares outstanding and assumed to be outstanding for EPS calculations. Shares sold or reacquired during the period (including treasury stock) should be weighted for the portion of the period they were outstanding.

	Shares outstanding at the beginning of the period
+	Shares sold during the period (on a time-weighted basis)
−	Shares reacquired during the period (on a time-weighted basis)
+	Stock dividends and stock splits (retroactively adjusted)
−	Reverse stock splits (retroactively adjusted)
	Weighted average number of common shares outstanding

3.3.1　Stock Dividends and Stock Splits

Stock dividends and stock splits (to the same class of shareholders in the same company) must be treated as though they occurred at the *beginning* of the period. The shares outstanding before the stock dividend or stock split must be restated for the portion of the period before the stock dividend/split. If prior periods are presented, the effects of stock dividends and stock splits must be retroactively adjusted for those periods.

- If a stock dividend or stock split occurs after the end of the period but before the financial statements are issued, those shares should enter into the shares outstanding for the EPS calculation for all periods presented.

- Reverse stock splits would retroactively reduce shares outstanding for all periods presented.

3.3.2 Rules for Stock Issued in a Business Combination

If the acquisition method is used, the weighted average is measured from the date of the combination.

Example 1	Weighted Average Number of Shares Outstanding Computation

Facts:

Date	Transaction	Change in Shares	Total Shares
1/1	Shares outstanding		1,000,000
3/31	2-for-1 stock split	1,000,000	2,000,000
4/1	Additional shares sold	3,000,000	5,000,000
12/1	Reacquired shares (treasury)	(500,000)	4,500,000

Required: Calculate the weighted average number of shares outstanding.

Solution:

Total Shares	× Period Outstanding	× Adjustment for Split	= Weighted Average
1,000,000	3/12 (Jan–Mar)	2	500,000
5,000,000	8/12 (April–Nov)		3,333,333
4,500,000	1/12 (Dec)		375,000
		Weighted average shares outstanding	4,208,333

Alternative Solution:

Date	Transaction	Gross Change in Shares	Adjustment to Weighted Average Shares	
1/1	Shares outstanding	(beginning number)	1,000,000	
3/31	2-for-1 stock split	1,000,000	1,000,000	[effective 1/1]
4/1	Additional shares sold	3,000,000	2,250,000	[3,000,000 × 9/12]
12/1	Reacquired shares	(500,000)	(41,667)	[500,000 × 1/12]
	Weighted average shares outstanding		4,208,333	

4 Complex Capital Structure (Report Basic and Diluted EPS)

An entity has a complex capital structure when it has securities that can potentially be converted to common stock and would therefore dilute (reduce) EPS (of common stock). Both basic and diluted EPS must be presented. The basic EPS calculation ignores potentially dilutive securities in the weighted average number of shares outstanding calculation. The objective of diluted EPS is to measure the performance of an entity over the reporting period while giving effect to all potentially dilutive common shares outstanding during the period. Potentially dilutive securities include:

- convertible securities (e.g., convertible preferred stock, convertible bonds, etc.);
- warrants and other options;
- contracts that may be settled in cash or stock; and
- contingent shares.

4.1   Diluted EPS Formula

$$\text{Diluted EPS} = \frac{\text{Income available to the common stock shareholder} + \text{Interest on dilutive securities}}{\text{Weighted average number of common shares (assuming all dilutive securities are converted to common stock)}}$$

4.2   Dilution From Options, Warrants, and Their Equivalents

The dilutive effect of options and warrants and their equivalents is applied using the treasury stock method. The treasury stock method assumes that the proceeds from the exercise of stock options, warrants, and their equivalents will be used by the company to repurchase treasury shares at the prevailing market price, resulting in an incremental increase in shares outstanding, but not the full amount of shares that are issued on exercise of the common stock equivalents. The equivalents of options and warrants include nonvested stock granted to employees, stock purchase contracts, and partially paid stock subscriptions. Any canceled or issued options or warrants during the period shall be included in the denominator of diluted EPS for the period they were outstanding.

4.2.1   Dilutive vs. Antidilutive

Options and similar instruments are only dilutive when the average market price of the underlying common stock exceeds the exercise price of the options or warrants because it is unlikely they would be exercised if the exercise price were higher than the market price. These options or warrants would be "out of the money" and antidilutive. Previously reported EPS should not be adjusted retroactively in the case of options or similar instruments to reflect subsequent changes in market prices of the common stock.

4.2.2   Treasury Stock Method

The treasury stock method is applied as follows:

- If the average market price of the stock is greater than the exercise price (called "in the money"), assume that the warrants or other options are exercised at the beginning of the period (or at the time of issue, if later).

- Also assume that the proceeds received (the option or exercise price) are used to purchase common shares at the average market price during the period.

- When the option/warrant is in the money (average market price > exercise price), the proceeds (assumed to be) received will not be sufficient to buy back an (assumed) equal number of shares. This will always result in dilution.

- The difference between the number of shares assumed issued to satisfy the options or warrants and the number of shares assumed to be purchased with the proceeds should be included in the number of shares (denominator) for diluted EPS.

- Previously reported EPS data should not be retroactively adjusted for changes in market price.

The formula to compute additional shares for options and similar instruments is:

$$\text{Additional shares outstanding} = \text{Number of shares} - \left(\frac{\text{Number of shares} \times \text{Exercise price}}{\text{Average market price}} \right)$$

Example 2 — Options and Warrants Treasury Stock Method

Facts:

1,000 options to purchase 1,000 common stock shares

$15.00 exercise price per share

$20.00 average market price

$25.00 period-end market price

Required: Compute the incremental shares to be added to WACSO when computing diluted EPS using the treasury stock method.

Solution:

		Diluted
Options/common stock shares	1,000 ⟶	1,000
Exercise price per share	× $ 15.00	
Cash corp. received (hypothetically)	$15,000	
Diluted "repurchase price"	÷ $ 20.00	
Repurchase shares (hypothetically)		<750>
Common shares added to WACSO when computing diluted EPS		250 shares

Formula Approach

$$1,000 - \frac{1,000 \times \$15.00}{\$20.00} = \underline{250} \text{ shares}$$

4.3 Dilution From Convertible Securities: Bonds or Preferred Stock

The "if-converted" method should be used to determine the dilutive effects of the convertible securities. The if-converted method assumes that the securities were converted to common stock at the *beginning* of the period (or at the time of issue, if later).

4.3.1 Convertible Bonds

Use the following steps to apply the if-converted method to convertible bonds:

1. Add to the numerator (i.e., income available to common shareholders) the interest expense, net of tax, due to the assumed conversion of bonds to common stock.

2. Add to the denominator (i.e., weighted average number of shares outstanding) the number of common shares associated with the assumed conversion.

3. If the convertible bonds were issued during the period, assume that the stock was issued at that date for the weighted average calculation.

Illustration 1	Convertible Bonds: If-Converted Method	

Actual	Income	Pretend
$100	Income	$100
<20>	Bond interest	<0>
80	Income before taxes	100
<32>	Taxes (40%)	<40>
$ 48	N.I. available to common stockholders	$ 60

4.3.2 Antidilution

Use the results of each assumed conversion only if it results in dilution (i.e., reduces EPS). Do not include the results of the *assumed* conversion if it is antidilutive (i.e., increases EPS). In determining whether potential common shares are dilutive or antidilutive, each issue will be considered separately in sequence from most to least dilutive, with options and warrants generally included first. The tests for dilutive or antidilutive effects should be based on income from continuing operations.

Example 3	Application of the If-Converted Method (Convertible Bonds)

Facts: X Company has outstanding 100,000 shares of common stock and $500,000 in 6 percent bonds convertible into 10 shares for each $1,000 bond. Net income for the year is $100,000.

Required: Compute the diluted EPS assuming a 34 percent tax rate.

Solution:

Diluted shares outstanding:

Common stock	$ 100,000
Convertible bonds (500 × 10)	5,000
Total common shares outstanding	105,000

Diluted net income:

Net income	$100,000
Add: Interest on bonds, less tax effects [0.06 × $500,000 × (1 − 0.34)]	19,800
Total net income	$119,800
Diluted EPS ($119,800 ÷ 105,000 shares)	$ 1.14

(continued)

(continued)

Compare basic EPS computed with the bonds to diluted EPS computed without the bonds to determine whether the inclusion of the convertible bonds in the computation of diluted EPS is antidilutive:

Basic EPS (without conversion) ($100,000 ÷ 100,000 shares)	$ 1.00

Diluted EPS with conversion of the convertible bonds ($1.14) is more than basic EPS without the conversion ($1.00). The convertible bonds are antidilutive and would be excluded.

4.3.3 Convertible Preferred Stock

Use the following steps to apply the if-converted method to convertible preferred stock:

1. Adjust the numerator (as preferred stock dividends do not affect net income).

2. Add to the denominator the number of shares associated with the assumed conversion.

Antidilution rules apply to convertible preferred stock.

Example 4	Application of the If-Converted Method (Convertible Preferred Stock)

Facts: Carlin Company has outstanding 100,000 shares of common stock and 10,000 shares of convertible preferred stock, convertible into five shares of common stock for each share of preferred. Net income for the year is $100,000. Dividends declared during the year were $20,000 on the preferred, and $30,000 on the common.

Required: Compute the diluted EPS assuming a 34 percent tax rate.

Solution:

Diluted shares outstanding:	
Common stock	$100,000
Convertible debentures (10,000 × 5)	50,000
Total common shares outstanding	150,000
Diluted net income:	$100,000
Diluted EPS ($100,000 ÷ 150,000)	$ 0.67

Note: The preferred stock dividends are not subtracted from net income. We assume that since the preferred stock was converted into common stock, the preferred stock dividends were not paid.

Antidilution is checked by comparing basic EPS with the calculated diluted EPS:

$$\text{Basic EPS:} \quad \frac{\$100,000 - \$20,000}{100,000} = \$0.80$$

Since diluted EPS is less than basic EPS (without conversion), the preferred stock is dilutive, and diluted EPS is $0.67.

4.4 Dilution From Contracts That May Be Settled in Cash or in Stock

If a contract could be settled in either stock or cash at the election of either the entity or the holder, the facts available each period determine whether it is reflected in the computation of EPS. It is presumed that the contract will be settled in common stock and the resulting shares included in diluted EPS if the effect is more dilutive.

4.5 Dilution From Contingent Shares

Contingent issuable shares do not require cash consideration and depend on some future event or on certain conditions being met. Contingent shares (that are dilutive) are also included in the calculation of *basic* EPS if (and as of the date) all conditions for issuance are met.

Issuable shares contingent on the attainment of a certain level of earnings are treated as follows, if dilutive:

- If the necessary conditions have been satisfied by the end of the period, those shares are included in basic EPS as of the beginning of the period in which the conditions were satisfied.

- If the necessary conditions have not been satisfied by the end of the period, the number of contingently issuable shares included in diluted EPS is based on the number of shares that would be issuable, if any, if the end of the reporting period were the end of the contingency period. These shares are included as of the beginning of the period (or as of the date of the contingent stock agreement, if later). If the contingency is due to attainment of future earnings and/or future prices of the shares, both earnings to date and current market price, as they exist at the end of the reporting period, are used.

5 Earnings per Share Disclosures

Cash flow per share should not be reported. In addition to reporting basic EPS and diluted EPS for both income from continuing operations and net income and the effects of discontinued operations, the following disclosure requirements must be met:

- A reconciliation of the numerators and the denominators of the basic and diluted per-share computations for income from continuing operations.

- The effect that has been given to preferred dividends in arriving at income available to common stockholders in computing basic EPS.

- Securities that could potentially dilute basic EPS in the future that were not included in the computation of diluted EPS because the effect was antidilutive for the period(s) presented.

- Description of any transaction that occurred after the period end that would have materially affected the number of actual and/or potential common shares outstanding.

Pass Key

	Weighted Average	Options and Warrants	Convertible Bond	Convertible P/S	Contingent Issues
Basic	Yes	N/A	N/A	N/A	Conditions have been fully satisfied
Diluted	Yes	Average market value > Exercise price **Treasury stock method** Repurchase common stock at the *average* price	Any dilutive **If-converted method** Adjust net income for interest expense (not incurred) reduced by taxes	Any dilutive **If-converted method** Do *not* reduce income available to common shareholders by the preferred stock dividend (pretend they were converted)	Based upon conditions having been met to date

3 Stockholders' Equity: Part 1

1 Overview

Stockholders' equity (also called shareholders' equity or owners' equity) is the owners' claim to the net assets (i.e., assets minus liabilities) of a corporation. It is generally presented on the statement of financial position (balance sheet) as the last major section (following liabilities). The various elements constituting stockholders' equity must be clearly classified according to source.

Capital Corp. Consolidated Shareholders' Equity—December 31, Year 1		
Capital Stock (capital equal to par or stated value)		
Preferred stock, noncumulative, $100 par value, authorized 1,000 shares issued and outstanding 500 shares		$ 50,000
Common stock, $10 par value, authorized 50,000 shares, issued 30,000 shares of which 5,000 are held in the treasury		300,000
		350,000
Additional Paid-in Capital (capital in excess of par or stated value)		
Excess of issue price over par value of common/preferred stock sold	$ 29,000	
Excess of sales price over cost of treasury shares sold	15,000	
Excess of FMV over par of stock issued as stock dividend	20,000	
Defaulted stock subscriptions	10,000	
FMV of common shares contributed by shareholders to corporation	75,000	
FMV of fixed assets contributed by local government	60,000	209,000
Retained Earnings		
Appropriated (reserved) for general contingencies	50,000	
Appropriated (reserved) for possible future inventory decline	20,000	
Appropriated (reserved) for plant expansion	40,000	
Appropriated (reserved) for higher replacement cost of fixed assets	60,000	
Unappropriated (unreserved)	$200,000	370,000
		929,000
Accumulated other comprehensive income		10,000
Less: Cost of shares in treasury		(85,000)
Total Capital Corp. shareholders' equity		854,000
Noncontrolling interest		25,000
Total equity		$879,000

2 Capital Stock (Legal Capital)

Legal capital is the amount of capital that must be retained by the corporation for the protection of creditors. The par or stated value of both preferred and common stock is legal capital and is frequently referred to as "capital" stock.

2.1 Par Value

Generally, preferred stock is issued with a par value, but common stock may be issued with or without a par value. No-par common stock may be issued as true no-par stock or no-par stock with a stated value. Any excess of the actual amount received over the par or stated value of the stock is accounted for as additional paid-in capital.

2.2 Authorized, Issued, and Outstanding

A corporation's charter contains the amounts of each class of stock that it may legally issue, and this is called "authorized" capital stock. When part or all of the authorized capital stock is issued, it is called "issued" capital stock. Because a corporation may own issued capital stock in the form of treasury stock, the amount of issued capital stock in the hands of shareholders is called "outstanding" capital stock. In summary, capital stock may be:

■ authorized;

■ authorized and issued; or

■ authorized, issued, and outstanding.

The number of shares of each class of stock authorized, issued, and outstanding must be disclosed.

2.3 Common Stock

Common stock is the basic ownership interest in a corporation. Common shareholders bear the ultimate risk of loss and receive the ultimate benefits of success, but they are not guaranteed dividends or assets upon dissolution. Common shareholders generally control management. They have the right to vote, the right to share in earnings of the corporation, and the right to share in assets upon liquidation after the claims of creditors and preferred shareholders are satisfied.

Pass Key

Common shareholders may have preemptive rights to a proportionate share of any additional common stock issued if granted in the articles of incorporation.

2.3.1   Book Value per Common Share

Book value per common share measures the amount that common shareholders would receive for each share if all assets were sold at their book (carrying) values and all creditors were paid. Book value per common share can be determined as follows:

$$\text{Book value per common share} = \frac{\text{Common shareholders' equity}}{\text{Common shares outstanding}}$$

2.3.2   Common Stockholders' Equity Formula

$$
\begin{array}{ll}
 & \text{Total shareholders' equity} \\
- & \text{Preferred stock outstanding (at greater of call price or par value} \\
- & \text{Cumulative preferred dividends in arrears} \\
\hline
= & \text{Common shareholders' equity}
\end{array}
$$

2.4   Preferred Stock

Preferred stock is an equity security with preferences and features not associated with common stock. Preferred stock may include a preference relating to dividends, which may be cumulative or noncumulative and participating or nonparticipating. Preferred stock may also include a preference relating to liquidation. Usually, preferred stock does not have voting rights.

2.4.1   Cumulative Preferred Stock

The *cumulative* feature provides that all or part of the preferred dividend not paid in any year *accumulates* and must be paid in the future before dividends can be paid to common shareholders. The accumulated amount is referred to as *dividends in arrears.* The amount of dividends in arrears is not a legal liability, but it must be disclosed in total and on a per-share basis either parenthetically on the balance sheet or in the footnotes.

2.4.2   Noncumulative Preferred Stock

With *noncumulative preferred stock,* dividends not paid in any year do not accumulate. The preferred shareholders lose the right to receive dividends that are not declared.

2.4.3   Participating Preferred Stock

The *participating* feature provides that preferred shareholders share (participate) with common shareholders in dividends in excess of a specific amount. The participation may be full or partial. *Fully participating* means that preferred shareholders participate in excess dividends without limit. Generally, preferred shareholders receive their preference dividend first, and then additional dividends are shared between common and preferred shareholders. *Partially participating* means preferred shareholders participate in excess dividends, but to a limited extent (e.g., a percentage limit).

2.4.4 Nonparticipating Preferred Stock

When preferred stock is *nonparticipating,* preferred shareholders are limited to the dividends provided by their preference. They do not share in excess dividends.

2.4.5 Preference Upon Liquidation

Preferred stock may include a preference to assets upon liquidation of the entity. If the liquidation preference is significantly greater than the par or stated value, the liquidation preference must be disclosed. The disclosure of the liquidation preference must be in the equity section of the balance sheet, not in the notes to the financial statements.

2.4.6 Convertible Preferred Stock

Convertible preferred stock may be exchanged for common stock (at the option of the stockholder) at a specified conversion rate.

2.4.7 Callable (Redeemable) Preferred Stock

Callable preferred stock may be called (repurchased) at a specified price (at the option of the issuing corporation). The aggregate or the per-share amount at which the preferred stock is callable must be disclosed either on the balance sheet or in the footnotes.

2.4.8 Mandatorily Redeemable Preferred Stock (Liability)

Mandatorily redeemable preferred stock is issued with a maturity date. Similar to debt, mandatorily redeemable preferred stock must be bought back by the company on the maturity date. Mandatorily redeemable preferred stock must be classified as a liability, unless the redemption is required to occur only upon the liquidation or termination of the reporting entity.

Example 1	Distribution of Dividends to Participating Preferred Stockholders

Facts: On January 1, Year 1, Samuel Co. issued 100,000 shares of $5 par common stock and 25,000 shares of $10 par fully participating 8 percent cumulative preferred stock. No dividends were paid in Year 1. Cash dividends of $101,000 were declared and paid in Year 2.

Required: Determine the dividend to be paid on the preferred and common stock.

Solution:

Schedule 1: Dividends Remaining for Distribution

Cash dividends	$101,000
Year 1 preferred dividends in arrears [(25,000 × $10) × 0.08]	(20,000)
Preferred dividends accumulated in Year 2	(20,000)
	61,000
Common stock [(100,000 × $5) × 0.08]*	(40,000)
Remaining for proration between preferred and common stock	$ 21,000

(continued)

(continued)

Schedule 2: Proration of Remaining Dividends According to Par Values

Preferred stock

$$\frac{250,000}{750,000} \times \$21,000 = \$7,000$$

Common stock

$$\frac{500,000}{750,000} \times \$21,000 = \$14,000$$

Schedule 3: Total Dividends Paid on Preferred and Common Stock

Preferred stock	$7,000 + $20,000 + $20,000 = $ 47,000
Common stock	$14,000 + $40,000 = 54,000
Total cash dividends distributed	$101,000

*The principle applied here is that, with participating cumulative preferred stock, before any proration of dividends may exist, the common shareholders must receive an equal dividend as the preferred shareholders. In this case, preferred shareholders receive an 8 percent dividend first; common shareholders receive an 8 percent dividend second; and the balance ($21,000) is shared pro rata.

3   Additional Paid-in Capital

Additional paid-in capital is generally contributed capital in excess of par or stated value. It can also arise from many other different types of transactions. Additional paid-in capital may be aggregated and shown as one amount on the balance sheet.

Examples include:

- Sale of treasury stock at a gain
- Liquidating dividends
- Conversion of bonds
- Small stock dividends

4   Retained Earnings

Retained earnings (or deficit) is accumulated earnings (or losses) during the life of the corporation that have not been paid out as dividends The amount of accumulated retained earnings is reduced by distributions to stockholders and transfers to additional paid-in capital for stock dividends. Retained earnings does not include treasury stock or accumulated other comprehensive income If the retained earnings account has a negative balance, it is called a deficit.

4.1   Formula

> **Net income/loss**
> − **Dividends (cash, property, and stock) declared**
> ± **Prior period adjustments**
> ± **Accounting changes reported retrospectively**
>
> **Retained earnings**

4.2   Classification of Retained Earnings (Appropriations)

Retained earnings may be classified as either appropriated or unappropriated. The purpose of appropriating retained earnings is to disclose to the shareholders (usually the common shareholders) that some of the retained earnings are not available to pay dividends because they have been restricted for legal or contractual reasons (e.g., a bond indenture) or as a discretionary act of management for specific contingency purposes (e.g., plant expansion). An appropriation of retained earnings may not be used to absorb costs or losses and may not be transferred to income.

The following entry should be recorded when an appropriation is to be made (and should be reversed when the purpose of the appropriation has occurred):

DR	Retained earnings (unappropriated)	$XXX	
CR	Retained earnings appropriated for [purpose]		$XXX

5   Accumulated Other Comprehensive Income

Components of accumulated other comprehensive income include pension adjustments, unrealized gains and losses on available-for-sale debt securities and hedges, and foreign currency translation adjustments.

These components of other comprehensive income are not included in determining net income and, therefore, do not enter into retained earnings. Rather, they are recognized in the period in which they occur and are combined with net income to determine comprehensive income. Total accumulated other comprehensive income must be shown in the shareholders' equity section separate from capital stock, additional paid-in capital, and retained earnings.

6   Treasury Stock

Treasury stock is a corporation's own stock that has been issued to shareholders and subsequently reacquired (but not retired). Treasury stockholders are not entitled to any of the rights of ownership given to common shareholders, such as the right to vote or to receive dividends. In addition, a portion of retained earnings equal to the cost of treasury stock may be restricted and may not be used as a basis for the declaration or payment of dividends (depending on applicable state law).

6.1   Methods of Accounting for Treasury Stock

Two methods of accounting for treasury stock are permitted:

1. Cost method

2. Legal (or par/state value) method

The primary difference between the two methods is the timing of the recognition of "gain or loss" on treasury stock transactions. Note that under both methods, the "gains and losses" are recorded as a direct adjustment to stockholders' equity and are not included in the determination of net income. Also, under both methods, shares held as treasury stock are not considered to be outstanding shares.

6.1.1   Cost Method (Used by Entities Approximately 95 Percent of the Time)

Under the cost method, the treasury shares are recorded and carried at their reacquisition cost. A gain or loss will be determined when treasury stock is reissued or retired, and the original issue price and book value of the stock do not enter into the accounting. The account "additional paid-in capital from treasury stock" is credited for gains and debited for losses when treasury stock is reissued at prices that differ from the reacquisition cost. Losses may also decrease retained earnings if the additional paid-in capital from treasury stock account does not have a balance large enough to absorb the loss. Net income or retained earnings will never be increased through treasury stock transactions.

Illustration 1   Cost Method

Original issue

10,000 shares $10 par value common stock sold for $15 per share.

DR	Cash	$150,000	
CR	Common stock (10,000 × $10 par)		$100,000
CR	Additional paid-in capital—C/S		50,000

Buy back above issue price

200 shares were repurchased for $20 per share.

DR	Treasury stock (200 × $20)	$4,000	
CR	Cash		$4,000

Reissue above cost

100 shares repurchased for $20 were resold for $22.

DR	Cash (100 × $22)	$2,200	
CR	Treasury stock (100 × $20)		$2,000
CR	Additional paid-in capital—T/S		200

The following journal entry was made after the preceding entry:

Reissue below cost

100 shares repurchased for $20 were resold for $13.

DR	Cash (100 × $13)	$1,300	
DR	Additional paid-in capital—T/S	200	
DR	Retained earnings	500	
CR	Treasury stock (100 × $20)		$2,000

6.1.2   Legal (or Par/Stated Value) Method (Used by Entities Approximately 5 Percent of the Time)

Under the legal method, the treasury shares are recorded by reducing the amounts of par (or stated) value and additional paid-in capital received at the time of the original sale. Treasury stock is debited for its par (or stated) value. APIC—Common Stock is debited (reduced) for the pro rata share of the original issue price attributable to the reacquired shares. Additional paid-in capital from treasury stock is credited for gains and debited for losses when treasury stock is repurchased at prices that differ from the original selling price. Losses may also decrease retained earnings if the "additional paid-in capital from treasury stock" account does not have a balance large enough to absorb the loss. Note that, under this method, the sources of capital associated with the original issue are maintained.

Illustration 2   Par Value Method

Original issue

10,000 shares $10 par value common stock sold for $15 per share.

DR	Cash	$150,000	
CR	Common stock (10,000 × $10 par)		$100,000
CR	Additional paid-in capital—C/S		50,000

Buy back above issue price

200 shares were repurchased for $20 per share.

DR	Treasury stock (200 × $10 par)	$2,000	
DR	Additional paid-in capital—C/S	1,000	
DR	Retained earnings*	1,000	
CR	Cash		$4,000

*This entry should be made to retained earnings if there is no balance in the additional paid-in capital–T/S account.

Buy back below issue price

200 shares repurchased for $12 per share.

DR	Treasury stock (200 × $10 par)	$2,000	
DR	Additional paid-in capital—C/S (200 × $5)	1,000	
CR	Cash (200 × $12)		$2,400
CR	Additional paid-in capital—T/S		600

Reissue shares

100 shares repurchased for $20 were resold for $22.

DR	Cash (100 × $22)	$2,200	
CR	Treasury stock (100 × $10 par)		$1,000
CR	Additional paid-in capital—C/S		1,200

Reissue shares

100 shares repurchased for $20 were resold for $13.

DR	Cash (100 × $13)	$1,300	
CR	Treasury stock (100 × $10 par)		$1,000
CR	Additional paid-in capital—C/S		300

Illustration 3	Effect of Cost and Par Value Methods on Balance Sheet Presentation

The equity sections of the cost balance sheet and par value balance sheet would appear as follows, assuming that the treasury shares were repurchased for $20 per share:

Cost Method		Par Value Method	
Common stock (par value)	$100,000	Common stock (par value)	$100,000
Additional paid-in capital	50,000	Less: Treasury stock at par	(2,000)
Total paid-in capital	150,000	Common stock o/s at par	98,000
Retained earnings	75,000	Additional paid-in capital	49,000
	225,000		147,000
Less: Treasury stock at cost	(4,000)	Retained earnings	74,000
Total stockholders' equity	$221,000	Total stockholders' equity	$221,000

6.2 Retirement of Treasury Stock

When treasury stock is acquired with the intent of retiring the stock (regardless of whether it is accomplished) and the price paid is in excess of the par or stated value, that excess may be charged against either (1) all paid-in capital arising from past transactions in the same class of stock or (2) retained earnings. When the price paid for the acquired treasury stock is less than par or stated value, the difference must be credited to paid-in capital.

The retirement of treasury stock would be accomplished with the following journal entries under the cost method and the par value method:

Illustration 4	Retirement of Treasury Stock

If all 200 treasury shares reacquired for $20 were retired rather than reissued, the following entry would be made:

Retirement of Shares (Cost Method)

200 shares of $10 par common stock originally sold for $15 and reacquired for $20 are retired.

DR	Common stock (200 × $10)	$2,000	
DR	Additional paid-in capital—C/S (200 × $5)	1,000	
DR	Retained earnings	1,000	
CR	Treasury stock (200 × $20)		$4,000

To retire treasury stock under the par value method, debit common stock at par and credit treasury stock at par.

Retirement of Shares (Par Value Method)

DR	Common stock (200 × $10 par)	$2,000	
CR	Treasury stock (200 × $10 par)		$2,000

6.3   Donated Stock

Donated stock is a company's own stock received as a donation from a shareholder. There is no change in total shareholders' equity as a result of the donation, but the number of shares outstanding decreases, resulting in higher book value per common share. The company should record donated stock at fair market value, as follows:

DR	Donated treasury stock (@FMV)	$XXX	
CR	Additional paid-in capital (@FMV)		$XXX

If the donated stock is sold, the journal entry would be:

DR	Cash (@ sales price)	$XXX	
DR	Additional paid-in capital (if SP < original FMV)	XXX	
CR	Additional paid-in capital (if SP > original FMV)		$XXX
CR	Donated treasury stock (@ book value, or original FMV)		XXX

NOTES

1 Accounting for a Stock Issuance (to Nonemployees)

If par (or stated) value exists, stock may be issued above, at, or below par (or stated) value. Often, stock subscriptions are sold before the stock is actually issued.

1.1 Stock Issued Above Par Value

If stock is issued above par value, cash will be debited for the proceeds, common (or preferred) capital stock will be credited for par (or stated) value, and additional paid-in capital will be credited for the excess over par (or stated) value.

1.2 Stock Issued at Par Value

If stock is issued at par value, cash will be debited and common (or preferred) capital stock will be credited for the proceeds. There is no entry to additional paid-in capital.

1.3 Stock Issued Below Par Value

If stock is issued at less than par (or stated) value, additional paid-in capital would be debited to reflect a discount on the stock. The discount represents a contingent liability to the original owners.

1.4 Stock Subscriptions

Frequently, a corporation sells its capital stock by subscription. This means that a contractual agreement to sell a specified number of shares at an agreed-upon price on credit is entered into. Upon full payment of the subscription, a stock certificate evidencing ownership in the corporation is issued.

1.4.1 Sale of Subscriptions

When the subscription method is used to sell capital stock, a subscriptions receivable account is debited and a capital stock subscribed account is credited, as is a regular additional paid-in capital account. Subscriptions not paid for at year-end are treated as a contra-equity item, offsetting the amount of par (or stated) value and additional paid-in capital related to subscriptions not paid for at year-end (if subscriptions are paid after year-end but before the financial statements are issued, the subscriptions receivable may be reported as an asset and will increase paid-in capital at year-end).

The journal entry to record subscriptions receivable is as follows:

DR	Subscriptions receivable (1,000 shares @ sales price of $100/share)	$100,000	
CR	Common stock subscribed ($10 par × 1,000 shares)		$10,000
CR	Additional paid-in capital (1,000 shares × $90 share)		90,000

1.4.2 Collection of Subscriptions

Upon payment of the subscription, the subscription receivable account is credited and cash or other assets are debited, as follows. Assume that $85,000 of the $100,000 subscription from above is collected, including $80,000 in full payment of subscriptions and $5,000 in partial subscription payments (common stock cannot be issued until partial payments are paid in full).

DR	Cash	$85,000	
CR	Subscriptions receivable		$85,000

1.4.3 Issuance of Stock Previously Subscribed

On the actual issuance of the stock certificates, the capital stock subscribed account is debited and the regular capital stock account is credited, as follows (assume that the $80,000 in fully paid subscriptions from above become issued shares):

DR	Common stock subscribed (800 shares @ $10)	$8,000	
CR	Common stock (issued)		$8,000

1.4.4 Default/Forfeiture of a Subscription

If all or part of a subscription is not collected, the terms of the subscription agreement and corporate policy will determine the appropriate accounting treatment. Generally, the treatment is to reverse the applicable portion of the original entry and either:

- issue stock in proportion to the amount paid;

- refund the partial payment; or

- retain the partial payment (as liquidated damages for breach of contract) by a credit to additional paid-in capital.

1.5 Stock Rights

A stock right provides an existing shareholder with the opportunity to buy additional shares. The right usually carries a price below the stock's market price on the date the rights are granted. The issuance of stock rights requires a memorandum entry only. It is possible that the rights may subsequently be redeemed by the company, which will cause a decrease in stockholders' equity in the amount of the redemption price. The exercise of stock rights requires the following journal entry:

DR	Cash	[amount received]	
CR	Common stock		[par value]
CR	Additional paid-in capital		[residual]

1.6 Other Stock Valuation Issues

Stock issued for *outside services* should be recorded at the fair value of the stock, and the trading price of the stock is the best evidence of fair value. Stock issued in a *basket sale* with other securities (e.g., bonds) should be allocated a portion of the sales proceeds based on the relative fair market values of the different securities.

2 Distributions to Shareholders

A dividend is a pro rata distribution by a corporation based on the shares of a particular class of stock and usually represents a distribution of earnings. Cash dividends are the most common type of dividend distribution, although there are many other types (covered below). Preferred stock usually pays a fixed dividend, expressed in dollars or as a percentage.

2.1 Terminology

- **Date of Declaration:** the date the board of directors formally approves a dividend. On the declaration date, a liability is created (dividends payable) and retained earnings is reduced (debited).

- **Date of Record:** the date the board of directors specifies as the date the names of the shareholders to receive the dividend are determined.

- **Date of Payment:** the date on which the dividend is actually disbursed by the corporation or its paying agent.

2.2 Cash Dividends

Cash dividends distribute cash to shareholders and may be declared on common or preferred stock. They are paid from retained earnings. Dividends are paid only on authorized, issued, and outstanding shares. They are not paid (or declared) on treasury stock.

2.3 Property (In-Kind) Dividends

Property dividends distribute noncash assets (e.g., inventory, investment securities, etc.) to shareholders. They are nonreciprocal transfers of nonmonetary assets from the company to its shareholders. On the date of declaration, the property to be distributed should be restated to fair value and any gain or loss should be recognized in income. The dividend liability and related debit to retained earnings should be recorded at the fair value of the assets transferred.

2.4 Scrip Dividends

Scrip dividends are simply a special form of notes payable whereby a corporation commits to paying a dividend at some later date. Scrip dividends may be used when there is a cash shortage. On the date of declaration, retained earnings is debited and notes payable (instead of dividends payable) is credited. Some scrip dividends even bear interest from the declaration date to the date of payment (and, thus, require accrual).

2.5 Liquidating Dividends

Liquidating dividends occur when dividends to shareholders exceed retained earnings. Dividends in excess of retained earnings would be charged (debited) first to additional paid-in capital and then to common or preferred stock (as appropriate). Liquidating dividends reduce total paid-in capital.

2.6   Stock Dividends

Stock dividends distribute additional shares of a company's own stock to its shareholders. The treatment of stock dividends depends on the size (percentage) of the dividend in proportion to the total shares outstanding before the dividend.

2.6.1   Treatment of a Small Stock Dividend (< 20–25 Percent)

When less than 20 to 25 percent of the shares previously outstanding are distributed, the dividend is treated as a small stock dividend because the issuance is not expected to affect the market price of the stock. The fair market value of the stock dividend at the date of declaration is transferred from retained earnings to capital stock and additional paid-in capital. There is no effect on total shareholders' equity, as paid-in capital is substituted for retained earnings (i.e., retained earnings is "capitalized" and made part of paid-in capital).

Example 1   Small Stock Dividend

Facts: Capital Corporation has 100,000 shares of $10 par value common stock outstanding. The company declares a stock dividend of 5,000 shares when the fair market value is $15 (on the date of declaration). 5,000 shares/100,000 shares = 5%, which is considered a small stock dividend.

Required: Prepare the journal entry to record the dividend.

Solution:

Journal entry:

DR	Retained earnings (5,000 × $15 FV)	$75,000	
CR	Common stock (5,000 × $10 par value)		$50,000
CR	Paid-in capital (difference = $75,000 − 50,000)		25,000

2.6.2   Treatment of a Large Stock Dividend (> 20–25 Percent)

When more than 20 to 25 percent of the previously issued shares outstanding are distributed, the dividend is treated as a large stock dividend, as it may be expected to reduce the market price of the stock (similar to a stock split). The par (or stated) value of the stock dividend is normally transferred from retained earnings to capital stock to meet legal requirements. The amount transferred is the number of shares issued multiplied by the par (or stated) value of the stock. However, if state law does not require capitalization of retained earnings for stock dividends (which is rare because it requires amendment to the articles of incorporation), record the stock dividend distribution (like a stock split) by changing the number of shares outstanding and the par (or stated) value per share.

| Example 2 | Stock Dividend Greater Than 20–25 Percent of Previous Outstanding Shares |

Facts: LMT Corp. declares a 40 percent stock dividend on its 1,000,000 shares of outstanding $10 par common stock (5,000,000 authorized). On the date of declaration, LMT stock is selling for $20 per share.

Total stock dividend (0.40 × 1,000,000)	400,000 shares
Value of 400,000 shares @ $10 per share (par)	$4,000.000

Required: Prepare the journal entries to record the declaration and distribution of the stock dividend.

Solution:

Journal entry to record the declaration of the stock dividend at par:

DR	Retained earnings	$4,000,000	
CR	Common stock distributable		$4,000,000

Journal entry to record the distribution of the stock dividend at par:

DR	Common stock distributable	$4,000,000	
CR	Capital stock, $10 par common		$4,000,000

2.6.3   Stock Dividends on Treasury Stock

Stock dividends are generally not distributed on treasury stock because such stock is not considered outstanding. However, an exception is made when:

1. The company is maintaining a ratio of treasury shares to shares outstanding in order to meet stock option or other contractual commitments or

2. State law requires that treasury stock be protected from dilution.

2.7   Stock Splits

Stock splits occur when a corporation issues additional shares of its own stock (without charge) to current shareholders and reduces the par (or stated) value per share proportionately. There is no change in the total book value of the shares outstanding. Thus, the memo entry to acknowledge a stock split is merely a formality.

A stock split usually does not affect retained earnings or total shareholders' equity, as is exhibited below:

Before the Split		
Common stock (10,000 shares outstanding @ $10 par)		$100,000
After the Split (× 2)	(÷ 2)	
Common stock (20,000 shares outstanding @ $5 par)		$100,000

2.7.1 Reverse Stock Splits

A reverse stock split would involve reducing the number of shares outstanding and increasing the par (or stated) value proportionately. One way to reduce the amount of outstanding shares is to recall outstanding stock certificates and issue new certificates.

2.7.2 Stock Splits on Treasury Stock

Stock splits are usually not applied to treasury stock because such stock is not considered outstanding. However, an exception is made when:

- the company is maintaining a ratio of treasury shares to shares outstanding in order to meet stock option or other contractual commitments; or

- state law requires that treasury stock be protected from dilution.

3 Statement of Changes in Shareholders' Equity

The statement of changes in shareholders' equity provides specific information about changes in an entity's primary equity components, including capital transactions and distributions to shareholders, a reconciliation of retained earnings, and a reconciliation of the carrying amount of each class of equity capital, paid-in capital, and accumulated other comprehensive income.

<table>
<tr><td colspan="5" align="center">Sydney Technologies Inc.
Statement of Changes in Stockholders' Equity
For the Year Ended December 31, Year 1</td></tr>
<tr><th></th><th>Total</th><th>Retained earnings</th><th>Accumulated other comprehensive income</th><th>Common stock</th></tr>
<tr><td>Beginning balance</td><td>$30,000,000</td><td>$8,500,000</td><td>$1,500,000</td><td>$20,000,000</td></tr>
<tr><td>Comprehensive income:</td><td></td><td></td><td></td><td></td></tr>
<tr><td>Net income</td><td>1,200,000</td><td>1,200,000</td><td></td><td></td></tr>
<tr><td>Other comprehensive income</td><td>200,000</td><td></td><td>200,000</td><td></td></tr>
<tr><td>Common stock issued</td><td>1,000,000</td><td></td><td></td><td>1,000,000</td></tr>
<tr><td>Dividends declared on common stock</td><td>(700,000)</td><td>(700,000)</td><td></td><td></td></tr>
<tr><td>Ending balance</td><td>$31,700,000</td><td>$9,000,000</td><td>$1,700,000</td><td>$21,000,000</td></tr>
</table>

FAR
2

Financial Reporting and Disclosures

Module

1 Overview and Scope

Revenue recognition occurs when an entity satisfies a performance obligation by transferring either a good or a service to a customer. Revenue should be recognized at an amount that reflects the expected consideration the entity is entitled to receive in exchange for the good or service provided.

All entities (public, private, not-for-profit) that either enter into contracts with customers to transfer goods, services, or nonfinancial assets (unless governed by other standards) are subject to the revenue recognition standard. Certain contracts, such as those covering leases, insurance, non-warranty guarantees, and financial instruments, are covered under other standards.

2 The Five-Step Approach

In order to properly apply the revenue recognition standard, an entity should implement the five-step approach described below:

- **Step 1:** Identify the contract with the customer
- **Step 2:** Identify the separate performance obligations in the contract
- **Step 3:** Determine the transaction price
- **Step 4:** Allocate the transaction price to the separate performance obligations
- **Step 5:** Recognize revenue when or as the entity satisfies each performance obligation

2.1 Step 1: Identify the Contract(s) With the Customer

A contract is defined as an agreement between two or more parties that creates enforceable rights and obligations. Depending on an entity's typical business practices, contracts can be verbal, written, or implied.

A customer is a party that has contracted with an entity to exchange consideration in order to obtain goods or services that are an output of the entity's ordinary activities.

2.1.1 Criteria for Identifying the Contract

The five-step approach is applied only when a contract with a customer meets all of the following criteria:

- All parties have approved the contract and have committed to perform their obligations.
- The rights of each party regarding contracted goods or services are identified.
- Payment terms can be identified.
- The contract has commercial substance, meaning future cash flows (amount, risk, and timing) are expected to change as a result of the contract.
- It is probable (based on the customer's intent and ability to pay when due) that the entity will collect substantially all of the consideration due under the contract.

The criteria assessment is performed at contract inception and, if all criteria are met, reassessments should only be needed if significant changes occur. If all of the criteria are not met at inception, regular reassessments should follow.

If the criteria are not met but consideration has been paid by the customer, an entity can recognize revenue if the consideration is nonrefundable and either there are no remaining obligations to transfer goods/services or the contract has terminated. If not recognized as revenue, the consideration received is booked as a liability.

2.1.2 Combination of Contracts

When two or more contracts are entered into with the same customer or with related parties of the customer at or near the same time, the contracts should be combined and accounted for as a single contract if either the contracts are negotiated as a package with a single commercial objective, consideration for one contract is tied to the performance or price of another contract, or the goods/services promised represent a single performance obligation.

2.1.3 Contract Modification

A contract modification represents a change in the price or scope (or both) of a contract approved by both parties. When a modification occurs, it is either treated as a new contract or as a modification of the existing contract. The modification is treated as a new contract if:

- the scope increases due to the addition of distinct goods or services; and
- the price increase appropriately reflects the stand-alone selling prices of the additional goods/services.

If not accounted for as a new contract, the modification is treated as part of the existing contract (for non-distinct goods and services) with an adjustment to revenue to reflect the change in the transaction price.

2.2 Step 2: Identify the Separate Performance Obligations in the Contract

A performance obligation is a promise to transfer a good or a service to a customer. The transfer can be either an individual good or service (or a bundle of goods or services) that is distinct, or a series of goods or services that are substantially the same and are thereby transferred in the same manner. If the promise to transfer a good or a service is not distinct from other goods or services, they will all be combined into a single performance obligation.

In order to be distinct, both criteria below must be met:

1. The promise to transfer the good or service is separately identifiable from other goods or services in the contract; and

2. The customer can benefit either from the good or service independently or when combined with the customer's available resources.

2.2.1 Separately Identifiable

A transfer of a good or service is separately identifiable if:

- the entity does not integrate the good or service with other goods or services in the contract;
- the good or service does not customize or modify another good or service in the contract; or
- the good or service does not depend on or relate to other goods or services promised in the contract.

2.2.2   Not Separately Identifiable

Factors that indicate two or more promises to transfer a good or a service to a customer are not separately identifiable include (but are not limited to) the following:

- The goods or services are highly interrelated or interdependent.
- The entity provides a significant service of integrating the good or service with other goods or services promised in the contract into a bundle of goods or services that represent the combined output contracted for by the customer.

Example 1	Single Performance Obligation

Facts: Tanner Co. is building a multi-unit residential complex. The entity enters into a contract with a customer for a specific unit that is under construction. The goods and services to be provided in the contract include procurement, construction, piping, wiring, installation of equipment, and finishing.

Required: Identify the performance obligation(s) in this contract.

Solution: Although the goods and services provided by the contractor are capable of being distinct, they are not distinct in this contract because the goods and services cannot be separately identified from the promise to construct the unit. The contractor will integrate the goods and services into the unit, so all the goods and services are accounted for as a single performance obligation.

Example 2	Separately Identifiable Performance Obligations

Facts: A software developer enters into a contract with a customer to transfer a software license, perform installation, and provide software updates and technical support for five years. The developer sells the license, installation, updates, and technical support separately. The entity determines that each good or service is separately identifiable because the installation does not modify the software and the software is functional without the updates and technical support.

Required: Identify the performance obligation(s) in this contract.

Solution: The software is delivered before the installation, updates, and technical support and is functional without the updates and technical support, so the customer can benefit from each good or service on its own. The developer has also determined that the software license, installation, updates, and technical support are separately identifiable. On this basis, there are four performance obligations in this contract:

1. Software license
2. Installation service
3. Software updates
4. Technical support

2.3   Step 3: Determine the Transaction Price

The transaction price represents the amount of consideration that an entity can expect to be entitled to receive in exchange for transferring promised goods or services to a customer. The transaction price should be determined based on considering the effects of: variable consideration (and any constraining estimates), significant financing if applicable, noncash considerations, and any consideration payable to the customer (if applicable).

2.3.1   Variable Consideration

The amount of variable consideration should be estimated by taking a range of possible amounts and using either the expected value (which sums probability-weighted amounts) or the most likely amount—whichever is assumed to be the better predictor. Variable consideration should only be included in the price if it is probable that a significant revenue reversal will not be required once any uncertainty tied to the consideration is resolved.

2.3.2   Significant Financing

Time value of money should be an adjustment to the transaction price if the timing of the payments per the contract provides either the customer or the entity with a significant benefit in regard to financing the transfer of goods or services. Revenue should be recognized based on the price that would have been paid in cash by the customer at the time of transfer. If the time between the transfer of goods/services and the payment by the customer is anticipated to be less than one year, discounting the transaction price is unnecessary.

2.3.3   Noncash Consideration

Noncash consideration should be measured at fair value at contract inception.

2.3.4   Consideration Payable to a Customer

Any consideration (cash, credits, vouchers, etc.) that is payable to a customer should be treated as a reduction in the transaction price and revenue recognized by the entity unless the entity is receiving goods or services transferred by the customer.

Example 3	Time Value of Money

Facts: On January 1, Year 5, SDF sold furniture to a customer for $4,000 with three years' interest-free credit. The customer took delivery of the furniture on that day. The $4,000 is payable to SDF on December 31, Year 7. The applicable discount rate based on the customer's credit profile is 8 percent.

Required: Determine the transaction price for the sale of furniture.

Solution: The transaction price is $3,175 ($4,000 × $1/(1.08)^3$) because the time value of money must be considered when determining the transaction price.

Note that interest income will also be recognized each year as follows:

Year 5: $3,175 × 8% = $254

Year 6: ($3,175 + $254) × 8% = $274

Year 7: ($3,175 + $254 + $274) × 8% = $296

2.4   Step 4: Allocate the Transaction Price to the Performance Obligations in the Contract

If there is more than one performance obligation within a contract, the transaction price should be allocated to each separate performance obligation based on the amount of consideration that would be expected for satisfying each unique obligation. The stand-alone selling price (and any applicable discount or variable consideration) of each distinct good or service underlying each performance obligation should be determined at contract inception.

2.4.1   Stand-alone Selling Price

The price an entity would sell the promised good or service to a customer on a stand-alone basis. Once this price is determined for each obligation within the contract, the total transaction price should be allocated in proportion to the stand-alone selling prices.

2.4.2   Discounts

A discount exists when the sum of the stand-alone prices for each obligation within a contract exceeds the total consideration for the contract. A discount should be allocated proportionally to all obligations within the contract.

2.4.3   Variable Consideration

If applicable, variable consideration may be attributable to the entire contract, individual performance obligations within a contract, or distinct goods or services within a single performance obligation.

2.4.4   Transaction Price Changes

If the transaction price changes after contract inception, the change should be allocated to the performance obligations in the contract on the same basis that was used at inception. Changes in stand-alone selling prices after inception should not be reallocated.

Example 4	Allocating the Transaction Price

Facts: A software company enters into a $250,000 contract with a customer to transfer a software license, perform installation service, and provide technical support for a three-year period. The entity sells the license, installation service, and technical support separately. The license is usually sold for $160,000, the installation service is $20,000, and technical support runs $30,000 per year. The installation service and technical support could be performed by other entities and the software remains functional in the absence of these services. The contract price must be paid on installation of the software, which is planned for March 1, Year 1.

Required: How should the software company recognize revenue for these transactions?

(continued)

(continued)

Solution: The entity identifies three performance obligations in the contract for the following goods and services:

1. Software license

2. Installation service

3. Technical support

The stand-alone selling price can be determined for each performance obligation. The fair value of the contract is determined to be $270,000 ($160,000 for the license, $20,000 for the installation service, and $90,000 for three years of technical support). Based on the relative fair values, the allocation of revenue is as follows:

Software license	[($160,000/$270,000) × $250,000] = $148,148
Installation service	[($20,000/$270,000) × $250,000] = $18,519
Technical support	[($90,000/$270,000) × $250,000] = $83,333

The journal entry to record the $250,000 payment received on March 1 appears below.

March 1, Year 1

DR	Cash	$250,000	
CR	License revenue		$148,148
CR	Service revenue		18,519
CR	Unearned service revenue		83,333

Revenue is recorded for the sale of the license and the installation at the time of sale. The technical support will be recognized on a monthly basis as the support is provided.

The journal entry to record the first month of technical support revenue on March 31 is shown below.

March 31, Year 1

DR	Unearned service revenue	$2,314.80	
CR	Service revenue		$2,314.80

At year-end, after all adjusting entries for months March through December are recorded, service revenue earned will total $23,148 ($83,333/36 = $2,314.80; $2,314.80 × 10 = $23,148). The remaining technical support will be recorded in Years 2, 3, and 4.

2.5   Step 5: Recognize Revenue When (or as) the Entity Satisfies a Performance Obligation

An entity should recognize revenue when the entity satisfies a performance obligation by transferring the good or service to the customer, who thereby obtains control of the asset. Control implies the ability to obtain the benefits from and direct the usage of the asset while also preventing other entities from obtaining benefits and directing usage. Performance obligations may be satisfied either over time or at a point in time.

2.5.1   Satisfied Over Time

Revenue is recognized over time if any one of the criteria below is met:

- The entity's performance creates or enhances an asset (e.g., work in process) that the customer controls as the asset is created or enhanced.

- The customer simultaneously receives and consumes the benefits of the entity's performance as the entity performs it (e.g., service contracts, such as a cleaning service or a monthly payroll processing service).

- The entity's performance does not create an asset with alternative use to the entity (assessed at inception) and the entity has an enforceable right to receive payment for performance completed to date.

In order to recognize revenue, the entity must be able to reasonably measure progress toward completion. Progress can be measured using output and input methods.

1. **Output Methods**

    When using output methods, revenue is recognized based on the value to the customer of the goods or services transferred to date relative to the remaining goods or services promised. Examples of output methods include: units produced or delivered, time elapsed, milestones achieved, surveys of performance completed to date, and appraisals of results achieved. These methods should only be used when the output selected represents the entity's performance toward complete satisfaction of the performance obligation. When the outputs used to measure progress are not available or directly observable, an input method may be necessary.

2. **Input Methods**

    When using input methods, revenue is recognized based on the entity's efforts or inputs to the satisfaction of the performance obligation relative to the total expected inputs. Examples of input methods include: costs incurred relative to total expected costs, resources consumed, labor-hours expended, and time elapsed. A disadvantage of input methods is that there may not be a direct relationship between an entity's inputs and the transfer of control of goods and services to a customer. If inputs are used evenly throughout the performance period, revenue can be recognized on a straight-line basis.

Illustration 1   Straight-Line Basis

A health club enters into a contract with a customer for one year of unlimited health club access for $75 per month. The health club determines that the customer simultaneously receives and consumes the benefits of the club's performance, so the contract is a performance obligation satisfied over time. Because the customer benefits from the club's services evenly throughout the year, the best measure of progress toward complete satisfaction of the performance obligation is a time-based measure. Revenue will be recognized on a straight-line basis throughout the year at $75 per month.

In the absence of reliable information used to measure progress, if an entity expects to recover its costs, revenue may be recognized to the extent that costs are recovered until the point at which it can reasonably measure the outcome of the performance obligation.

2.5.2 Satisfied at a Point in Time

If the performance obligation is not satisfied over time, then it is satisfied at a point in time. Revenue should be recognized at the point in time when the customer obtains control of the asset.

Control would generally require the following:

- The entity has a right to payment and the customer has an obligation to pay for an asset.
- The customer has legal title to the asset.
- The entity has transferred physical possession of the asset.
- The customer has the significant rewards and risks of ownership.
- The customer has accepted the asset.

Example 5   Performance Obligation Satisfied Over Time

Facts: Tanner Co. is building a multi-unit residential complex. The entity enters into a contract with a customer for a specific unit that is under construction. The contract has the following terms:

- The customer pays a nonrefundable security deposit upon entering the contract.
- The customer agrees to make progress payments during construction.
- If the customer fails to make the progress payments, the entity has the right to all of the consideration in the contract if it completes the unit.
- The terms of the contract prevent the entity from directing the unit to another customer.

Required: Determine whether this performance obligation is satisfied over time or at a point in time.

Solution: This performance obligation is satisfied over time because:

- The unit does not have an alternative future use to the entity because it cannot be directed to another customer.
- The entity's performance creates an asset that the customer controls because the terms of the contract prevent the entity from directing the unit to another customer.

Example 6	Performance Obligation Satisfied at a Point in Time

Facts: Tanner Co. is building a multi-unit residential complex. The entity enters into a contract with a customer for a specific unit that is under construction. The contract has the following terms:

- The customer pays a deposit upon entering the contract that is refundable if the entity fails to complete the unit in accordance with the contract.

- The remainder of the purchase price is due on completion of the unit.

- If the customer defaults on the contract before completion, the entity only has the right to retain the deposit.

Required: Determine whether this performance obligation is satisfied over time or at a point in time.

Solution: This is a performance obligation satisfied at a point in time because it is not a service contract, the customer does not control the unit as it is created, and the entity does not have an enforceable right to payment for performance completed to date (i.e., the entity only has a right to the deposit until the unit is completed).

3   Presentation

A contract asset or liability should be presented in the statement of financial position when either party has performed in a contract.

A *contract asset* reflects the entity's right to consideration in exchange for goods or services that the entity has transferred to the customer. Essentially, the entity has performed prior to the customer paying or prior to the payment due date. The conditions associated with this right are something other than the passage of time.

Note: If the payment due date is conditioned only by the passage of time, the entity should present this separately as a *receivable*.

A *contract liability* must be booked when an entity has an obligation to transfer goods or services to a customer. In this situation, the entity has either already received consideration from the customer or the customer owes consideration and it is unconditional (the customer pays or owes payment before the entity performs).

Example 7   Contract Liability and Receivable

Facts: On January 1, Anderson Co. enters into a noncancelable contract with Tanner Co. for the sale of an excavator for $350,000. The excavator will be delivered to Tanner on April 1. The contract requires Tanner to pay the $350,000 in advance on February 1, and Tanner makes the payment on March 1.

Required: Prepare the journal entries that would be used by Anderson to account for this contract.

Solution:

February 1 journal entry: Anderson recognizes a receivable because it has an unconditional right to the consideration (i.e., the contract is noncancelable).

DR	Receivable	$350,000	
CR	Contract liability		$350,000

March 1 journal entry: When Tanner makes the payment, Anderson recognizes the cash collection.

DR	Cash	$350,000	
CR	Receivable		$350,000

April 1 journal entry: Anderson recognizes revenue when the excavator is delivered to Tanner.

DR	Contract liability	$350,000	
CR	Revenue		$350,000

Example 8	Contract Asset and Receivable

Facts: On January 1, Anderson Co. enters into a contract with Tanner Co. for the sale of two excavators for $350,000 each. The contract requires one excavator to be delivered on February 1 and states that the payment for the delivery of the first excavator is conditional on the delivery of the second excavator. The second excavator is delivered on June 1.

Required: Prepare the journal entries that would be used by Anderson to account for this contract.

Solution:

February 1 journal entry: Anderson recognizes a contract asset and revenue when it satisfies the performance obligation to deliver the first excavator.

DR	Contract asset	$350,000	
CR	Revenue		$350,000

Note that a receivable is not recognized on February 1, because Anderson does not have an unconditional right to the consideration until the second excavator is delivered.

June 1 journal entry: Anderson recognizes a receivable and revenue when it satisfies the performance obligation to deliver the second excavator.

DR	Receivable	$700,000	
CR	Contract asset		$350,000
CR	Revenue		350,000

4 Applications of Revenue Recognition: Long-Term Construction Contracts

The revenue from long-term construction contracts may be recognized over time or at a point in time.

4.1 Construction Contract Revenue Recognized Over Time

Revenue on a construction contract is recognized over time if any one of the criteria below is met:

- The entity's performance creates or enhances an asset (e.g., work in process) that the customer controls as the asset is created or enhanced.

- The entity's performance does not create an asset with alternative use to the entity, and the entity has an enforceable right to receive payment for performance completed to date.

Example 9	Recognized Over Time

Facts: Tanner Co. is building a multiunit residential complex. The entity enters into a contract with a customer for a specific unit that is under construction. The contract has the following terms:

- The customer pays a nonrefundable security deposit upon entering the contract.

- The customer agrees to make progress payments during construction.

- If the customer fails to make the progress payments, the entity has the right to all of the consideration in the contract if it completes the unit.

- The terms of the contract prevent the entity from directing the unit to another customer.

Required: Determine whether this performance obligation is satisfied over time or at a point in time.

Solution: This performance obligation is satisfied over time because:

- The unit does not have an alternative future use to the entity because it cannot be directed to another customer.

- The entity's performance creates an asset that the customer controls because the terms of the contract prevent the entity from directing the unit to another customer.

4.1.1 Using Input Methods

When a long-term construction contract meets the criteria for recognizing revenue over time and it is expected to be profitable, it is appropriate to use an input method such as cost-to-cost (costs incurred relative to total expected costs) if the entity's accounting system can:

1. reasonably estimate profitability; and

2. provide a reliable measure of progress toward completion.

4.1.2 Determination of Revenues Recognized

Income recognized is the percentage of estimated total income either:

1. that incurred costs to date bear to total estimated costs based on the most recent cost information; or

2. that may be indicated by such other measure of progress toward completion appropriate to the work performed.

4.1.3 Balance Sheet Presentation

When long-term construction contract revenue is recognized over time, construction costs and estimated gross profit earned are accumulated in the *construction in progress* account (an inventory account) and billings on construction are accumulated in the *progress billings* account (a contra-inventory account). The two accounts are netted against each other for balance sheet reporting.

4.1.4 Accounting for Construction Revenue Recognized Over Time

The following are important points to remember in accounting for contracts where revenue is recognized over time:

- Journal entries and interim balance sheet treatment are the same as they are for construction contract revenue recognized at a point in time (described in the next section), except that the amount of estimated gross profit earned in each period is recorded by charging the construction in progress account and crediting realized gross profit.

- Gross profit or loss is recognized in each period by the following steps:

Step 1	Compute gross profit of completed contract:	Contract price
		< Estimated total cost >
		Gross profit
Step 2	Compute percentage of completion:	Total cost to date
		Total estimated cost of contract
Step 3	Compute gross profit earned (profit to date):	Step 1 × Step 2 = PTD
Step 4	Compute gross profit earned for current year:	PTD at current FYE
		< PTD at beginning of period >
		Current year-to-date GP

- An estimated loss on the total contract is recognized immediately in the year it is discovered. However, any previous gross profit or loss reported in prior years must be adjusted for when calculating the total estimated loss.

Pass Key

Pay attention to the terminology in long-term construction contract questions. Estimated total costs can be confused with estimated costs to complete. Estimated total costs is the total costs for a long-term contract from inception to completion. Estimated costs to complete would be added to costs incurred to date to arrive at estimated total costs.

4.2   Construction Contract Revenue Recognized at a Point in Time

When a long-term construction contract does not meet the criteria for recognizing revenue over time, revenue and gross profit are recognized when the contract is completed.

Example 10   Revenue Recognized at a Point in Time

Facts: Tanner Co. is building a multiunit residential complex. The entity enters into a contract with a customer for a specific unit that is under construction. The contract has the following terms:

- The customer pays a deposit upon entering the contract that is refundable if the entity fails to complete the unit in accordance with the contract.

- The remainder of the purchase price is due on completion of the unit.

- If the customer defaults on the contract before completion, the entity only has the right to retain the deposit.

Required: Determine whether this performance obligation is satisfied over time or at a point in time.

Solution: This is a performance obligation satisfied at a point in time because the customer does not control the unit as it is created, and the entity does not have an enforceable right to payment for performance completed to date (i.e., the entity only has a right to the deposit until the unit is completed).

4.2.1   Balance Sheet Presentation

When construction contract revenue is recognized at a point in time, construction costs are accumulated in the *construction in progress* account (an inventory account) and billings on construction are accumulated in the *progress billings* account (a contra-inventory account). The two accounts are netted against each other for balance sheet reporting.

4.2.2   Accounting for Construction Revenue Recognized at a Point in Time

The following are important points to remember in accounting for contracts when revenue is recognized at a point in time:

- Estimated gross profit is not recognized each period as part of construction in progress. Unless a loss is recognized on the contract, no gross profit is recognized until the contract is completed.

- At completion of the contract, gross profit or loss is recognized as follows:

> **Gross profit or loss = Contract price − Total costs**

- At interim balance sheet dates, the excess of either the construction in progress account or the progress billings account over the other is classified as a current asset or a current liability.

- Losses should be recognized in full in the year they are discovered.

- An expected loss on the total contract is determined by:

  1. Adding to advances any additional revenue expected to arrive at total contract revenue.

  2. Adding estimated costs to complete to the recorded costs to date to arrive at total contract costs.

  3. Subtracting (2) from (1) to arrive at estimated profit or loss.

- Losses are recorded immediately. Any profit would be recorded at completion of the contract.

Example 11   Long-Term Contract Gross Profit Computation

Facts:

	Year 1	Year 2	Year 3	Year 4
Sales price	$4,000	$4,000	$4,000	$4,000
Total (estimated) cost of contract	3,000	3,200	4,200	4,300
Costs incurred to date	1,500	2,400	3,600	4,300

Required: Compute gross profit in Years 1 through 4 assuming revenue is recognized over time and at a point in time.

Solution:

Revenue Recognized Over Time

	Year 1	Year 2	Year 3	Year 4
Step 1 Compute GP of completed contract:				
Total contract sales price	$ 4,000	$ 4,000	$ 4,000	$ 4,000
Less: Total estimated cost of contract	(3,000)	(3,200)	(4,200)	(4,300)
Total gross profit	$ 1,000	$ 800	$ (200)	$ (300)
Step 2 Compute percentage of completion:				
Costs incurred to date	$ 1,500	$ 2,400	$ 3,600	$ 4,300
Total estimated cost of contract	$ 3,000	$ 3,200	$ 4,200	$ 4,300
Percentage of completion	50%	75%	100%	100%
			(Loss Rule)	
Step 3 Compute GP earned to date:				
Total contract GP	$ 1,000	$ 800	$ (200)	$ (300)
× Percentage of completion	50%	75%	100%	100%
GP earned to date (cumulative)	$ 500	$ 600	$ (200)	$ (300)
Step 4 Compute GP earned each year—percentage of completion:				
Previously recognized	$ -0-	$ 500	$ 600	$ (200)
Current year gross profit	$ 500	$ 100	$ (800)	$ (100)

Revenue Recognized at a Point in Time

Compute GP earned each year—revenue recognized at a point in time:

	Year 1	Year 2	Year 3	Year 4
Computations	$ -0-	$ -0-	$ (200)	$ (100)

Long-Term Construction Contract Accounting Journal Entries

Revenue Recognized Over Time	Revenue Recognized at a Point in Time

Journal Entries During Construction Period

Journal entry to record costs incurred:

DR	Construction in progress
CR	Materials, cash, etc.

Journal entry to record costs incurred:

DR	Construction in progress
CR	Materials, cash, etc.

Journal entry to record billings on contract:

DR	Accounts receivable
CR	Progress billings on construction contract

Journal entry to record billings on contract:

DR	Accounts receivable
CR	Progress billings on construction contract

Journal entry to record payments received:

DR	Cash
CR	Accounts receivable

Journal entry to record payments received:

DR	Cash
CR	Accounts receivable

Journal entry to record estimated gross profit during construction:

DR	Cost of long-term construction contracts
DR	Construction in progress
CR	Revenue from LT construction contracts*

*Determined based on costs to date relative to total costs. Losses recognized in full in the period incurred.

N/A if project is profitable. Losses are recognized in full in the period incurred.

Balance Sheet Presentation During Construction Period

CIP > Progress billings = Current asset (costs of uncompleted contracts in excess of progress billings)

Progress billings > CIP = Current liability (progress billings on uncompleted contracts in excess of costs)

CIP includes costs incurred and estimated gross profit earned to date.

CIP > Progress billings = Current asset (costs of uncompleted contracts in excess of progress billings)

Progress billings > CIP = Current liability (progress billings on uncompleted contracts in excess of costs)

CIP includes only costs incurred.

Journal Entries When Construction Completed

Journal entry to close construction accounts:

DR	Progress billings
CR	Construction in progress

Journal entry to close billings to revenue:

DR	Progress billings
CR	Revenue

Journal entry to close construction in progress to expense:

DR	Cost of LT construction contract
CR	Construction in progress

5 Other Applications of Revenue Recognition

5.1 Incremental Costs of Obtaining a Contract

The incremental costs of obtaining a contract are costs incurred that would not have been incurred if the contract had not been obtained, and are recognized as an asset (capitalized and amortized) if the entity expects that it will recover these costs. An entity will recognize an expense if the costs would have been incurred regardless of whether the contract was obtained.

Example 12   Incremental Costs of Obtaining a Contract

Facts: A software developer enters into a contract with a customer to transfer a software license, perform installation, and provide software updates and technical support for three years in exchange for $240,000. In order to win this contract, the developer incurred the following costs:

Legal fees for drawing up the contract	$10,000
Travel costs to deliver proposal	20,000
Commissions to sales employee	12,000
Total	$42,000

Required: Determine which costs should be recognized as an asset and which should be expensed.

Solution: The travel costs ($20,000) should be expensed because they would have been incurred even if the developer did not get the contract. The legal fees ($10,000) and sales commissions ($12,000) should be recognized as assets because they are costs of obtaining the contract, assuming that the developer expects to recover the costs.

5.2 Costs to Fulfill a Contract

The costs that are incurred to fulfill a contract that are not within the scope of another standard will be recognized as an asset if they meet *all* of the following criteria:

- Relate directly to a contract (such as direct labor, materials, allocated costs, and other costs that are explicitly chargeable to the customer per the contract).

- They generate or enhance the resources of the entity.

- They are expected to be recovered.

Costs to be expensed include selling, general and administrative costs, wasted labor and materials costs, and costs tied to satisfied performance obligations.

Example 13	Costs to Fulfill a Contract

Facts: A software developer enters into a contract with a customer to transfer a software license, perform installation, and provide software updates and technical support for three years in exchange for $240,000. In order to fulfill the technical support portion of the project, the developer purchases an additional workstation for the technical support team for $8,000 and assigns one employee to be primarily responsible for providing the technical support for the customer. This employee also provides services for other customers. The employee is paid $30,000 annually and is expected to spend 10 percent of his time supporting the customer.

Required: Determine which costs should be recognized as an asset and which should be expensed.

Solution: The additional workstation ($8,000) should be recognized as an asset. The cost of the employee assigned to the contract ($30,000) should be recognized as a payroll expense because, although the costs relate to the contract and are expected to be recovered, the employee was already working for the developer and therefore the costs do not generate or enhance the resources of the developer.

5.3 Contract Modifications

A contract modification represents a change in the price or scope (or both) of a contract approved by both parties. When a modification occurs, it is either treated as a new contract or as a modification of the existing contract. The modification is treated as a new contract if:

- the scope increases due to the addition of distinct goods or services; and
- the price increase appropriately reflects the stand-alone selling prices of the additional goods/services.

If not accounted for as a new contract, the modification is treated as part of the existing contract (for non-distinct goods and services) with an adjustment to revenue to reflect the change in the transaction price.

5.4 Principal vs. Agent

Whenever an entity uses another party to provide goods or services to a customer, the entity needs to determine whether it is acting as a principal or an agent.

- **Principal:** The entity controls the good or service before it is transferred to the customer. When this is the case, the revenue recognized is equal to the gross consideration an entity expects to receive.
- **Agent:** The entity arranges for the other party to provide the good or service to the customer. When this is the case, the revenue recognized is equal to the fee or commission for performing the agent function.

Indicators that an entity is an agent and does not control the good or service before it is provided to the customer include:

- another party (the principal) is primarily responsible for fulfilling the contract;
- the entity does not have inventory risk; and
- the entity does not have discretion in establishing prices for the other party's goods or services.

Example 14   Principal vs. Agent

Facts: On January 1, Anderson Co. enters into a contract with Tanner Co. for the sale of an excavator with unique specifications. Anderson and Tanner develop the specifications and Anderson contracts with a construction equipment manufacturer to produce the equipment. The manufacturer will deliver the equipment to Tanner when it is completed.

Anderson agrees to pay the manufacturer $350,000 on delivery of the excavator to Tanner. Anderson and Tanner agree to a selling price of $385,000, which will be paid by Tanner to Anderson. Anderson's profit is $35,000. Anderson's contract with Tanner requires Tanner to seek remedies for defects from the manufacturer, but Anderson is responsible for any corrections due to errors in specifications.

Required: Determine whether Anderson is acting as principal or agent in its contract with Tanner.

Solution: Anderson is acting as principal in the contract based on the following indicators:

- Anderson is responsible for fulfilling the contract because it is responsible for ensuring that the excavator meets specifications.

- Anderson has inventory risk because it is responsible for correcting errors in specifications, even though the manufacturer has inventory risk during production.

- Anderson has discretion in establishing the selling price.

5.5   Repurchase Agreements

A repurchase agreement is a contract by which an entity sells an asset and also either promises to or has the option to repurchase the asset. The three main forms of repurchase agreements include: an entity's obligation to repurchase the asset (a forward); an entity's right to repurchase the asset (a call option); and an entity's obligation to repurchase the asset at the customer's request (a put option).

5.5.1   Forward or Call Option

The entity's accounting for the contract will be based on whether it must (forward) or can (call) repurchase the asset for either:

- less than the original selling price (it will be a lease); or

- equal to/more than the original price (it will be a financing arrangement).

If the contract is a financing arrangement, the entity will recognize the asset, recognize a financial liability for any consideration received from the customer, and recognize as interest expense the difference between the amount of consideration received from the customer and the amount of consideration to be paid by the customer.

Example 15   Forward or Call Option

Facts: On January 1, Anderson Co. enters into a contract with Tanner Co. for the sale of an excavator for $350,000. The contract includes a call option that gives Anderson the right to repurchase the excavator for $385,000 on or before December 31. Tanner pays the entity $350,000 on January 1. On December 31, the option lapses unexercised.

Required: Explain how Anderson should account for the transaction on January 1, during the year, and on December 31.

Solution: Anderson should account for the transaction as a financing arrangement because the repurchase price is greater than the original selling price.

On January 1, Anderson recognizes a financial liability of $350,000:

DR	Cash	$350,000	
CR	Financial liability		$350,000

During the year, Anderson recognizes interest expense of $35,000, the difference between the repurchase price of $385,000 and the cash received of $350,000.

DR	Interest expense	$35,000	
CR	Financial liability		$35,000

On December 31, when the option lapses, Anderson derecognizes the liability and records a sale:

DR	Financial liability	$385,000	
CR	Revenue		$385,000

5.5.2 Put Option

If the entity has an obligation to repurchase the asset at the customer's request for less than the original selling price, the entity will account for the contract as either:

- a lease (if the customer has a significant economic incentive to exercise the right); or
- a sale with a right of return (if the customer does not have a significant economic incentive to exercise the right).

If the repurchase price is equal to or greater than the original selling price, the entity accounts for the contract as either:

- a financing arrangement (if the repurchase price is more than the expected market value of the asset); or
- a sale with a right of return (if the repurchase price is less than or equal to the expected market value of the asset and the customer does not have a significant economic incentive to exercise the right).

Example 16	Put Option

Facts: On January 1, Anderson Co. enters into a contract with Tanner Co. for the sale of an excavator for $350,000. The contract includes a put option that obliges Anderson to repurchase the excavator at Tanner's request for $315,000 on or before December 31. The market value is expected to be $275,000 on December 31. Tanner pays Anderson $350,000 on January 1.

Required: Determine whether Anderson should account for this transaction as a lease, a financing arrangement, or a sale with a right of return.

Solution: The transaction should be accounted for as a lease because Anderson has an obligation to repurchase the excavator for less than the original selling price, and Tanner has a significant economic incentive to exercise the option because the repurchase price is greater than the market value expected on December 31.

5.6 Bill-and-Hold Arrangements

Bill-and-hold arrangements are contracts in which the entity bills a customer for a product that it has not yet delivered to the customer. Revenue cannot be recognized in a bill-and-hold arrangement until the customer obtains control of the product. Generally, control is transferred to the customer when the product is shipped to or delivered to the customer (depending on the terms of the contract). For a customer to have obtained control of a product in a bill-and-hold arrangement, *all* of the following criteria must be met:

- There must be a substantive reason for the arrangement (e.g., the customer has requested the arrangement because it does not have space for the product).
- The product has been separately identified as belonging to the customer.
- The product is currently ready for transfer to the customer.
- The entity cannot use the product or direct it to another customer.

Example 17   Bill and Hold

Facts: On January 1, Anderson Co. enters into a contract with Tanner Co. for the sale of an excavator and spare parts. The manufacturing lead time is 18 months. On July 1 of the following year, Tanner pays for the machine and spare parts, but only takes possession of the machine. Tanner inspects and accepts the spare parts, but requests that the parts be stored in Anderson's warehouse because Tanner does not have a place to store the parts and its premises are very close to Anderson's warehouse.

Anderson expects to store the spare parts in a separate section of its warehouse for three years. The parts are available for immediate delivery to Tanner. Anderson cannot use the spare parts or transfer them to another customer.

Required: Identify the performance obligation(s) in this contract and determine when revenue is recognized on each performance obligation.

Solution: There are three performance obligations in this contract:

1. Promise to provide the excavator

2. Promise to provide spare parts

3. Custodial services related to the spare parts

Tanner obtains control of the spare parts on July 1 because all of the criteria are met (i.e., there is a substantive reason for Anderson to hold the spare parts, the parts are separately identified and ready to transfer, and Anderson cannot use the parts or transfer them to another customer).

Anderson recognizes revenue for the excavator and spare parts on July 1 when the excavator is transferred to Tanner and Tanner has obtained control of the spare parts.

Anderson recognizes revenue on the custodial services over the three years that the services are provided.

5.7   Consignment

Consignment is when the dealer or distributor has not obtained control of the product. Revenue is recognized when the dealer or distributor sells the product to a customer, or when the dealer or distributor obtains control of the product (i.e., after a specified period of time expires).

Indicators of a consignment arrangement include:

- The entity controls the product until a specified event occurs (the sale of the product to the customer or a specific time period expires).

- The dealer does not have an unconditional obligation to pay the entity for the product (although it might be required to pay a deposit).

- The entity can require the return of the product or transfer the product to another party.

Example 18	Sale or Consignment

Facts: FMC, a large multinational car manufacturer, delivers cars to a car dealer on the following terms:

- Legal title passes on sale to the public.

- The car dealer must pay for the car when legal title passes. The price to the car dealer is determined on the date FMC delivers the cars to the dealership.

- FMC can require the return of the cars and, if not sold by the car dealer, can transfer the cars to another dealer.

Required: Determine whether FMC should account for the delivery of the cars to the car dealer as a sale or a consignment arrangement.

Solution: FMC should account for the delivery of cars to the car dealer as a consignment arrangement because the dealer has not obtained control of the cars, as evidenced by the fact that FMC can require the return or transfer of the cars and the dealer does not have an unconditional obligation to pay FMC for the cars. Revenue should not be recognized until the dealer sells a car.

5.8 Warranties

The accounting for a warranty will depend on whether a customer has the option to purchase the warranty separately. If it can be purchased separately, the warranty will be considered a distinct service because it is promised to the customer in addition to the product covered by the contract. An entity will therefore account for the warranty as a performance obligation and allocate a portion of the overall transaction price to that obligation. If the warranty cannot be purchased separately, then there is no separate performance obligation.

The following factors should be considered when determining whether the warranty represents a service in addition to the assurance that a product is compliant with agreed-upon specifications:

- If the law requires the warranty, this would indicate that it is not a performance obligation.

- The longer the coverage period, the higher the likelihood that it is a performance obligation.

- If an entity must perform specific tasks to provide assurance regarding product compliance with agreed-upon specifications, these tasks are likely not a performance obligation.

If a warranty provides a service to a customer that is beyond the assurance that the product will comply with agreed-upon specifications, the promised service will represent a performance obligation that will require the transaction price be allocated to both the product itself and the service.

5.9   Refund Liabilities and the Right to Return

An entity should recognize a refund liability if it receives or will receive consideration from a customer and anticipates having to refund a portion or all of that consideration. The refund liability represents the amount an entity does not expect to be entitled to receive.

For products with a right of return (which may involve the customer receiving a refund, a credit, or another product in exchange for the original product), an entity should recognize:

- Revenue for transferred products equaling the amount of consideration the entity expects to be entitled to receive (revenue will not be recognized for products that entities anticipate having to return)

- A refund liability

- An asset related to the subsequent recovery of products when the refund liability is settled

---

Illustration 2   Sales Returns

Journal entry to record an initial liability on a cash sale of $50,000 where 10 percent of items purchased tend to be returned:

DR	Cash	$50,000	
CR	Refund liability		$ 5,000
CR	Sales revenue		45,000

Journal entry to record cash paid to customer who returns $3,000 in goods purchased:

DR	Refund liability	$3,000	
CR	Cash		$3,000

NOTES

1 Changes in Accounting Estimate (Prospective Application)

A change in accounting estimate occurs when it is determined that the estimate previously used by the company is incorrect.

1.1 Events Resulting in Estimate Changes

- Changes in the lives of fixed assets.
- Adjustments of year-end accrual of officers' salaries and/or bonuses.
- Write-downs of obsolete inventory.
- Material, nonrecurring IRS adjustments.
- Settlement of litigation.
- Changes in accounting principle that are inseparable from a change in estimate (e.g., a change from the installment method to immediate recognition method because uncollectible accounts can now be estimated).
- Revisions of estimates regarding discontinued operations.

Example 1	Change in Accounting Estimate

Facts: Carlin Company buys a truck for $90,000. The truck is expected to last 10 years. During the third year, Carlin Company realizes that the truck is only going to last a total of five years. The truck is depreciated on the straight-line basis and has no estimated salvage value.

Required: Create a depreciation schedule for the life of the truck (five years).

Solution:

Depreciation Schedule

Year	Depreciation
1	$ 9,000 [$90,000/10]
2	$ 9,000 [$90,000/10]
3	$24,000 [$72,000/3]
4	$24,000 [$72,000/3]
5	$24,000 [$72,000/3]
	$90,000

1.2 Reporting a Change in Estimate

1.2.1 Prospectively

Changes in accounting estimate are accounted for prospectively (i.e., implement in the current period and continue in future periods). They do not affect previous periods (i.e., no effect on previously reported retained earnings).

1.2.2 Change in Estimate Affecting Future Periods

If a change in accounting estimate affects several future periods (e.g., a revision of service lives of depreciable assets), the effect on income from continuing operations, net income, and the related per share information for the current year should be disclosed in the notes to the financial statements.

Note: Changes in ordinary accounting estimates (e.g., uncollectible accounts and inventory adjustments) usually made each period do not have to be disclosed unless they are material.

2 Changes in Accounting Principle (Retrospective Application)

A change in accounting principle is a change in accounting from one accounting principle to another acceptable accounting principle (e.g., GAAP to GAAP).

2.1 Rule of Preferability

An accounting principle may be changed only if required by GAAP (a newly issued codification update) or if the alternative principle is preferable and more fairly presents the information.

2.2 Effects of a Change

2.2.1 Direct Effects

The direct effects of a change in accounting principle are adjustments that would be necessary to restate the financial statements of prior periods.

2.2.2 Indirect Effects

The indirect effects of a change in accounting principle are differences in nondiscretionary items based on earnings (e.g., bonuses) that would have occurred if the new principle had been used in prior periods.

2.2.3 Cumulative Effect

If noncomparative financial statements are being presented, then the cumulative effect of a change in accounting principle is equal to the difference between the amount of beginning retained earnings in the period of change and what the retained earnings would have been if the accounting change had been retroactively applied to all prior affected periods. It includes direct effects and only those indirect effects that are entered in the accounting records. If comparative financial statements are being presented, then the cumulative effect is equal to the difference between beginning retained earnings in the first period presented and what retained earnings would have been if the new principle had been applied to all prior periods. The cumulative effect of a change in accounting principle is presented net of tax as an adjustment to beginning retained earnings in the statement of stockholders' equity.

Illustration 1	Cumulative Effect of a Change in Accounting Principle

On January 1, Year 5, Harbor Company decided to switch to the weighted average method of inventory accounting. Prior to Year 5, Harbor used FIFO to account for its inventory. Harbor's effective tax rate is 30 percent.

Pretax income information is as follows:

	Pretax Income Under	
	Weighted Average	**FIFO**
Prior to Year 5	$800,000	$600,000

Cumulative effect adjustment as of 1/1/Year 5	$200,000
Less income tax effect at 30 percent	(60,000)
Cumulative effect net of income tax	$140,000

The $140,000 cumulative effect net of income tax would adjust the beginning retained earnings balance within the statement of stockholders' equity.

2.3   Reporting Changes in an Accounting Principle

The general rule is that changes in accounting principle should be recognized by adjusting beginning retained earnings in the earliest period presented for the cumulative effect of the change, and, if prior period (comparative) financial statements are presented, they should be restated (retrospective application).

2.3.1   Exceptions to the General Rule

- **Impracticable to Estimate:** To prepare a change in accounting principle handled retrospectively, the amount of the cumulative effect adjustment must be calculated as of the beginning of the first period presented. If it is considered "impractical" to accurately calculate this cumulative effect adjustment, then the change is handled prospectively (like a change in estimate). An example of a change handled in this manner is a change in inventory cost flow assumption to LIFO (under U.S. GAAP). Since a cumulative effect adjustment to LIFO would require the reestablishment and recalculation of old inventory layers, it is considered impractical to try to rebuild those old cost layers. This change is therefore handled prospectively. The beginning inventory of the year of change is the first LIFO layer. Additional LIFO layers are added from that point forward.

- **Change in Depreciation Method:** A change in the method of depreciation, amortization, or depletion is considered to be both a change in accounting principle and a change in estimate. These changes should be accounted for as changes in estimate and are handled prospectively. The new depreciation method should be used as of the beginning of the year of the change in estimate and should start with the current book value of the underlying asset. No retroactive or retrospective calculations should be made, and no adjustment should be made to retained earnings.

2.3.2 Applications of the General Rule

- The amount of cumulative effect to be reported on the retained earnings statement is the difference between:
  - retained earnings at the beginning of the earliest period presented; and
  - retained earnings that would have been reported at the beginning of the earliest period presented if the new accounting principle had been applied retrospectively for all prior periods, by recognizing only the direct effects and related income tax effect.
- The new accounting principle is used for all periods presented (prior periods are restated).
- If an accounting change is not considered material in the year of change but is reasonably expected to become material in later periods, it should be fully disclosed in the year of change.

2.3.3 Nonrecurring Changes

An accounting change should not be made for a transaction or event in the past that has been terminated or is nonrecurring.

3   Changes in Accounting Entity (Retrospective Application)

Under U.S. GAAP, a change in accounting entity occurs when the entity being reported on has changed composition. Examples include consolidated or combined financial statements that are presented in place of statements of the individual companies and changes in the companies included in the consolidated or combined financial statements from year to year.

3.1   Restatement to Reflect Information for the New Entity (if Comparative Financial Statements Are Presented)

If a change in accounting entity occurs in the current year, all previous financial statements that are presented in comparative financial statements along with the current year should be restated to reflect the information for the new reporting entity.

3.2   Full Disclosure

Full disclosure of the cause and nature of the change should be made, including changes in income from continuing operations, net income, and retained earnings.

4   Error Correction (Prior Period Adjustment)

Error corrections are not accounting changes. Error corrections include:

- Corrections of errors in recognition, measurement, presentation, or disclosure in financial statements resulting from mathematical mistakes, mistakes in the application of U.S. GAAP, or oversight or misuse of facts that existed at the time the financial statements were prepared.
- Changes from a non-GAAP method of accounting to a GAAP method of accounting (e.g., cash basis to accrual basis), which is a specific correction of an error.

4.1   Comparative Financial Statements Presented

4.1.1   Correct the Information (if the Year Is Presented)

If comparative financial statements are presented and financial statements for the year with the error are presented, merely correct the error in those prior financial statements.

4.1.2   Adjust Beginning Retained Earnings of the Earliest Year Presented (if the Year Is Not Presented)

If comparative financial statements are presented and financial statements for the year with the error are not presented (e.g., because it is too far back in years), adjust (net of tax) the opening retained earnings of the earliest year presented.

4.2   Comparative Financial Statements Not Presented

If comparative financial statements are not presented, the error correction should be reported as an adjustment to the opening balance of retained earnings (net of tax).

4.3   Effect on the Statement of Retained Earnings

The purpose of the statement of retained earnings is to reconcile the beginning balance of retained earnings with the ending balance. It is usually presented immediately following the income statement or as a component of the statement of stockholders' equity.

Example 2   Accounting Changes and Error Corrections

Facts: In Year 4, Jordan Manufacturing discovered that depreciation expense was incorrectly calculated in Years 1 and 2. In total, $4,500,000 of depreciation expense was not recorded during these two years.

At the beginning of Year 4, Jordan Manufacturing decided to change inventory methods from the last-in first-out (LIFO) cost flow assumption to the first-in first-out (FIFO) cost flow assumption. The following information details the pretax income under LIFO and FIFO for Years 1 through 3.

	Pretax Income Under		
	LIFO	**FIFO**	**Difference**
Year 1	$3,000,000	$3,750,000	$ 750,000
Year 2	3,400,000	5,500,000	2,100,000
Year 3	4,100,000	6,250,000	2,150,000

Jordan's tax rate is 40 percent.

Required:

1. Calculate the required adjustment for the depreciation error and indicate how this correction should be presented in the financial statements.

2. Calculate the cumulative adjustment for the change in principle and indicate how the adjustment should be reported in the financial statements.

(continued)

(continued)

Solution:

1. As Jordan is presenting financial information for the current Year 4 only, the depreciation error should be reported as an adjustment to retained earnings net of tax. The $4,500,000 depreciation not recorded in Years 1–3 results in a $2,700,000 adjustment to beginning retained earnings:

    $4,500,000 × (1 − 40%) = $2,700,000

2. The change in accounting principle (from LIFO to FIFO) should also be reported as an adjustment to retained earnings net of tax. The sum of the increases in pretax income in Years 1–3 as a result of the change is $5,000,000 ($750,000 + $2,100,000 + $2,150,000), and the net of tax adjustment is:

    $5,000,000 × (1 − 40%) = $3,000,000

3 Adjusting Journal Entries

1 Matching Revenues and Related Expenses

Accrual basis accounting is in accordance with U.S. GAAP and matches revenues with expenses. In order to properly match revenues with expenses in the periods in which they occur, it is sometimes necessary to *defer* or *accrue* revenues or expenses.

- In the case of unearned (deferred) revenues, cash is received before the revenue is earned (e.g., magazine subscription revenues are collected January 1, Year 1, for the calendar year ending December 31, Year 1).

- In the case of prepaid (deferred) expenses, cash is paid before the expense is incurred (e.g., prepaying rent today for the upcoming year).

- In the case of accrued revenues (receivables), cash is received after the revenue has been earned (e.g., you made a sale on credit and the customer actually pays you 30 days later).

- In the case of accrued expenses (accrued liabilities, accounts payable, or other payables), cash is paid after the expense has been incurred (e.g., you incur utilities expense but don't pay the bill until next month).

2 Adjusting Journal Entries

In order for financial statements to be prepared in accordance with the accrual basis of accounting, adjusting entries must be recorded.

2.1 Unearned Revenues and Prepaid Expenses

If revenue has been deferred, the company must calculate the amount of revenue that has been earned through year-end and make the appropriate adjusting journal entry.

Journal entry to record unearned revenue:

DR	Cash	$XXX	
CR	Unearned revenue		$XXX

Adjusting journal entry to record unearned revenue that has been earned:

DR	Unearned revenue	$XXX	
CR	Revenue		$XXX

If expenses have been deferred (prepaid), the company must calculate the amount of expenses that have been incurred through year-end and make the appropriate adjusting journal entry.

Journal entry to record prepaid expense:

DR	Prepaid expense (asset)	$XXX	
CR	Cash		$XXX

Adjusting journal entry to reverse prepaid expense and record incurred expense:

DR	Expense	$XXX	
CR	Prepaid expense		$XXX

2.2 Accrued Revenues and Expense

An entity must assess whether revenues have been earned prior to the cash being received. If so, revenues must be accrued by recording a receivable.

Journal entry to record accrued revenue:

DR	Accounts receivable	$XXX	
CR	Revenue		$XXX

An entity must also assess if expenses have been incurred prior to the cash being paid. If so, expenses must be accrued by recording accrued liabilities, accounts payable, or other payable (e.g., wages payable).

DR	Expense	$XXX	
CR	Accrued liability		$XXX

2.3 Error Corrections

In some instances, an entity may record cash receipts (disbursements) to a revenue/expense account when they should have been recorded to an asset/liability account. An adjusting entry may be required in this case to ensure that the financial statements are in accordance with the accrual basis of accounting (e.g., recording the prepayment of insurance directly to insurance expense rather than prepaid insurance).

2.4 Rules for Recording Adjusting Journal Entries

- Adjusting journal entries must be recorded by the end of the entity's fiscal year, before the preparation of financial statements.

- Adjusting journal entries *never* involve the cash account.

- All adjusting entries will hit one income statement account and one balance sheet account.

Example 1 — Adjusting Journal Entries: Unearned Revenue

Facts: On December 1, Year 1, Impact Inc. received $250,000 in cash for services to be performed equally during December Year 1, and January Year 2. Impact Inc. recorded the entry as a credit to unearned service revenue.

Required: Prepare the journal entry to record the unearned revenue on December 1, Year 1, and the adjusting journal entry required at year-end.

Solution:

December 1, Year 1—journal entry to record deferred revenue:

DR	Cash	$250,000	
CR	Unearned service revenue		$250,000

December 31, Year 1—adjusting journal entry to record revenue earned during Year 1:

DR	Unearned service revenue	$125,000	
CR	Service revenue		$125,000

Example 2 — Adjusting Journal Entries: Accrued Interest

Facts: On November 1, Year 1, Impact Inc. borrowed $2,000,000 from Federal Bank at a rate of 3 percent with interest due annually on November 1. The principal will be paid back on November 1, Year 11.

Required: Prepare the journal entry to record the loan on November 1, Year 1, and the adjusting journal entry for the accrued interest at year-end.

Solution:

November 1, Year 1—journal entry to record loan from Federal Bank:

DR	Cash	$2,000,000	
CR	Note payable		$2,000,000

December 31, Year 1—adjusting journal entry to record the interest accrued from November–December of Year 1 ($2,000,000 × 3% × 2/12 = $10,000):

DR	Interest expense	$10,000	
CR	Interest payable		$10,000

Example 3	Adjusting Journal Entries: Comprehensive Example

Facts: Titan Company reported pretax income in Year 2 of $8,000. Upon review of the general ledger, the following information listed in the first column was discovered.

Required: If necessary, record an adjustment to pretax income in the table provided so that the income statement and balance sheet will be presented in accordance with the accrual basis of accounting. Prepare the adjusting journal entries required to record these adjustments.

Solution:

	Adjustment to Year 2 Pretax Income	Adjustments to Balance Sheet	
		Assets	Liabilities and Equity
Unadjusted Year 2 pretax income	$8,000		
1. The company purchased a $300, three-year insurance policy on 1/1/Year 2 and expensed it all on the payment date.	200	$ 200	
2. $2,000 of credit sales made during Year 2 were not recorded in the ledger because they had not been collected in cash.	2,000	2,000	
3. Cash totaling $3,000 that was received in advance from customers was recorded to service revenue. Only 30 percent of the services had been performed by year-end.	(2,100)		$2,100
4. The accountant discovered that a $450 utility bill covering the month of December had not been entered in the AP system at year-end.	(450)		450
5. $4,000 of rent was prepaid on 1/1/Year 1, covering a four-year rental period. No entry was recorded in Year 2 related to this prepayment.	(1,000)	(1,000)	
6. The direct write-off method (non-GAAP method) was used to write off a $650 bad debt in Year 2, although the company uses the allowance approach to estimate bad debts.	650	650	
7. The company purchased $1,300 of raw materials at year-end which were shipped FOB shipping point and were in transit at the end of the year. The goods were not included in the actual year-end inventory count (the effect of this correction on the financial statements is the same whether the perpetual or periodic inventory system is used.)		1,300	1,300
8. The company purchased available-for-sale securities during Year 2 for $1,500. The fair value at year-end totaled $2,000 but no adjustment to fair value was recorded in the ledger.		500	500
Total adjustments	$ (700)	$3,650	$4,350
Adjusted Year 2 pretax income	$7,300		

(continued)

(continued)

1. The $300 paid for insurance during the year should have been debited to *prepaid insurance*. At year-end, two years of insurance coverage are left and one year has expired. The $200 reduction in expense increases pretax income for the year. The $200 debit under balance sheet reflects the correct balance of *prepaid insurance* as of that date. At year-end, two years of insurance coverage remain.

DR	Prepaid insurance	$200	
CR	Insurance expense		$200

2. According to the revenue recognition principle and accrual accounting, sales should be recorded when the performance obligation is satisfied. The $2,000 credit to income properly records the sale, and the debit to the balance sheet properly reflects the claim to cash that exists at year-end.

DR	Accounts receivable	$2,000	
CR	Sales revenue		$2,000

3. The receipt of cash in advance from a customer should not have been recorded as service revenue because it represents unearned revenue. At year-end, 30 percent of the services had been performed, so $900 is valid service revenue. $2,100 had to be removed from income and recorded as an obligation on the balance sheet at year-end to reflect remaining services to be performed.

DR	Sales revenue	$2,100	
CR	Unearned revenue		$2,100

4. Expenses should be recorded in the period incurred. The $450 charge to income records the correct expense incurred. The year-end balance sheet now reflects the $450 as accounts payable (utilities payable).

DR	Utilities expense	$450	
CR	A/P (Utilities payable)		$450

5. There was no cash outflow in the current year related to the rent expense, but one year of rent expense must be charged to income. The $1,000 reflects the expense incurred in the current year. The prepaid rent balance from the prior year-end is reduced and the current year-end prepaid balance would total $2,000, as two years of benefit remain.

DR	Rent expense	$1,000	
CR	Prepaid rent		$1,000

(continued)

(continued)

6. Because the company uses the allowance approach to record estimated bad debts, we can assume that an estimate of bad debt was recorded when the sale was originally recorded. The direct write-off was recorded to bad debt expense when it should have been recorded to the allowance account. The effect of this correction is to increase income and increase assets (assets increase because we are reducing a contra-asset account).

DR	Allowance for doubtful accounts	$650	
CR	Bad debt expense		$650

7. The correct journal to record the inventory in transit at year-end:

DR	Inventory (perpetual system, *or:* Purchases (periodic system)	$1,300	
CR	Accounts payable		$1,300

8. Available-for-sale securities must be reported on the balance sheet at fair value. The valuation account increases the value of the investment on the balance sheet. The unrealized gain affects equity through accumulated other comprehensive income.

DR	Valuation account (fair value adjustment)	$500	
CR	Unrealized gain on available-for-sale securities)		$500

4 Notes to Financial Statements

1 Summary of Significant Accounting Policies

U.S. GAAP requires that a description of all significant policies be included as an integral part of the financial statements. The preferred presentation is to include the "Summary of Significant Accounting Policies" as the first or second note to the financial statements. Policies presented in other notes should not be duplicated.

1.1 Disclosures

The summary of significant accounting policies includes disclosures of:

- Measurement bases used in preparing the financial statements.
- Specific accounting principles and methods used during the period, including:
  - Basis of consolidation
  - Depreciation methods
  - Amortization of intangibles
  - Inventory pricing
  - Use of estimates
  - Fiscal year definition
  - Special revenue recognition issues (e.g., long-term construction contracts, franchising, leasing operations, etc.)

1.2 Items Not Included

The summary of significant accounting policies would not include the following items:

- Composition and detailed dollar amounts of account balances
- Details relating to changes in accounting principles
- Dates of maturity and amounts of long-term debt
- Yearly computation of depreciation, depletion, and amortization

2 Remaining Notes to the Financial Statements

The remaining notes contain all other information relevant to decision makers (e.g., investors, creditors, etc.) These notes are used to disclose facts not presented in either the body of the financial statements or in the Summary of Significant Accounting Policies. Examples of relevant note information include the following:

- Material information regarding inventory, property, plant, and equipment, and other significant asset/liability balances that require specific disclosures;

- Changes in stockholders' equity, including capital stock, paid-in capital, retained earnings, treasury stock, stock dividends, and other capital changes;

- Required marketable securities disclosure, including carrying value and gross unrealized gains and losses;

- Fair value estimates;

- Contingency losses;

- Contingency gains (if highly probable, but care should be exercised to avoid misleading implications as to the likelihood of realization);

- Contractual obligations (including bonds payable and notes payable), including restrictions on specific assets or liabilities;

- Pension plan description;

- Segment reporting;

- Subsequent events; and

- Changes in accounting principles or implementation of new accounting standards update.

3 Disclosure of Risks and Uncertainties

U.S. GAAP requires the disclosure of risks and uncertainties existing at the date(s) of the financial statements in the following areas:

3.1 Nature of Operations

The footnotes should include a description of the entity's major products or services and its principal markets, including the locations of those markets. If the entity operates multiple businesses, the disclosure should describe the relative importance of each business.

3.2 Use of Estimates in the Preparation of Financial Statements

The footnotes should include the following statement (or a similar statement):

The preparation of financial statements in conformity with generally accepted accounting principles (GAAP) requires management to make estimates and assumptions that affect the reported amounts of assets and liabilities, the disclosure of contingent assets and liabilities at the date of the financial statements, and the reported amounts of revenues and expenses during the reporting period. Actual results could differ from those estimates.

3.3   Certain Significant Estimates

When it is reasonably possible that an estimate will change in the near term and that the effect of the change will be material, an estimate of the effect of the change should be disclosed.

The following are examples of assets and liabilities and related revenues and expenses, including gain and loss contingencies that may be based on estimates that are particularly sensitive to change:

- Inventory or equipment subject to rapid technological obsolescence.
- Deferred tax asset valuation allowances.
- Capitalized computer software costs.
- Loan valuation allowances.
- Litigation-related obligations.
- Amounts reported for long-term obligations, such as pension and postretirement benefits.
- Amounts reported in long-term contracts.

3.4   Current Vulnerability Due to Certain Concentrations

3.4.1   Definition

Vulnerability due to concentrations arise when an entity is exposed to risk of loss that could be mitigated through diversification.

3.4.2   Disclosure Requirements

Concentrations should be disclosed if all of the following criteria are met:

- The concentration exists at the financial statement date.
- The concentration makes the entity vulnerable to the risk of a near-term severe impact (a significant financially disruptive effect on the normal functioning of an entity).
- It is at least reasonably possible that the events that could cause the severe impact will occur in the near term.

3.4.3   Examples of Concentrations

The following are common examples of concentrations:

- Concentrations in the volume of business transacted with a particular customer, supplier, lender, grantor, or contributor.
- Concentrations in revenue from particular products, services, or fund-raising events.
- Concentrations in the available supply of resources, such as materials, labor, or services.
- Concentrations in market or geographic area.

NOTES

1 Definition of a Subsequent Event

A subsequent event is an event or transaction that occurs after the balance sheet date but before the financial statements are issued or are available to be issued. Subsequent events can be divided into two categories:

1.1 Recognized Subsequent Events

Recognized subsequent events provide additional information about conditions that existed at the balance sheet date. Entities must recognize the effects of all recognized subsequent events in the financial statements. The following subsequent events are considered to be recognized subsequent events:

- **Settlement of Litigation:** If litigation that arose before the balance sheet date is settled after the balance sheet date but before the date that the financial statements are issued or available to be issued, the settlement amount should be considered when determining the liability to be reported on the balance sheet date.

- **Loss on an Uncollectible Receivable:** The effects of a customer's bankruptcy filing after the balance sheet date but before the date that the financial statements are issued or available to be issued should be considered when determining the amount of the uncollectible receivable to be recognized in the financial statements on the balance sheet date.

1.2 Nonrecognized Subsequent Events

An entity should not recognize subsequent events that provide information about conditions that did not exist at the balance sheet date.

The following subsequent events occurring after the balance sheet date but before the date the financial statements are issued or are available to be issued are considered to be nonrecognized subsequent events:

- Sale of bond or capital stock
- Business combination
- Settlement of litigation, if the litigation arose after the balance sheet date
- Loss of plant or inventory due to fire or natural disaster
- Changes in the fair value of assets, liabilities, or foreign exchange rates
- Entering into significant commitments or contingent liabilities
- Loss on receivables resulting from conditions occurring after the balance sheet date

A nonrecognized subsequent event should be disclosed if disclosure is necessary to keep the financial statements from being misleading. Disclosure should include the nature of the subsequent event and an estimate of the financial effect of the event or a statement that no estimate can be made. Pro forma financial statements showing the effect of the subsequent event if it had occurred on the balance sheet date may also be presented.

2 Subsequent Event Evaluation Period

An entity that files financial statements with the Securities and Exchange Commission (SEC) must evaluate subsequent events through the *date that the financial statements are issued*. All other entities must evaluate subsequent events through the *date that the financial statements are available to be issued*. Financial statements are considered to be issued when they have been widely distributed to financial statement users in a form and format that complies with GAAP. Financial statements are available to be issued when they are in a form and format that complies with GAAP and all approvals for issuance have been obtained.

If an entity is not an SEC filer, then the entity must disclose the date through which subsequent events have been evaluated, including whether that date is the date the financial statements were issued or the date that the financial statements were available to be issued. This disclosure is not required for SEC filers to avoid potential conflicts with current SEC guidance.

3 Reissuance of Financial Statements

When an entity reissues its financial statements, the entity should not recognize events that occurred between the date the original financial statements were issued or available to be issued and the date that the financial statements were reissued, unless an adjustment is required by GAAP or other regulatory requirements.

4 Revised Financial Statements

Revised financial statements are financial statements that have been revised to correct an error or to reflect the retrospective application of U.S. GAAP. Revised financial statements are considered reissued financial statements. If an entity is not an SEC filer, the entity should disclose in its revised financial statements the dates through which subsequent events have been evaluated in both its issued/available-to-be-issued financial statements and its revised financial statements. This disclosure is not required for SEC filers.

Example 1	Subsequent Events

Facts: Friends of Fido is an SEC filer and has a balance sheet date of December 31, Year 3. The entity will file financial statements by the end of March, Year 4. The following events occurred after the balance sheet date.

1. A lawsuit filed in Year 2 was settled in early February. Friends of Fido must pay $600,000 as a result of the lawsuit. The financial statements currently reflect a contingency amount of $725,000.

2. The entity announced in early March that it will acquire Dawghouse Inc. for $1.5 million. The acquisition, which is planned for September, Year 4, will be made with cash and stock.

3. A customer that had significant aged invoices at year-end announced bankruptcy in January.

4. A second customer that is typically a timely payer had multiple outstanding invoices at year-end. The customer experienced a flood in February and the entire retail location was wiped out. The customer has decided to close its business permanently and is not returning phone calls regarding payment.

Required: Determine how these subsequent events should be treated in the financial statements.

Solution:

1. This subsequent event relates to a condition that existed at the December 31, Year 3, balance sheet date and should be treated as a recognized subsequent event. The contingency in the financial statements should be adjusted to reflect the settlement amount of $600,000 rather than the current estimate of $725,000.

2. The expected acquisition of Dawghouse Inc. is an example of a nonrecognized subsequent event. The expected acquisition is a material event and should be disclosed in the financial statements but does not required adjustment in the financial statements at December 31, Year 3.

3. The bankruptcy of a customer whose account balances were significantly past due results in a recognized subsequent event. Because the condition (the customer's inability to pay) has occurred over time and existed at the financial statement year-end, the declaration of bankruptcy needs to be accounted for in the analysis of accounts receivable and bad debt expense for December 31, Year 3.

4. Although this customer's receivable balance may be past due, this subsequent event is a nonrecognized subsequent event for two reasons. First, there was no evidence at year-end that this customer, which has always been a timely payer, was not going to pay the past-due invoices. Second, the flood and subsequent decision to close the retail shop did not occur until after year-end. If the outstanding invoices are considered material, this information may require disclosure in the financial statements, but no adjustment is required. If not material, no disclosure would be required.

NOTES

6 Fair Value Measurements

1 Fair Value Overview

U.S. GAAP has standardized the definition of fair value, established a framework for measuring fair value, and outlined required fair value disclosures for all areas that require or permit fair value measurement, *except*:

- share-based compensation;

- measurements based on or using vendor-specific objective evidence of fair value; and

- fair value measurements used for lease classification or measurement.

1.1 Fair Value Defined

Fair value is the price that would be received to sell an asset or paid to transfer a liability in an orderly transaction between market participants in the principal (or most advantageous) market at the measurement date under current market conditions.

- Fair value is measured for a specific asset or liability, a group of assets and/or liabilities, or an entity's own equity instrument (e.g., an equity interest issued as consideration in a business combination).

- Fair value is a market-based measure, not an entity-based measure.

- Fair value is measured in the principal market for the asset or liability, or the most advantageous market in the absence of a principal market.

- Fair value is an exit price (the price to sell an asset or transfer a liability), not an entrance price (the price to acquire an asset or assume a liability).

- A fair value measure should reflect all of the assumptions that market participants would use in pricing the asset or liability, including assumptions about risk.

- Fair value does not include transaction costs, but may include transportation costs if location is an attribute of the asset or liability.

- The fair value of a nonfinancial asset assumes the highest and best use of the asset.

- The fair value of a liability should include the liability's nonperformance risk, which is the risk that the obligation will not be fulfilled.

- The fair value of an entity's own equity instrument should be measured from the perspective of a market participant who holds that instrument as an asset.

- Fair value measurement assumes that a liability or an entity's own equity instrument is transferred to a market participant at the measurement date and assumes that the liability or equity interest would remain outstanding and would not be settled, canceled, or extinguished on the measurement date.

2 Fair Value Terminology

2.1 Orderly Transaction

An orderly transaction is one in which the asset or liability is exposed to the market, for a period before the measurement date, long enough to allow for marketing activities that are usual and customary for transactions involving such assets or liabilities. An orderly transaction cannot be a forced transaction.

2.2 Market Participants

Market participants are buyers and sellers who are independent (not related parties), knowledgeable about the asset or liability, able to transact for the asset or liability, and willing to transact for the asset or liability. They are considered to be acting in their economic best interest.

2.3 Principal Market

The principal market is the market with the greatest volume or level of activity for the asset or liability. If there is a principal market for an asset or liability, the price in that market will be the fair value measurement, even if there is a more advantageous price in a different market. The reporting entity must have access to the principal market at the measurement date.

2.4 Most Advantageous Market

The most advantageous market is the market with the best price for the asset (maximizes selling price of the asset) or liability (minimizes payment to transfer liability), after considering transaction costs. Note that although transactions costs are used to determine the most advantageous market, transaction costs are not included in the final fair value measurement (see the example below). The price in the most advantageous market will be the fair value measurement only if there is no principal market.

Example 1   Most Advantageous Market

Facts:

- Gearty Inc. holds Foxy Co. stock, which trades on two exchanges (Gearty Inc. can access both the New York and London markets).

- The stock price and transaction costs at the measurement date are as follows:

Exchange	Quoted Stock Price	Transactions Costs	Net
New York	$52	$6	$46
London	50	2	48

Required: Determine the fair value of Foxy stock if New York is the principal market, if London is the principal market, and if there is no principal market.

Solution:

If New York is the principal market	= $52
If London is the principal market	= $50
If no principal market, with London's price (net of transaction costs) having the most advantageous result	= $50

2.5   Highest and Best Use

2.5.1   Nonfinancial Assets

The fair value measurement of a nonfinancial asset takes into account the market participant's ability to generate economic benefits by using the asset in its highest and best use or by selling it to another market participant that would use the asset in its highest and best use.

A reporting entity's current use of a nonfinancial asset is presumed to be its highest and best use, unless market or other factors suggest that a different use by market participants would maximize the value of the asset. The highest and best use of a nonfinancial asset may be to use the asset in combination with other assets, with other assets and liabilities, or on a stand-alone basis.

2.5.2   Liabilities and Financial Assets

The highest and best use concept is not relevant when measuring the fair value of financial assets or the fair value of liabilities because such items do not have alternative uses and their fair values do not depend on their use within a group of other assets or liabilities.

Illustration 1   Fair Value Measurement

As part of a business combination, a reporting entity acquires land that is currently the site of a factory. Similar sites in the area were recently developed for other purposes, including residential and retail space. The highest and best use of the land would be determined by comparing both of the following:

- The value of the land as currently developed for industrial use (value of the land plus the value of the assets/liabilities related to the land, such as the building cost, debt on the land/building, etc.).

- The value of the land as a vacant site for residential or retail use. The cost of tearing down the factory and any related costs must be considered, as well as any uncertainty in converting the land to a vacant site for residential or retail space.

Fair value will be determined based on whichever use results in the highest value.

---

3   Fair Value Measurement Framework

U.S. GAAP has established a framework for measuring fair value. This framework for measuring fair value (i) outlines the *valuation techniques* that can be used to measure fair value, and (ii) establishes a *hierarchy* of the inputs that can be used in these valuation techniques.

3.1   Valuation Techniques

Entities can use the market approach, the income approach, the cost approach, or a combination of these, as appropriate, when measuring the fair value of an asset or a liability. The valuation technique should be appropriate to the circumstances and should maximize the use of observable inputs and minimize the use of unobservable inputs. A change in valuation technique or its application is accounted for as a change in accounting estimate (which is accounted for prospectively).

3.1.1   Market Approach

The *market approach* uses prices and other relevant information from market transactions involving identical or comparable assets or liabilities to measure fair value.

3.1.2 Income Approach

The *income approach* converts future amounts, including cash flows or earnings, to a single discounted amount to measure fair value. This method can be applied to assets or liabilities.

3.1.3 Cost Approach

The *cost approach* uses current replacement cost to measure the fair value of assets.

3.2 Hierarchy of Inputs

The fair value hierarchy prioritizes the inputs that can be used in the valuation techniques described above. Level 1 inputs have the highest priority, and Level 3 inputs have the lowest priority. The level in the fair value hierarchy in which a fair value measurement falls is determined by the lowest level input that is significant to the fair value measurement. Valuation techniques should maximize the use of observable inputs (Level 1 and Level 2) and minimize the use of unobservable inputs (Level 3).

3.2.1 Level 1 Inputs

Level 1 inputs are quoted prices in active markets for identical assets or liabilities that the reporting entity has access to on the measurement date. Quoted prices may be obtained from exchange markets (NYSE), dealer markets, brokered markets and principal-to-principal markets. Level 1 inputs are the most reliable measures of fair value and should be used when available.

3.2.2 Level 2 Inputs

Level 2 inputs are inputs other than quoted market prices (Level 1) that are directly or indirectly observable for the asset or liability. Level 2 inputs include:

- Quoted prices for similar assets or liabilities in active markets.

- Quoted prices for identical or similar assets in markets that are not active.

- Quoted prices for identical liabilities when traded as assets, if adjustments to the quoted market price of the assets are required.

- Quoted prices for similar liabilities when traded as assets.

- Inputs other than quoted prices that are observable for the asset or liability.

- Inputs that are derived from or corroborated by observable market data.

3.2.3 Level 3 Inputs

Level 3 inputs are unobservable inputs for the asset or liability. Unobservable inputs reflect the reporting entity's assumptions and should be based on the best available information. Level 3 inputs should be used only when there are no observable (Level 1 or Level 2) inputs or when undue cost and effort is required to obtain observable inputs.

4   Fair Value Disclosures

The objective of fair value disclosures is to provide users of financial statements with information about assets and liabilities measured at fair value, including:

1. The valuation techniques and inputs the entity uses to arrive at its measures of fair value, including judgments and assumptions that the entity makes;

2. The uncertainty in the fair value measurements as of the reporting date; and

3. How changes in fair value measurements affect the entity's performance and cash flows.

Specifically, an entity must provide the following disclosures regarding fair value measurements:

■   Quantitative information about significant unobservable inputs.

■   Discussion of the sensitivity of Level 3 measurements to changes in unobservable inputs disclosed.

■   Information about nonfinancial assets and liabilities for which measurements differ from highest and best use.

■   Hierarchy for items that are not measured on the balance sheet but are disclosed in the notes to the financial statements.

Example 2   Fair Value Measurement

Facts: During the year, Marker Eight Company purchased 3,000 shares of Milledge Inc.'s common stock. At the time of purchase, the stock was trading at a price of $24 per share. The quoted stock price for Milledge Inc. at year-end according to the public exchange was $21.50 per share.

Required: Calculate the fair value of the stock at year-end and explain how Marker Eight should record any change in fair value.

Solution:

	Original Cost	Fair Value at Year-End
Investment in Milledge Inc.	3,000 × $24.00/share = $72,000	3,000 × $21.50/share = $64,500

Marker Eight must record a $7,500 ($72,000 – $64,500) adjusting entry to decrease the value of the investment on the balance sheet to its fair value of $64,500 at year-end. The other side of the entry will affect net income because the stock is an equity security. This is an example of the market approach as the identical asset is used to determine fair value. The market price for the stock is a Level 1 input.

---

5   Exceptions to Fair Value Measurement

Exemptions to the requirement to measure fair value exist when:

■   it is not practicable to measure fair value;

■   fair value cannot be reasonably determined; or

■   fair value cannot be measured with sufficient reliability.

NOTES

7 Special Purpose Frameworks

1 Special Purpose Frameworks

Special purpose frameworks, also known as other comprehensive bases of accounting (OCBOA), are non-GAAP presentations that have widespread understanding and support. OCBOA presentations include:

- The cash basis and modified cash basis of accounting.

- The tax basis of accounting.

- A definite set of criteria have substantial support that is applied to all material financial statement elements, such as price-level adjusted financial statements.

- A regulatory basis of accounting.

The cash basis, modified cash basis, and tax basis of accounting are the most commonly used special purpose frameworks.

1.1 General Presentation Guidelines

The following guidelines apply to all OCBOA financial statement presentations:

- Financial statement titles should differentiate the OCBOA financial statements from accrual basis financial statements.

- The required financial statements are the equivalents of the accrual basis balance sheet and income statement.

- The financial statements should explain changes in equity accounts.

- A statement of cash flows is not required.

- Disclosures in OCBOA financial statements should be similar to the disclosures in GAAP financial statements and should include:

  - A summary of significant accounting policies.

  - Informative disclosures similar to those required by GAAP for all financial statement items that are the same as or similar to those in GAAP financial statements.

  - Disclosures related to items not shown on the face of the financial statements, such as related party transactions, subsequent events, and uncertainties.

1.2 Cash Basis and Modified Cash Basis Financial Statements

Entities that are not required to use the accrual basis of accounting may choose to present cash basis or modified cash basis financial statements because they are simple to prepare and easy to understand. Cash basis financial statements are not well-suited for entities that have complex operations.

1.2.1 Cash Basis Financial Statements

Under the cash basis of accounting, revenues are recognized when cash is received and expenses are recognized when cash is paid. Cash basis financial statements are generally used by estates and trusts, civic ventures, and political campaigns and committees.

Cash basis financial statements include a statement of cash and equity and a statement of cash receipts and disbursements.

- **Statement of Cash and Equity**

  In pure cash basis financial statements, cash is the only asset, no liabilities are recorded, and equity is equal to cash.

- **Statement of Cash Receipts and Disbursements**

  The statement of cash receipts and disbursements includes the following:

  - Revenues received
  - Debt and equity proceeds
  - Proceeds from asset sales
  - Expenses paid
  - Debt repayments
  - Dividend payments
  - Payments for purchases of assets

1.2.2 Modified Cash Basis Financial Statements

Most for-profit and not-for-profit organizations that produce cash basis financial statements use the modified cash basis of accounting. The modified cash basis is a hybrid method that includes elements of both cash basis and accrual basis accounting. Modifications should not be so extensive that the modified cash basis financial statements become accrual basis financial statements.

- **Common Modifications**

  Modifications made to cash basis financial statements should have substantial support. Substantial support means that the modification is logical and equivalent to the accrual basis of accounting for that item. Common modifications include:

  - Capitalizing and depreciating fixed assets.
  - Accrual of income taxes.
  - Recording liabilities for long-term and short-term borrowings and the related interest expense.
  - Capitalizing inventory.
  - Reporting investments at fair value and recognizing unrealized gains and losses.

- **Presentation**

  Modified cash basis financial statements include the following:

  - A statement of assets and liabilities (modified cash basis) or a statement of assets and liabilities arising from cash transactions.
  - A statement of revenues and expenses and retained earnings (modified cash basis) or a statement of revenues collected and expenses paid.

  The specific elements included in these financial statements depend on the modifications made by the entity.

1.3 Income Tax Basis Financial Statements

Entities that are not required to use the accrual basis of accounting may choose to present income tax basis financial statements. In contrast to cash basis financial statements, tax basis financial statements are well-suited for entities that have complex operations.

1.3.1 Accounting Issues

Tax basis financial statements are prepared based on the methods and principles used to prepare the entity's tax return. Special accounting treatment must be given to nontaxable revenues and expenses not reported on the tax return.

Nontaxable revenues and expenses must be recognized in tax basis financial statements in the period received or paid for cash-basis taxpayers and in the period accruable for accrual-basis taxpayers. Nontaxable revenues and expenses may be reported as:

- Separate line items in the revenue and expense sections of the statement of revenues and expenses;

- Additions and deductions to net income; or

- A disclosure in a note.

1.3.2 Presentation

Tax-basis financial statements include the following:

- A statement of assets and liabilities and equity (income tax basis) or a balance sheet (income tax basis).

- A statement of revenues and expenses and retained earnings (income tax basis) or a statement of income (income tax basis).

The specific elements included in an entity's tax basis financial statements depend on the income and deductions reported on the entity's tax return.

2 Converting Cash Basis Financial Statements to the Accrual Basis

Many small businesses use the cash basis or modified cash basis of accounting to account for day-to-day operations. In certain circumstances (e.g., to obtain a loan from a bank, to report to owners, or to go public) such entities may be required to convert cash basis financial statements to accrual basis financial statements.

In order to make this conversion, it is essential to understand the differences between cash basis and accrual basis accounting:

	Cash Basis	Accrual Basis
Revenue Recognition	Cash received	Realized or realizable and earned
Expense Recognition	Cash paid	Incurred/owed/benefit received

2.1 Balance Sheet Conversion

The pure cash basis balance sheet reports only cash and equity. The modified cash basis balance sheet may also include inventory, investments at fair value, fixed assets net of accumulated depreciation, short-term and long-term debt, and/or accrued income taxes. To convert from a cash basis or modified cash basis balance sheet to an accrual basis balance sheet, all assets and liabilities existing at year-end that are not already included on the balance sheet must be added to the balance sheet, with equity equal to the difference between total assets and total liabilities.

Common balance sheet accounts to be recognized (if not already recognized under the modified cash basis) include:

- Accounts receivable
- Inventory
- Prepaid expenses
- Investments at fair value
- Fixed assets, net of accumulated depreciation
- Accounts payable
- Accrued liabilities
- Unearned revenue
- Interest payable
- Income taxes payable
- Short-term and long-term debt

2.2 Income Statement Conversion

The primary adjustments required to convert from a cash basis or modified cash basis income statement to an accrual basis income statement include:

- Converting cash basis revenue to accrual basis revenue.
- Converting cash paid for purchases to accrual basis cost of goods sold.
- Converting cash paid for operating expenses to accrual basis operating expenses.

Pass Key

The process of converting from the cash basis income statement to the accrual basis income statement is the OPPOSITE of the process used to prepare the statement of cash flows from the accrual basis financial statements. If you understand how to prepare the operating section of the statement of cash flows, then you can reverse those calculations to convert cash basis revenues and expenses to accrual basis revenues and expenses.

Additional adjustments may be required to:

- Recognize noncash expenses (i.e., depreciation and amortization).
- Capitalize purchases of fixed assets (fixed asset purchases are cash disbursements under the cash basis).
- Reduce the fixed asset balance for assets sold during the period (fixed asset sales are cash receipts under the cash basis) and recognize gains/losses on the sale.
- Record debt proceeds received during the period as liabilities (debt proceeds are cash receipts under the cash basis).
- Record debt repayments as reductions in liabilities (debt repayments are cash disbursements under the cash basis).

2.2.1   Converting Cash Basis Revenue to Accrual Basis Revenue

The following formula can be used to convert from cash basis revenue to accrual basis revenue:

Formula	Explanation
Cash basis revenue	From the cash basis income statement
+ Ending AR	Revenue earned during the period but not yet collected from customers
− Beginning AR	Cash collected during the current period that was earned in prior periods
− Ending unearned revenue	Cash collected during the current period that will not be earned until future periods
+ Beginning unearned revenue	Cash collected in prior periods that was earned in the current period
Accrual basis revenue	

Pass Key

This conversion process requires knowledge of beginning and ending balance sheet accounts (i.e., accounts receivable and unearned revenue). This is also true when converting cash paid for purchases to cost of goods sold, and when converting from cash paid for operating expenses to accrual basis operating expenses. These balance sheet account balances will be provided to you in any CPA Exam question requiring you to do the cash-to-accrual conversion, just as they are provided to you in questions related to the preparation of the statement of cash flows.

2.2.2   Converting Cash Paid for Purchases to Cost of Goods Sold

The following formula can be used to convert from cash paid for purchases to accrual basis cost of goods sold:

Formula	Explanation
Cash paid for purchases	From the cash basis income statement
+ Ending AP	Expenses incurred during the period but not yet paid
− Beginning AP	Expenses incurred during the prior period and paid in the current period
− Ending inventory	Purchases made during the current period that have not yet been sold
+ Beginning inventory	Purchases made in prior periods that were sold during the current period
Cost of goods sold	

2.2.3   Converting Cash Paid for Operating Expenses to Accrual Basis Operating Expenses

The following formula can be used to convert from cash payments for operating expenses to accrual basis operating expenses:

Formula	Explanation
Cash paid for operating expenses	From the cash basis income statement
+ Ending accrued liabilities	Expenses incurred during the period but not yet paid
− Beginning accrued liabilities	Expenses incurred during the prior period and paid in the current period
− Ending prepaid expenses	Payments made during the current period that will benefit future periods
+ Beginning prepaid expenses	Payments made in prior periods that benefited the current period
Accrual basis operating expenses	

Pass Key

This formula can be used to convert any operating expense, such as wages payable, from the cash basis to the accrual basis and can also be used to determine accrual basis interest payable or income taxes payable.

2.2.4   Converting Cash Basis Net Income to Accrual Basis Net Income

The above adjustments and calculations can be combined to calculate accrual basis net income from cash basis net income.

Example 1   Converting From Cash Basis to Accrual Basis

Facts: ABC Company had cash collections of $50,000, made cash payments of $20,000, and reported cash basis net income of $30,000 for Year 6. The company has determined the following balance sheet amounts for the beginning and ending of Year 6.

Balance Sheet Account	12/31/Year 6	1/1/Year 6	Change
Accounts Receivable	$15,000	$10,000	$ 5,000
Prepaid Insurance	4,000	2,000	2,000
Unearned Service Revenue	5,000	20,000	(15,000)
Salaries Payable	7,000	3,000	4,000

ABC Company also purchased a piece of equipment on 1/1/ Year 6 for $5,000 in cash. The equipment has no salvage value and will be depreciated on a straight-line basis over five years.

Required: Compute ABC Company's Year 6 accrual basis revenue, expenses, and net income.

(continued)

(continued)

Solution: Calculate accrual basis revenue for Year 6:

Formula	Explanation
$50,000	Cash collections
+ 15,000	Revenue earned during Year 6 but not yet collected from customers
– 10,000	Cash collected from customers in Year 6 that was earned in prior periods
– 5,000	Cash collected during Year 6 that will not be earned until future periods
+ 20,000	Cash collected in prior periods that was earned in Year 6
$70,000	Accrual basis revenue

Calculate accrual basis expenses for Year 6:

Formula	Explanation
$20,000	Cash payments
– 5,000	Capitalized fixed asset purchase (not a Year 6 expense)
+ 1,000	Depreciation
+ 7,000	Salaries owed for Year 6 that are not yet paid
– 3,000	Salaries from Year 5 paid in Year 6
– 4,000	Insurance paid in Year 6 that will benefit future periods
+ 2,000	Insurance paid in prior years that benefitted Year 6
$18,000	Accrual basis expenses

Accrual basis net income = $70,000 – $18,000 = $52,000

NOTES

8 Ratio and Variance Analysis

1 Ratio Analysis Overview

Ratios are financial indicators that distill relevant information about a business entity by quantifying the relationship among selected items on the financial statements. An entity's ratios may be compared with ratios of a different period for that entity. An entity's ratios may also be compared with competitor ratios and industry ratios. These comparative analyses identify trends that may be important to investors, lenders, and other interested parties.

Key financial ratios and metrics that are used to analyze a company's performance are classified into four high-level categories: profitability ratios, liquidity ratios, solvency ratios, and performance metrics. Depending on the area of focus, each of these categories includes measures that an analyst, investor, or stakeholder can use to evaluate the strength of an entity and whether its performance is improving over time or trending unfavorably. Gi Company's financial statements provide the financial data for the ratio calculations throughout this module.

Pass Key

Ratio questions on the financial exam may require a simple ratio calculation, an interpretation of what the ratio means, or an analysis of the effects of a change.

When asked to analyze whether a ratio is likely to increase or decrease, you can gain efficiency by knowing the following:

- The numerator has a direct relationship with the ratio. For example, an increase in the numerator results in an increase in the ratio.

$$\uparrow \frac{\text{Numerator}}{\text{Denominator}} = \text{Resulting ratio} \uparrow$$

- The denominator has an inverse relationship with the ratio. For example, an increase in the denominator results in a decrease in the ratio.

$$\frac{\text{Numerator}}{\uparrow \text{Denominator}} = \text{Resulting ratio} \downarrow$$

Sometimes, when both the numerator and denominator are affected by a given change, the final result (increase or decrease) is not easy to determine. The best way to answer questions such as these is to make up numbers and plug them into the ratio formula.

Gi Company
Balance Sheet

Current Assets:	12/31/Year 2	12/31/Year 1
Cash and cash equivalents	$ 50,000	$ 35,000
Trading securities (at fair value)	75,000	65,000
Accounts receivable	300,000	390,000
Inventory (at lower of cost or market)	290,000	275,000
Total current assets	715,000	765,000
Investments available for sale (at fair value)	350,000	300,000
Fixed Assets:		
Property, plant, and equipment (at cost)	1,900,000	1,800,000
Less: accumulated depreciation	(180,000)	(150,000)
	1,720,000	1,650,000
Goodwill	30,000	35,000
Total assets	$2,815,000	$2,750,000
Current Liabilities:		
Accounts payable	$ 150,000	$ 125,000
Notes payable	325,000	375,000
Accrued and other liabilities	220,000	200,000
Total current liabilities	695,000	700,000
Long-Term Debt:		
Bonds and notes payable	650,000	700,000
Total liabilities	1,345,000	1,400,000
Stockholders' Equity:		
Common stock (100,000 shares outstanding)	500,000	500,000
Additional paid-in capital	670,000	670,000
Retained earnings	300,000	180,000
Total equity	1,470,000	1,350,000
Total liabilities and equity	$2,815,000	$2,750,000

Income Statement for Year Ended:	Year 2	Year 1
Sales	$1,800,000	$1,700,000
Cost of goods sold	(1,000,000)	(940,000)
Gross profit	800,000	760,000
Operating expenses	(486,970)	(476,970)
Interest expense	(10,000)	(10,300)
Net income before income taxes	303,030	272,730
Income taxes (34 percent)	(103,030)	(92,730)
Net income after income taxes	$ 200,000	$ 180,000
Earnings per share	$ 2	$ 1.80

Other Financial Information:		
Depreciation and amortization (part of operating expenses)	$30,000	$25,000
Operating cash flows	275,000	265,000
Dividends per share	0.80	-0-
Market price per share	12	11

2 Profitability Ratios

Profitability ratios are measures of the success or failure of an enterprise for a given time period.

2.1 Gross (Profit) Margin

$$\text{Gross (profit) margin} = \frac{\text{Sales (net)} - \text{Cost of goods sold}}{\text{Sales (net)}}$$

$$\text{Year 2} = \frac{\$800,000}{\$1,800,000}$$

$$= 44.44\%$$

2.2 Profit Margin

$$\text{Profit margin} = \frac{\text{Net income}}{\text{Sales (net)}}$$

$$\text{Year 2} = \frac{\$200,000}{\$1,800,000}$$

$$= 11.11\%$$

2.3 Return on Sales

$$\text{Return on sales} = \frac{\text{Income before interest income, interest expense, and taxes}}{\text{Sales (net)}}$$

$$\text{Year 2} = \frac{\$303,030 + \$10,000}{\$1,800,000}$$

$$= 17.39\%$$

2.4   Return on Assets (ROA)

$$\text{Return on assets} = \frac{\text{Net income}}{\text{Average total assets}}$$

$$\text{Year 2} = \frac{\$200,000}{\$2,782,500}$$

$$= 7.2\%$$

2.5   DuPont Return on Assets

$$\text{DuPont return on assets} = \text{Profit margin} \times \text{Asset turnover}$$

$$\text{Year 2} = \frac{\text{Net income}}{\text{Sales (net)}} \times \frac{\text{Sales (net)}}{\text{Average total assets}}$$

$$= 11.11\% \times 0.65 \text{ times} = 7.22\%$$

Note that this ratio uses both profit margin and the asset turnover. This ratio allows for increased analysis of the changes in the percentages. The profit margin indicates the percentage return on each sale, and the asset turnover indicates the effective use of assets in generating that sale.

2.6   Return on Equity

$$\text{Return on equity} = \frac{\text{Net income}}{\text{Average total equity}}$$

$$\text{Year 2} = \frac{\$200,000}{(\$1,470,000 + \$1,350,000) / 2}$$

$$= 14.18\%$$

2.7   Operating Cash Flow Ratio

$$\text{Operating cash flow ratio} = \frac{\text{Cash flow from operations}}{\text{Current liabilities}}$$

$$\text{Year 2} = \frac{\$275,000}{\$695,000}$$

$$= 0.396$$

3   Liquidity Ratios

Liquidity ratios are measures of a firm's short-term ability to pay maturing obligations.

3.1   Current Ratio

$$\text{Current ratio} = \frac{\text{Current assets}}{\text{Current liabilities}}$$

$$\text{Year 2} = \frac{\$715,000}{\$695,000} = 1.03$$

$$\text{Year 1} = \frac{\$765,000}{\$700,000} = 1.09$$

(Industry average = 1.50)

The ratio, and therefore Gi's ability to meet its short-term obligations, is low compared with the industry's average.

3.2   Quick Ratio

$$\text{Quick ratio} = \frac{\text{Cash and cash equivalents} + \text{Short-term marketable securities} + \text{Receivable (net)}}{\text{Current liabilities}}$$

$$\text{Year 2} = \frac{\$50,000 + \$75,000 + \$300,000}{\$695,000} = 0.61$$

$$\text{Year 1} = \frac{\$35,000 + \$65,000 + \$390,000}{\$700,000} = 0.70$$

(Industry average = 0.80)

The industry average of 0.80 is higher than Gi's ratio, which indicates that Gi may have trouble meeting short-term needs.

Pass Key

Turnover ratios generally use average balances [i.e., (beginning balance + ending balance) / 2] for balance sheet components. However, on some recent CPA Exam questions, candidates have been instructed to use year-end balances instead. Please be sure to read the question carefully to determine the appropriate method to use.

The ratios given in this module match the most recent ratios provided by the AICPA as an exhibit on task-based simulations requiring ratio calculations.

3.3 Accounts Receivable Turnover

$$\text{Accounts receivable turnover} = \frac{\text{Sales (net)}}{\text{Average accounts receivable (net)}}$$

$$\text{Year 2} = \frac{\$1,800,000}{(\$300,000 + \$390,000) / 2}$$

$$= \frac{\$1,800,000}{\$345,000}$$

$$= 5.22 \text{ times}$$

This ratio indicates the receivables' quality and indicates the success of the firm in collecting outstanding receivables. Faster turnover gives credibility to the current and acid-test ratios.

3.4 Days Sales in Accounts Receivable

$$\text{Days sales in accounts receivable} = \frac{\text{Ending accounts receivable (net)}}{\text{Sales (net) / 365}}$$

$$\text{Year 2} = \frac{\$300,000}{\$1,800,000 / 365}$$

$$= 60.83 \text{ days}$$

This ratio indicates the average number of days required to collect accounts receivable.

3.5   Inventory Turnover

$$\text{Inventory turnover} = \frac{\text{Cost of goods sold}}{\text{Average inventory}}$$

$$\text{Year 2} = \frac{\$1,000,000}{(\$290,000 + \$275,000) / 2}$$

$$= \frac{\$1,000,000}{\$282,500}$$

$$= 3.54 \text{ times}$$

This measure of how quickly inventory is sold is an indicator of enterprise performance. The higher the turnover, in general, the better the performance.

3.6   Days in Inventory

$$\text{Days in inventory} = \frac{\text{Ending inventory}}{\text{Cost of goods sold} / 365}$$

$$\text{Year 2} = \frac{\$290,000}{\$1,000,000 / 365}$$

$$= 105.85 \text{ days}$$

This ratio indicates the average number of days required to sell inventory.

3.7   Accounts Payable Turnover

$$\text{Accounts payable turnover} = \frac{\text{Cost of goods sold}}{\text{Average accounts payable}}$$

$$\text{Year 2} = \frac{\$1,000,000}{(\$150,000 + \$125,00) / 2}$$

$$= 7.27 \text{ times}$$

This ratio indicates the number of times trade payables turn over during the year. A low turnover may indicate a delay in payment, such as from a shortage of cash.

3.8   Days of Payables Outstanding

$$\text{Days of payables outstanding} = \frac{\text{Ending accounts payable}}{\text{Cost of goods sold} / 365}$$

$$\text{Year 2} = \frac{\$150,000}{\$1,000,000 / 365}$$

$$= 54.75 \text{ days}$$

This ratio indicates the average length of time trade payables are outstanding before they are paid.

3.9   Cash Conversion Cycle

$$\text{Cash conversion cycle} = \frac{\text{Days sales}}{\text{in accounts receivable}} + \frac{\text{Days in}}{\text{inventory}} - \frac{\text{Days of payables}}{\text{outstanding}}$$

$$\text{Year 2} = 60.83 \text{ days} + 105.85 \text{ days} - 54.75 \text{ days}$$

$$= 111.93 \text{ days}$$

This ratio indicates the average length of time it takes from when the company pays cash for an inventory purchase to when the company receives cash from a sale.

4   Solvency Ratios

Solvency ratios are measures of security or protection for long-term creditors/investors.

4.1   Debt-to-Equity

$$\text{Debt-to-equity ratio} = \frac{\text{Total liabilities}}{\text{Total equity}}$$

$$\text{Year 2} = \frac{\$1,345,000}{\$1,470,000} = 0.91$$

$$\text{Year 1} = \frac{\$1,400,000}{\$1,350,000} = 1.04$$

This ratio indicates the degree of protection to creditors in case of insolvency. The lower this ratio the better the company's position.

4.2   Total Debt Ratio

$$\text{Total debt ratio} = \frac{\text{Total liabilities}}{\text{Total assets}}$$

$$\text{Year 2} = \frac{\$1,345,000}{\$2,815,000} = 47.78\%$$

$$\text{Year 1} = \frac{\$1,400,000}{\$2,750,000} = 50.91\%$$

This debt ratio indicates that approximately half of the assets are financed by creditors.

4.3   Equity Multiplier

$$\text{Equity multiplier} = \frac{\text{Total assets}}{\text{Total equity}}$$

$$\text{Year 2} = \frac{\$2,815,000}{\$1,470,000} = 1.91$$

$$\text{Year 1} = \frac{\$2,750,000}{\$1,350,000} = 2.04$$

4.4   Times Interest Earned

$$\text{Times interest earned} = \frac{\text{Income before interest expense and taxes}}{\text{Interest expense}}$$

Or:

$$= \frac{\text{Earnings before interest and taxes}}{\text{Interest expense}}$$

$$\text{Year 2} = \frac{\$303,030 + \$10,000}{\$10,000}$$

$$= 31.30 \text{ times}$$

This ratio reflects the ability of a company to cover interest charges. It uses income before interest and taxes to reflect the amount of income available to cover interest expense.

5 Performance Metrics

Performance metrics are measures used to evaluate operating performance and elements of a company's stock performance from the perspective of current and potential investors.

5.1 EBITDA (Earnings Before Interest, Taxes, Depreciation, and Amortization)

EBITDA can be calculated from the income statement using either a "top-down" or "bottom-up" approach.

- **Top-down:** Sales – Cost of goods sold – Operating expenses (excluding depreciation and amortization)

  - Year 2 = $1,800,000 – $1,000,000 – ($486,970 – $30,000) = $343,030

  - Year 1 = $1,700,000 – $940,000 – ($476,970 – $25,000) = $308,030

- **Bottom-up**: Net income + Income tax expense + Interest expenses + Depreciation and amortization

  - Year 2 = $200,000 + $103,030 + $10,000 + $30,000 = $343,030

  - Year 1 = $180,000 + $92,730 + $10,300 + $25,000 = $308,030

5.2 Earnings per Share

$$\text{Earnings per share} = \frac{\text{Income available to common shareholders}}{\text{Weighted average common shares outstanding}}$$

$$\text{Year 2} = \frac{\$200,000}{100,000 \text{ shares}}$$

$$= \$2/\text{share}$$

5.3 Price-to-Earnings Ratio

$$\text{Price-to-earnings ratio} = \frac{\text{Price per share}}{\text{Basic earnings per share}}$$

$$\text{Year 2} = \frac{\$12}{\$2}$$

$$= 6$$

This statistic indicates the investment potential of an enterprise; a rise in this ratio indicates that investors are pleased with the firm's opportunity for growth.

5.4   Dividend Payout

$$\text{Dividend payout} = \frac{\text{Cash dividends}}{\text{Net income}}$$

$$\text{Year 2} = \frac{\$0.80 \text{ dividend per share} \times 100{,}000 \text{ shares outstanding}}{\$200{,}000}$$

$$= 40\%$$

This ratio indicates the portion of current earnings being paid out in dividends. (Alternatively, calculate dividend payout as Dividends per share / Earnings per share = $0.80 / $2 = 40%.)

5.5   Asset Turnover

$$\text{Asset turnover} = \frac{\text{Sales (net)}}{\text{Average total assets}}$$

$$\text{Year 2} = \frac{\$1{,}800{,}000}{(\$2{,}815{,}000 + \$2{,}750{,}000) / 2}$$

$$= \frac{\$1{,}800{,}000}{\$2{,}782{,}500}$$

$$= 0.65 \text{ times}$$

This ratio is an indicator of how Gi makes effective use of its assets. A high ratio indicates effective asset use to generate sales.

6   Limitations of Ratios

Although ratios are easy to compute, they depend entirely on the reliability of the data on which they are based (e.g., estimates, historical costs, fair value, etc.). Additional information is also valuable when analyzing a company. Horizontal analysis measures the dollar and percentage change over a period of time, which is useful in evaluating trends and noting material changes from period to period. Vertical analysis is helpful in reducing statement items to a common size, as all elements are expressed as a percentage of a common number (e.g., income statement elements are expressed as a percentage of sales revenue). Vertical analysis assists in period-to-period comparison, but also allows for comparability among other entities as the statement is in a common size format.

7 Variance Analysis (Actual Versus Budget)

Variance analysis is a tool for comparing some measure of performance to a plan, budget, or standard for that measure. Variance analysis is used for planning and control purposes, and can be used to evaluate revenues and costs. Comparison of actual results to the annual business plan is the first and most basic level of control and evaluation of operations.

Costs are categorized as either variable or fixed. Variable costs in total change as production levels change, while fixed costs are assumed to remain constant regardless of production or sales levels. Budgets are created based on a set sales price per unit, a set variable cost per unit, and set fixed costs (in total). The contribution margin (CM) is equal to revenues (or sales) less all variable costs.

7.1 Performance Report

Actual results may be easily compared with budgeted results. However, usefulness is limited by the existence of budget variances that may be strictly related to volume.

Example 1   Budget vs. Plan Performance Report

Facts: Neostar Corporation has prepared its annual business plan for Year 1. The organization anticipated that it would sell 10,000 units of its product at $15 apiece, that its contribution margin percentage would be 20 percent, and that its fixed costs would be $25,000. Actual units sold numbered only 8,000 (totaling $112,000 in revenue); variable expenses materialized at $100,800 and fixed costs materialized at $24,000.

Required: Prepare a performance report comparing actual versus budgeted results.

Solution:

	Budget	Actual	Variance	
Revenue	$150,000	$112,000	$(38,000)	Unfavorable
Variable expenses	(120,000)	(100,800)	19,200	Favorable
Contribution margin	30,000	11,200	(18,800)	Unfavorable
Fixed costs	(25,000)	(24,000)	1,000	Favorable
Operating income	$ 5,000	$ (12,800)	$(17,800)	Unfavorable

Variances need significant analysis before they are useful. The favorable variance in variable expenses, for example, does not represent efficiencies. Budgeted contribution margin ratios are 20 percent; actual contribution margin ratios are 10 percent. Sales in units were off budget by 20 percent, yet revenue was down by 25 percent. Something is very wrong at Neostar, but what?

7.2   Use of Flexible Budgets to Analyze Performance

Budget variance analysis becomes progressively more sophisticated as managers review flexible budget comparisons. The flexible budget allows managers to identify how an individual change in a cost or revenue driver affects the overall cost of a process.

Example 2	Flexible Budget Performance Report

Facts: Management at Neostar has heard that flexible budgeting can provide more meaningful information.

Required: Prepare a flexible budget using the same information described in Example 1.

Solution:

Neostar Corporation
Flexible Budget Performance Report
For the year ended December 31, Year 1

	Actual Results @ Actual	Flexible Budget Variances	Flexible Budget @ Actual (Planned Cost)	Sales Activity (Volume) Variances	Master Budget
Units	8,000		8,000		10,000
Sales	$112,000	$ (8,000)	$120,000	$(30,000)	$150,000
Variable costs	(100,800)	(4,800)	(96,000)	24,000	(120,000)
Contribution margin	11,200	(12,800)	24,000*	(6,000)	30,000*
Fixed costs	(24,000)	1,000	(25,000)	–	(25,000)
Operating income	$ (12,800)	$(11,800)	$ (1,000)	$ (6,000)	$ 5,000

Flexible budget variances	(11,800)	
Sales activity (volume) variances		(6,000)
Total master budget variances		(17,800)

*24,000 / 120,000 = 20%
30,000 / 150,000 = 20%

Flexible budget variances show that revenue per unit was less than expected and variable costs per unit were greater than expected. The company has performed $11,800 worse than expected. Meanwhile, differences in volume produced a $6,000 unfavorable variance, yielding a total variance from the budget of $17,800.

Although we still do not know what is wrong with Neostar, we know where to look. Revenue is not materializing as expected despite efforts to discount our selling price (producing an unfavorable sales price variance of $8,000), and expenses are over budget (producing an unfavorable variable cost variance of $4,800 despite a favorable fixed-cost variance of $1,000).

NOTES

FAR
3

Assets and Related Topics

Module

1 Cash and Cash Equivalents

1 Definition and Classifications

Cash includes both currency and demand deposits with banks and/or other financial institutions. It also includes deposits that are similar to demand deposits (can be added to or withdrawn at any time without penalty).

The term cash equivalents broadens the definition of cash to include short-term, highly liquid investments that are both readily convertible to cash and so near their maturity when acquired by the entity (90 days or less from date of purchase) that they present insignificant risk of changes in value.

1.1 Examples of Cash and Cash Equivalents

- Coin and currency on hand (including petty cash)
- Checking accounts
- Savings accounts
- Money market funds
- Deposits held as compensating balances against borrowing arrangements with a lending institution that are *not* legally restricted
- Negotiable paper
  - Bank checks, money orders, traveler's checks, bank drafts, and cashier's checks
  - Commercial paper and Treasury bills
  - Certificates of deposit (having original maturities of 90 days or less)

1.2 Items Not Cash or Cash Equivalents

- Time certificates of deposit (if original maturity over 90 days)
- Legally restricted deposits held as compensating balances against borrowing arrangements with a lending institution

1.3 Restricted or Unrestricted

Cash is classified as *unrestricted* or *restricted*. Restricted cash is cash that has been set aside for a specific use or purpose (e.g., the purchase of property, plant, and equipment). Unrestricted cash is used for all current operations. The nature, amount, and timing of restrictions should be disclosed in the footnotes.

- If the restriction is associated with a current asset or current liability, classify as a current asset but separate from unrestricted cash.
- If the restriction is associated with a non-current asset or non-current liability, classify as a non-current asset but separate from either the Investments or Other Assets section.

■ **Examples of Restrictions**

- If any portion of cash and cash equivalents is contractually restricted because of financing arrangements with a credit institution (called a compensating balance), that portion should be separately reported as "restricted cash" in the balance sheet.

- If any portion of cash and cash equivalents is restricted by management, it should be reported as restricted cash and as a current or long-term asset (depending on the anticipated date of disbursement).

- Some industries (such as public utilities) report the amount of cash and cash equivalents as the last asset on the balance sheet because they report assets in inverse order of liquidity.

Example 1	Items Included in Cash Balance

Facts: Smith Corporation's cash ledger balance on December 31, Year 7, was $160,000. On the same date Smith held the following items in its safe:

- A $5,000 check payable to Smith, dated January 2, Year 8, that was not included in the December 31 checkbook balance.

- A $3,500 check payable to Smith, deposited December 22 and included in the December 31 checkbook balance, which was returned non-sufficient funds (NSF). The check was redeposited January 2, Year 8, and cleared January 7.

- A $25,000 check, payable to a supplier and drawn on Smith's account, that was dated and recorded December 31, but was not mailed until January 15, Year 8.

Required: Determine the amount of cash that Smith should report in its December 31, Year 7, balance sheet.

Solution: Smith's cash balance is calculated as follows:

Unadjusted balance of Smith's cash ledger account, December 31, Year 7	$160,000
Add: check payable to supplier dated and recorded on December 31, Year 7, but not mailed until January 15, Year 8	25,000
Less: NSF check returned by bank on December 30, Year 7	(3,500)
Adjusted balance, December 31, Year 7	$181,500

2 Bank Reconciliations

There are two general forms of bank reconciliations. One form is called a simple reconciliation. The other widely used form is entitled reconciliation of cash receipts and disbursements.

2.1 Components of a Simple Reconciliation

Differences between the cash balance reported by the bank and the cash balance per the depositor's records are explained through the preparation of the bank reconciliation. Several factors bring about this differential.

■ **Deposits in Transit**

Funds sent by the depositor to the bank that have not been recorded by the bank and deposits made after the bank's cutoff date will not be included in the bank statement. In both cases, the balance per the depositor's records will be higher than those of the bank.

■ **Outstanding Checks**

Checks written for payment by the depositor that have not been presented to the bank will result in a higher balance per bank records than per depositor records.

■ **Service Charges**

Service charges are deducted by the bank. The depositor will not deduct this amount from its records until it is made aware of the charge, usually in the following month. Balance per books is overstated until this amount is subtracted.

■ **Bank Collections**

The bank may make collections on the depositor's behalf, increasing the depositor's bank balance. If the depositor is not aware the collection was credited to its balance, the balance per depositor's records will be understated.

■ **Errors**

Errors made by either the bank or the depositors are another cause for difference.

■ **Non-sufficient Funds (NSF)**

The bank may have charged the depositor's account for a dishonored check and the check may not have been redeposited until the following month. This would overstate the depositor's book balance as of the balance sheet date.

■ **Interest Income**

Usually the depositor does not keep track of average daily cash balances, and so will add this amount to its records once made aware of this revenue. Balance per books is understated until this amount is added.

2.2 Steps in a Simple Bank Reconciliation

Although other methods can be used, the most common procedure is to reconcile both book and bank balances to a common "true" balance. That balance should then appear on the balance sheet under the caption "cash and cash equivalents."

Procedures:

1. Book balance is adjusted to reflect any corrections reported by the bank (e.g., NSF checks, notes collected by the bank and credited to the account, monthly service charges, and other bank charges, such as check printing charges).

2. After the above adjustments are made:

> **Adjusted book balance = True balance**

3. The bank balance per the bank statement is reconciled to the "true balance," determined above.

Example 2   Simple Bank Reconciliation

Facts: Burbank Company's records reflect a $12,650 cash balance on November 30, Year 3. Burbank's November bank statement reports the following amounts:

Cash balance	$10,050
Bank service charge	10
NSF check	90

Deposits in transit equal $3,000 and outstanding checks are $500.

Required: Determine Burbank's November 30, Year 3, adjusted cash balance.

Solution: Bank reconciliation for November Year 3.

Balance per books		$12,650
Less: bank service charge	$10	
NSF check	90	(100)
Adjusted cash balance		$12,550
Balance per bank		$10,050
Add: deposits in transit		3,000
		$13,050
Less: outstanding checks		(500)
Adjusted cash balance		$12,550

2.3   Reconciliation of Cash Receipts and Disbursements

The reconciliation of cash receipts and disbursements, commonly referred to as the four-column reconciliation, or proof of cash, serves as a proof of the proper recording of cash transactions.

Additional information is required in preparing the four-column reconciliation. The bank reconciliation information for the present month and that of the prior month must be obtained.

The object of the four-column approach is to reconcile any differences between the amount the depositor has recorded as cash receipts and the amount the bank has recorded as deposits. Likewise, this approach determines any differences between amounts the depositor has recorded as cash disbursements and amounts the bank has recorded as checks paid.

Illustration 1   Four-Column Reconciliation

Based on the information in the previous example and additional information for the month of December, Burbank's reconciliation of cash receipts and disbursements follows:

Burbank Company
Reconciliation of Cash Receipts and Cash Disbursements
For the Month of December, Year 3

	Balance 11/30/Year 3	December Receipts	December Payments	Balance 12/31/Year 3
Balance per depositor's books	$12,550	$12,950	$4,948	$20,552
Note collected by bank		3,050		3,050
Bank service charge			15	(15)
NSF check received from customer		(285)		(285)
Error in recording check No. 350			54	(54)
Adjusted balances	$12,550	$15,715	$5,017	$23,248
Balance per bank records	$10,050	$15,000	$2,400	$22,650
Deposit in transit:				
November 30	3,000	(3,000)		
December 31		4,000		4,000
Outstanding checks:				
November 30	(500)		(500)	
December 31			3,402	(3,402)
NSF check		(285)	(285)	
Adjusted balances	$12,550	$15,715	$5,017	$23,248

NOTES

1 Accounts Receivable

Accounts receivable are oral promises to pay debts and are generally classified as current assets. They are classified either as trade receivables (accounts receivable from purchasers of the company's goods and services) or nontrade receivables (accounts receivable from persons other than customers, such as advances to employees, tax refunds, etc.).

The net realizable value of accounts receivable is the balance of the accounts receivable account adjusted for allowances for receivables that may be uncollectible, sales discounts, and sales returns and allowances.

1.1 Account Analysis Format

The preparation of an account analysis may increase your ability to "squeeze" or otherwise derive various answers to CPA Exam questions regarding accounts receivable, allowance for current expected credit losses (CECL), and many other accounts.

Blank Analysis Format

Beginning balance	$ _____
Add:	_____
	_____
	_____
Subtotal	_____
Subtract:	_____
	_____
	_____
Ending balance	$ _____

Pass Key

The blank analysis format is a tool that is merely an "add-subtract" form of a t-account that can be used to obtain the correct result to many examination questions. You will find that this format will assist you in "squeezing" answers to many questions related to balance sheet accounts on the CPA Exam.

Illustration 1	Accounts Receivable Account Analysis Format		

Beginning balance			$ 90,000
Add:	Credit sales		800,000
	Subtotal		890,000
Subtract:	Cash collected on account	$810,000	
	Accounts receivable converted to notes receivable	7,000	
	Accounts receivable written off as credit losses	23,000	(840,000)
Ending balance			$ 50,000

1.2 Valuation of Accounts Receivable With Discounts

In general, accounts receivable should be initially valued at the original transaction amount (i.e., historical cost) net of estimated credit losses; however, that amount may be adjusted for sales or cash discounts.

The offer of a cash discount on payments made within a specified period is widely used by many companies. This practice encourages prompt payment and assumes that customers will take advantage of the discount.

1.2.1 Sales or Cash Discounts

The discount is generally based on a percentage of the sales price. For example, a discount of 2/10, n/30 offers the purchaser a discount of 2 percent of the sales price if the payment is made within 10 days. If the discount is not taken, the entire (gross) amount is due in 30 days. The calculation of cash discounts typically follows one of two forms; the determination of which method to use is generally based on the company's experience with its customers taking discounts.

1. **Gross Method**

   The gross method records a sale without regard to the available discount. If payment is received within the discount period, a sales discount (contra-revenue) account is debited to reflect the sales discount.

2. **Net Method**

   The net method records sales and accounts receivable net of the available discount. An adjustment is not needed if payment is received within the discount period. However, if payment is received after the discount period, a sales discount not taken account (revenue) must be credited.

Example 1   Sales Discounts, Gross and Net Methods

Facts: Gearty Company sells $100,000 worth of goods to Smith Company. There are no estimated expected credit losses for the sales of goods to Smith Company. The terms of the sale are 2/10, n/30.

Required: Prepare the journal entries for the accounts receivable Gearty Company would record using both the gross method and the net method.

Solution:

The journal entries at the date of sale:

		Gross		Net	
DR	Accounts receivable	$100,000		$98,000	
CR	Sales		$100,000		$98,000

The journal entries if payment is <u>received within</u> the discount period:

		Gross		Net	
DR	Cash	$98,000		$98,000	
DR	Sales discounts taken	2,000			
CR	Accounts receivable		$100,000		$98,000

The journal entries if payment is <u>not received within</u> the discount period.

		Gross		Net	
DR	Cash	$100,000		$100,000	
CR	Accounts receivable		$100,000		$98,000
CR	Sales discounts not taken				2,000

1.2.2 Trade Discounts

Trade discounts (quantity discounts) are quoted in percentages. Sales revenues and accounts receivable are recorded net of trade discounts. Trade discounts are applied sequentially.

Example 2	Application of Trade Discounts

Facts: Caitlyn & Brown sells coats with a list price of $1,000. They are sold to stores for list price minus trade discounts of 40 percent and 10 percent.

Required: Calculate the Caitlyn & Brown accounts receivable balance if 100 coats are sold on credit. Assume there are no estimated expected credit losses for the sale.

Solution:

List price	$100,000
Less: 40% discount	(40,000)
List price after 40% discount	60,000
Less: 10% discount	(6,000)
Accounts receivable balance	$ 54,000

1.3 Estimating Credit Losses

Accounts receivable should be presented on the balance sheet at their net realizable value. Thus, the amount recorded at initial transaction should reflect the amount an entity expects to collect from its customers and includes consideration of customer credit risk. Two methods of recognizing credit losses exist, the direct write-off method and the current expected credit loss (CECL) method. However, only the CECL method is consistent with accrual accounting (and thus acceptable for GAAP).

1.3.1 Direct Write-off Method (Not GAAP)

Under the direct write-off method, the account is written off and the bad debt (or credit loss) is recognized when the account becomes uncollectible. The direct write-off method is not GAAP because it does not properly match the bad debt (or credit loss) expense with the revenue (note, however, that the direct write-off method is the method used for federal income tax purposes). An additional weakness of this method is that accounts receivable are always overstated because no attempt is made to account for the unknown bad debts (or estimate of current expected credit loss) included in the balance on the financial statements.

Example 3   Direct Write-off Method

Facts: On December 15, Year 1, Roe Company recorded a credit sale of $10,000. On July 1, Year 2, the company determined that the account receivable was uncollectible.

Required: Prepare the journal entry.

Solution:

Journal entry to record the account balance of $10,000 as uncollectible:

DR	Bad debt (or credit loss) expense	$10,000	
CR	Accounts receivable		$10,000

The revenue recorded in Year 1 is not properly matched to the bad debt (or credit loss) expense recorded in Year 2.

1.3.2 Current Expected Credit Loss (CECL) Method (GAAP)

Under the current expected credit losses (CECL) model, once the selling entity determines that collection for goods or services provided is probable, an estimate of expected credit losses over the life of the receivable (along with the related receivable) should be recorded. There is no set or prescribed methodology for measuring expected credit losses, but entities should consider historical loss rates (categorized by age, industry, region, and customer credit ratings), historical recoveries of estimated credit losses, and account for future economic conditions such as recession, unemployment, and industry forecasts in determining the appropriate credit risk loss adjustment.

A percentage of each period's ending accounts receivable is estimated to be uncollectible. The amount determined is charged to credit loss expense (formerly known as "bad debt expense") in the period and the credit is made to a valuation account such as "allowance for credit losses" (formerly known as "allowance for doubtful accounts"). The allowance for credit losses is reviewed and adjusted each reporting period for changes to customer credit risk.

The method used to determine the estimate of current expected credit loss should be applied consistently by management each reporting period.

The method for many companies is similar to a traditional aged trade receivable analysis whereby a schedule is prepared categorizing customer invoices by number of days or months outstanding. Each category's total amount outstanding is then multiplied by a percentage representing a credit loss rate for that aging category.

Example 4   Aging Schedule of Trade Receivables

Facts: DEF Co. manufactures and sells sports balls to a broad range of customers with similar risk characteristics. Customers typically receive payment terms of 45 days with a 5% discount if payment is received within 30 days. DEF Co. maintains historical loss information for its trade receivables and has the following historical loss percentages:

5% for receivables aged as current

10% for receivables that are 1–30 days past due

20% for receivables that are 31–60 days past due

30% for receivables that are 61–90 days past due

50% for receivables that are more than 90 days past due

DEF Co. believes that historical loss information is a reasonable basis on which to determine expected credit losses for trade receivables held at the reporting date. However, DEF Co. believes that this historical loss information reflects the declining general economic conditions rather than the current improvement in general economic conditions. DEF Co. expects the improvement in general economic conditions to continue into future periods. DEF Co. estimates the loss rates to decrease by 20% in each age bucket based on its knowledge of past experiences for which there were similar improvements in the economy.

DEF Co.'s schedule of aged receivables as of December 31, Year 1, is:

Current	$850,000
1–30 days past due	50,000
31–60 days past due	20,000
61–90 days past due	8,000
More than 90 days past due	2,000
	$930,000

The unadjusted allowance for credit losses is $50,000 on December 31, Year 1.

Required: Prepare a journal entry to record the adjustment to the allowance for credit losses on December 31, Year 1.

Solution:

DEF Co. needs to adjust its historical loss percentages for each aging receivable category based on its revised assumptions to reflect the expected 20% improvement in loss rates. Below is a summary of the required allowance for credit losses calculation on December 31, Year 1:

Aged Receivable Category	Balance	Credit Loss %	Expected Credit Loss Estimate $
Current	$850,000	4.0%	$34,000
1–30 days past due	50,000	8.0%	4,000
31–60 days past due	20,000	16.0%	3,200
61–90 days past due	8,000	24.0%	1,920
More than 90 days past due	2,000	40.0%	800
	$930,000		$43,920

(continued)

(continued)

The required allowance for credit losses ($43,920) is less than the unadjusted allowance for credit losses on December 31, Year 1 ($50,000).

Journal entry to record adjustment to allowance for credit losses on December 31, Year 1:

DR	Allowance for credit losses ($50,000 − $43,920)	$6,080	
CR	Credit loss expense ($50,000 − $43,920)		$6,080

1.4 Credit Loss Expense

The amount of credit loss expense (formerly known as "bad debt expense") recognized in net income stated for a reporting period includes the following:

- An estimate of expected credit loss (or bad debt) for each sale recognized
- An adjustment for changes to the estimate of expected credit losses if needed

1.5 Sales Returns

Customers may return goods provided by a company after sales (revenues) have been recorded. The journal entry associated with the return is shown below:

DR	Sales return allowance	$XXX	
CR	Cash (or accounts receivable)		$XXX
DR	Inventory	XXX	
CR	Cost of goods sold		XXX

Illustration 2   Sales Returns

Jacobs Inc. sells $500 in goods to Bennit, who pays in cash. The goods originally cost Jacobs $350. 20 percent of the goods are returned by Bennit to Jacobs due to poor quality. Jacobs will record the following journal entries associated with the initial sale and the subsequent return:

Original sale:

DR	Cash	$500	
CR	Revenue		$500
DR	Cost of goods sold	350	
CR	Inventory		350

Return:

DR	Sales return allowance	$100	
CR	Cash		$100
DR	Inventory	70	
CR	Cost of goods sold		70

Note that 20 percent of the $500 sale is $100, and 20 percent of the original inventory of $350 is $70.

Sales return allowance is a contra-revenue account. If the company had initially recorded a refund liability to account for any returns, the refund liability is debited when the return is processed instead of sales return allowance (to the extent there is enough in the refund liability account).

1.6 Write-off of a Specific Account Receivable

When a receivable is formally determined to be uncollectible, the following entry is made:

DR	Allowance for credit losses	$XXX	
CR	Accounts receivable		$XXX

1.7 Subsequent Collection of Accounts Receivable Written Off

If a collection is made on a receivable that was previously written off, the accounting procedure depends on the method of accounting used.

1.7.1 Direct Write-off Method

The "uncollectible accounts (or credit losses) recovered" account is a revenue account.

DR	Cash	$XXX	
CR	Uncollectible accounts (or credit losses) recovered		$XXX

1.7.2 CECL Method

To restore the account previously written off:

DR	Accounts receivable	$XXX	
CR	Allowance for credit losses		$XXX

To record the cash collection on the account:

DR	Cash	$XXX	
CR	Accounts receivable		$XXX

Example 5 — Calculation of Allowance for Credit Losses

Facts: Bost Company manufactures and sells high-end beauty products to customers with similar risk characteristics. Customers typically receive payment terms of 45 days with a 10 percent discount if payment is received within 30 days.

The unadjusted allowance for credit losses balance is $10,000 on December 31, Year 1. Credit loss expense recognized through November 30, Year 1, was $35,000.

Bost Company determines its allowance for credit losses on December 31, Year 1, should be $15,850 based on historical recoveries of estimated credit losses.

The following transactions occurred in December Year 1:

- Bost Company lost two customers who filed for bankruptcy. Total receivables outstanding on November 30, Year 1, for these customers was $16,000, and they were in the 31–60 days past due receivable aging category. This was not recorded in December Year 1.

- Bost Company successfully received $5,000 from a collections agency for old receivables previously written off.

(continued)

(continued)

Required

1. Prepare the journal entries to record the activity during December Year 1.
2. Calculate the adjustment needed to the allowance for credit losses balance on December 31, Year 1.

Solution

1. The loss of receivables for two customers who filed for bankruptcy should be written off against the allowance for credit losses.

Journal entry to record receivable credit loss adjustment during December Year 1 due to bankruptcy:

DR	Allowance for credit losses	$16,000	
CR	Accounts receivable		$16,000

The successful receipt of funds from the credit agency should be reflected within credit loss expense as a recovery.

Journal entry to reclassify recoveries from collection agency during December 31, Year 1:

DR	Cash	$5,000	
CR	Credit loss expense		$5,000

The unadjusted balance of accounts related to credit losses on December 31, Year 1, is as follows:

Allowance for Credit Losses

Unadjusted beginning balance, 12/31/Year 1	$10,000 CR
Less: Year 1 write-off	(16,000) DR
Ending unadjusted balance, 12/31/Year 1	($6,000) DR

Credit Loss Expense

Beginning balance, 12/31/Year 1	$35,000
Less: Year 1 recovery	(5,000)
Ending unadjusted balance, 12/31/Year 1	$30,000

2. The required allowance for credit losses balance on December 31, Year 1, as determined by Bost Company (based on historical recoveries of estimated credit losses) is $15,850. This amount is higher than the ending unadjusted allowance for credit losses debit balance of $6,000. Therefore, the required adjustment to the allowance for credit losses is $21,850.

Journal entry to record adjustment to allowance for credit losses on December 31, Year 1:

DR	Credit loss expense ($15,850 + $6,000)	$21,850	
CR	Allowance for credit losses ($15,850 + $6,000)		$21,850

1.8   Pledging (Assignment)

Pledging is the process whereby the company uses existing accounts receivable as collateral for a loan. The company retains title to the receivables but "pledges" that it will use the proceeds to pay the loan. Pledging requires only note disclosure. The accounts receivable account is not adjusted.

1.9   Factoring of Accounts Receivable

Factoring is a process by which a company can convert its receivables into cash by assigning them to a "factor" either without or with recourse. Under factoring arrangements, the customer may or may not be notified.

1.9.1   Without Recourse

If a sale is nonrecourse, it means that the sale is final and that the assignee (the factor) assumes the risk of any losses on collections. If the buyer is unable to collect all of the accounts receivable, it has no recourse against the seller.

Journal entry to factor accounts receivable without recourse:

DR	Cash	$XXX	
DR	Due from factor (factor's margin)	XXX	
DR	Loss on sale of receivable	XXX	
CR	Accounts receivable		$XXX

The entry to the asset account "Due from Factor" reflects the proceeds retained by the factor. This amount protects the factor against sales returns, sales discounts, allowances, and customer disputes. If the returns, discounts, and allowances are less than the retained amount, the balance will be returned to the seller.

1.9.2   With Recourse

If a sale is on a recourse basis, it means that the factor has an option to re-sell any uncollectible receivables back to the seller.

If accounts receivable are transferred to a factor *with recourse*, two treatments are possible. The transfer may be considered either a sale or a borrowing (with the receivables as mere collateral).

- In order to be considered a sale, the transfer must meet the following conditions:
  - The transferor's (seller's) obligation for uncollectible accounts can reasonably be estimated.
  - The transferor surrenders control of the future economic benefits of the receivables to the buyer.
  - The transferor cannot be required to repurchase the receivables, but may be required to replace the receivables with other similar receivables.
- If any of the above conditions are not met, the transfer is treated as a loan.

1.10   Securitization

In a securitization, accounts receivable are transferred to a different entity, such as a trust or subsidiary. The entity then sells securities that are collateralized by the accounts receivable. Investors receive cash as the accounts receivable are paid.

2   Reconciliation of Subledger to General Ledger

2.1   Subledgers

When there are large volumes of transactions, a subsidiary ledger is often used to record the details. A subledger is used to record and store the more detailed information that is summarized in the control account in the general ledger. The control account from the general ledger will reflect single-line totals for items such as trade receivables, inventory, property, plant, and equipment (PP&E), and accounts payable and accrued liabilities.

- **Trade Receivable Subledger**

  The trade receivables subledger is used to manage the company's customers and receipts from those customers. The subledger will include details on all credit sales by customer, the dates of the invoice, the invoice numbers, any discounts provided, applicable returns and allowances, and payments made on outstanding invoices.

- **Inventory Subledger**

  The inventory subledger is used to manage the movement of inventory and prices. Each item of inventory has a separate account in the subledger, which is used for tracking purchases, sales, and balances.

- **Property, Plant, and Equipment Subledger**

  The PP&E subledger contains detailed information for each asset categorized as PP&E, such as date of purchase, original cost, residual value, estimated useful life, depreciation method, accumulated depreciation, and carrying value.

- **Accounts Payable and Accrued Liabilities**

  The accounts payable and accrued liabilities subledger is used to manage amounts owed to suppliers and subsequent payments made. Included in the subledger is an account for each vendor/supplier, along with the date and amounts incurred and paid.

2.2   Reconciliation to the General Ledger

At a high level, the balance in the control accounts in the general ledger must equal the total from the accounts in the subledger. When there are differences, a reconciliation is needed to identify and correct the differences.

2.2.1   The Reconciliation Process: Trade Receivables

The reconciliation process should be done on a monthly basis and is often performed electronically due to the volume of data. The process involves first comparing the total from the receivables subledger accounts to the overall balance in receivables in the general ledger. If there are differences, transactions in both ledgers must be reviewed and compared. Once the discrepancies are identified and the location of the necessary adjustments is determined, adjusting journal entries will be recorded in the general ledger or updates will be made to the subledger. The process is complete when the adjusted balances for the general ledger and subledger are equal.

There is a myriad of reasons why differences initially exist between the receivables subledger and the general ledger. Examples of the types of differences often found and the corrections needed include:

- Incorrect entries may have been recorded in the receivables' general ledger control account, which will require adjusting journal entries to the general ledger to correct the balance.

- Adjusting journal entries posted to the general ledger at month-end may not have been reflected in the receivables subledger and must subsequently be updated in the subledger.

- Automatic posting errors may cause transactions to post to ledger account codes other than trade receivables, which will require a change in the posting rules and adjusting entries to the general ledger.

- Discounts and allowances may be reflected as direct offsets to receivables in the subledger but appear under different accounts in the general ledger. Actual adjustments are not needed, but the reconciliation should include all accounts related to sales to fully capture these discounts and allowances.

Illustration 3	Trade Receivables Subledger

In the subledger below, the trade receivables beginning balance is $15,000, and the ending balance is $8,900. If the receivables control account in the general ledger reflects an amount different than $8,900, adjustments must be made to ensure the balances are equal in both the ledger and subledger.

Trade Receivable Subledger (January, Year 2)						
Customer: ABC Goods						
Invoice Date	Invoice No.	Description	Debit	Credit	Balance	Notes
		Balance forwarded			$15,000	Includes 2 credit sales: $11,400 (invoice # 247298), $3,600 (invoice # 247610) in December, Year 1.
Jan. 14, Year 2	248674	Credit sale	$4,000		$19,000	Credit sales for Invoice # 248674
Jan. 23, Year 2	248935	Credit sale	$3,500		$22,500	Credit sales for Invoice # 248935
Jan. 28, Year 2		Payment		$19,000	$3,500	Payment for December credit sales and for invoice # 248674
Jan. 31, Year 2	249177	Credit sale	$5,400		$8,900	10% discount on sale of $6,000 if customer pays by Feb. 10.

3   Notes Receivable

Notes receivable are written promises to pay a debt, and the writing is called a promissory note. Notes receivable are classified the same as accounts receivable. They are either a current asset or a long-term asset, depending on when collection will occur.

3.1   Valuation and Presentation

Notes receivable are similar to trade receivables in that the initial value of the note receivable is adjusted for current expected credit losses. In addition, the initial and ongoing value of the note receivable must reflect an adjustment for expected losses that may occur due to changes in macroeconomic conditions.

For financial statement purposes, unearned interest and finance charges are deducted from the face amount of the related promissory note. This is necessary in order to state the receivable at its present value.

Also, if the promissory note is noninterest bearing or the interest rate is below market, the value of the note should be determined by imputing the market rate of interest and determining the value of the promissory note by using the effective interest method. Interest-bearing promissory notes issued in an arm's-length transaction are presumed to be issued at the market rate of interest.

3.2   Discounting Notes Receivable

Discounted notes receivable arise when the holder endorses the note (with or without recourse) to a third party and receives a sum of cash. The amount received by the holder is determined by applying a *discount rate* to the maturity value of the note. The difference between the amount of cash received by the holder and the maturity value of the note is the *discount*.

3.2.1   With Recourse

If the note is discounted with recourse, the holder remains contingently liable for the ultimate payment of the note when it becomes due. Notes receivable that have been discounted with recourse are reported on the balance sheet with a corresponding contra-account (Notes Receivable Discounted) indicating that they have been discounted to a third party. Alternatively, the notes receivable may be removed from the balance sheet and the contingent liability disclosed in the notes to the financial statements.

3.2.2   Without Recourse

If the note is discounted without recourse, the holder assumes no further liability. Notes receivable that have been discounted without recourse have essentially been sold outright and should, therefore, be removed from the balance sheet.

Example 6   Discounting a Note at a Bank

Facts: Jordan Corporation has a $40,000, 90-day note from a customer dated September 30, Year 3, due December 30, Year 3, and bearing interest at 12 percent. On October 30, Year 3 (30 days after issue), Jordan Corporation takes the note to its bank, which is willing to discount it at a 15 percent rate. The note was paid by Jordan's customer at maturity on December 30, Year 3 (60 days later).

Required: Compute the amount to be paid by the bank for the note. Determine the amount that Jordan Corporation should report as net interest income from the note.

Solution

1. Calculate the *maturity value* of the note by *adding the interest to the face* amount of the note, as follows:

Face value of the note	$40,000
Interest on note to maturity	1,200 ($40,000 × 12% × 90/360)
Payoff value of note at maturity	$41,200

2. Calculate the *bank discount on the payoff value at <u>maturity</u>*, as follows:

    15% discount × 60/360 days × $41,200 = $1,030

3. Compute the amount *paid by the bank* for the note.

Payoff value at maturity	$41,200
Less: bank's discount	(1,030)
Amount paid by bank for note	$40,170

4. Determine the *interest income* (or expense) by subtracting the face value of the note from the amount paid by the bank for the note, as follows:

Amount paid by bank for the note	$40,170
Less: face value of the note	(40,000)
Interest income to Jordan Corporation	$ 170

3.2.3 Dishonored Discounted Notes Receivable

When a discounted note receivable is dishonored, the contingent liability should be removed by a debit to Notes Receivable Discounted and a credit to Notes Receivable. Notes Receivable Dishonored should be recorded to the estimated recoverable amount of the note. A loss is recognized if the estimated recoverable amount is less than the amount required to settle the note and any applicable penalties.

1 Types of Inventories

Inventories of goods must be periodically counted, valued, and recorded in the books of account of a business. In general, there are four types of inventories, which are assets that are held for resale.

- **Retail Inventory:** Retail inventory is inventory that is resold in substantially the same form in which it was purchased.

- **Raw Materials Inventory:** Raw materials inventory is inventory that is being held for use in the production process.

- **Work-in-Process Inventory (WIP):** WIP is inventory that is in production but incomplete.

- **Finished Goods Inventory:** Finished goods inventory is production inventory that is complete and ready for sale.

2 Goods and Materials to Be Included in Inventory

The general rule is that any goods and materials in which the company has legal title should be included in inventory, and legal title typically follows possession of the goods. Of course, there are many exceptions and special applications of this general rule.

2.1 Goods in Transit

Title passes from the seller to the buyer in the manner and under the conditions explicitly agreed on by the parties. If no conditions are explicitly agreed on ahead of time, title passes from the seller to the buyer at the time and place where the seller's performance regarding delivery of goods is complete.

FOB means "free on board" and requires the seller to deliver the goods to the location indicated as FOB. The following terminology is most commonly used in passing title from the seller to the buyer:

- **FOB Shipping Point:** With FOB shipping point, title passes to the buyer when the seller delivers the goods to a common carrier. Goods shipped in this manner should be included in the buyer's inventory upon shipment.

- **FOB Destination:** With FOB destination, title passes to the buyer when the buyer receives the goods from the common carrier.

2.2 Shipment of Nonconforming Goods

If the seller ships the wrong goods, the title reverts to the seller upon rejection by the buyer. Thus, the goods should not be included in the buyer's inventory, even if the buyer possesses the goods prior to their return to the seller.

2.3 Consigned Goods

In a consignment arrangement, the seller (the "consignor") delivers goods to an agent (the "consignee") to hold and sell on the consignor's behalf. The consignor should include the consigned goods in its inventory because title and risk of loss is retained by the consignor even though the consignee possesses the goods.

If all of the conditions in 2.3 (above) are not met, there is no revenue recognition from a sale. Revenue will be recognized when the goods are sold to a third party. Until the sale, the goods remain in the consignor's inventory. Title passes directly to the third-party buyer (not to the consignee and then to the third-party buyer) at the point of sale.

2.4 Public Warehouses

Goods stored in a public warehouse and evidenced by a warehouse receipt should be included in the inventory of the company holding the warehouse receipt. The reason is that the warehouse receipt evidences title even though the owner does not have possession.

2.5 Sales With a Mandatory Buyback

Occasionally, as part of a financing arrangement, a seller has a requirement to repurchase goods from the buyer. If so, the seller should include the goods in inventory even though title has passed to the buyer.

2.6 Installment Sales

If the seller sells goods on an installment basis but retains legal title as security for the loan, the goods should be included in the seller's inventory if the percentage of uncollectible debts cannot be estimated. However, if the percentage of uncollectible debts can be estimated, the transaction would be accounted for as a sale, and an allowance for uncollectible debts would be recorded.

3   Valuation of Inventory

U.S. GAAP requires that inventory be stated at its *cost*. Where evidence indicates that cost will be recovered with an approximately normal profit on a sale in the ordinary course of business, no loss should be recognized even though replacement or reproduction costs are lower.

3.1   Cost

Inventories are generally accounted for at cost, which is defined as the price paid or consideration given to acquire an asset. Methods used to determine the cost of inventory include first-in, first-out (FIFO); last-in, first-out (LIFO); average cost; and the retail inventory method.

3.2   Departures From the Cost Basis

3.2.1   Precious Metals and Farm Products

Gold, silver, and other precious metals, and meat and some agricultural products are valued at *net realizable value*, which is net selling price less costs of disposal. When inventory is stated at a value in excess of cost, this fact should be fully disclosed in the financial statements. Inventories reported at net realizable value include:

- Inventories of gold and silver, when there is effective government-controlled market at a fixed monetary value.

- Inventories of agricultural, mineral, or other products meeting all of the following criteria:

    - Immediate marketability at quoted prices;

    - Unit interchangeability; and

    - Inability to determine appropriate costs.

3.2.2   Lower of Cost or Market, and Lower of Cost and Net Realizable Value

In the ordinary course of business, when the utility of goods is no longer as great as their cost, a departure from the cost basis principle of measuring inventory is required. This is usually accomplished by stating such goods at market value or net realizable value, as appropriate. The purpose of reducing inventory to an amount below cost is to show the probable loss sustained (conservatism) in the period in which the loss occurred (matching principle).

3.2.3   Recognize Loss in Current Period

Under U.S. GAAP, the write-down of inventory is usually reflected in cost of goods sold, unless the amount is material, in which case the loss should be identified separately in the income statement.

3.2.4   Reversal of Inventory Write-Downs

Under U.S. GAAP, reversals of inventory write-downs are prohibited.

3.2.5 Exceptions

The lower of cost or market and lower of cost and net realizable value rules will not apply when:

- the subsequent sales price of an end product is not affected by its market value; or
- the company has a firm sales price contract.

3.3 Lower of Cost and Net Realizable Value

Under U.S. GAAP, the lower of cost and net realizable value method is used for all inventory that is *not* costed using LIFO or the retail inventory method. The lower of cost and net realizable value principle may be applied to a single item, a category, or total inventory, provided that the method most clearly reflects periodic income.

3.3.1 Net Realizable Value

Net realizable value is an item's net selling price less the costs to complete and dispose of the inventory. Net realizable value is the same as the "market ceiling" in the lower of cost or market method.

3.4 Lower of Cost or Market

Under U.S. GAAP, the lower of cost or market method is used when inventory is costed using LIFO or the retail inventory method. The lower of cost or market principle may be applied to a single item, a category, or total inventory, provided that the method most clearly reflects periodic income.

3.4.1 Market Value

Under U.S. GAAP, the term *market* in the phrase *lower of cost or market* generally means current replacement cost (whether by purchase or reproduction), provided the current replacement cost does not exceed net realizable value (the *market ceiling*) or fall below net realizable value reduced by normal profit margin (the *market floor*).

3.4.2 Definitions

- **Market Value**

  Under U.S. GAAP, market value is the median (middle value) of an inventory item's replacement cost, its market ceiling, and its market floor.

- **Replacement Cost**

  Replacement cost is the cost to purchase the item of inventory as of the valuation date.

- **Market Ceiling**

  Market ceiling is an item's net selling price less the costs to complete and dispose (called the net realizable value).

- **Market Floor**

  Market floor is the market ceiling less a normal profit margin.

Example 1   Lower of Cost or Market

Facts: The following information pertains to a company's inventory at the end of the current year. The company uses LIFO and values its ending inventory using the lower of cost or market method.

Item	Cost	Replacement Cost	Selling Price	Costs of Completion	Normal Profit
1	$20.50	$19.00	$25.00	$1.00	$6.00
2	26.00	20.00	30.00	2.00	7.00
3	10.00	12.00	15.00	1.00	3.00
4	40.00	55.00	60.00	6.00	4.00

Required: Calculate the lower of cost or market for the above four items.

Solution:

Item 1: Determine the maximum ("ceiling") and minimum ("floor") limits for the replacement cost.

    Ceiling = $24.00 ($25 − $1)

    Floor = $18.00 ($25 − $1) − $6

Since replacement cost ($19) falls between the maximum and minimum, market price is $19.00. Market ($19.00) is lower than cost ($20.50); therefore inventory would be valued at market ($19.00).

Item 2: Determine the maximum and minimum limits for the replacement cost.

    Ceiling = $28.00 ($30 − $2)

    Floor = $21.00 ($30 − $2) − $7

Since replacement cost ($20) is less than the minimum, market value is the minimum, or $21.00. Market ($21.00) is lower than cost ($26.00), therefore inventory would be valued at market ($21.00).

Item 3: Determine the maximum and minimum limits for the replacement cost.

    Ceiling = $14.00 ($15 − $1)

    Floor = $11.00 ($15 − $1) − $3

Replacement cost ($12) falls within these limits. Since cost ($10.00) is less than replacement cost ($12.00), the cost of $10.00 is used.

Item 4: Determine the maximum and minimum limits for the replacement cost.

    Ceiling = $54.00 ($60 − $6)

    Floor = $50.00 ($60 − $6) − $4

Since the replacement cost ($55) exceeds the maximum limit, the maximum ($54.00) is compared with cost ($40.00). Inventory is valued at cost ($40.00).

When market is lower than cost, the maximum prevents a loss in future periods by valuing the inventory at its estimated selling price less costs of completion and disposal. The minimum prevents any future periods from realizing any more than a normal profit.

Journal entry to record the write-down to a separate account:

DR	Inventory loss due to decline in market value	$XXX	
CR	Inventory		$XXX

Example 2   Lower of Cost and Net Realizable Value

Facts: The following information pertains to a company's year-end inventory. The company uses FIFO and values its ending inventory using the lower of cost and net realizable value method.

Item	Cost	Selling Price	Costs of Completion
1	$28.50	$30.00	$3.00
2	21.00	26.00	4.00

Required: Calculate the net realizable value and determine the lower of cost or net realizable value for the above two items.

Solution

Item 1: Determine the net realizable value (NRV):

   NRV = $27.00 ($30 − $3)

Net realizable value ($27.00) is lower than cost ($28.50); therefore, inventory would be valued at net realizable value ($27.00).

Item 2: Determine the net realizable value:

   NRV = $22.00 ($26 − $4)

Net realizable value ($22.00) is greater than cost ($21.00); therefore, inventory would be valued at cost ($21.00).

3.5 Disclosure

Substantial and unusual losses from the subsequent measurement of inventory should be disclosed in the financial statements. Small losses from a decline in value are included in the cost of goods sold.

The basic principle of consistency must be applied in the valuation of inventory and the method should be disclosed in the financial statements. In the event that a significant change takes place in the measurement of inventory, adequate disclosure of the nature of the change and, if material (materiality principle), the effect on income should be disclosed in the financial statements.

4   Periodic Inventory System vs. Perpetual Inventory System

Two types of inventory systems are used to count inventory.

4.1   Periodic Inventory System

With a periodic inventory system, the quantity of inventory is determined only by physical count, usually at least annually. Therefore, units of inventory and the associated costs are counted and valued at the end of the accounting period. The actual cost of goods sold for the period is determined after each physical inventory by "squeezing" the difference between beginning inventory plus purchases less ending inventory, based on the physical count.

The periodic method does not keep a running total of the inventory balances. Ending inventory is physically counted and priced. Cost of goods sold is calculated as shown below:

	Beginning inventory	$ 70,000
+	Purchases	300,000
	Cost of goods available for sale	370,000
−	Ending inventory (physical count)	(270,000)
	Cost of goods sold	$ 100,000

4.2   Perpetual Inventory System

With a perpetual inventory system, the inventory record for each item of inventory is updated for each purchase and each sale as they occur. The actual cost of goods sold is determined and recorded with each sale. Therefore, the perpetual inventory system keeps a running total of inventory balances.

4.3   Hybrid Inventory Systems

4.3.1   Units of Inventory on Hand: Quantities Only

Some companies maintain a perpetual record of quantities only. A record of units on hand is maintained on the perpetual basis, and this is often referred to as the *modified perpetual system*. Changes in quantities are recorded after each sale and purchase.

4.3.2   Perpetual With Periodic at Year-End

Most companies that maintain a perpetual inventory system still perform either complete periodic physical inventories or test count inventories on a random (or cyclical) basis.

Example 3 — Comparison of Periodic and Perpetual Inventory Methods (Sales)

Facts: ABC Company sold 20,000 units of inventory for $7 per unit. The inventory had originally cost $5 per unit.

Required: Prepare the journal entries to record the sale using the periodic and perpetual methods.

Solution:

Journal entry to record sale under periodic method (cost of goods sold will be recorded after the periodic inventory count):

DR	Cash	$140,000	
CR	Sales		$140,000

Journal entry to record sale under perpetual method:

DR	Cash	$140,000	
CR	Sales		$140,000
DR	Cost of goods sold	100,000	
CR	Inventory		100,000

Example 4 — Comparison of Periodic and Perpetual Inventory Methods (Purchases)

Facts: ABC Company purchased 50,000 units of merchandise for $6 a unit to be held as inventory.

Required: Prepare the journal entries to record the purchase of inventory under the periodic and the perpetual methods.

Solution: The periodic method debits purchases; the perpetual method debits inventory.

Journal entry to record purchase under periodic method:

DR	Purchases	$300,000	
CR	Cash		$300,000

Journal entry to record purchase under perpetual method:

DR	Inventory	$300,000	
CR	Cash		$300,000

5 Primary Inventory Cost Flow Assumptions

Inventory valuation is dependent on the cost flow assumption underlying the computation. Under U.S. GAAP, the cost flow assumption used by a company is not required to have a rational relationship with the physical inventory flows; however, the primary objective is the selection of the method that will most clearly reflect periodic income.

When similar goods are purchased at different times, it may not be possible to identify and match the specific costs of the item sold. Frequently, the identity of goods and their specific related costs are lost between the time of acquisition and the time of sale. This has resulted in the development and general acceptance of several assumptions with respect to the flow of cost factors (FIFO, LIFO, and average cost) to provide practical bases for the measurement of periodic income.

5.1 Specific Identification Method

Under the specific identification method, the cost of each item in inventory is uniquely identified to that item. The cost follows the physical flow of the item in and out of inventory to cost of goods sold. Specific identification is usually used for physically large or high-value items and allows for greater opportunity for manipulation of income.

5.2 First In, First Out (FIFO) Method

Under FIFO, the first costs inventoried are the first costs transferred to cost of goods sold. Ending inventory includes the most recently incurred costs; thus, the ending balance approximates replacement cost. Ending inventory and cost of goods sold are the same whether a periodic or perpetual inventory system is used.

Pass Key

In periods of rising prices, the FIFO method results in the highest ending inventory, the lowest costs of goods sold, and the highest net income (i.e., current costs are not matched with current revenues).

Example 5   **FIFO Method**

Facts: During its first year of operations, Helix Corporation has purchased all of its inventory in three batches. Batch 1 was for 4,000 units at $4.25 per unit. Batch 2 was for 2,000 units at $4.50 per unit. Batch 3 was for 3,000 units at $4.75 per unit. In total, 4,000 units were sold, 3,000 units after the first purchase and 1,000 units after the second purchase.

Required: Determine the amounts of ending inventory and cost of goods sold using the FIFO method and the periodic and perpetual systems.

Solution:

FIFO: Periodic Inventory System

Units Bought	Cost/Unit	Ending Inventory	Goods Available for Sale
4,000	$4.25		$17,000
2,000	4.50	$ 9,000	9,000
3,000	4.75	14,250	14,250
		$23,250	40,250
Ending inventory			23,250
Cost of goods sold			$17,000

FIFO: Perpetual Inventory System

Units Bought	Units Sold	Cost/Unit	Change in Inventory	Inventory Balance	COGS
4,000		$4.25	$17,000		
	3,000	4.25	(12,750)	4,250	$12,750
2,000		4.50	9,000	13,250	
	1,000	4.25	(4,250)	9,000	4,250
3,000		4.75	14,250	23,250	
Ending inventory			$23,250		
Cost of goods sold					$17,000

Note that the ending inventory under both methods is $23,250 and the amount of cost of goods sold under both methods is $17,000.

5.3   Weighted Average Method

Under the weighted average method, at the end of the period, the average cost of each item in inventory would be the weighted average of the costs of all items in inventory. The weighted average is determined by dividing the total costs of inventory available by the total number of units of inventory available, remembering that the beginning inventory is included in both totals. This method is particularly suitable for homogeneous products and a periodic inventory system.

Example 6   **Weighted Average Method**

Facts: Assume the same information for Helix Corporation as in the previous example for FIFO.

Requirement: Determine the amounts of ending inventory and cost of goods sold under the weighted average method.

Solution:

Unit Cost	Units Purchased	Total
$4.25	4,000	$17,000
4.50	2,000	9,000
4.75	3,000	14,250
Total	9,000	$40,250

Weighted average cost per unit = $4.4722 ($40,250/9,000)

Cost of goods sold = $17,889 (4,000 units × $4.4722)

Ending inventory = $22,361 (5,000 units × $4.4722)

5.4   Moving Average Method

The moving average method computes the weighted average cost after each purchase by dividing the total cost of inventory available after each purchase (inventory plus current purchase) by the total units available after each purchase. The moving average is more current than the weighted average. A *perpetual inventory* system is necessary to use the moving average method.

Example 7   **Moving Average Method**

Facts: Assume the same information for Helix Corporation as in the previous example for FIFO.

Required: Determine the amounts of ending inventory and cost of goods sold under the moving average method.

Solution:

Purchases/(Sales)			Inventory Balances (Rounded)		
Quantity	Cost	Total	Quantity	Average Cost	Total
4,000	$4.25	$17,000	4,000	$4.25	$17,000
(3,000)	4.25	(12,750)	1,000	4.25	4,250
2,000	4.50	9,000	3,000	4.4167*	13,250
(1,000)	4.4167	(4,417)	2,000	4.4167	8,833
3,000	4.75	14,250	5,000	4.6166**	23,083

*Weighted average cost per unit = ($4,250 + $9,000) / 3,000 = $4.4167

**Weighted average cost per unit = ($8,833 + $14,250) / 5,000 = $4.6166

Cost of goods sold is $17,167 ($12,750 + $4,417)

Ending inventory is $23,083

5.5 Last In, First Out (LIFO) Method

Under LIFO, the last costs inventoried are the first costs transferred to cost of goods sold. Therefore, the ending inventory value will generally be lower than under FIFO, given the assumptions that the items of inventory on hand are the oldest, and the value of goods purchased tends to increase over time. The ending balance of inventory will typically not approximate replacement cost.

■ LIFO does not generally relate to actual flow of goods in a company because most companies sell or use their oldest goods first to prevent holding old or obsolete items.

■ If LIFO is used for tax purposes, it must also be used in the GAAP financial statements.

5.5.1 LIFO Financial Statement Effects

The use of the LIFO method generally better matches expense against revenues because it matches current costs with current revenues; thus, LIFO eliminates holding gains and reduces net income during times of inflation.

■ If sales exceed production (or purchases) for a given period, LIFO will result in a distortion of net income because old inventory costs (called "LIFO layers") will be matched with current revenue.

■ LIFO is susceptible to income manipulation by intentionally reducing purchases in order to use old layers at lower costs.

Pass Key

In periods of rising prices, the LIFO method generally results in the lowest ending inventory, the highest costs of goods sold, and the lowest net income.

Remember: LIFO = Lowest

5.5.2 LIFO: Specific Goods Method

The specific goods method for LIFO requires a company to identify each item or similar types of inventory as a group. The company then establishes a base-year inventory amount from which additional layers may be added on an annual basis.

■ After an original LIFO amount is created (base year), it may decrease, or additional layers may be created in each year according to the amount of ending inventory. An additional LIFO layer is created in any year in which the ending inventory is greater than the beginning inventory.

■ An additional LIFO layer is priced at the earliest costs of the year in which it was created, because the LIFO method matches the most current costs incurred with current revenues, leaving the first cost incurred to be included in any inventory increase.

■ The specific goods method requires companies to maintain both quantity and pricing information for each item or group identified. Therefore, it is normally only used when there is a limited amount of inventory or relatively homogeneous products.

Illustration 1   LIFO Layer Container

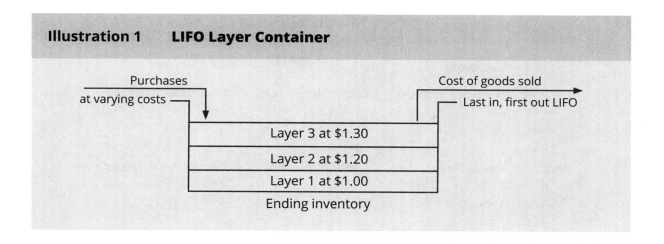

Example 8   LIFO: Specific Goods Method

Facts: Assume the same facts for Helix Corporation as in previous examples.

Required: Determine the amounts of ending inventory and cost of goods sold using the LIFO method and periodic and the perpetual systems.

Solution

LIFO: periodic inventory system

Units Bought	Cost/Unit	Ending Inventory	Goods Available for Sale
4,000	$4.25	$17,000	$ 17,000
2,000	4.50	4,500	9,000
3,000	4.75	_____	14,250
			40,250
Ending inventory		**$21,500**	(21,500)
Cost of goods sold			**$18,750**

LIFO: perpetual inventory system

Units Bought	Units Sold	Cost/Unit	Inventory Balance	COGS
4,000		$4.25	$17,000	
	3,000	4.25	(12,750)	$12,750
2,000		4.50	9,000	
	1,000	4.50	(4,500)	4,500
3,000		4.75	14,250	
			$23,000	**$17,250**

Under the *periodic inventory system,* ending inventory is $21,500 and cost of goods sold is $18,750.

Under the *perpetual inventory system,* ending inventory is $23,000 and cost of goods sold is $17,250.

Pass Key

Comparison of FIFO, LIFO, and the average methods:

Periodic Inventory System	Ending Inventory	Cost of Goods Sold
FIFO	$23,250	$17,000
Weighted Average	22,361	17,889
LIFO	21,500	18,750

Perpetual Inventory System	Ending Inventory	Cost of Goods Sold
FIFO	$23,250	$17,000
Moving Average	23,083	17,167
LIFO	23,000	17,250

These examples illustrate that in a period of rising prices, FIFO results in the highest ending inventory and the lowest cost of goods sold, LIFO results in the lowest ending inventory and the highest cost of goods sold, and the average method balances fall between the LIFO and FIFO balances. Note that the moving average method results in higher ending inventory and lower cost of goods sold than with the weighted average method.

5.5.3   LIFO: Dollar Value Method

Under the specific goods LIFO method, inventory is measured in units and is priced at unit prices. Under the dollar-value LIFO method, inventory is measured relative to base-year dollar values and is adjusted for changing price levels. When computing dollar-value LIFO, a price index will be used to adjust the inventory value based on units on hand at the end of the period for each inventory layer. In some problems the price index will be internally computed. In other problems, the price index will be supplied.

■   **Internally Computed Price Index:** When the price index is computed internally by the company, the price index will be ending inventory at current year cost divided by ending inventory at base year cost:

$$\text{Price index } = \frac{\text{Ending inventory at current year cost}}{\text{Ending inventory at base year cost}}$$

■   To compute the LIFO layer added in the current year at dollar-value LIFO, the LIFO layer at base year cost is multiplied by the internally generated price index.

Example 9	Dollar-Value LIFO—Internally Computed Price Index

Facts: Brock Co. adopted the dollar-value LIFO inventory method as of January 1, Year 1. A single inventory pool and an internally computed price index are used to compute Brock's LIFO inventory layers. Information about Brock's dollar-value inventory follows:

Date	At Base Year Cost	At Current Year Cost	At Dollar-Value LIFO
1/1/Year 1	$40,000	$40,000	$40,000
Year 1 layer	5,000	14,000	6,000*
12/31/Year 1	$45,000	$54,000	46,000**
Year 2 layer	15,000	26,000	20,000***
12/31/Year 2	$60,000	$80,000	$66,000****

Required: Compute the LIFO layers added and ending inventory for Years 1 and 2 at dollar-value LIFO.

Solution:

$$\text{Year 1 price index} = \frac{\$54,000}{\$45,000} = \frac{6}{5}$$

*Year 1 LIFO layer added = 6/5 × $5,000 = $6,000

**Year 1 ending inventory = $40,000 + $6,000 = $46,000

$$\text{Year 2 price index} = \frac{\$80000}{\$60,000} = \frac{4}{3}$$

***Year 2 LIFO layer added = 4/3 × $15,000 = $20,000

****Year 2 ending inventory = $46,000 + $20,000 = $66,000

■ **Price Index Supplied:** Where the price index is given in the problem, the year-end price index is multiplied by the LIFO layer at the base year cost to calculate the LIFO layer added at dollar-value LIFO.

Example 10   Dollar-Value LIFO—Price Index Supplied

Facts: Walt Company adopted the dollar-value LIFO inventory method as of January 1, Year 1, when its inventory was valued at $500,000. Walt's entire inventory constitutes a single pool. Using a relevant price index of 1.10, Walt determined that its December 31, Year 1, inventory was $577,500 at current year cost, and $525,000 at base year cost.

Required: Calculate Walt's dollar-value LIFO inventory at December 31, Year 1.

Solution:

Date	At Base Year Cost	At Current Year Cost	At Dollar-Value LIFO
1/1/Year 1	$500,000	$500,000	$500,000
Year 1 layer			
12/31/Year 1	525,000	577,500	

The Year 1 layer at base year cost is $525,000 − $500,000 = $25,000

The Year 1 layer at current year cost is $577,500 − $500,000 = $77,500

The Year 1 layer at dollar-value LIFO is $25,000 (base year layer) × 1.10 = $27,500

The dollar-value LIFO ending inventory is $500,000 + $27,500 = $527,500

---

6 Gross Profit Method

The gross profit method is used for interim financial statements as part of a periodic inventory system. Inventory is valued at retail, and the average gross profit percentage is used to determine the inventory cost for the interim financial statements. The gross profit percentage is known and is used to calculate cost of sales.

Example 11   Gross Profit Method

Facts: Dahl Co. sells soap at a gross profit percentage of 20 percent. The following figures apply to the eight months ended August 31, Year 1:

Sales	$200,000
Beginning inventory	100,000
Purchases	100,000

On September 1, Year 1, a flood destroys all of Dahl's soap inventory.

Required: Estimate the cost of the destroyed inventory.

Solution:

Sales	$200,000
COGS % (1.00 − 0.20)	× 80%
Cost of goods sold	$160,000

Cost of goods sold is deducted from the total goods available to determine ending inventory, as follows:

Beginning inventory	$100,000
Add: purchases	+ 100,000
Cost of goods available	$200,000
Less: cost of goods sold	(160,000)
Estimated cost of inventory destroyed	$ 40,000

7 Firm Purchase Commitments

A firm purchase commitment is a legally enforceable agreement to purchase a specified amount of goods at some time in the future. All material firm purchase commitments must be disclosed in either the financial statements or the notes thereto.

If the contracted price exceeds the market price and if it is expected that losses will occur when the purchase is actually made, the loss should be recognized at the time of the decline in price. A description of losses recognized on these commitments must be disclosed in the current period's income statement.

Example 12	Loss on Purchase Commitments

Facts: J and S Inc. signed timber-cutting contracts in Year 1 to be executed at $5,000,000 in Year 2. The market price of the rights at December 31, Year 1, is $4,000,000 and it is expected that the loss will occur when the contract is effected in Year 2.

Required: Determine the amount that should be reported as a loss on purchase commitments at December 31, Year 1.

Solution:

Price of purchase commitment	$5,000,000
Market price at 12/31/Year 1	(4,000,000)
Loss on purchase commitments	$1,000,000

Journal entry to record the loss:

DR	Estimated loss on purchase commitment	$1,000,000	
CR	Estimated liability on purchase commitment		$1,000,000

Note that the loss is recognized in the period in which the price declined. The estimated loss on purchase commitment is reported in the income statement under other expenses and losses.

1 Property, Plant, and Equipment

- Property, plant, and equipment (PP&E), or fixed assets, are assets that are acquired for use in operations and not for resale.

- They possess physical substance, are long-term in nature, and are subject to depreciation.

The following fixed assets must be shown separately on the balance sheet (or footnotes) at original cost (historical cost):

- **Land (Property)**

- **Buildings (Plant)**

- **Equipment:** May show machinery, tools, furniture, and fixtures separately, if these categories are significant.

- **Accumulated Depreciation Account (Contra-Asset):** May be combined for two or more asset categories.

2 Valuation of Fixed Assets

2.1 Historical Cost

Historical cost is the basis for valuation of purchased fixed assets. Historical cost is measured by the cash or cash equivalent price of obtaining the asset and bringing it to the location and condition necessary for its intended use.

2.2 Donated Fixed Assets

Donated fixed assets are recorded at fair market value along with incidental costs incurred. Donated fixed assets result in the recognition of a gain on the income statement.

DR	Fixed asset (FMV)	$XXX	
CR	Gain on nonreciprocal transfer		$XXX

3 Property

3.1 Cost of Land

When land has been purchased for the purpose of constructing a building, all costs incurred up to excavation for the new building are considered land costs. All the following expenditures are included.

- Purchase price
- Brokers' commissions
- Title and recording fees
- Legal fees
- Draining of swamps
- Clearing of brush and trees
- Site development (e.g., grading of mountain tops to make a "pad")
- Existing obligations assumed by buyer, including mortgages and back taxes
- Costs of razing (tearing down) an old building (demolition)
- Less proceeds from sale of existing buildings, standing timber, etc.

3.2 Land Improvements

Land improvements are depreciable, and include the following:

- Fences
- Water systems
- Sidewalks
- Paving
- Landscaping
- Lighting

3.3 Interest Costs

Interest costs during the construction period should be added to the cost of land improvements based on the weighted average of accumulated expenditures.

4 Plant

4.1 Cost of Plant

Cost of plant or buildings includes:

- Purchase price, etc.
- All repair charges neglected by the previous owner ("deferred maintenance")
- Alterations and improvements
- Architect's fees
- Possible addition of construction-period interest

Pass Key

When preparing the land for the construction of a building:
- Land cost: filling in a hole or leveling
- Building cost: digging a hole for the foundation

4.2 "Basket Purchase" of Land and Building

Allocate the purchase price based on the ratio of appraised values of individual items.

5 Equipment

Equipment includes office equipment, machinery, furniture, fixtures, and factory equipment.

5.1 Cost of Equipment

Cost includes all expenditures related directly to the acquisition or construction of the equipment:

- Invoice price
- Less cash discounts and other discounts (if any)
- Add freight-in (and insurance while in transit and while in construction)
- Add installation charges (including testing and preparation for use)
- Add sales and federal excise taxes
- Possible addition of construction period interest

5.2 Capitalize vs. Expense

Proper accounting is determined based on the purpose of the expenditure.

5.2.1 Additions

Additions increase the quantity of fixed assets and are capitalized:

DR	Asset (machinery, etc.)	$XXX	
CR	Cash/accounts payable		$XXX

5.2.2 Improvements and Replacements

Improvements (betterments) improve the quality of fixed assets and are capitalized to the fixed asset account (e.g., a tile or steel roof is substituted for an old asphalt roof). In a replacement, a new, similar asset is substituted for the old asset (e.g., an asphalt shingle roof is replaced with a roof of similar material).

■ If the carrying value of the old asset is *known*, remove it and recognize any gain or loss. Capitalize the cost of the improvement/replacement to the asset account.

■ If the carrying value of the old asset is *unknown*, and:

• *The asset's life is extended, debit accumulated depreciation for the cost of the improvement/replacement:*

DR	Accumulated depreciation	$XXX	
CR	Cash/accounts payable		$XXX

■ The usefulness (utility) of the asset is increased, capitalize the cost of the improvement/replacement to the asset account.

5.2.3 Repairs

■ Ordinary repairs should be expensed as repair and maintenance.

■ Extraordinary repairs should be capitalized. Treat the repair as an addition, improvement, or replacement, as appropriate.

Summary Chart		Expense	Capitalize	Reduce Accumulated Depreciation
Additions: Increase quantity			✓	
Improvement/replacement:	Increase life			✓
	Increase usefulness		✓	
Ordinary repair		✓		
Extraordinary repair:	Increase life			✓
	Increase usefulness		✓	

6 Fixed Assets Constructed by a Company

6.1 Costs to Capitalize

When a fixed asset is constructed by a company, the cost of the fixed asset includes:

- Direct materials and direct labor.
- Repairs and maintenance expenses that add value to the fixed asset.
- Overhead, including direct items of overhead (any "idle plant capacity" expense).
- Construction period interest.

6.2 Capitalization of Interest Costs

Construction period interest should be capitalized based on weighted average of accumulated expenditures as part of the cost of producing fixed assets, such as:

- Buildings, machinery, or land improvements, constructed or produced for others or to be used internally.
- Fixed assets intended for sale or lease and constructed as discrete projects, such as real estate projects.
- Land improvements. If a structure is placed on the land, charge the interest cost to the structure, not the land.

6.2.1 Computing Capitalized Cost

- **Weighted Average Amount of Accumulated Expenditures:** Capitalized interest costs for a particular period are determined by applying an interest rate to the average amount of accumulated expenditures for the qualifying asset during the period (this is known as the avoidable interest).

- **Interest Rate on Borrowings:** The interest rate paid on borrowings (specifically for asset construction) during a particular period should be used to determine the amount of interest cost to be capitalized for the period. Where a qualifying asset is related to a specific new borrowing, the allocated interest cost is equal to the amount of interest incurred on the new borrowing.

- **Interest Rate on Excess Expenditures (Weighted Average):** If the average accumulated expenditures outstanding exceed the amount of the related specific new borrowing, interest cost should be computed on the excess. The interest rate that should be used on the excess is the weighted average interest rate for other borrowings of the company.

- **Not to Exceed Actual Interest Costs:** Total capitalized interest costs for any particular period may not exceed the total interest costs actually incurred by an entity during that period. In consolidated financial statements, this limitation should be applied on a consolidated basis.

- **Do Not Reduce Capitalizable Interest:** Do not reduce capitalizable interest by income received on the unexpended portion of the loan.

Pass Key

For the CPA Exam, it is important to remember two rules concerning capitalized interest:

Rule 1: Only capitalize interest on money actually spent, not on the total amount borrowed.

Rule 2: The amount of capitalized interest is the lower of:

- actual interest cost incurred, or
- computed capitalized interest (avoidable interest).

Example 1   Capitalized Interest

Facts: On January 1, Year 1, Conviser Soup Kitchen Inc. signed a fixed-price contract to have a new kitchen built for $1,000,000. On the same day, Conviser borrowed $500,000 to finance the construction. The loan is payable in five $100,000 annual payments plus interest at 11 percent. Conviser planned to finance the balance of the construction costs using the company's existing debt, which had a weighted average interest rate of 9 percent. During Year 1, Conviser had average accumulated expenditures of $600,000 and incurred actual interest costs on all borrowings of $150,000.

Required: Calculate Conviser's capitalized interest cost?

Solution:

Weighted Average of Accumulated Expenditures	×	Applicable Interest Rate	=	Amount of Interest to Be Capitalized
$500,000	×	11%	=	$55,000
100,000	×	9%	=	9,000
		Total capitalizable interest		$64,000

Note that because the capitalizable interest of $64,000 is less than the actual interest of $150,000, the full $64,000 is capitalized. The remainder of the actual interest is expensed.

6.2.2   Capitalization of Interest Period

- Begins when three conditions are present:
    - Expenditures for the asset have been made.
    - Activities that are necessary to get the asset ready for its intended use are in progress.
    - Interest cost is being incurred.
- Continues as long as the three conditions are present.
- Stops during intentional delays in construction, but continues during ordinary construction delays.
- Ends when the asset is (or independent parts of the asset are) substantially complete and ready for the intended use (regardless of whether it is actually used).

6.2.3   Disclose in Financial Statements

- Total interest cost incurred during the period.
- Capitalized interest cost for the period, if any.

Illustration 1	Construction Period		

		Interest	
Date		**Capitalized**	**Expense**
1/2/Year 1	Purchased $1,000,000 parcel of land for speculation; paid $600,000 down, borrowed $400,000 at 12% per year		
3/1	Paid interest cost of $8,000 (2 months)		$8,000
3/2	Decision made to build condo project on the land, and attorneys apply for zoning permits*		
5/1	Paid interest cost of $8,000 (2 months) (charge to building)	$ 8,000	
5/2	Permits received—*architects begin plans*		
9/1	Begin grading and developing land and foundation; paid four months' interest (charge building)	16,000	
9/2	Incurred expenses to date for attorney, architect, and land development = $300,000, all paid with additional borrowed money		
12/31/Year 1	Paid four months interest**	28,000	
	Total interest	$52,000	$8,000
12/31/Year 1	Required disclosure of interest:		
	Total interest cost incurred during year = $60,000 **Interest cost capitalized = $52,000*** **		
1/2/Year 2	Wildcat strike stops construction (unintentional delay)	$$$	
2/1	Wildcat strike over—*construction continues*	$$$	
4/1	Glut on condo market; construction delayed intentionally		$$$
8/1	Construction continued	$$$	
10/1	Floors 1–3 of the 10-story condo building are completed and ready for sale (except for light fixtures and wall coverings)	Floors 4–10	Floors 1–3
12/15/Year 2	Building and project completed		$$$

*Construction period begins at point the decision is made to build on land, and ends when asset is substantially complete and ready for intended use.

**$400,000 + 300,000 = $700,000 × 12% × 4/12 = $28,000

***Capitalizable interest is based on weighted average of accumulated expenditures to date.

NOTES

1 Overview

The basic principle of matching revenue and expenses is applied to long-lived assets that are not held for sale in the ordinary course of business. The systematic and rational allocation used to achieve "matching" is usually accomplished by depreciation, amortization, or depletion, according to the type of long-lived asset involved.

1.1 Types of Depreciation

- **Physical Depreciation:** This type of depreciation is related to an asset's deterioration and wear over a period of time.

- **Functional Depreciation:** Functional depreciation arises from obsolescence or inadequacy of the asset to perform efficiently. Obsolescence may result from diminished demand for the product that the depreciable asset produces or from the availability of a new depreciable asset that can perform the same function for substantially less cost.

1.2 Definitions

- **Salvage Value:** Salvage or residual value is an estimate of the amount that will be realized at the end of the useful life of a depreciable asset. Frequently, depreciable assets have little or no salvage value at the end of their estimated useful life and, if immaterial, the amount(s) may be ignored in calculating depreciation.

- **Estimated Useful Life:** Estimated useful life is the period of time over which an asset's cost will be depreciated. It may be revised at any time, but any revision must be accounted for prospectively, in current and future periods only (change in estimate).

Pass Key

The CPA Exam frequently will have an asset placed in service *during* the year. Therefore, it requires computing depreciation for a part of the year rather than the full year. Candidates must always check the date the asset was placed in service.

2 Composite Depreciation and Component Depreciation

2.1 Component Depreciation

Component depreciation is the separate depreciation of each part of an item of property, plant, and equipment that is significant to the total cost of the fixed asset. Component depreciation is permitted but rarely used under U.S. GAAP.

2.2 Composite or Group Depreciation

Composite depreciation is the process of averaging the economic lives of a number of property units and depreciating the entire class of assets over a single life (e.g., all at five years), thus simplifying record keeping of assets and depreciation calculations.

2.2.1 Asset Retirement

When a group or composite asset is sold or retired, the accumulated depreciation is treated differently from the accumulated depreciation of a single asset. If the average service life of the group of assets has not been reached when an asset is retired, the gain or loss that results is absorbed in the accumulated depreciation account. The accumulated depreciation account is debited (credited) for the difference between the original cost and the cash received.

2.2.2 Depreciation Methods

Composite and component depreciation can be done using any acceptable depreciation method, including the straight-line, sum-of-the-years'-digits, and declining balance methods.

Example 1   Composite (Group) Depreciation

Facts: A schedule of machinery owned by Lester Manufacturing Company is presented below:

	Total Cost	Estimated Salvage Value	Estimated Life in Years
Machine A	$550,000	$50,000	20
Machine B	200,000	20,000	15
Machine C	40,000	–	5

Lester computes depreciation on the straight-line method.

Required: Depreciate the machinery using composite depreciation.

Solution: Based on the information presented, the composite life of these assets (in years) should be 16 years, computed as follows:

Machine	Total Cost	Estimated Salvage Value	Depreciable Cost	Estimated Life in Years	Annual Depreciation
A	$550,000	$50,000	$500,000	20	$25,000
B	200,000	20,000	180,000	15	12,000
C	40,000	–	40,000	5	8,000
Totals	$790,000	– $70,000	= $720,000		$45,000

Average composite life = $720,000 divided by $45,000 = 16 years

---

Illustration 1   Disposal of Group or Composite Asset

Assume that the Lester Company sells Machine A in 10 years for $260,000. Because the loss on disposal is not recognized, accumulated depreciation must be reduced or debited.

The journal entry is as follows:

DR	Cash	$260,000	
DR	Accumulated depreciation	290,000	
CR	Asset A		$550,000

---

3   Basic Depreciation Methods

The goal of a depreciation method should be to provide for a reasonable, consistent matching of revenue and expense by systematically allocating the cost of the depreciable asset over its estimated useful life.

The actual accumulation of depreciation in the books is accomplished by using a contra-account, such as accumulated depreciation or allowance for depreciation.

3.1   Straight-Line Depreciation

Straight-line depreciation is determined by the formula:

$$\frac{\text{Cost} - \text{Salvage value}}{\text{Estimated useful life}} = \text{Depreciation}$$

Estimated useful life is usually stated in periods of time, such as years or months.

Illustration 2   Straight-Line Depreciation

Assume that an asset cost $11,000, has a salvage value of $1,000, and has an estimated useful life of five years.

$$\frac{\$11,000 - \$1,000}{5 \text{ years}} = \$2,000 \text{ depreciation per year}$$

If the asset was acquired within the year instead of at the beginning of the year, a partial depreciation expense is taken in the first year.

3.2 Sum-of-the-Years'-Digits Depreciation

The sum-of-the-years'-digits method is one of the accelerated methods of depreciation that provides higher depreciation expense in the early years and lower charges in the later years.

3.2.1 Calculation

To find the sum-of-the-years'-digits, each year is progressively numbered and then added. For example, the sum-of-the-years'-digits for a five-year life would be: 1 + 2 + 3 + 4 + 5 = 15

> For four years: 1 + 2 + 3 + 4 = 10

> For three years: 1 + 2 + 3 = 6

3.2.2 Formula

The sum-of-the-years'-digits becomes the denominator. The numerator is the remaining life of the asset at the beginning of the current year. For example, the first year's depreciation for a five-year life would be 5/15 of the depreciable base of the asset.

$$\text{Depreciation expense} = (\text{Cost} - \text{Salvage value}) \times \frac{\text{Remaining life of asset}}{\text{Sum-of-the-years' digits}}$$

3.2.3 Calculating the Sum-of-the-Years' Digits

When dealing with an asset with a long life, use the general formula for finding the sum-of-the-years'-digits:

$$S = \frac{N \times (N + 1)}{2}$$

Where:

N = Estimated useful life

Note: The CPA Exam rarely tests sum-of-the-years'-digits depreciation for asset lives longer than five years.

Example 2   Sum-of-the-Years'-Digits Method

Facts: Assume that an asset cost $11,000, has a salvage value of $1,000, and has an estimated useful life of four years.

Required: Calculate the amount of depreciation expense for each of the four years of the asset's useful life.

Solution: The first step is to determine the depreciable base:

Cost of asset	$11,000
Less: salvage value	(1,000)
Depreciable base	$10,000

The sum-of-the-years'-digits for four years is:

$1 + 2 + 3 + 4 = 10$

The first year's depreciation is 4/10, the second year's is 3/10, the third year's is 2/10, and the fourth year's is 1/10, as follows:

1st Year:	4/10 × $10,000	=	$4,000
2nd Year:	3/10 × $10,000	=	3,000
3rd Year:	2/10 × $10,000	=	2,000
4th Year:	1/10 × $10,000	=	1,000
Total depreciation		=	$10,000

3.3   Units-of-Production (Productive Output) Depreciation

The units-of-production method relates depreciation to the estimated production capability of an asset and is expressed in a rate per unit or hour.

The formula is:

$$\frac{\text{Cost} - \text{Salvage value}}{\text{Estimated units or hours}} = \text{Rate per unit or hour}$$

$$\begin{array}{c}\text{Rate per unit} \\ \text{(or hour)}\end{array} \times \begin{array}{c}\text{Number of units produced} \\ \text{(or hours worked)}\end{array} = \begin{array}{c}\text{Depreciation} \\ \text{expense}\end{array}$$

3.4   Declining Balance Depreciation

The most common of these accelerated methods is the double-declining-balance method, although other alternative (less than double) methods are acceptable.

3.4.1   Calculation

Under double-declining balance, each year's depreciation rate is double the straight-line rate. In the final year, the asset is depreciated to its salvage value, if any.

Double-declining-balance depreciation is calculated using the following formula:

$$\text{Depreciation expense} = 2 \times \frac{1}{N} \times (\text{Cost} - \text{Accumulated depreciation})$$

3.4.2   Salvage Value

No allowance is made for salvage value because the method always leaves a remaining balance, which is treated as salvage value. However, the asset should not be depreciated below the estimated salvage value.

Pass Key

The only methods that ignore salvage value in the annual calculation of depreciation are the declining balance methods. Salvage value is only used as the limitation on total depreciation.

Example 3	Double-Declining-Balance Method

Facts: An asset costing $10,000 with a salvage value of $2,000 has an estimated useful life of 10 years.

Required: Using the double-declining-balance method, calculate the depreciation expense for each year of the useful life of the asset.

Solution: First, the regular straight-line method percentage is determined, which in this case is 10 percent (10-year life). The amount is doubled to 20 percent and applied each year to the remaining book value, as follows:

Year	Double Percentage	Net Book Value Remaining	Amount of Depreciation Expense
1	20	$10,000	$2,000
2	20	8,000	1,600
3	20	6,400	1,280
4	20	5,120	1,024
5	20	4,096	819
6	20	3,277	655
7	20	2,622	524
8	20	2,098	98
Salvage value		2,000	0

Note: Had the preceding illustration been 1½ times declining balance (150 percent), the rate would have been 15 percent of the remaining book value.

If the asset had been placed in service halfway through the year, the first year's depreciation would have been $1,000 (one-half of $2,000), and the second year's depreciation would have been 20 percent of $9,000 (remaining value after the first year), or $1,800.

In Year 8, only $98 depreciation expense is taken because book value cannot drop below salvage value. In addition, no depreciation expense is recorded in Years 9 and 10.

3.5 Partial-Year Depreciation

When an asset is placed in service during the year, the depreciation expense is typically taken only for the portion of the year that the asset is used. For example, if an asset (of a company on a calendar year basis) is placed in service on July 1, only six months' depreciation is taken.

Some companies may choose to use other specific variations for assets placed in service during the year. The half-year convention means one-half year's depreciation is taken in both the year of acquisition and the year of disposal. Other variations include taking no depreciation in the year of acquisition and a full year's depreciation in the year of disposal, or taking a full year's depreciation in the year of acquisition and no depreciation in the year of disposal.

4   Disposals

4.1   Sale of an Asset During Its Useful Life

DR	Cash received from sale	$XXX	
DR	Accumulated depreciation of sold asset	XXX	
CR	Sold asset at cost		$XXX
CR/DR	The difference is gain/loss		XXX

4.2   Write-off Fully Depreciated Asset

DR	Accumulated depreciation (100 percent)	$XXX	
CR	Old asset at full cost (100 percent)		$XXX

4.3   Total and Permanent Impairment

DR	Accumulated depreciation per records	$XXX	
DR	Loss due to impairment (the difference)	XXX	
CR	Asset at full cost		$XXX

5   Disclosure

Allowances for depreciation and depletion should be deducted from the assets to which they relate.

The following disclosures of depreciable assets and depreciation should be made in the financial statements or notes thereto:

- Depreciation expense for the period.
- Balance of major classes of depreciable assets by nature or function.
- Accumulated depreciation allowances by classes or in total.
- The methods used, by major classes, in computing depreciation.

6   Depletion

Depletion is the allocation of the cost of wasting natural resources such as oil, gas, timber, and minerals to the production process.

6.1   Definitions

- **Purchase Cost:** Purchase cost includes any expenditures necessary to purchase and then prepare the land for the removal of resources, such as drilling costs or the costs for tunnels or shafts for the oil industry (intangible development costs) or to prepare the asset for harvest, such as in the lumber industry.

- **Residual Value:** The residual value is similar to salvage value. It is the monetary worth of a depleted asset after the resources have been removed.

- **Depletion Base (Cost − Residual Value):** The depletion base is the cost to purchase the property minus the estimated net residual value remaining after all resources have been removed from the property.

6.2   Methods

6.2.1   Cost Depletion (GAAP)

Cost depletion is computed by dividing the current estimated recoverable units into unrecovered cost (less salvage) to arrive at a cost depletion rate, which is multiplied by units produced to allocate the costs to production.

6.2.2   Percentage Depletion (Not GAAP/Tax Only)

- Percentage depletion is based on a percentage of sales. It is allowed by Congress as a tax deduction to encourage exploration in very risky businesses.

- Percentage depletion can (and usually does) exceed cost depletion.

- It is limited to 50 percent of net income from the depletion property computed before the percentage depletion allowance.

6.3   Calculation of Depletion

Depletion for a period is calculated as follows:

$$\text{Total depletion} = \text{Unit depletion rate} \times \text{Number of units extracted}$$

6.3.1   Unit Depletion Rate (Depletion per Unit)

Unit depletion is the amount of depletion recognized per unit (e.g., ton, barrel, etc.) extracted.

$$\text{Unit depletion rate} = \frac{\text{Depletion base}}{\text{Estimated recoverable units}}$$

6.3.2   Depletion Base

The depletion base may be calculated as:

Cost to purchase property
Plus: development costs to prepare the land for extraction
Plus: any estimated restoration costs
Less: residual value of land after the resources (e.g., mineral ore, oil, etc.) are extracted

6.3.3   Recognition of Depletion

If all units extracted are not sold, then depletion must be allocated between cost of goods sold and inventory. The amount of depletion to be included in cost of goods sold is calculated by multiplying the unit depletion rate by the number of units sold. Depletion applicable to units extracted but not sold is allocated to inventory as direct materials.

Example 4   Total Depletion and Cost of Goods Sold Depletion

Facts: In Year 1, Happy Mine Corp. purchased a mineral mine for $3,400,000 with removable ore estimated by geological surveys at 4,000,000 tons. The property has an estimated value of $200,000 after the ore has been extracted. The company incurred $800,000 of development costs preparing the mine for production. During Year 1, 400,000 tons were removed and 375,000 tons were sold.

Required:

1. Calculate the depletion base for the mineral mine.

2. Calculate the amount of depletion the mine should record for Year 1.

3. Determine the amount of depletion the mine should include in cost of goods sold for Year 1.

Solution:

1. **Depletion base:**

    Cost of land + Development costs + Restoration − Residual value

    $4,000,000 = $3,400,000 + $800,000 + 0 − $200,000

    Then, calculate unit depletion rate:

    $$\text{Unit depletion} = \frac{\text{Depletion base}}{\text{Estimated recoverable units}} = \frac{\$4,000,000}{4,000,000 \text{ tons}} = \$1 \text{ per ton}$$

2. **Depletion for Year 1:**

    = Unit depletion × Units extracted

    = $1 per unit × 400,000 units

    = $400,000

3. **Depletion to be included in cost of goods sold:**

    = Unit depletion × Units sold

    = $1 per unit × 375,000 units

    = $375,000

    Note that the remaining $25,000 would be included in inventory as direct materials ($400,000 − $375,000 = $25,000).

Pass Key

When computing depletion on land, remember it is **REAL** property:

Residual value (subtract)

Extraction/development cost

Anticipated restoration cost

Land purchase price

7 Impairment of Property, Plant, and Equipment

The carrying amounts of fixed assets held for use and to be disposed of need to be reviewed whenever events or changes in circumstances indicate that the carrying amount may not be recoverable.

7.1 Test for Recoverability

When a fixed asset is tested for impairment, the future cash flows expected to result from the use of the asset and its eventual disposition need to be estimated. If the sum of *undiscounted* expected (future) cash flows is less than the carrying amount, an impairment loss needs to be recognized.

7.2 Calculation of the Impairment Loss

The impairment loss is calculated as the amount by which the carrying amount exceeds the fair value of the asset.

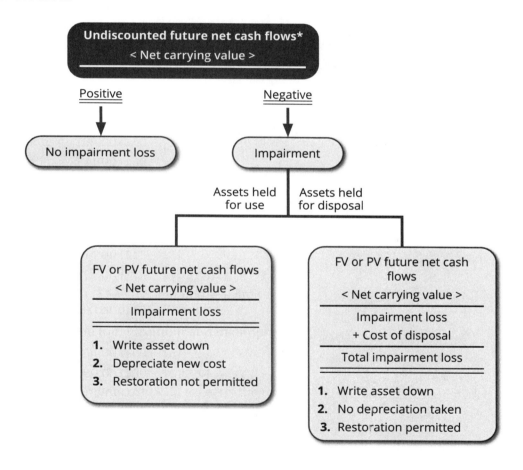

7.3   Reporting the Impairment Loss: General

The impairment loss is reported as a component of income from continuing operations before income taxes or in a statement of activities (related to not-for-profit entities). The impairment loss is recognized by reducing the carrying value of the asset to its lower fair value. Restoration of previously recognized impairment losses is prohibited under U.S. GAAP unless the asset is held for disposal.

Pass Key

It is important to remember the following rules when performing your calculations:

- **Determining the Impairment:** Use undiscounted future net cash flows.
- **Amount of the Impairment:** Use fair value (FV) or discounted (PV) future net cash flows.

1 Intangible Assets

Intangible assets are long-lived legal rights and competitive advantages developed or acquired by a business enterprise. They are typically acquired to be used in operations of a business and provide benefits over several accounting periods.

1.1 Classification of Intangible Assets

Patents, copyrights, franchises, trademarks, and goodwill are the common intangible assets tested on the CPA Examination.

1.1.1 Manner of Acquisition

■ **Purchased Intangible Assets**

Intangible assets acquired from other enterprises or individuals should be recorded as an asset at cost. Legal and registration fees incurred to obtain an intangible asset should also be capitalized.

■ **Internally Developed Intangible Assets**

- Under U.S. GAAP, the cost of intangible assets not acquired from others (i.e., developed internally) should be expensed when incurred because U.S. GAAP prohibits the capitalization of research and development costs.

- Examples (must be expensed):

  —Trademarks (except for the capitalizable costs identified below)

  —Goodwill from advertising

  —The cost of developing, maintaining, or restoring goodwill

- The exception is that certain costs associated with internally developed intangibles that are specifically identifiable can be capitalized, such as:

  —Legal fees and other costs related to a successful defense of the asset

  —Registration or consulting fees

  —Design costs (e.g., of a trademark)

  —Other direct costs to secure the asset

1.1.2 Expected Period of Benefit (Finite vs. Indefinite Life)

Classification of the intangible asset depends on whether the economic life can be determined or is indeterminable. An intangible asset has a finite life when it is possible to estimate the useful life of the asset (e.g., customer lists, patents, copyrights). If it is not possible to determine the useful life, then the asset has an indefinite (not finite) life (e.g., goodwill, trademarks, licenses, crypto assets).

Crypto assets represent a digital value or right. The value or rights of the digital assets are created or reside on a distributed ledger, such as blockchain. Crypto assets are classified as indefinite-lived intangible assets when the assets possess all of the following criteria:

- The assets meet the definition of intangible assets under GAAP.

- The assets do not provide the asset holder with enforceable rights to or claims on an underlying good, service, or other asset.

- The assets are created or reside on a distributed ledger based on blockchain or similar technology.

- The assets are secured through cryptography.

- The assets are fungible.

- The assets are not created or issued by the reporting entity or its related parties.

1.1.3 Separability

The classification of an intangible asset depends on whether the asset can be separated from the entity, also referred to as specifically identifiable (e.g., patents, copyrights, franchises, etc.), or is substantially inseparable from it, also referred to as not specifically identifiable (e.g., a trade name or goodwill).

1.2 Capitalization of Costs

A company should record the cost of intangible assets acquired from other enterprises or individuals in an "arm's-length" transaction as assets.

- Cost is measured by:
  - the amount of cash disbursed or the fair value of other assets distributed;
  - the present value of amounts to be paid for liabilities incurred; and
  - the fair value of consideration received for stock issued.

- Cost may be determined either by the fair value of the consideration given or by the fair value of the property acquired, whichever is more clearly evident.

1.3 Amortization

The value of intangible assets eventually disappears; therefore, the cost of each type of intangible asset (except for goodwill and assets with indefinite lives) should be amortized by systematic charges to income over the period estimated to be benefited (useful economic life).

1.3.1 Method

The straight-line method of amortization should be applied, unless a company demonstrates that another systematic method is more appropriate. The method and estimated useful lives of intangible assets should be adequately disclosed in the notes to the financial statements. Expenses that increase the useful life of the intangible asset require an adjustment to the calculation of the annual amortization.

1.3.2 Change in Useful Life

If the life of an existing intangible asset is reduced or extended, the remaining net book value is amortized over the new remaining life.

Pass Key

A patent is amortized over the shorter of its estimated life or remaining legal life.

1.4   Sale of Intangible Assets

If an intangible asset is sold, compare its carrying value at the date of sale with the selling price to determine the gain or loss.

1.5   Valuation

Under U.S. GAAP, finite life intangible assets are reported at cost less amortization and impairment. Indefinite life intangible assets are reported at cost less impairment. Crypto assets are similar to indefinite-lived intangible assets, but U.S. GAAP outlines different recognition and measurement requirements. Crypto assets are measured at fair value each reporting period on the statement of financial position with changes from remeasurement reflected in current period net income.

2   Impairment of Finite-Lived Intangible Assets

Intangible assets with finite useful lives are tested for impairment whenever events or changes in circumstances indicate that the carrying amount may not be recoverable.

2.1   Two-Step Impairment Test

An intangible asset with a finite life is tested for impairment using a two-step impairment test.

Step 1: The carrying amount of the asset is compared with the sum of the undiscounted cash flows expected to result from the use of the asset and its eventual disposition.

Step 2: If the carrying amount exceeds the total undiscounted future cash flows, then the asset is impaired and an impairment loss equal to the difference between the carrying amount of the asset and its fair value is recorded.

Pass Key

It is important to note the following when testing an intangible asset with a finite life for impairment:

- **Determining the Impairment:** Use undiscounted future net cash flows.
- **Amount of Impairment:** Use fair value (FV).

2.2   Reporting an Impairment Loss

An impairment loss is reported as a component of income from continuing operations before income taxes, unless the impairment loss is related to discontinued operations. The carrying amount of the asset is reduced by the amount of the impairment loss. Restoration of previously recognized impairment losses is prohibited, unless the asset is held for disposal.

2.3   Calculation of the Impairment Loss

The impairment loss is calculated as the amount by which the carrying amount exceeds the fair value of the asset.

Impairment Test for Finite-Lived Intangibles

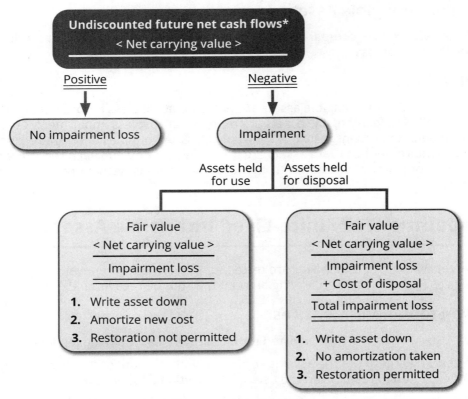

*When testing indefinite-life intangible assets for impairment, fair value must be used instead of undiscounted future net cash flows:

> Fair value − Net carrying value = Positive (no impairment) or negative (impairment)

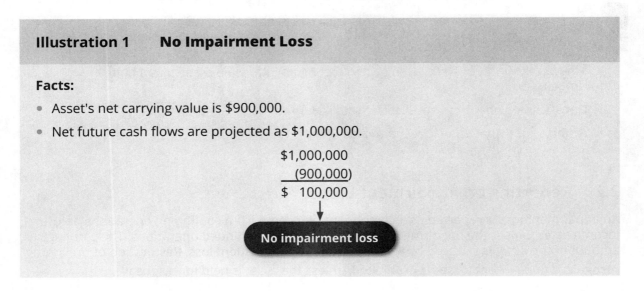

Illustration 1   No Impairment Loss

Facts:

- Asset's net carrying value is $900,000.
- Net future cash flows are projected as $1,000,000.

$$\begin{array}{r} \$1,000,000 \\ \underline{(900,000)} \\ \$\ \ \ 100,000 \end{array}$$

No impairment loss

Illustration 2   Impairment Loss

Facts:

- Asset's net carrying value is $1,200,000.
- Net future cash flows are projected as $1,000,000.
- Assumption 1: Asset held for use, and
  - FV/PV net cash flows are $700,000.
- Assumption 2: Asset is held for disposal, and
  - FV/PV net cash flows are $700,000.
  - Cost of disposal will be $100,000.

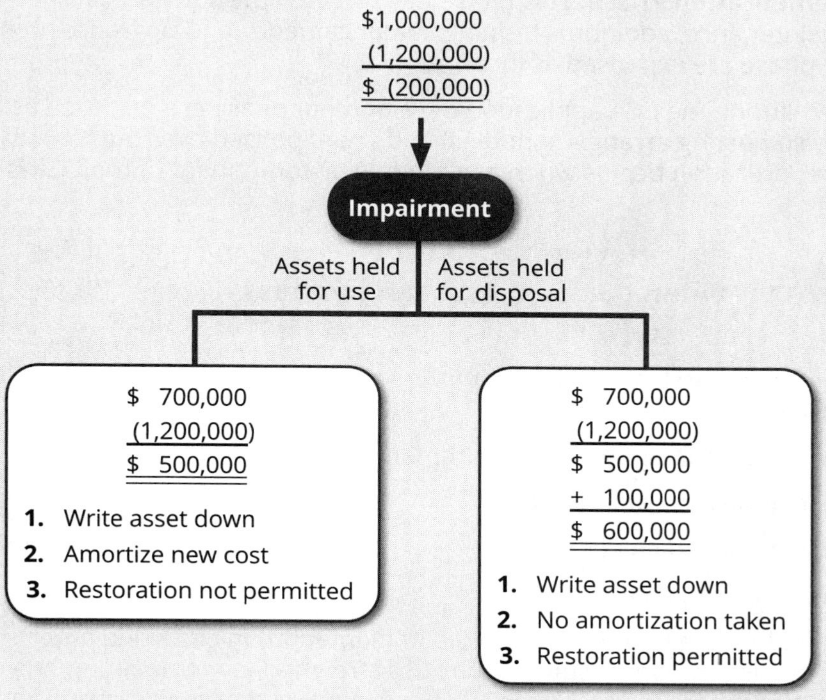

$1,000,000
(1,200,000)
$ (200,000)

Impairment

Assets held for use | Assets held for disposal

$ 700,000
(1,200,000)
$ 500,000

1. Write asset down
2. Amortize new cost
3. Restoration not permitted

$ 700,000
(1,200,000)
$ 500,000
+ 100,000
$ 600,000

1. Write asset down
2. No amortization taken
3. Restoration permitted

3   Purchased Software and Cloud Computing Arrangements

3.1   Purchased Software

Software purchased for use by an organization is recorded on the balance sheet as an intangible asset at the purchase price. The asset is amortized over the shorter of the legal life (the contractual term of the asset) or the economic life (the period over which the software provides cash flows to the organization).

3.2 Cloud Computing

Cloud computing arrangements (CCA) involve paying a vendor a fee in exchange for the right to use software over the internet. The vendor is responsible for hosting the software on its computing infrastructure.

CCAs involve three phases:

1. **Preliminary Project Phase:** Determining the system requirements for software. Costs incurred during this phase are expensed as incurred.

2. **Application Development Phase:** Work performed to customize or change infrastructure or configurations. Costs incurred during this phase are either capitalized or expensed.

   - **Capitalize:** Implementation costs involving software, software licensing, third-party software development fees, external materials, coding fees, and testing fees.

   - **Expense:** Training, manual data conversion, maintenance costs, and support costs.

3. **Post-Implementation Phase:** This phase begins when the software is placed in service and includes maintenance, additional training, enhancements, and upgrades. Costs incurred during this phase are expensed as incurred.

Costs capitalized during the CCA application development phase are recorded as an intangible asset (e.g., prepaid hosting arrangement fees) and are expensed over the term of the arrangement. Amortization begins when any module or component of the CCA is ready for intended use.

Illustration 3   Cloud Computing Arrangements

Beyta Co. contracts with Linc Inc. for a cloud computing arrangement for five years. Beyta incurs the following costs:

- $2 million in determining system requirements

- $8 million in implementation costs

- $1 million in manual data conversion

- $1 million in maintenance costs

The company will capitalize the $8 million in implementation costs and amortize it over the five-year hosting period. Assuming they use straight-line amortization, the expense will be $1.6 million per year. The other costs (determining system requirements, manual data conversion, and maintenance costs) will be expensed as incurred.

3.3 Testing Purchased Software and Capitalized CCA costs for Impairment

Purchased software and capitalized CCA costs should be tested for impairment using the two-step process used for other finite-lived intangible assets. If the sum of the undiscounted future cash flows is below the carrying value, the asset is deemed impaired, and an impairment loss equal to the difference between the fair value and the carrying amount is recorded.

4 Franchisee Accounting

4.1 Initial Franchise Fees

The present value of the amount paid (or to be paid) by a franchisee is recorded as an intangible asset on the balance sheet and amortized over the expected period of benefit of the franchise (i.e., the expected life of the franchise).

4.2 Continuing Franchise Fees

These fees are received for ongoing services provided by the franchisor to the franchisee (often referred to as franchise royalties). Usually, such fees are calculated based on a percentage of franchise revenues. Such services might include management training, promotion, and legal assistance. Fees should be reported by the franchisee as an expense and as revenue by the franchisor, in the period incurred.

Example 1   Franchisee's Intangible Assets

Facts: Peter signed an agreement on July 1, Year 1, with Disco Records to operate as a franchisee in New York City. The initial franchise fee was $75,000 and was paid by a $25,000 down payment with the balance payable in five equal annual payments of $10,000 beginning July 1, Year 2. The expected life of the franchise is 10 years. The present value of the five annual payments is $37,908. The amount to be capitalized as an intangible franchise asset on July 1, Year 1, is $62,908 ($25,000 + $37,908).

Required: Prepare the journal entry to record the franchise on Peter's books at the acquisition date. Explain the accounting treatment required over the life of the franchise for the discount account. Calculate the amortization of the franchises account for Year 1.

Solution:

Franchisee's journal entry to record the franchise at July 1, Year 1:

DR	Franchises	$62,908	
DR	Discount on notes payable (contra-liability)	12,092	
CR	Notes payable		$50,000
CR	Cash		25,000

The discount will be recognized as interest expense by the franchisee over the payment period on an effective interest basis. The franchise account would appear in the franchisee's intangible assets section of the balance sheet and would be amortized over the expected life of the franchise:

Year 1 amortization = (Franchise balance / Expected life) × Months
= ($62,908 / 10) × 6/12 (July through December, Year 1)
= $3,145

---

5   Start-up Costs

Expenses incurred in the formation of a corporation (e.g., legal fees) are considered organizational costs and are an example of start-up costs.

Start-up costs, including organizational costs, should be expensed when incurred.

- Start-up costs include costs of the one-time activities associated with:
  - Organizing a new entity (e.g., legal fees for preparing a charter, partnership agreement, bylaws, original stock certifications, filing fees, etc.)
  - Opening a new facility
  - Introducing a new product or service
  - Conducting business in a new territory or with a new class of customer
  - Initiating a new process in an existing facility
- Start-up costs do not include costs associated with:
  - Routine, ongoing efforts to refine, enrich, or improve the quality of existing products, services, processes, or facilities
  - Business mergers or acquisitions
  - Ongoing customer acquisition

Pass Key

Remember that organizational expenses are *not* capitalized as an intangible asset. Rather, they are expensed immediately.

FAR

4

Liabilities

Module

Payables and Accrued Liabilities

1 Overview

Liabilities are probable future sacrifices of economic benefits arising from present obligations of an entity to transfer assets or provide services to other entities in the future as a result of past transactions or events.

Liabilities must be identified as current or non-current for financial reporting purposes. Current liabilities are obligations whose liquidation is reasonably expected to require the use of current assets, the creation of other current liabilities, or the provision of services within the next year or operating cycle, whichever is longer.

Regular business operations can result in current liabilities as can bank borrowings to meet the cash needs of the entity. Current liabilities are valued on the balance sheet at their settlement value. Current liabilities are an important indication of financial strength and solvency. The ability to pay current debts as they mature is analyzed by interested parties both within and outside the company.

1.1 Trade Accounts Payable

Trade accounts payable are amounts owed for goods, raw materials, and supplies that are not evidenced by a promissory note. Purchases of goods and services on credit are usually determinable as to amounts due and the due date. Cash discounts associated with accounts payable can be anticipated and journalized. The purchase may be recorded gross or net.

- **Gross Method**

  The gross method records the purchase without regard to the discount. If invoices are paid within the discount period, a purchase discount is credited.

- **Net Method**

  Under the net method, purchases and accounts payable are recorded net of the discount. If payment is made within the discount period, no adjustment is necessary. If payment is made after the discount period, a purchase discount lost account is debited.

Example 1   Trade Accounts Payable

Facts: An entity purchases $5,000 of inventory with terms 2/10, net 45 days near the end of Year 1. The entity accounts for discounts using the gross method. Assume that the entity pays for the invoice after year-end, but prior to expiration of the discount period.

Required: Prepare the journal entries when the trade payable is initially recorded in Year 1 and when the account is paid in Year 2.

Solution: *The following entry will be recorded when the trade payable is initially recorded in Year 1:*

DR	Inventory/purchases	$5,000	
CR	Accounts payable		$5,000

The accounts payable balance is current as it will be paid within 45 days. *The following entry would be recorded when the account is paid:*

DR	Accounts payable	$5,000	
CR	Cash		$4,900
CR	Purchase discounts*		100

*The Inventory account would be credited if the entity uses a perpetual inventory system.

1.2   Trade Notes Payable

Trade notes payable are formal, written promises to pay on a certain date that arise from the purchase of goods, supplies, or services. Trade notes payable may include a stated interest rate.

Example 2   Trade Notes Payable

Facts: To purchase supplies, Dogs and Cats LLC borrows $50,000 from Credit Hall Bank on March 1, signing a 12-month, 5 percent note. Interest payments are due quarterly.

Required: Prepare the journal entries that Dogs and Cats records when the note is issued, when interest is paid on June 1, September 1, December 1, and at year-end.

Solution: *The following entry records the issuance of the note:*

DR	Cash	$50,000	
CR	Notes payable		$50,000

On June 1, September 1, and December 1, the following entries related to interest expense will be recorded:

DR	Interest expense (50,000 × 5% × 3/12)	$625	
CR	Cash		$625

(continued)

(continued)

At the end of December, one month of interest must be accrued as the interest expense has been incurred but not yet paid in cash (cash payment will not be made until March 1).

DR	Interest expense (50,000 × 5% × 1/12)	$208	
CR	Interest payable		$208

1.3 Interest Payable

Short-term and long-term debt instruments with a stated interest rate whose payment date does not coincide with the fiscal year-end will result in an interest payable balance at year-end. The amount accrued should represent the interest expense incurred that has not been paid in cash as of the balance sheet date. The previous example includes an accrual for interest expense.

1.4 Current Portions of Long-Term Debt

Debt instruments may be set up such that periodic principal payments are made during the life of the borrowing. In this case the principal due within the next year (or operating cycle) will be classified as a current liability.

1.4.1 Current Obligations Expected to Be Refinanced

Under U.S. GAAP, a short-term obligation may be excluded from current liabilities and included in non-current debt if the company intends to refinance it on a long-term basis and the intent is supported by the ability to do so as evidenced either by:

- the actual refinancing prior to the issuance of the financial statements; or
- the existence of a noncancelable financing agreement from a lender having the financial resources to accomplish the refinancing.

The amount excluded from current liabilities and a full description of the financing agreement shall be fully disclosed in the financial statements or notes thereto.

The following journal entry would be used to record the reclassification:

DR	Short-term liability	$XXX	
CR	Long-term liability		$XXX

1.5 Accrued Liabilities/Expenses

Accrued salaries and wages payable is the unpaid portion of salaries and wages as of the balance sheet date. Unpaid salaries and wages generally result from pay periods that overlap the balance sheet date. Accruals are calculated as the ratio of days occurring prior to the balance sheet date divided by the total days in the pay period times the amount of the affected payroll.

Other accrued liabilities relate to expenses incurred that have not been paid in cash at the financial statement date (such as utilities, rent, etc.).

Example 3   **Accrued Liabilities/Expenses**

Facts: An employee works five days during the last week of the year and earns $1,250 a week. Three of the days fall in fiscal Year 1 and two of the days fall in fiscal Year 2.

Required: Prepare the journal entry to record the accrued liability at the end of fiscal Year 1 and when the employee is paid in fiscal Year 2.

Solution: *The following journal entry is recorded at the end of Year 1:*

DR	Salaries and wages expense	$750	
CR	Salaries and wages payable ($1,250 × 3/5)		$750

When the employee is paid the next year, the following journal entry is recorded:

DR	Salaries and wages payable	$750	
DR	Salaries and wages expense	500	
CR	Cash		$1,250

1.6 Taxes Payable

Several types of taxes payable may exist on an entity's balance sheet.

1.6.1 Property Taxes Payable

Property taxes are often invoiced in arrears. There are two methods of accrual:

1. Property taxes payable may be accrued prior to the receipt of the tax invoice and matched in the year for which the invoice pertains.

2. Property taxes also may be recorded as a payable upon the receipt of the tax invoice and expensed in the year of receipt (which is often different from the year to which the invoice pertains).

Either method is acceptable, provided the method used is consistently applied.

1.6.2 Sales Taxes Payable

Sales taxes payable are sales taxes collected from customers on behalf of the taxing authority and held in trust until remission to the taxing authority. Sales taxes payable should be credited to a payable account after collection and until remitted. Sales taxes are not an expense of the company collecting the sales taxes from customers.

Example 4   **Sales Taxes Payable**

Facts: Jewelry Unlimited sells a $10,000 bracelet and collects 7 percent sales tax.

Required: Prepare the journal entry for the sale.

Solution: *The following entry will be recorded:*

DR	Cash	$10,700	
CR	Sales revenue		$10,000
CR	Sales tax payable		700

1.7   Employee-Related Liabilities

1.7.1   Unemployment Taxes and Employer's Share of Payroll Taxes

Unemployment taxes and the employer's share of payroll taxes (e.g., Social Security and Medicare) should be accrued by the employer as an expense. The liability will not be liquidated until the amounts are remitted to the appropriate taxing authority.

1.7.2   Payroll Deductions

Payroll deductions for Social Security, Medicare, and income taxes are withheld from employees out of the gross pay of their paychecks. These deductions are the responsibility of the employee and are therefore not recorded as an expense, but credited to a payable account until remitted.

Example 5   Payroll Deductions

Facts: Hodge Corporation's weekly payroll totals $25,000. The entire balance is subject to FICA and Medicare (7.65 percent) and unemployment taxes (2 percent). The company withholds $3,000 for income taxes.

Required: Prepare the journal entries to record the weekly payroll and the employer's weekly tax expense.

Solution: *The following entry will be recorded for the weekly payroll:*

DR	Salaries and wages expense	$25,000	
CR	FICA taxes payable		$ 1,913
CR	Withholding taxes payable		3,000
CR	Cash		20,087

An additional entry related to the employer's tax expense must also be recorded:

DR	Payroll tax expense	$2,413	
CR	FICA taxes payable		$1,913
CR	Unemployment taxes payable		500

1.8   Bonuses

Companies may pay employees bonuses in addition to their regular salaries or wages. These amounts should be recorded to salaries and wages expense. The amount of the bonus is normally based on company profits. Computation problems result because although the bonuses are based on net income, they are a business expense that also reduces net income. The example that follows illustrates the difficulties.

Example 6	Bonuses

Facts: X Corp. offers its sales vice president a bonus equal to 10 percent of net income after deducting taxes but before deducting the bonus. Income without taxes or the bonus is $100,000, and the tax rate is 40 percent.

Required: Calculate the bonus.

Solution: Although the bonus is based on after-tax income, the bonus is deductible from pretax income.

1. Bonus = 10% ($100,000 − Taxes)

2. Taxes = 40% ($100,000 − Bonus)

Substitute equation 2 for "Taxes" in equation 1.

$$
\begin{aligned}
\text{Bonus} &= 10\% \,[\$100,000 - 40\% \,(\$100,000 - \text{Bonus})] \\
B &= 10\% \,[\$100,000 - 40\% \,(\$100,000 - B)] \\
B &= 10\% \,[\$100,000 - \$40,000 + 40\% \, B] \\
B &= \$6,000 + 4\% \, B \\
96\% \, B &= \$6,000 \\
B &= \underline{\$6,250}
\end{aligned}
$$

1.9 Accrued Vacation

Vacation accruals are recorded in the year earned if *all* of the following conditions are met:

1. The employer's obligation to compensate employees for accrued vacations is attributable to services already rendered by employees.

2. The obligation relates to rights that vest (are not contingent on an employee's future service) or *accumulate* (may be carried forward to one or more accounting periods subsequent to that in which earned).

3. Payment of the compensation is probable.

4. The amount can be reasonably estimated.

If only the first three conditions are met, disclosure in a note to the financial statements is adequate.

Example 7   Accrued Vacation

Facts: Taney Company began operations on January 1, Year 1. Taney's employees earn four weeks of paid vacation for each year of employment. Unused vacation time is carried forward and paid at the current salary in effect at the balance sheet date. In Year 1, James had taken no vacation. His salary as of December Year 1 was $300 per week. In Year 2 his salary increased to $400 per week.

Required: Calculate the amount Taney Company should carry as a liability for James' accumulated vacation time and prepare the journal entries recorded at the end of Year 1 and when James takes four weeks of vacation in Year 2.

Solution:

Accrued vacation at 12/31/Year 1 = Current salary rate × Number of weeks of accumulated vacation

= $300 × 4

= $1,200

Taney Company would record the following journal entry at the end of Year 1:

DR	Salaries and wages expense	$1,200	
CR	Salaries and wages payable		S1,200

Even if James' salary is raised in Year 2, Taney Company would still record the liability at the end of Year 1 based on the $300-per-week salary, as the vacation was earned during that period.

When the four weeks of vacation are taken in the following year, the additional expense for increased wages would be recorded to salaries and wage expense.

DR	Salaries and wages payable	$1,200	
DR	Salaries and wages expense	400	
CR	Cash		$1,600

1.10 Self-Insurance Liabilities

Self-insurance occurs when an entity is liable for risk they choose to bear themselves rather than obtaining third-party insurance. By saving the costs of premiums, the entity can set aside savings to cover future claims.

The entity should accrue estimated losses for unpaid claims that have already been filed and for those which may occur in the future. Discounting the liability is possible when future payments can be reasonably estimated, and liabilities may be both current and non-current depending on expected timing.

Example 8   Self-Insurance Liabilities

Facts: In preparing year-end financial statements, actuaries for Brige Inc. determine that the company should record $350,000 for potential claims where the company chose to self-insure. In the past year, the company had to pay out $145,000 in actual claims where they had no outside insurance coverage.

Required: Prepare the journal entries for both the claims accrual and the actual payout.

Solution:

Claims accrual:

DR	Claims expense (or provision for claims)	$350,000	
CR	Unpaid claims liability (or accrued liability—self-insurance)		$350,000

Actual payout:

DR	Unpaid claims liability (or accrued liability—self-insurance)	$145,000	
CR	Cash		$145,000

---

2   Exit or Disposal Activities

A liability must be recognized for the costs associated with an exit or disposal activity.

2.1 Exit and Disposal Costs

Costs associated with exit and disposal activities include:

- Involuntary employee termination benefits.
- Costs to terminate a contract that is not a lease.
- Other costs associated with exit or disposal activities, including costs to consolidate facilities or relocate employees.

2.2   Criteria for Liability Recognition

An entity's commitment to an exit or disposal plan, by itself, is not enough to result in liability recognition. A liability associated with an exit or disposal activity should be recognized only when a transaction or event occurs that creates a present obligation of an entity to transfer an economic benefit.

Future operating losses expected to be incurred as part of an exit or disposal activity are recognized in the period(s) incurred.

An exit cost liability for employee termination benefits is recorded when the plan of termination meets all of the following criteria and the plan for exit has been communicated to employees:

- Management commits to a plan of termination;

- The plan identifies the employees to be terminated and the expected completion date;

- The plan establishes the terms of the benefits that employees will receive upon termination; and

- Actions required to complete the plan indicate that it is unlikely that significant changes will be made to the plan or that the plan will be withdrawn.

2.3   Liability Measurement

The liability should be measured at fair value. The liability may be adjusted in future periods as a result of revisions to the timing of, or estimated cash flows from, the exit or disposal activity. Revisions are accounted for prospectively (change in estimate).

2.4   Income Statement Presentation

Costs associated with an exit or disposal activity related to a discontinued operation will be reported in discontinued operations. Costs associated with an exit or disposal activity not related to a discontinued operation will be reported in income from continuing operations.

2.5   Disclosure

All of the following must be disclosed in the notes to the financial statements in the period the exit or disposal activity is initiated and all subsequent periods until the activity is completed:

- A description of the exit or disposal activity, including the facts and circumstances leading to the expected activity and the expected completion date.

- For each major cost associated with an activity:

    - The total amount expected to be incurred in connection with the activity, the amount incurred in the period, and the cumulative amount incurred to date.

    - A reconciliation of the beginning and ending liability balances showing the changes during the period for costs incurred, costs paid or otherwise settled, and any other adjustments with an explanation of the reasons.

- The line item(s) in the income statement in which the costs are aggregated.

- For each reportable segment, the total amount of costs expected to be incurred, the amount incurred in the period and incurred to date, net of any adjustments with an explanation of the reasons.

- If a liability for a cost associated with the activity is not recognized because fair value cannot be reasonably estimated, that fact and the reasons for that should be disclosed.

Illustration 1	Exit and Disposal Activities

An entity plans to close its facility in a particular location and determines that it no longer needs the 100 employees who work at the facility. The entity notifies the employees that they will be terminated in six months. A termination benefit will be provided to each employee totaling $5,000 on the date the employee stops working. On the communication date (the obligating event), a liability of $500,000 will be recognized.

3 Asset Retirement Obligations (AROs)

An asset retirement obligation is a legal obligation associated with the retirement of a tangible long-lived asset that results from the acquisition, construction or development, and/or normal operation of a long-lived asset, except for certain lease obligations (minimum lease payment and contingent rentals).

Asset retirement obligations were initially required for nuclear decommissioning and were then expanded to other similar closure or removal-type costs in other industries, such as oil and gas and mining industries.

A balance sheet approach is required to recognize AROs.

3.1 ARO Recognition

An ARO qualifies for recognition when it meets the definition of a liability:

- Duty or responsibility
- Little or no discretion to avoid
- Obligating event

Uncertainty about whether performance will be required does not defer the recognition of a retirement obligation; rather, that uncertainty is factored into the measurement of the fair value of the liability through assignment of probabilities to cash flows.

3.2 Initial Measurement (Balance Sheet Approach)

When an asset retirement obligation exists and qualifies for recognition, an entity records an asset and a liability on the balance sheet equal to the fair value of the asset retirement obligation, if a reasonable estimate of fair value can be made. Fair value is generally equal to the present value of the future obligation. If a reasonable estimate of fair value cannot be made, the liability and related asset are recognized when a reasonable estimate of fair value can be made.

- **Asset Retirement Obligations (ARO)**

    The ARO is the obligation (liability) associated with the retirement of a tangible long-lived asset.

■ **Asset Retirement Cost (ARC)**

The ARC is the amount capitalized (asset) that increases the carrying amount of the long-lived asset when a liability for an ARO is recognized.

DR	Asset retirement cost (asset)	$XXX	
CR	Asset retirement obligation (liability)		$XXX

3.3 Subsequent Measurement

3.3.1 Accretion and Depreciation

In periods after the initial measurement, the ARO liability is adjusted for accretion expense due to the passage of time, and the ARC asset is depreciated.

■ **Accretion Expense**

Accretion expense is the increase in the ARO liability due to the passage of time calculated using the appropriate accretion rate. The accretion expense is added to the ARO liability each period. At the end of the accretion period, the ARO liability reported on the balance sheet should be (approximately) equal to the asset retirement obligation to be paid.

Journal entry to record accretion expense associated with the ARO (liability):

DR	Accretion expense	$XXX	
CR	Asset retirement obligation (liability)		$XXX

Pass Key

The asset retirement obligation is recorded at a discounted amount. Accretion expense is the growth of the liability over time so that at the time the liability is satisfied, it is reported at its total non-discounted value.

■ **Depreciation Expense**

Depreciation expense decreases the ARC asset reported on balance sheet. At the end of the accretion period, the asset retirement cost (asset) should be fully depreciated.

Journal entry to record depreciation expense associated with the ARC (asset):

DR	Depreciation expense	$XXX	
CR	Accumulated depreciation (asset retirement cost)		$XXX

Pass Key

The cumulative accretion expense plus depreciation expense recognized on the income statements over the accretion period should be equal to the total asset retirement obligation:

$$\text{Cumulative accretion expense} + \text{Cumulative depreciation expense} = \text{Asset retirement obligation (ARO)}$$

3.3.2 Revisions to Cash Flow Estimates

Estimated cash flows are used to calculate the discounted ARO liability reported on the balance sheet. Under U.S. GAAP, these cash flow estimates may be revised over time.

- Upward revisions to undiscounted cash flows are "new" liabilities—use current discount rate.

- Downward revisions require removal of "old" liabilities—use historical (or weighted average) discount rate.

2 Contingencies and Commitments

1 Definition of Contingencies

A contingency is an existing condition, situation, or set of circumstances involving uncertainty as to possible gain (gain contingency) or loss (loss contingency) that will ultimately be determined when a future event occurs or fails to occur. The resolution may result in the acquisition of an asset, the reduction of a liability, the loss or impairment of an asset, or the incurrence of a liability.

1.1 Loss Contingencies

A loss contingency involves a possible future loss whose existence is proven by subsequent events. Examples of loss contingencies include:

- Collectibility of receivables
- Obligations regarding product warranties and defects and unredeemed coupons
- Risk of loss of property by fire, explosion, or other hazards
- Threat of expropriation of assets
- Pending or threatened litigation
- Actual or possible claims and assessments
- Risk of loss from catastrophes assumed by property and casualty insurance companies
- Guarantees of indebtedness of others
- Obligations of commercial banks under standby letters of credit
- Agreements to repurchase receivables (or related property) that have been sold
- Environmental damages

1.2 Gain Contingencies

Examples of gain contingencies include:

- Expected favorable settlement from a pending court case
- Possible refunds regarding tax disputes

2 Recognition and Measurement of Gain Contingencies

Gain contingencies are claims or rights to receive assets whose existence is uncertain but may become valid upon the occurrence of future events. Gain contingencies are not recognized in the financial statements because to do so may cause recognition of revenue prior to its realization. An entity should disclose a contingency that might result in a gain in the notes to the financial statements, but should be careful to avoid misleading implications about the likelihood of realization.

3 Recognition and Measurement of Loss Contingencies

The recognition of contingent losses in the financial statements depends on the likelihood that future events will confirm the contingent loss. GAAP classifies the likelihood of contingent losses as follows:

- **Probable:** Likely to occur.
- **Reasonably possible:** More than remote, but less than likely.
- **Remote:** Slight chance of occurring.

3.1 Loss Is Probable and Can Be Reasonably Estimated

Provision for a loss contingency should be accrued by a charge to income, providing that both of the following conditions exist:

1. *It is probable that as of the date of the financial statements an asset has been impaired or a liability incurred*, based on information available prior to the issuance of the financial statements.

2. *The amount of loss can be reasonably estimated*. In the event that a range of probable losses is given (e.g., $100,000 to $250,000), GAAP requires that the best estimate of the loss be accrued. If no amount in the range is a better estimate than any other amount within the range, the minimum amount in the range should be accrued (in this case $100,000), and a note disclosing the possibility of an additional $150,000 loss should be presented.

3.2 Loss Is Reasonably Possible

In the event that both of the conditions above are not met, a financial statement disclosure shall be made when there is at least a reasonable possibility that a loss or an additional loss may have been incurred. The disclosure should include:

- The nature of the contingency.
- An estimate of the possible loss or range of loss, or a statement that an estimate cannot be made.

3.3 Loss Is Remote

Generally, no disclosure is necessary for a remote loss contingency; however, disclosure (nature, amount of guarantee, and any expected recovery) should be made for "guarantee-type" remote loss contingencies, such as:

- **Debts** of others guaranteed (officers/related parties);
- **Obligations** of commercial banks under standby letters of credit; and
- **Guarantees** to repurchase receivables (or related property) that have been sold or assigned.

Example 1   Loss Contingency

Facts: Alton Company is the defendant in a wrongful death suit filed as the result of the death of an employee who was working on one of the company's production lines. The plaintiff filed suit in June and has asked for damages of $3,000,000. Alton carries insurance for potential claims of this nature, but the insurance coverage amounts to $1,500,000. Legal counsel for Alton believes that the judge will rule in the plaintiff's favor and that the company will have to pay about $2,200,000, but the settlement could reach $3,000,000.

Required: Identify the financial statement treatment for the contingency and prepare the journal entry.

Solution:

Alton should record the following entry at year-end:

DR	Lawsuit loss	$2,200,000	
CR	Lawsuit liability		$2,200,000

It is probable that the judge will rule against Alton. Because the estimate of the settlement is a range, the $2,200,000 should be recorded as the contingency amount, with disclosures indicating the maximum settlement amount of $3,000,000. The insurance proceeds that may result would be treated as a gain contingency and not recorded until received.

Contingency Treatments	Accrue Amounts	Disclose		
		Amount	Nature	Ignore
Loss contingency that is probable and: *Amount or range can be reasonably estimated*	✓ (or minimum)	range	✓	
Amount cannot be reasonably estimated		range	✓	
Loss contingency that is a reasonable possibility		range	✓	
Loss contingency that is remote				✓
Loss contingency that is remote, but is a guarantee for others		✓	✓	
Gain contingencies that are probable or reasonably possible		✓	✓	
Gain contingencies that are remote				✓

3.4 Potential Loss Contingencies

If it is probable that an unasserted claim will be filed, then it is treated similarly to any other loss contingency.

General or unspecified business risks (such as fire, floods, strikes, and war) do not meet the conditions for accrual, and no loss accrual shall be made (nor is disclosure required).

3.5 Appropriation of Retained Earnings

- Any appropriation of retained earnings (such as for general loss contingencies) must be shown within the stockholders' equity section and clearly identified.

- Costs or losses shall not be charged to an appropriation of retained earnings, and no part of the appropriation should be transferred to income.

- Any appropriation should be restored to retained earnings as soon as its purpose is no longer deemed necessary.

4 Premiums and Warranties

Premiums and warranties are loss contingencies that are generally accrued by an entity as the expected amounts are probable and can be reasonably estimated.

4.1 Premiums

Premiums are offers to customers for the purpose of stimulating sales. They are offered in return for coupons, box tops, labels, etc. The cost of the premium is charged to sales in the period(s) that benefit from the premium offer. Generally, all premiums will not be redeemed in the same period.

Therefore, the number of outstanding premium offers must be estimated accurately to reflect the current liability at the end of each period.

$$\text{Total number of coupons issued} \times \text{Estimated redemption rate} = \text{Total estimated coupon redemptions}$$

Example 2   Premiums

Facts: AAA Corp. kicked off a sales promotion on August 31, Year 1. AAA included a redeemable coupon on each can of soup sold. Five coupons must be presented to receive a premium that costs AAA $2.00. AAA estimates that 70 percent of the coupons will be redeemed. Information available at December 31, Year 1, is as follows:

Cans of Soup Sold	Premiums Purchased	Coupons Redeemed
1,500,000	200,000	600,000

Required: Calculate AAA Corp.'s estimated liability for premium claims.

Solution:

The calculation of the estimated liability for premium claims outstanding is as follows:

Total estimated coupon redemptions (1,500,000 × 70%)	1,050,000
Less: coupons redeemed	(600,000)
Coupons to be redeemed	450,000
Outstanding premium claims (450,000 ÷ 5)	**90,000**

The estimated liability for premium claims is 90,000 × $2 = $180,000. Note that you were given information about premiums purchased that was not used in the computation in determining estimated liability.

The entry to record the estimated liability for outstanding premium claims is:

DR	Premium expense	$180,000	
CR	Premium liability		$180,000

4.2 Warranties

Warranties are a seller's promise to "correct" any product defects. Sellers offering warranties must create a liability account if the cost of the warranty can be reasonably estimated.

The entire liability for the warranty should be accrued in the year of sale to "match" the cost with the corresponding revenue. The accrual should take place even if part of the warranty expenditure will be incurred in a later year.

Example 3   Warranties

Facts: ABC Corp. has a three-year warranty against defects in the machinery it sells. When a warranty claim is made, ABC Corp. satisfies the claim by replacing the machinery. Warranty costs are estimated at 2 percent of sales in the year of sale, and 4 and 6 percent in the succeeding years. ABC sales and actual warranty expenses for Year 1–Year 3 were as follows:

	Sales	Actual Warranty Costs
Year 1	$ 250,000	$10,000
Year 2	500,000	20,000
Year 3	750,000	30,000
	$1,500,000	$60,000

Required: Prepare the journal entries to account for the warranty in Years 1-3 and determine the balance in the warranty liability account at the end of Year 3.

Solution: ABC's total liability should be accrued in the year of sale even though it will not be incurred in that year.

The following journal entries will be recorded in Years 1-3.

Year 1:

DR	Warranty expense ($250,000 × 12%)	$30,000	
CR	Warranty liability		$30,000
DR	Warranty liability (actual costs)	10,000	
CR	Inventory		10,000

Year 2:

DR	Warranty expense ($500,000 × 12%)	$60,000	
CR	Warranty liability		$60,000
DR	Warranty liability	20,000	
CR	Inventory		20,000

Year 3:

DR	Warranty expense ($750,000 × 12%)	$90,000	
CR	Warranty liability		$90,000
DR	Warranty liability	30,000	
CR	Inventory		30,000

The balance in the account at the end of Year 3 is total liability less actual expenditures and is calculated as follows:

$$\text{Total liability} = \text{Sales} \times \text{Total estimated expense}$$
$$= \$1,500,000 \times 12\% \ [2\% + 4\% + 6\%]$$
$$= \$180,000$$

$$\text{Balance, liability account, 12/31/Year 3} = \text{Total liability} - \text{Actual expenditures}$$
$$= \$180,000 - \$60,000$$
$$= \underline{\$120,000}$$

3 Long-Term Liabilities

1 Time Value of Money

Problems involving interest, annuities, and present values, including problems related to long-term liabilities, are all concerned with the use of money over a period of time, which is referred to as the time value of money. The idea of present value is also the basis for the latest foundational concept, SFAC No. 7. The principles used in computing interest, annuities, and present values are applied to many accounting problems. Accounting for leases, pensions, bonds, and long-term debt are some of the more important applications.

1.1 Computations

For examination purposes, present value concepts are divisible into six separate types:

- Present value of $1
- Future value of $1
- Present value of an ordinary annuity
- Future value of an ordinary annuity
- Present value of an annuity due
- Future value of an annuity due

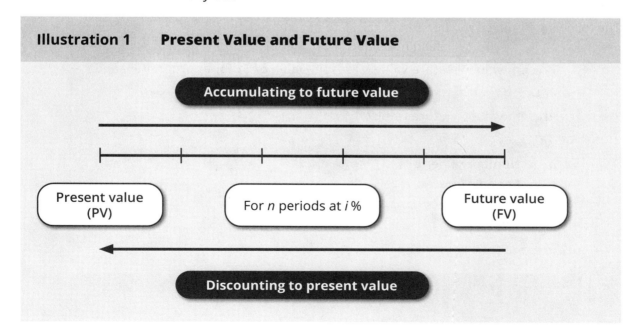

Illustration 1   Present Value and Future Value

Accumulating to future value

Present value (PV)

For *n* periods at *i* %

Future value (FV)

Discounting to present value

1.2 Annuities

A large number of business transactions involve multiple payments or receipts. Bond interest payments and lease rental payments are two examples. Annuities are transactions that result in identical periodic payments or receipts at regular intervals. Ordinary annuity (also called "annuity in arrears") payments are made at the end of each period. Annuity due payments occur at the beginning of each period.

The timing of payments is the only difference between an ordinary annuity and an annuity due. This applies to both present value and future value annuities.

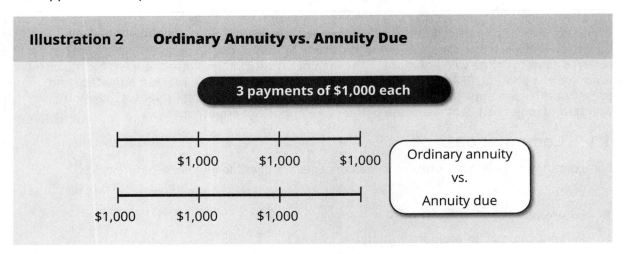

Illustration 2   Ordinary Annuity vs. Annuity Due

1.3 Present Value of $1

The present value of $1 is the amount that must be invested now at a specific interest rate so that $1 can be paid or received in the future.

The following formulas can be used to calculate present value:

> Present value = Future value × Present value of $1 for appropriate n and r
>
>   *Or:*
>
> Present value = Future value $/(1 + r)^n$
>
> **Where:**
> n = Number of periods
> r = Periodic interest rate

Example 1   Present Value of $1

Facts: On January 1, Year 1, ABC Corp. received an offer from a competitor to buy ABC's equipment at the end of Year 4. The competitor would pay $500,000 at the end of Year 4. The equipment is worth $300,000 now, and the prevailing interest rate is 10 percent, compounded annually.

Required: Using present value calculations, determine whether ABC should accept or reject the offer.

Solution: The present value of the $500,000 is calculated as follows:

Present value of $1 for 4 periods at 10% = 0.6830

$500,000 × 0.6830 = $341,500

Alternatively, the present value can be calculated as:

$$PV = \$500,000/(1 + 0.10)^4$$
$$= \$341,507$$

Note that the difference between these two calculations is due to the rounding of the present value factor in the first calculation.

ABC should accept the offer of payment at the end of Year 4. The current value of the Year 4 payment is $341,500, which is more than the equipment's current value.

Pass Key

If interest compounds on an other-than-annual basis, the number of periods and the interest rate must be adjusted. For example, if the annual interest rate is 12 percent and interest compounds quarterly over 10 years, then the periodic interest rate is 3 percent and the total number of compounding periods is 40.

1.4   Future Value of $1

The future value of $1 is more easily understood as compound interest. It is the amount that would accumulate at a future point in time if $1 were invested now. The interest factor causes the future value of $1 to be greater than $1.

The following formula can be used to calculate future value:

Future value = Present value × Future value of $1 for appropriate *n* and *r*

Or:

Future value = Present value × $(1 + r)^n$

Example 2   Future Value of $1

Facts: Your partner is retiring in five years. It will cost $300,000 to purchase her interest. Assume that you invest $200,000 now, earning 10 percent compounded annually.

Required: Using future value calculations, determine whether you will have enough money in five years to purchase your partner's interest.

Solution:

Future value of $1 at 10% for 5 periods = 1.6105

$200,000 × 1.6105 = $322,100

Alternatively, the future value can be calculated as:

FV = $200,000 × (1 + 0.10)^5

    = $322,102

Note that the difference between these two calculations is due to the rounding of the future value factor in the first calculation.

$322,100 > $300,000, so you will be able to purchase your partner's interest.

Pass Key

Note that the difference between present value and future value is the amount of interest earned over the period. Also note that the present value factors and future value factors are inverses of each other.

1.5   Present Value of an Ordinary Annuity

The present value of an ordinary annuity is the current worth of a series of identical periodic payments to be made in the future. To calculate the present value of an ordinary annuity, the following formula can be used:

$$\text{Present value of ordinary annuity} = \text{Annuity payment} \times \text{Present value of ordinary annuity of \$1 for appropriate } n \text{ and } r$$

Example 3   Present Value of an Ordinary Annuity

Facts: Parker Inc. enters into a 10-year, noncancelable lease requiring year-end payments of $100,000 each year for 10 years. Parker's borrowing rate is 10 percent compounded annually.

Required: Calculate the present value of the lease payments.

Solution:

Present value of an ordinary annuity of $1 at 10% for 10 periods = 6.1445

$100,000 × 6.1445 = $614,450

Parker should record the lease at $614,450.

1.6 Present Value of an Annuity Due

The only difference in the calculations of an annuity due and an ordinary annuity is the timing of the payments. For an annuity due, the payment occurs at the beginning of the period. When calculating the present value of an annuity due, it is calculated on the day of the first payment. There are several ways to calculate the present value of an annuity due. By adding 1.00 to the present value of an ordinary annuity of 1 for n periods, the present value of an annuity due of 1 for $n + 1$ periods may be found.

In addition, if you have the present value of an ordinary annuity of 1 for n periods and need the present value of an annuity due of 1 for n periods, the following calculation may be used:

> **Present value of annuity due = Present value of ordinary annuity × (1 + r)**

In an annuity due, each cash flow is discounted one less period; therefore, the value is higher by (1 + r).

Illustration 3   Ordinary Annuity vs. Annuity Due

Present value of an ordinary annuity of 1 at 6% for 2 periods = 1.8334

Present value of an annuity due of 1 at 6% for 2 periods = 1.8334 × 1.06 = 1.9434

Present value of an annuity due of 1 at 6% for 3 periods = 1.8334 + 1.00 = 2.8334

Example 4   Present Value of an Annuity Due

Facts: Avalanche Inc. enters into a 10-year lease requiring beginning-of-the-year payments of $100,000 each year for 10 years. Avalanche's borrowing rate is 10 percent compounded annually.

Required: Calculate the present value of the payments.

Solution:

Present value of an annuity due of $1 at 10% for 10 periods = 6.759

$100,000 × 6.759 = $675,900

1.7   Future Value of an Ordinary Annuity

The future value of an ordinary annuity is the value at a future date of a series of periodic payments. The following formula can be used to calculate the future value of an ordinary annuity:

$$\text{Future value of an ordinary annuity} = \text{Periodic payment} \times \text{Future value of an ordinary annuity of \$1 for appropriate } n \text{ and } r$$

Example 5   Future Value of an Ordinary Annuity

Facts: Jay Planner wants to save for his 12-year-old son's college education. Assume that he sets aside $5,000 at the end of each of the next five years, earning 10 percent compounded annually.

Required: Calculate how much money will be in Jay's account at the end of five years.

Solution:

Future value of an ordinary annuity of 1 at 10% for 5 periods = 6.1051

$5,000 × 6.1051 = $30,525.50

---

2 Long-Term Liabilities

Long-term liabilities are probable sacrifices of economic benefits associated with present obligations that are not payable within the current operating cycle or reporting year, whichever is greater.

2.1 Examples

Examples of long-term liabilities include:

- Long-term promissory notes payable
- Bonds payable
- Long-term leases
- Long-term contingent liabilities
- Purchase commitments
- Equipment purchase obligations
- Amounts due under deferred compensation agreements
- Postretirement pension and other benefits payable
- Other financial instruments
- Short-term debt expected to be refinanced (to the extent of post-balance sheet refinancing with support)
- Deferred income taxes payable

Most of these types of liabilities are covered in other sections of this course. This module will focus on notes payable.

2.2 Distinguishing Liabilities From Equity

Certain financial instruments have characteristics of both liabilities and equity. The following financial instruments must be classified as liabilities:

- Financial instruments in the form of shares that are mandatorily redeemable (i.e., mandatorily redeemable preferred stock) and represent an unconditional obligation to the issuer to redeem the instrument by transferring assets at a specified date or upon a future event, unless the redemption is required upon the liquidation or termination of the issuer.

- Financial instruments, other than outstanding shares, that represent an obligation to repurchase the issuer's equity shares by transferring assets.

- Financial instruments that represent an obligation to issue a variable number of shares.

3 Notes Payable

Notes payable (contractual rights to pay money at a fixed or determinable rate) must be recorded at present value at the date of issuance. If a note is non-interest bearing or the interest rate is unreasonable (usually below market), the value of the note must be determined by imputing the market rate of the note and by using the effective interest method.

Many of these rules apply when notes are exchanged for goods and services and the interest rate varies from the prevailing interest rates. Notes must be recorded at present value so that expense for the period is not distorted.

3.1 Stated Interest Factors

A note issued solely for cash equal to its face amount is presumed to earn the interest stated. However, if rights or privileges are attached to the note, they must be evaluated separately. If no rights or privileges are attached and the interest rate on the note reflects prevailing interest rates, record the note payable at face value without any present value considerations.

There is a general presumption that the interest stated on a note resulting from a business transaction entered into at arm's length is fair and adequate.

3.2 Imputing Interest

When a note contains either no interest or an unreasonable rate of interest, the substance rather than the form of the transaction must be recorded. This involves determining the present value of the obligation at the appropriate market interest rate, and:

1. recording the payable at its face amount;

2. recording the item received in exchange for the note at the present value of the obligation; and

3. recording any difference between the face amount of the note and its present value as a discount that must be amortized over the life of the note.

3.3 Imputing Interest Not Required

The present value calculation at the market rate of interest is not required for certain payables with low or no interest rate when those payables:

■ arise in the ordinary course of business, the terms of which do not exceed approximately one year (short-term notes).

■ are paid in property or services (not in cash).

■ represent security deposits.

■ bear an interest rate determined by a government agency.

■ arise from transactions between a parent and its subsidiaries.

3.4   Amortization of the Discount

Any discount resulting from imputing interest on a note payable must be amortized over the life of the note payable using the effective interest method.

The *effective interest method* is a method under which each payment on a note (or other loan) is allocated to interest and principal as though the note had a constant effective stated rate (or adequate rate) of interest.

3.5   Presentation and Disclosure

The *discount* is inseparable from the related note payable and is added to the note payable to determine the carrying value to be reported on the balance sheet.

A full description of the payable, the effective interest rate, and the face amount of the note should be disclosed in the financial statements or notes thereto.

Example 6   Effective Interest Method

Facts: Company A is making three annual loan payments of $1,000 each to Company B. There is no stated rate of interest. The present value of the aggregate loan payments at the appropriate interest rate of 10 percent is $2,486.

Required: Using the effective interest method, allocate the interest and principal for each payment.

Solution: Under the effective interest method, each payment would be allocated between interest and principal as follows:

(a) Cash Payment	(b) Interest Expense (d) × 10%	(c) Principal Paid (a) − (b)	(d) Carrying Value (d) − (c)
			$2,486
$1,000	$249	$ 751	1,735
1,000	174	826	909
1,000	91	909	-0-
	$514	$2,486	

This example presents an installment note that has fixed payments over the life of the note. Interest is determined using the remaining balance on the note and the 10 percent effective interest rate. The amount allocated to principal and interest changes as the carrying value of the note decreases.

Example 7   Imputed Interest

Facts: On January 1, Year 1, a company purchases a machine for $10,000 and issues a $10,000 note payable bearing no interest due in five years. Ten percent is an appropriate interest rate.

The present value of $1 at 10 percent for five years is 0.621. Because the issued note is non-interest bearing, the value of the machine purchased is not $10,000. The present value of the note is also the fair value of the machine.

Required: Prepare the journal entries to record the purchase and to amortize the discount on the note payable at the end of Year 1 using the effective interest method. Indicate how the notes payable would appear on the Year 1 balance sheet. Prepare an amortization table showing interest expense and carrying value for the five years of the note.

Solution: *Journal entry to record the purchase:*

DR	Machine	$6,210	
DR	Discount on note payable	3,790	
CR	Note payable		$10,000

Journal entry: Year 1 end of year to amortize the discount on notes payable using the effective interest method:

DR	Interest expense	$621	
CR	Discount on note payable		$621

Balance sheet presentation at the end of Year 1:

Notes payable	$10,000	
Less: discount on notes payable	(3,169)	[$3,790 − $621]
	$ 6,831	

In this example, the company records the note at its face amount but records the sale at the present value of the note. The difference between the face amount of the note and its present value is recorded as "discount on notes payable." This deferred interest is payment for the use of the seller's funds for the five years. Interest expense is recorded each year, using the effective interest method even though no cash interest payments are made during the five-year life of the loan. Interest is built into the face value of the note and will be paid at maturity.

Amortization Table: No Interest Note Payable					
Period	Beginning Carrying Value	Interest Expense (10%)	Cash Payment (0%)	Amortization	Ending Carrying Value
Year 1	$6,210	$621	–	$621	$ 6,831
Year 2	6,831	683	–	683	7,514
Year 3	7,514	751	–	751	8,266
Year 4	8,266	827	–	827	9,092
Year 5	9,092	909	–	909	10,000

(rounded)

4 Debt Covenants

Creditors use debt covenants in lending agreements to protect their interest by limiting or prohibiting the actions of debtors that might negatively affect the positions of the creditors.

4.1 Common Debt Covenants

Debt covenants vary widely. Common debt covenants include the following:

- Limitations on issuing additional debt
- Restrictions on the payment of dividends
- Limitations on the disposal of certain assets
- Minimum working capital requirements
- Collateral requirements
- Limitations on how the borrowed money can be used
- Maintenance of specific financial ratios, including:
  - Debt-to-equity ratio
  - Debt-to-total-capital ratio (debt ratio)
  - Interest coverage ratio (times interest earned)

4.2 Violation of Debt Covenants

When debt covenants are violated, the debtor is in technical default and the creditor can demand repayment. Most of the time, concessions are negotiated and real default, as opposed to technical default, is avoided. Concessions can result in the violated covenant(s) being waived temporarily or permanently. Concessions can also result in a change in the interest rate or other terms of the debt.

Example 8	Debt Covenants

Facts: On December 31, Bike Ride Inc. borrowed $1,000,000 in cash from Creditworthy Bank to purchase a building for the company's production facility. Bike Ride must make annual interest payments at a rate of 6.25 percent. The terms of the borrowing from Creditworthy include the following debt covenants:

- $100,000 of the borrowing must be kept in an account at Creditworthy Bank.
- Bike Ride may not issue any additional debt during the life of the borrowing.
- Bike Ride must maintain a times interest earned ratio of at least 5 during the life of the borrowing.

Bike Ride reported net income of $350,000 and income taxes of $140,000 for the first year.

Required: Prepare the journal entry to record the debt at issuance and determine whether Bike Ride's income for the year satisfies the debt covenant requirement.

(continued)

(continued)

Solution: *The entry to record the issuance of the debt is:*

DR	Cash	$900,000	
DR	Restricted cash	100,000	
CR	Notes payable		$1,000,000

Every year, Bike Ride must calculate times interest earned.

Times interest earned = Earnings before interest and taxes (EBIT)/Interest expense

= (350,000 + 140,000 + 62,500)/62,500

= 8.84

Bike Ride Inc. meets the terms of the debt covenants for the year.

1 Introduction to Bonds Payable

1.1 Terminology

Bonds payable are a very common type of long-term liability. The terms below are important to understand when accounting for debt securities such as bonds.

- **Bond Indenture:** The document that describes the contract between the issuer (borrower) and bond holders (lenders).

- **Face (Par) Value:** Face value is the total dollar amount of the bond and the basis on which periodic interest is paid. Bonds are issued at face (par) value when the stated rate of interest equals the market rate of interest.

- **Stated (Nominal or Coupon) Interest Rate:** The stated interest rate, also known as the nominal interest rate or the coupon rate, is the interest to be paid to the investors in cash. This rate is specified in the bond contract.

- **Market (Effective) Interest Rate:** The market interest rate is the rate of interest actually earned by the bondholder and is the rate of return for comparable contracts on the date the bonds are issued.

- **Discount:** If the market rate is higher than the stated rate, the bonds will be issued at a *discount*, in which case the bonds sell for less than the face amount to make up for the lower return being provided.

- **Premium:** If the market rate is lower than the stated rate, the bonds will be issued at a *premium* because the investor will pay more than face value due to the higher return offered.

1.2 Types of Bonds

Bonds are an important source of long-term funding for companies needing large amounts of capital. Bonds represent a contractual promise by the issuing corporation to pay investors (bondholders) a specific sum of money at a designated maturity date plus periodic, fixed interest payments (usually made semiannually) based on a percentage of the face amount of the bond. The following are various types of bonds:

- **Debentures:** Debentures are unsecured bonds.

- **Mortgage Bonds:** Mortgage bonds are bonds that are secured by real property.

- **Collateral Trust Bonds:** Collateral trust bonds are secured bonds.

- **Convertible Bonds:** Convertible bonds are convertible into common stock of the debtor (generally) at the option of the bondholder.

  - **Nondetachable Warrants:** The convertible bond itself must be converted into capital stock.

  - **Detachable Warrants:** The bond is not surrendered upon conversion, only the warrants plus cash representing the exercise price of the warrants. The warrants can be bought and sold separately from the bonds.

- **Participating Bonds:** Participating bonds are bonds that not only have a stated rate of interest but participate in income if certain earnings levels are obtained.

- **Term Bonds:** Term bonds are bonds that have a single fixed maturity date. The entire principal is paid at the end of this term/period.

- **Serial Bonds:** Serial bonds are prenumbered bonds that the issuer may call and redeem a portion by serial number (often redeemed pro rata annually/in a series of annual installments).

- **Income Bonds:** Income bonds are bonds that only pay interest if certain income objectives are met.

- **Zero Coupon Bonds:** Zero coupon bonds (also known as "deep discount bonds") are bonds sold with no stated interest but rather at a discount and redeemed at the face value without periodic interest payments.

- **Commodity-Backed Bonds:** Commodity-backed bonds (also known as "asset-linked bonds") are bonds that are redeemable either in cash or a stated volume of a commodity, whichever is greater.

2   Bonds Payable vs. Notes Payable

The accounting for long-term notes payable is similar to the accounting for bonds payable. The accounting for long-term, non-interest-bearing notes is similar to the accounting for short-term, non-interest-bearing notes. The following schedule identifies the typical differences between bonds and notes:

Attribute	Bonds	Notes
Implementing instrument	Bond	Note
Definitive agreement	Indenture	Loan agreement
Face amount increments	$1,000 (general)	Negotiated
Term	10 to 30 years	Negotiated
Payments prior to maturity	Interest only	Negotiated
Payments at maturity	Principal	Negotiated
Number of creditors	Many	Few
Publicly traded	Yes	No
Easily renegotiable	No	Yes
Secured	Yes and no	Yes
Registered (order) form	Yes	Yes
Bearer (coupon) form	Yes	No
Right of debtor to call/prepay	Yes	Yes
Right of creditor to put w/o default	Yes	No

3 Overview of Bond Terms

Bonds payable should be recorded as a long-term liability at face value and adjusted to the present value of their future cash outflows by either subtracting unamortized discounts or adding unamortized premiums. Bonds payable are recorded at the true present value at the date of issuance based on the market (effective) interest rate at that date.

- Bonds are usually issued in denominations of $1,000.

- Price is always quoted in 100s *(percentage of par value)*.

- Indenture is a contract for purchase of a bond.

- Coupon rate = The stated interest rate on the bond.

- Bond interest (check amount) = Coupon rate × Face. Bonds generally pay interest semiannually in the U.S. and annually in other countries.

- Principal payoff is always the full face amount.

- Premium/discount is the result of the buyer and seller "adjusting" the coupon rate to the prevailing market rate of interest.

4 Accounting for the Issuance of Bonds

4.1 Bond Selling Price

When a bond is issued, the price is computed as the sum of the present value of the future principal payment *plus* the present value of the future periodic interest payments. Both cash flows are discounted at the prevailing market rate of interest on the date of issuance. This recorded price is the value of the bond at its current cash equivalent.

4.1.1 Bonds Issued at Par Value

A bond is issued at par value when the stated rate on the bond is equal to the market (effective) interest rate on the date the bonds are issued.

Example 1	Bonds Issued at Par

Facts: Assume that Kristi Corporation issued a 10 percent, $1,000,000 bond due in five years. The bonds were issued January 1. Interest is due on June 30 and December 31. The yield or market rate is also 10 percent.

PV of $1 at 10% for 5 periods	0.620921
PV of $1 at 5% for 10 periods	0.613913
PV of an annuity of $1 at 10% for 5 periods	3.790787
PV of an annuity of $1 at 5% for 10 periods	7.721735

Required: Determine the selling price of the bond and prepare the journal entries for borrower and investor to record the bonds at issuance.

(continued)

(continued)

Solution:

	1		2		3		4		5		Principal
	6/30	12/31	6/30	12/31	6/30	12/31	6/30	12/31	6/30	12/31	12/31/X5
	$50,000	$50,000	$50,000	$50,000	$50,000	$50,000	$50,000	$50,000	$50,000	$50,000	$1,000,000

$ 386,087 = $50,000 × 7.721735 (PV of an annuity of $1 at 5% for 10 periods)

$ 613,913 = $1,000,000 × 0.613913 (PV of $1 at 5% for 10 periods)

$1,000,000   Net Present Value

Borrower			Investor		
DR Cash	$1,000,000		DR Investment in bonds	$1,000,000	
CR Bond payable		$1,000,000	CR Cash		$1,000,000

4.1.2 Bonds Issued at a Discount

A bond is issued at a discount when the stated rate on the bond is less than the market (effective) interest rate on the date the bonds are issued.

Example 2   Bonds Issued at Discount

Facts: Assume that Kristi Corporation issued a 10 percent, $1,000,000 bond due in five years. The bonds were issued January 1. Interest is due on June 30 and December 31. The yield or market rate is 12 percent.

Required: Determine the selling price of the bond, noting the amount of discount or premium, and prepare the journal entries for the borrower and investor to record the bonds at issuance.

Solution:

PV of $1 at 10% for 5 periods	0.620921
PV of $1 at 12% for 5 periods	0.567427
PV of $1 at 5% for 10 periods	0.613913
PV of $1 at 6% for 10 periods	0.558395
PV of an annuity of $1 at 10% for 5 periods	3.790787
PV of an annuity of $1 at 12% for 5 periods	3.604776
PV of an annuity of $1 at 5% for 10 periods	7.721735
PV of an annuity of $1 at 6% for 10 periods	7.360087

	1		2		3		4		5		Principal
	6/30	12/31	6/30	12/31	6/30	12/31	6/30	12/31	6/30	12/31	12/31/X5
	$50,000	$50,000	$50,000	$50,000	$50,000	$50,000	$50,000	$50,000	$50,000	$50,000	$1,000,000

$368,004 = $50,000 × 7.360087 (PV of an annuity of $1 at 6% for 10 periods)

$558,395 = $1,000,000 × 0.558395 (PV of $1 at 6% for 10 periods)

$926,399

(continued)

(continued)

	Borrower				Investor		
DR	Cash	$926,399		DR	Investment in bonds	$926,399	
DR	Discount on bond payable	73,601		CR	Cash		$926,399
CR	Bond payable		$1,000,000				

4.1.3 Bonds Issued at a Premium

A bond is issued at a premium when the stated rate on the bond is greater than the market (effective) interest rate on the date the bonds are issued.

Example 3   Bonds Issued at Premium

Facts: Assume that Kristi Corporation issued a 10 percent, $1,000,000 bond due in five years. The bonds were issued January 1. Interest is due on June 30 and December 31. The yield or market rate is 8 percent.

Required: Determine the selling price of the bond, noting the amount of discount or premium, and prepare the journal entries for borrower and investor to record the bonds at issuance.

Solution:

PV of $1 at 10% for 5 periods	0.620921
PV of $1 at 8% for 5 periods	0.680583
PV of $1 at 5% for 10 periods	0.613913
PV of $1 at 4% for 10 periods	0.675564
PV of an annuity of $1 at 10% for 5 periods	3.790787
PV of an annuity of $1 at 8% for 5 periods	3.992710
PV of an annuity of $1 at 5% for 10 periods	7.721735
PV of an annuity of $1 at 4% for 10 periods	8.110896

	1		2		3		4		5		Principal
	6/30	12/31	6/30	12/31	6/30	12/31	6/30	12/31	6/30	12/31	12/31/X5
	$50,000	$50,000	$50,000	$50,000	$50,000	$50,000	$50,000	$50,000	$50,000	$50,000	$1,000,000

$ 405,545 = $50,000 × 8.110896 (PV of an annuity of $1 at 4% for 10 periods)

$ 675,564 = $1,000,000 × 0.675564 (PV of $1 at 4% for 10 periods)

$1,081,109

	Borrower				Investor		
DR	Cash	$1,081,109		DR	Investment in bonds	$1,081,109	
CR	Premium on bond payable		$ 81,109	CR	Cash		$1,081,109
CR	Bond payable		1,000,000				

4.2   Stated Interest Rate

The stated rate of interest of a bond is typically printed on the bond and included in the bond indenture before the bond is brought to market. The stated rate of a bond does not change, regardless of the market rate at the date of issuance. The amount of cash received by a bondholder at regular interest payment intervals throughout the life of the bonds will always be at the stated rate applied to the face amount of the bond.

Interest is typically paid on bonds twice a year (semiannually), although interest expense will accrue monthly.

4.3   Effective Interest Rate

Because the amount of cash to be received in the future is fixed at the time the bond is sold, the market will automatically adjust the issue price of the bond so that the purchaser receives the *market rate of interest* for comparable risk bonds (i.e., the effective interest rate). A discount or premium on the bonds will exist when the bonds are issued with a stated rate that differs from the market rate at the date of issuance.

4.4   Discounts

If the market rate of interest is higher than the stated rate of interest on the bond, the bonds will sell at a discount. This means that the bond will sell for *less* than the face value of the bond (at less than 100 percent of par). The difference between the face value of the bond and the sales price of the bond (i.e., the discount) will cause interest expense to be greater than the interest paid in cash to the bondholders.

4.4.1   Unamortized Discount

The unamortized discount on bonds payable is a contra-account to bonds payable, which means that it is presented on the balance sheet as a direct reduction from the face (par) value of the bonds to arrive at the bond's carrying value at any particular point in time. The unamortized discount will decrease as the discount is amortized.

Long-term liabilities:	
Bonds payable, 10%, due 12/31/Year X	$1,000,000
Less: unamortized discount	(73,601)
	$ 926,399

4.4.2   Amortization of the Discount

Bond discount represents additional interest to be paid to investors at the bond maturity and is amortized over the life of the bond. The discount is amortized over the life of the bond, with amortized amounts *increasing interest expense* each period. Therefore, the amortization of the discount is added to the amount of cash paid at the stated rate to obtain GAAP interest expense (remember that the amount of cash paid could be zero if the bond is a zero coupon bond).

4.5   Premiums

If the market rate of interest is lower than the stated interest rate on the bond, the bonds will sell at a premium. This means that the bonds will sell for more than the face value of the bond (at more than 100 percent of par). The difference between the face value of the bond and the sales price of the bond (i.e., the premium) will cause interest expense to be less than the interest paid in cash.

4.5.1 Unamortized Premium

The unamortized premium on bonds payable is presented on the balance sheet as a direct addition to the face (par) value of the bonds to arrive at the bond's carrying value at any particular point in time. The unamortized premium will decrease as the premium is amortized.

Long-term liabilities:	
Bonds payable, 10%, due 12/31/Year X	$1,000,000
Add: unamortized premium	81,109
	$1,081,109

4.5.2 Amortization of the Premium

The bond premium represents interest paid in advance to the issuer by bondholders who then receive a return of this premium in the form of larger periodic interest payments (at the stated rate). The bond premium is amortized over the life of the bond, with amortized amounts *decreasing interest expense* each period. Therefore, the amortization of the premium is subtracted from the amount of cash paid at the stated rate to obtain GAAP interest expense.

4.6 Carrying Value

The carrying value of a bond equals face plus the balance of unamortized premium or face minus the balance of unamortized discount. As bonds approach maturity, their carrying values approach face value, so that the carrying value of the bonds equals face value at maturity. The carrying value of a bond with a discount increases to maturity value as the discount is amortized. The carrying value of a bond with a premium decreases to maturity value as the premium is amortized.

	FACE		FACE
+	Unamortized premium	−	Unamortized discount
	Carrying value		Carrying value

4.7 Bond Issuance Costs

Bond issuance costs are transaction costs incurred when bonds are issued. Examples include legal fees, accounting fees, underwriting commissions, and printing. When bonds are accounted for at amortized cost, bond issuance costs are accounted for as follows:

- Bond issuance costs are presented on the balance sheet as a direct reduction to the carrying amount of the bond, similar to bond discounts.

- When bonds are issued, the bond proceeds are recorded net of the bond issuance costs.

- Bond issuance costs are amortized as interest expense over the life of the bond using the effective interest method.

Example 4   Bond With Bond Issuance Costs

Facts: On December 31, Year 1, Kristi Corporation issued a 10 percent $1,000,000 bond due in five years. Interest is due on June 30 and December 31. The yield or market rate is 12 percent and the bond sold for $926,399. Bond issuance costs of $20,000 were incurred. The effective interest rate is 12.58 percent.

Required: Prepare the journal entry to record the bonds at issuance and indicate how the bonds should be reported on the December 31, Year 1, balance sheet.

Solution:

DR	Cash	$906,399	
DR	Discount and bond issuance costs	93,601*	
CR	Bonds payable		$1,000,000

*$93,601 = $73,601 discount + $20,000 bond issuance costs

The bonds would be reported as follows on the December 31, Year 1, balance sheet:

Long-term liabilities:

Principal amount	$1,000,000
Less: unamortized discount and bond issuance costs	93,601
Long-term debt less unamortized discount and bond issuance costs	$ 906,399

4.7.1   Effective Interest Rate

The inclusion of bond issuance costs and bond discount/premium in the calculation of the carrying amount of the bond results in an effective interest rate for the bond that differs from the market rate. The effective interest rate is used to determine the interest expense for the period as the bond discount/premium and bond issuance costs are amortized. The effective interest rate must be disclosed in the footnotes.

Pass Key

Some CPA Exam questions may make the simplifying assumption that bond issuance costs are recognized as interest expense on a straight-line basis.

4.7.2   Deferred Bond Issuance Costs

Bond issuance costs incurred before the issuance of the bonds are deferred on the balance sheet until the bond liability is recorded.

Example 5   Deferred Bond Issuance Costs

Facts: On November 1, Year 1, Kristi Corporation incurred bond issuance costs of $20,000 related to bonds issued on December 31, Year 1 for $926,399.

Required: Prepare the journal entries for Kristi to record these transactions.

Solution: *On November 1, Kristi Corporation recorded the following journal entry:*

DR	Deferred bond issuance costs	$20,000	
CR	Cash		$20,000

On December 31, Kristi recorded the following journal entry:

DR	Cash	$926,399	
DR	Discount and bond issuance costs	93,601	
CR	Bonds payable		$1,000,000
CR	Deferred bond issuance costs		20,000

NOTES

5 Bonds: Part 2

1 Bond Amortization Methods

1.1 Amortization Period

Under U.S. GAAP, the period over which to amortize a bond premium or discount and bond issuance costs is the period that the bonds are outstanding (i.e., from the date the bonds are sold). In general, U.S. GAAP amortization is done over the contractual life of the bond.

Illustration 1	Bond Amortization Period

A five-year bond dated January 1 doesn't actually sell until November 1. In this case, the period of amortization is 50 months (not 60 months).

1.2 Straight-Line Method

To amortize a discount, premium, or bond issuance cost using the straight-line method, simply divide the unamortized discount or premium by the number of periods the bonds are outstanding and amortize the same amount of discount or premium each period. This method of amortization results in a *constant dollar amount of interest expense* each period. The straight-line method is *not GAAP* but is allowed under U.S. GAAP if the results are not materially different from the effective interest method.

Interest expense is calculated as follows:

$$\frac{\text{Premium/discount and bond issuance cost}}{\text{Number of periods bond is outstanding}} = \text{Period amortization}$$

$$\text{Interest expense} = (\text{Face value} \times \text{Stated interest rate}) \begin{array}{l} - \text{ Premium amortization} \\ \textit{Or:} \\ + \text{ Discount and bond issuance cost amortization} \end{array}$$

Example 1	Bond Discount Amortization: Straight-Line Method

Continuing with the Kristi Corporation example, this is an example of amortization and interest expense calculated under the straight-line method.

Facts: Assume that Kristi Corporation issued a 10 percent, $1,000,000 bond due in five years. The bonds were issued January 1. Interest is due on June 30 and December 31. The yield or market rate is 12 percent.

Required: Determine the selling price of the bond, noting the amount of discount or premium, and prepare the journal entries for borrower and investor to record the bonds at issuance and for the first interest payment.

Solution: $1,000,000 − $926,399 = ($73,601 ÷ 10 periods = $7,360.10)

			Journal Entry Impact	
			Balance Sheet	Income Statement
Date	Net Carrying Value	Straight-Line Amortization	Interest Payment Face × Coupon	Interest Expense Cash Paid + Discount
06/30/Year 1	$ 926,399.00	$7,360.10	$50,000	$57,360.10
12/31/Year 1	933,759.10	7,360.10	50,000	57,360.10
06/30/Year 2	941,119.20	7,360.10	50,000	57,360.10
12/31/Year 2	948,479.30	7,360.10	50,000	57,360.10
06/30/Year 3	955,839.40	7,360.10	50,000	57,360.10
12/31/Year 3	963,199.50	7,360.10	50,000	57,360.10
06/30/Year 4	970,559.60	7,360.10	50,000	57,360.10
12/31/Year 4	977,919.70	7,360.10	50,000	57,360.10
06/30/Year 5	985,279.80	7,360.10	50,000	57,360.10
12/31/Year 5	992,639.90	7,360.10	50,000	57,360.10
12/31/Year 5	$1,000,000.00			

Borrower			
January 1, Year 1			
DR	Cash	$926,399	
DR	Discount on bond payable	73,601	
CR	Bond payable		$1,000,000
June 30, Year 1			
DR	Bond interest expense	$57,360.10	
CR	Discount on bond payable		$ 7,360.10
CR	Cash		50,000.00

Investor			
January 1, Year 1			
DR	Investment in bonds	$926,399	
CR	Cash		$926,399
June 30, Year 1			
DR	Cash	$50,000.00	
DR	Investment in bonds	7,360.10	
CR	Bonds interest revenue		$57,360.10

Example 2 — Bond Premium Amortization: Straight-Line Method

Continuing with the Kristi Corporation example, this is an example of amortization and interest expense calculated under the straight-line method.

Facts: Assume that Kristi Corporation issued a 10 percent, $1,000,000 bond due in five years. The bonds were issued January 1. Interest is due on June 30 and December 31. The yield or market rate is 8 percent.

Required: Determine the selling price of the bond, noting the amount of discount or premium, and prepare the journal entries for borrower and investor to record the bonds at issuance and the first interest payment.

Solution: $1,081,109 − $1,000,000 = ($81,109 ÷ 10 periods = $8,110.90)

| | | | Journal Entry Impact | |
| | | | Balance Sheet | Income Statement |
Date	Net Carrying Value	Straight-Line Amortization	Interest Payment Face × Coupon	Interest Expense Cash Paid − Premium
06/30/Year 1	$1,081,109.00	$8,110.90	$50,000	$41,889.10
12/31/Year 1	1,072,998.10	8,110.90	50,000	41,889.10
06/30/Year 2	1,064,887.20	8,110.90	50,000	41,889.10
12/31/Year 2	1,056,776.30	8,110.90	50,000	41,889.10
06/30/Year 3	1,048,665.40	8,110.90	50,000	41,889.10
12/31/Year 3	1,040,554.50	8,110.90	50,000	41,889.10
06/30/Year 4	1,032,443.60	8,110.90	50,000	41,889.10
12/31/Year 4	1,024,332.70	8,110.90	50,000	41,889.10
06/30/Year 5	1,016,221.80	8,110.90	50,000	41,889.10
12/31/Year 5	1,008,110.90	8,110.90	50,000	41,889.10
12/31/Year 5	$1,000,000.00			

Borrower

January 1, Year 1

DR	Cash	$1,081,109	
CR	Premium on bond payable		$ 81,109
CR	Bond payable		1,000,000

June 30, Year 1

DR	Bond interest expense	$41,889.10	
DR	Premium on bond payable	8,110.90	
CR	Cash		$50,000.00

Investor

January 1, Year 1

DR	Investment in bonds	$1,081,109	
CR	Cash		$1,081,109

June 30, Year 1

DR	Cash	$50,000.00	
CR	Investment in bonds		$ 8,110.90
CR	Bonds interest revenue		41,889.10

1.3   Effective Interest Method

Use of the effective interest method of accounting for the amortization of unamortized discounts/premiums is required by U.S. GAAP. Under the effective interest method, interest expense is calculated by multiplying the carrying value of the bond at the *beginning* of the period by the effective interest rate. This method of amortization results in a *constant rate* of interest each period. The difference between interest expense and the cash paid for interest is the amortization for the period of the discount or premium. Interest expense and amortization for the period is calculated as follows:

1.3.1   Interest Expense

> Interest expense = Carrying value at the beginning of the period × Effective (market) interest rate

1.3.2   Discount/Premium Amortization

> Amortization of the discount = Interest expense − Interest payment

> Amortization of the premium = Interest payment − Interest expense

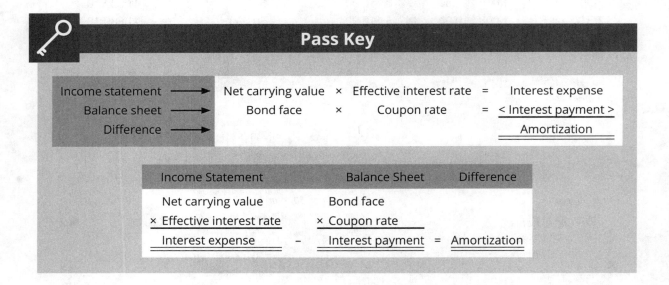

Pass Key

Income statement ⟶	Net carrying value	×	Effective interest rate	=	Interest expense
Balance sheet ⟶	Bond face	×	Coupon rate	=	< Interest payment >
Difference ⟶					Amortization

Income Statement	Balance Sheet	Difference
Net carrying value	Bond face	
× Effective interest rate	× Coupon rate	
Interest expense −	Interest payment =	Amortization

Example 3   Bond Premium Amortization: Effective Interest Method

Facts: Assume that Kristi Corporation issued a 10 percent, $1,000,000 bond due in five years. The bond sold for $1,081,109 on January 1, Year 1, to yield 8 percent. Interest is paid semiannually on June 30 and December 31.

Required: Determine the interest expense by the effective interest method and prepare the journal entries for borrower and investor to record the bonds at issuance and for the first two interest payments. Also show the borrower's balance sheet presentation and income statement effect on the Year 1 financial statements.

Solution:

			Journal Entry Impact			
			Income Statement	**Balance Sheet**	**Difference**	
Date	Beginning of Period Net Carrying Value	4% Semiannual Amortization Interest	Interest Expense N.C.V. × Effective	Interest Payment Face × Coupon	Amortization	End of Period Net Carrying Value
06/30/Year 1	$1,081,109	4%	$43,244	$50,000	$ 6,756	$1,074,353
12/31/Year 1	1,074,353	4%	42,974	50,000	7,026	1,067,327
06/30/Year 2	1,067,327	4%	42,693	50,000	7,307	1,060,021
12/31/Year 2	1,060,021	4%	42,401	50,000	7,599	1,052,421
06/30/Year 3	1,052,421	4%	42,097	50,000	7,903	1,044,518
12/31/Year 3	1,044,518	4%	41,781	50,000	8,219	1,036,299
06/30/Year 4	1,036,299	4%	41,452	50,000	8,548	1,027,751
12/31/Year 4	1,027,751	4%	41,110	50,000	8,890	1,018,861
06/30/Year 5	1,018,861	4%	40,754	50,000	9,246	1,009,615
12/31/Year 5	1,009,615	4%	40,385	50,000	9,615	1,000,000
					$81,109	

(continued)

(continued)

Borrower				Investor			

January 1, Year 1

DR	Cash	$1,081,109	
CR	Premium on bonds payable		$ 81,109
CR	Bond payable		1,000,000

January 1, Year 1

DR	Investment in bonds	$1,081,109	
CR	Cash		$1,081,109

June 30, Year 1

DR	Bond interest expense	$43,244	
DR	Premium on bonds payable	6,756	
CR	Cash		$50,000

June 30, Year 1

DR	Cash	$50,000	
CR	Investment in bonds		$ 6,756
CR	Bond interest revenue		43,244

December 31, Year 1

DR	Bond interest expense	$42,974	
DR	Premium on bonds payable	7,026	
CR	Cash		$50,000

December 31, Year 1

DR	Cash	$50,000	
CR	Investment in bonds		$ 7,026
CR	Bond interest revenue		42,974

Balance Sheet Presentation

Carrying value of the bond at December 31, Year 1:

Face value	$1,000,000
+ Unamortized premium	67,327
	$1,067,327

Income statement effect:

Interest expense for Year 1 = $86,218 [43,244 + 42,974]

Example 4   Bond Discount Amortization: Effective Interest Method

Facts: Assume that Kristi Corporation issued a 10 percent, $1,000,000 bond due in five years. The bond sold for $926,399 on January 1, Year 1, to yield 12 percent. Interest is paid semiannually on June 30 and December 31.

Required: Determine the interest expense by the effective interest method and prepare the journal entries for borrower and investor to record the bonds at issuance and for the first two interest payments. Also show the borrower's balance sheet presentation and income statement effect on the Year 1 financial statements.

(continued)

(continued)

Solution:

Journal Entry Impact

			Income Statement	Balance Sheet	Difference	
Date	**Beginning of Period Net Carrying Value**	**6% Semiannual Amortization Interest**	**Interest Expense N.C.V. × Effective**	**Interest Payment Face × Coupon**	**Amortization**	**End of Period Net Carrying Value**
06/30/Year 1	$926,399	6%	$55,584	$50,000	$ 5,584	$931,983
12/31/Year 1	931,983	6%	55,919	50,000	5,919	937,902
06/30/Year 2	937,902	6%	56,274	50,000	6,274	944,176
12/31/Year 2	944,176	6%	56,651	50,000	6,651	950,827
06/30/Year 3	950,827	6%	57,050	50,000	7,050	957,876
12/31/Year 3	957,876	6%	57,473	50,000	7,473	965,349
06/30/Year 4	965,349	6%	57,921	50,000	7,921	973,270
12/31/Year 4	973,270	6%	58,396	50,000	8,396	981,666
06/30/Year 5	981,666	6%	58,900	50,000	8,900	990,566
12/31/Year 5	990,566	6%	59,434	50,000	9,434	1,000,000
					$73,601	

Borrower	Investor

January 1, Year 1

DR	Cash	$926,399	
DR	Discount on bonds payable	73,601	
CR	Bond payable		$1,000,000

January 1, Year 1

DR	Investment in bonds	$926,399	
CR	Cash		$926,399

June 30, Year 1

DR	Bond interest expense	$55,584	
CR	Discount on bonds payable		$ 5,584
CR	Cash		50,000

June 30, Year 1

DR	Cash	$50,000	
DR	Investment in bonds	5,584	
CR	Bond interest revenue		$55,584

December 31, Year 1

DR	Bond interest expense	$55,919	
CR	Discount on bonds payable		$ 5,919
CR	Cash		50,000

December 31, Year 1

DR	Cash	$50,000	
DR	Investment in bonds	5,919	
CR	Bond interest revenue		$55,919

Balance Sheet Presentation

Carrying value of the bond at December 31, Year 1:

Face value	$1,000,000
– Unamortized discount	62,098
	$ 937,902

Income statement effect:
Interest expense for Year 1 = $111,503 [55,584 + 55,919]

1.3.3 Bond Amortization Including Bond Issuance Costs

Example 5	Bond Discount Amortization Including Bond Issuance Costs: Effective Interest Method

Facts: Assume that Kristi Corporation issued a 10 percent, $1,000,000 bond due in five years. The yield or market rate is 12 percent and the bond sold for $926,399. Bond issuance costs of $20,000 were incurred. The effective interest rate on this bond is 12.58 percent.

Required: Determine the interest expense by the effective interest method and prepare the journal entries for borrower and investor to record the bonds at issuance and for the first two interest payments. Also show the borrower's balance presentation and income statement effect on the Year 1 financial statements.

Solution:

			Journal Entry Impact			
			Income Statement	Balance Sheet	Difference	
Date	Beginning of Period Net Carrying Value	6.29% Semiannual Amortization Interest	Interest Expense N.C.V. × Effective	Interest Payment Face × Coupon	Amortization of Discount and Bond Issuance Costs	End of Period Net Carrying Value
06/30/Year 1	$906,399	6.29%	$57,012	$50,000	$7,012	$913,411
12/31/Year 1	913,411	6.29%	57,454	50,000	7,454	920,865
06/30/Year 2	920,865	6.29%	57,922	50,000	7,922	928,787
12/31/Year 2	928,787	6.29%	58,421	50,000	8,421	937,208
06/30/Year 3	937,208	6.29%	58,950	50,000	8,950	946,159
12/31/Year 3	946,159	6.29%	59,513	50,000	9,513	955,672
06/30/Year 4	955,672	6.29%	60,112	50,000	10,112	965,784
12/31/Year 4	965,784	6.29%	60,748	50,000	10,748	976,532
06/30/Year 5	976,532	6.29%	61,424	50,000	11,424	987,955
12/31/Year 5	987,955	6.29%	62,045*	50,000	12,045	1,000,000

*This amount is adjusted for rounding.

(continued)

(continued)

Borrower				Investor*			
January 1, Year 1				*January 1, Year 1*			
DR	Cash	$906,399		DR	Investment in bonds	$926,399	
DR	Discount and bond issuance costs	93,601		CR	Cash		$926,399
CR	Bond payable		$1,000,000				
June 30, Year 1				*June 30, Year 1*			
DR	Bond interest expense	$57,012		DR	Cash	$50,000	
CR	Discount and bond issuance costs		$ 7,012	DR	Investment in bonds	5,584	
CR	Cash		50,000	CR	Bond interest revenue		$55,584
December 31, Year 1				*December 31, Year 1*			
DR	Bond interest expense	$57,454		DR	Cash	$50,000	
CR	Discount and bond issuance costs		$ 7,454	DR	Investment in bonds	5,919	
CR	Cash		50,000	CR	Bond interest revenue		$55,919

*Note that the investor accounting is not affected by the bond issuance costs.

Balance Sheet Presentation

Carrying value of the bond at December 31, Year 1:

Face value	$1,000,000
− Unamortized discount	79,135
	$ 920,865

Income statement effect:

Interest expense for Year 1 = $114,466 [57,012 + 57,454]

2 Bonds Issued Between Interest Dates

Interest payments on bonds are generally made semiannually. However, bonds are usually sold between interest dates, which requires additional entries for accrued interest at the time of sale. The amount of interest that has accrued since the last interest payment is added to the price of the bond. The purchaser pays such interest and is reimbursed at the next payment date on receipt of a full period's interest.

Example 6	Bonds Issued Between Interest Dates

Facts: On April 1, Year 1, Kristi Corporation issued 10 percent bonds dated January 1, Year 1, in the face amount of $1,000,000. Interest is due on June 30 and December 31. The bonds were issued for $926,399, plus accrued interest for three months (January through March).

Required: Determine the cash received and prepare the journal entries to record the sale of the bonds and the first interest payment.

Solution:

Selling price ($1,000,000 face)	$926,399
Plus: Accrued interest ($1,000,000 × 10% × 3/12)	25,000
Total cash received	$951,399

Journal entry to record the sale on April 1:

DR	Cash	$951,399	
DR	Discount on bonds payable	73,601	
CR	Bonds payable		$1,000,000
CR	Bond interest expense (or payable)		25,000

*Journal entry to record the first interest payment on June 30 ($1,000,000 × 10% × 6/12):

DR	Bond interest expense (or payable)	$50,000	
CR	Cash		$50,000

The interest expense account would then contain a debit balance of $25,000, the proper amount of interest expense for three months at 10% ($1,000,000 × 10% × 3/12 = $25,000).

*Journal entry to record amortization should also be recorded.

3   Year-End Bond Interest Accrual

When the date of a scheduled interest payment and the issuer's year-end do not agree, it is necessary to accrue interest by an adjusting entry on the issuer's books at year-end. The accrual must take into account a prorated share of discount or premium amortization.

Example 7   Year-End Bond Interest Accrual

Facts: Kristi Corporation, whose year-end is December 31, issued $1,000,000 of five-year, 10 percent bonds with interest payable on July 1 and January 1. The bonds sold at a discount for $926,399.

Required: Calculate the amount of the year-end accrual for interest and discount amortization and prepare the journal entry to record the accrued interest at year-end.

Solution:

Year-end adjustment:

Interest payable

Face value × Coupon rate × Period = $1,000,000 × 10% × 6/12   = $50,000

Amortization (per prior schedule)   5,919

Journal entry on December 31, Year 1:

To record interest accrual and discount amortization from July 1, Year 1–December 31, Year 1:

DR	Interest expense	$55,919	
CR	Interest payable		$50,000
CR	Discount on bonds payable		5,919

---

4   Disclosure Requirements

Companies with many debt issues often report only one balance sheet total, which is supported by comments and schedules in the accompanying notes. Notes often show details regarding the liability maturity dates, interest rates, call and conversion privileges, assets pledged as security, and borrower-imposed restrictions.

NOTES

1 Troubled Debt Restructuring

A troubled debt restructuring is one in which the creditor allows the debtor certain concessions to improve the likelihood of collection that would not be considered under normal circumstances. Concessions include items such as reduced interest rates, extension of maturity dates, reduction of the face amount of the debt, and reduction of the amount of accrued interest. The concessions must be made in light of the debtor's financial difficulty, and the objective of the creditor must be to maximize recovery of the investment. Troubled debt restructurings are often the result of legal proceedings or of negotiation between parties.

1.1 Accounting and Reporting by Debtors

A debtor accounts for a troubled debt restructuring according to the type, as follows:

1.1.1 Transfer of Assets

The debtor will recognize a gain in the amount of the excess of the carrying amount of the payable (face amount of the payable plus accrued interest, premiums, etc.) over the fair value of the assets given up. The gain or loss on disposition of the asset (i.e., difference between book value and fair value) is reported in income of the period.

- **Recognize Gain/Loss**

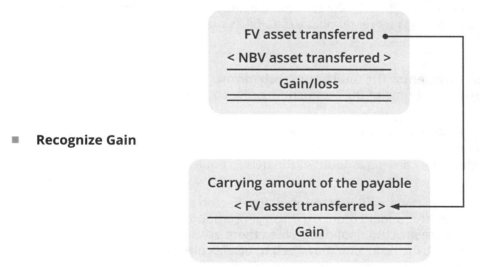

- **Recognize Gain**

1.1.2 Transfer of Equity Interest

The difference between the carrying amount of the payable and the fair value of the equity interest is recognized as a gain (gain on restructuring of debt) under U.S. GAAP.

■ **Recognize Gain**

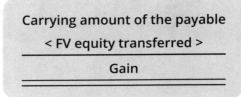

Carrying amount of the payable
< FV equity transferred >
_____
Gain

Pass Key

Whether transfer of assets or transfer of equity interest, once the transfer has taken place, the debt has been extinguished.

1.1.3 Modification of Terms

A restructuring that does not involve the transfer of assets or equity will often involve the modification of the terms of the debt. In a modification, the debtor usually accounts for the effects of the restructuring prospectively. The debtor does not change the carrying amount unless the carrying amount exceeds the total future cash payments specified by the new terms.

Pass Key

Under a modification of terms, the debt has not been extinguished; the terms have been adjusted so that the debtor has a greater ability to fulfill its obligation.

■ **Total Future Cash Payments:** The total future cash payments are the principal and any accrued interest at the time of the restructuring that continues to be payable by the new terms.

■ **Interest Expense:** Interest expense is computed by a method that causes a constant effective rate (e.g., the effective interest method). The new effective rate of interest is the discount rate at which the carrying amount of the debt is equal to the present value of the future cash payments.

■ **Future Payments:** When the total (undiscounted) future cash payments are less than the carrying amount, the debtor should reduce the carrying amount accordingly and recognize the difference as a gain restructuring of debt. When there are several related accounts (discount, premium, etc.), the reduction may need to be allocated among them. All cash payments after the restructuring reduce the carrying amount, and no interest expense is recognized after the date of restructure.

When there are indeterminate future payments, or any time the future payments might exceed the carrying amount, the debtor recognizes no gain and does not adjust the carrying value of the note. When there are indeterminate future payments, the debtor should assume that the future contingent payments will have to be made at least to the extent necessary to obviate any gain.

1.1.4 Combination of Type

When a restructuring involves a combination of asset or equity transfers and modification of terms, the fair value of any asset or equity is used first to reduce the carrying amount of the payable. The difference between the fair value and the carrying amount of any assets transferred is recognized as gain or loss. No gain on restructuring can be recognized unless the carrying amount of the payable exceeds the total future cash payments.

All gains on debt restructuring are aggregated and included in net income for the period. They are treated and classified along with other gains of the company, typically in the continuing operations section of the income statement.

1.2 Accounting and Reporting by Creditors

1.2.1 Recognition of Impairment

A loan is considered impaired if it is probable (likely to occur) that the creditor will be unable to collect all amounts due under the original contract when due. Normal loan procedures should be used to judge whether a loan is impaired. A loan restructured in a troubled debt restructuring is an impaired loan.

1.2.2 Measurement of Impairment

- **Receipt of Assets or Equity:** When the creditor receives either assets or equity as full settlement of a receivable, these are accounted for at their fair value at the time of the restructuring. The fair value of the receivable satisfied can be used if it is more clearly determinable than the fair value of the asset or equity acquired. In a partial payment, the creditor must use the fair value of the asset or equity received.

  The excess of the recorded receivable over the fair value of the asset received is recognized as a loss. The creditor accounts for these assets as if they were acquired for cash.

- **Modification of Terms:** Impairment should be captured as part of an entity's overall assessment of credit losses. Any losses with troubled debt restructuring should be incorporated into a creditor's estimate of its allowance for credit losses. Entities may employ a variety of methods to estimate credit losses. If a discounted cash flow approach is used, the post-restructuring effective interest rate must be used as the discount rate.

  The impairment is recorded by creating a valuation allowance with a corresponding charge to bad debt expense:

| DR | Bad debt expense | $XXX | |
| CR | Allowance for credit losses | | $XXX |

Example 1   Transfer of Assets

Facts: Hull Company is indebted to Apex under a $500,000, 12 percent, three-year note dated December 31, Year 1. Because of Hull's financial difficulties developing in Year 3, Hull owed accrued interest of $60,000 on December 31, Year 3. Under a troubled debt restructuring, on December 31, Year 3, Apex agreed to settle the note and accrued interest for a tract of land having a fair value of $450,000. Hull's acquisition cost of the land is $360,000.

Required:

1. Calculate the gain recognized by Hull on the troubled debt restructuring.

2. Prepare the journal entry to record the transaction on Hull's books.

3. Prepare the journal entry to record the transaction on Apex's books.

Solution:

1. Hull's total debt is the $500,000 face value of the note plus $60,000 of accrued interest, or $560,000.

The debt was forgiven in exchange for Hull giving Apex (the lender) land worth $450,000, with a cost to Hull of $360,000.

Hull's total gain is:

Debt forgiven	$560,000	
Carrying value of asset given	(360,000)	
Total gain	$200,000 ($90,000 + $110,000, per below)	

Breakout of gain

Gain on disposal of land (adjustment to fair value)

Fair value of land	$ 450,000	
Acquisition cost	(360,000)	
Holding gain on sale of land	$ 90,000	

Gain on restructuring

Three-year note	$500,000	
Accrued interest	60,000	
Amount owed		560,000
Settlement amount (fair value of land)		(450,000)
Gain on restructuring of debt		$ 110,000

2. *Journal entry to record the troubled debt restructuring on the books of Hull*:

DR	Notes payable	$500,000	
DR	Interest payable	60,000	
CR	Land		$360,000
CR	Gain on disposal of land		90,000
CR	Gain on restructuring		110,000

(continued)

(continued)

3. *Journal entry to record the troubled debt restructuring on the books of Apex:*

DR	Land	$450,000	
DR	Allowance for credit losses	110,000	
CR	Note receivable		$500,000
CR	Interest receivable		60,000

Example 2   Transfer of Equity

Facts: The same facts as in the previous example, except that on December 31, Year 3, Apex agreed to settle the note and accrued interest for an equity interest in Hull Company having a fair value of $450,000 (100,000 shares of common stock with a market value of $4.50/share and a par value of $2.00/share).

Required:

1. Calculate the gain recognized by Hull on the troubled debt restructuring.

2. Prepare the journal entry to record the transaction on Hull's books.

3. Prepare the journal entry to record the transaction on Apex's books.

Solution:

1. Hull's total debt is the $500,000 face value of the note plus $60,000 of accrued interest, or $560,000.

The debt was forgiven in exchange for Hull giving Apex (the lender) equity worth $450,000.

Gain on restructuring:

Carrying amount of payable	$560,000
Settlement amount (fair value of equity)	(450,000)
Gain on restructuring of debt	$110,000

2. *Journal entry to record the troubled debt restructuring on the books of Hull:*

DR	Notes payable	$500,000	
DR	Interest payable	60,000	
CR	Common stock		$200,000
CR	Additional paid-in capital		250,000
CR	Gain on restructuring		110,000

3. *Journal entry to record the troubled debt restructuring on the books of Apex:*

DR	Equity investments	$450,000	
DR	Allowance for credit losses	110,000	
CR	Note receivable		$500,000
CR	Interest receivable		60,000

Example 3   Modification of Terms

Facts: The same facts as in the previous example, except that on December 31, Year 3, Apex agreed to modify the terms of the debt. The accrued interest was forgiven, the interest rate was lowered to 3 percent, and the maturity date was extended to December 31, Year 5.

Required:

1. Indicate how Hull should report the troubled debt restructuring on its Year 3 income statement.

2. Prepare the journal entry to record the transaction on Hull's books.

3. Prepare the journal entry to record the transaction on Apex's books, assuming the company utilizes a discounted cash flow approach and the post-restructuring effective interest rate of 3.50 percent.

Solution:

1. Hull's total debt is the $500,000 face value of the note plus $60,000 of accrued interest, or $560,000.

Total future cash payments under modified terms:

Face amount of note	$500,000
Year 4 interest	15,000 = $500,000 × 3%
Year 5 interest	15,000 = $500,000 × 3%
Total	$530,000

Gain on restructuring:

Carrying amount of payable	$560,000
Total future cash payments	(530,000)
Gain on restructuring of debt	$ 30,000

2. *Journal entry to record the troubled debt restructuring on the books of Hull:*

DR	Notes payable	$500,000	
DR	Interest payable	60,000	
CR	Note payable		$530,000*
CR	Gain on restructuring		30,000

*All future payments (principal and interest) will reduce the note payable.

3. *Journal entry to record the impairment on the books of Apex:*

DR	Bad debt expense	$64,745	
CR	Allowance for credit losses		$64,745*

*This amount is calculated as the difference between the pre-restructured note balance and the present value of future cash flows ($500,000 and two interest payments of $15,000) discounted at the loan's effective interest rate of 3.50 percent.

Pre-restructure carrying amount	$ 560,000
Present value of restructured cash flows	(495,255)
Creditor's loss on restructuring	$ 64,745

(continued)

(continued)

The present value of restructured cash flows is calculated as follows:

Present value of $500,000 due in two years at 3.50 percent = 0.9335 × $500,000 = $466,755

Present value of $15,000 interest payable annually for two years at 3.5 percent = 1.900 × $15,000 = $28,500

Present value of restructured cash flows = $466,755 + $28,500 = $495,255

2 Extinguishment of Debt

Corporations issuing bonds may call or retire them prior to maturity. Callable bonds can be retired after a certain date at a stated price. Refundable bonds allow an existing issue to be retired and replaced with a new issue at a lower interest rate.

2.1 Definition of Extinguishment

A liability cannot be derecognized in the financial statements until it has been extinguished. A liability is considered extinguished if the debtor pays or the debtor is legally released.

2.1.1 Debtor Pays

A liability is considered extinguished if the debtor pays the creditor and is relieved of its obligation for the liability.

- **Bond Extinguishment at Maturity**

   If a bond is paid at maturity, the carrying value of the bond is equal to the face amount of the bond and no gain or loss is recorded:

   Journal entry retirement at maturity of a bond issued for $1,081,109 with a face value of $1,000,000. The premium has been fully amortized by maturity.

DR	Bonds payable	$1,000,000	
CR	Cash		$1,000,000

- **Bond Extinguished Before Maturity**

   If a bond is extinguished before maturity, a gain or loss is generally recorded. The gain or loss is the difference between the carrying value of the bond (Face value less Unamortized discount *or* plus Unamortized premium) and the cash paid to extinguish the bond.

2.1.2 Debtor Legally Released

A liability is considered extinguished if the debtor is legally released from being the primary obligor under the liability, either judicially or by the creditor. A troubled debt restructuring would result in the extinguishment of debt only if the debt were forgiven by the creditor as the result of a transfer of assets or the transfer of equity interest. A modification of terms is not extinguishment.

2.2 In-Substance Defeasance Not Extinguishment

An in-substance defeasance is an arrangement in which a company places purchased securities into an irrevocable trust and pledges them for the future principal and interest payments on its long-term debt. Because the company remains the primary obligor while there is outstanding debt, the liability is not considered extinguished by an in-substance defeasance.

2.3 Gain or Loss on Bond Extinguishment Before Maturity

2.3.1 Adjust Items in the Financial Statements

In any bond reacquisition, the following items must be accounted for and adjusted in the financial statements:

- Any related unamortized bond issuance costs;
- Any related unamortized discount or premium; and
- The difference between the bond's face value and the reacquisition proceeds.

2.3.2 Calculation of the Gain or Loss

Gain or loss on extinguishment of debt is the difference between the reacquisition price and the net carrying amount of the bond at the date of extinguishment. Any gain or loss on extinguishment of debt is recognized as income from continuing operations (gross of tax) in the income statement.

> (Gain) or loss = Reacquisition price − Net carrying amount

- **Reacquisition Price**

  Reacquisition price is usually shown as a percentage of the bond's face value (e.g., $100,000 at 102 or $100,000 at 95). To calculate the reacquisition price, multiply the percentage by the face value (e.g., $100,000 × 102% = $102,000 or $100,000 × 95% = $95,000).

- **Net Carrying Amount**

  The net carrying amount of the bond is the carrying value (i.e., face value of the bond plus unamortized premium or minus unamortized discount and minus unamortized bond issuance costs).

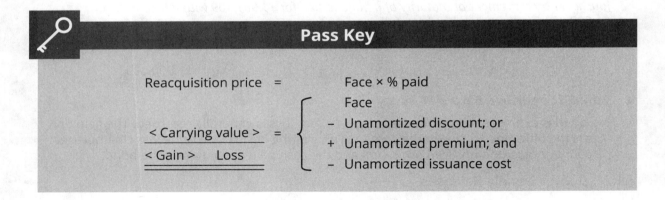

Pass Key

Reacquisition price = Face × % paid

< Carrying value > = Face
− Unamortized discount; or
+ Unamortized premium; and
− Unamortized issuance cost

< Gain >   Loss

Example 4   Loss on Extinguishment of Bonds

Facts: Assume that $1,000,000 bonds due in five years were issued on January 1, Year 1, at a discount for $926,399. Bond issuance costs of $20,000 were incurred. Two years later, on January 1, Year 3, the entire issue is redeemed at 101 and canceled (ignore income tax considerations). On this date, unamortized discount and bond issuance costs totaled $62,792.

Required: Calculate the gain or loss recorded when the bonds are extinguished and record the journal entry.

Solution:

Reacquisition price:

Face × % paid ($1,000,000 × 101)		$1,010,000
Bond carrying value:		
Face	$1,000,000	
Less: unamortized discount and bond issuance costs	(62,792)	
Net carrying value		(937,208)
Total loss on extinguishment		$ 72,792

Components of the loss are:

Unamortized bond discount and bond issuance costs	$ 62,792
Premium paid to retire ($1,000,000 × 1%)	10,000
Total loss	$ 72,792

Journal entry:

DR	Bonds payable	$1,000,000	
DR	Loss on extinguishment of bonds	72,792	
CR	Discount on bonds payable and bond issuance costs		$ 62,792
CR	Cash		1,010,000

Example 5   Gain on Extinguishment of Bonds

Facts: Assume that $1,000,000 bonds due in five years are issued on January 1, Year 1, at a premium for $1,081,109. The entire issue is redeemed two years later, on January 1, Year 3, for 96 and canceled. (Ignore income tax considerations.) On this date, unamortized premium totaled $52,421.

Required: Calculate the gain or loss recorded when the bonds are extinguished and record the journal entry.

Solution:

Reacquisition price:		
Face × % paid ($1,000,000 × 96%)		$ 960,000
Bond carrying value:		
Face	$1,000,000	
Plus: unamortized premium	52,421	
Net carrying value		(1,052,421)
Total gain on extinguishment		$ (92,421)

Components of the gain are:

Unamortized bond premium	$ 52,421
Discount to retire ($1,000,000 × 4%)	40,000
Total gain	$ 92,421

Journal entry:

DR	Bonds payable	$1,000,000	
DR	Premium on bond payable	52,421	
CR	Cash		$ 960,000
CR	Gain on extinguishment of bonds		92,421

7 Lessee Accounting

1 Overview

1.1 Definitions

Leases are used by public and private entities as a means of gaining access to assets and reducing their exposure to the full risks of asset ownership. A lease is defined as a contractual agreement between a *lessor* who conveys the right to use real or personal property (an asset) and a *lessee* who agrees to pay consideration for this right over a specific period of time. In order for a contract to be a lease or contain a lease, *both* of the criteria below must be met.

- The contract must depend on an identifiable asset. There is no identifiable asset if the supplier (lessor) has a substantive substitution right. The right to substitute an asset is substantive if:

    - the supplier has the ability to substitute alternative assets throughout the period of use (rather than at a specified point in time); and

    - the supplier would benefit economically from the substitution.

    If these conditions are met, the customer would not have the right to control the use of the specific asset, and the contract would not be considered a lease. On the other hand, the supplier's right or obligation to substitute an asset for repairs or maintenance is not considered a substantive substitution right because it does not prevent the customer from having the right to use an identified asset.

- The contract must convey the right to control the use of the asset over the lease term to the lessee. The lessee will have the right to obtain substantially all of the economic benefits from using the asset and have the right to direct its use.

Illustration 1   Definition of a Lease

Bentley Corp. has a written agreement in place to allow Riggs Inc. to use scientific equipment with a book value of $75,000 for the next five years. Bentley does not have the substantive right to replace the equipment during the term and Riggs is able to use the asset as it wishes for the next five years while keeping any cash inflows associated with outputs from the equipment.

This is an example of a lease, as there is a contract in place that defines the asset itself, recognizes that Bentley does not have a *substantive* substitution right, and provides Riggs with the economic benefits of and direction for the use of the asset.

---

2   Lease Contracts

2.1   Lease vs. Nonlease Components

The decision as to whether a contract is a lease or contains a lease must be made at contract inception, and only may be reassessed if the terms and conditions of the contract change. As noted earlier, for a contract or a portion of a contract to be considered a lease, the contract must include an identified asset and must convey the right to control this asset.

Once the determination is made that the contract is or contains a lease, the lessee must:

- assess whether multiple contracts should be combined;

- identify the separate lease components within a given contract (or combined contracts); and

- if applicable, determine whether separate lease components within the contract should be combined or separated from any related nonlease components.

2.1.1   Combining Contracts

For accounting purposes, contracts should be combined if they meet *all* of the following criteria.

- One or more contracts contains or is a lease.

- The contracts are entered into at approximately the same time.

- The parties to the contract are the same, or are related parties.

- One or more of the following:

  - Performance or price of one contract affects the consideration paid in the other contract(s).

  - The contracts have the same commercial objectives and were negotiated as part of a package.

  - Regarding the use of underlying assets, the rights to use them do not meet the accounting criteria for separate lease components (thereby resulting in a single lease component).

2.1.2   Separate Lease Components

Accounting for separate lease components from a lessee perspective is a two-step process.

Step 1: Identify each right to use an underlying asset within the contract.

- One right to use an asset = One separate lease component.

- More than one right to use an asset = Lessee must determine whether each right equates to a separate lease component for accounting purposes.

  - Separate if *both* are met:

    —The right benefits the lessee either on a stand-alone basis or together with other resources that are readily available to the lessee.

    —Rights are neither highly dependent on each other nor highly interrelated.

Note: The right to use land should be accounted for as a separate lease component unless the accounting effect of doing so would be insignificant.

Step 2: For a contract that includes both lease and nonlease components, the lessee has two options:

Option 1	Option 2
Lease components are separate units of account from nonlease components.	Each separate lease component is combined with related nonlease components into one unit of account.

2.2 Contract Allocations

Consideration associated with a contract is calculated as:

All components of lease payments	+	Other required payments in contract	−	Incentives owed/provided to lessee not accounted for in lease payments

If Option 1 described above is chosen, contract consideration can be allocated to the separate lease and nonlease components based on relative stand-alone prices. If Option 2 above is chosen, contract consideration will be allocated to each combined unit of account based on relative stand-alone prices. Observable stand-alone prices are the preference, but if those are not available, estimated prices may be used.

Example 1   Combining Contracts

Facts: Fast Science leases two electron microscopes to a university for four years each. Microscope FE is leased for monthly payments of $7,750 and comes with maintenance services. Microscope SQ is leased for monthly payments of $8,600 and also comes with maintenance services. Stand-alone prices for each unit are listed below, with price differentials reflecting the difference in microscope power offered at two distinct university locations.

Unit	Stand-alone Price
Microscope FE	$400,000
Microscope SQ	450,000
Maintenance, FE	30,000
Maintenance, SQ	35,000
	$915,000

The university will not pay maintenance fees for the microscopes outside of the agreed upon monthly payments noted above.

(continued)

(continued)

Required: Calculate the consideration allocation under a scenario in which (1) the lease and nonlease components are treated separately; and (2) the lease and related nonlease components are combined into a single unit of account.

Solution:

Scenario 1:

The consideration total of $784,800 equals the two monthly payments of $7,750 and $8,600 (total of $16,350) multiplied by 48 months. The stand-alone prices are used to determine the relative percentage values, and those values are each multiplied by $784,800 to determine the allocation. (Note that the percentages have been rounded.)

Unit	Stand-alone Price	Relative Value— Stand-alone Price	Consideration Allocation
Microscope FE	$400,000	44%	$345,312
Microscope SQ	450,000	49%	384,552
Maintenance, FE	30,000	3%	23,544
Maintenance, SQ	35,000	4%	31,392
	$915,000	**100%**	**$784,800**

Scenario 2:

The same logic is applied here that was applied in Scenario 1, except the microscope and the related maintenance are combined for each individual microscope.

Unit	Stand-alone Price	Relative Value— Stand-alone Price	Consideration Allocation
FE: Microscope and Maintenance	$430,000	47%	$368,856
SQ: Microscope and Maintenance	485,000	53%	415,944
	$915,000	**100%**	**$784,800**

3 Lease Classification as Operating or Finance

Leases transfer substantially all of the benefits and direct the use of the identified asset to the lessee throughout the period of use.

- This is an accounting transaction, which is in substance an installment purchase in the form of a leasing arrangement.

- The lessee accounts for a lease as either an operating or a finance lease, reflective of the acquisition of both an asset and a related liability.

Based on the criteria described below, a lease will be considered either an operating or a finance lease.

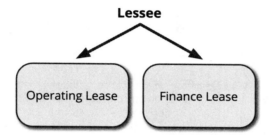

3.1 Criteria

At the onset of a lease, the lessee must determine whether the lease will be classified as an operating lease or a finance lease. The assessment, based on a defined set of criteria, shown below, will focus on whether the lessee will in effect assume control of the underlying asset.

The criteria below are applicable to lessors and lessees. If any one of the five criteria is met, the lease will be classified as a finance lease by the lessee.

- **Ownership** of the underlying asset transfers from the lessor to the lessee by the end of the lease term.

- The lessee has the **written option** to purchase the underlying asset; the option is one that the lessee is "reasonably certain" to exercise.

- The **net present** value of all lease payments and any guaranteed residual value equals or exceeds substantially all of the underlying asset's fair value.

- The term of the lease represents the major part of the **economic life** remaining for the underlying asset.

- The asset is **specialized** such that it will not have an expected, alternative use to the lessor when the lease term ends.

If none of the above criteria are met, or if the lease is considered short term (less than 12 months), it should be treated as an operating lease by the lessee.

3.2   Lessee Decision Tree

In applying the **OWNES** criteria to determine whether a lease should be treated as a finance or an operating lease, the following tree can be used:

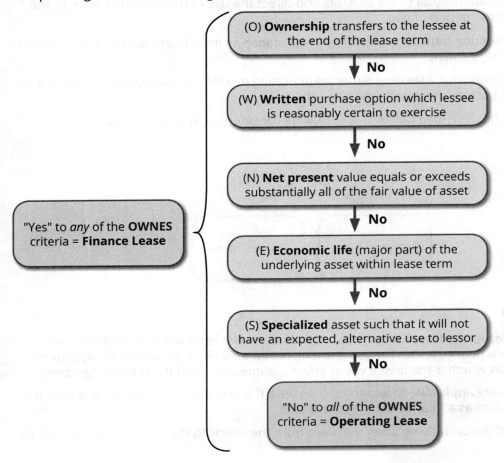

3.3   Quantitative Approach

Although the criteria above do not provide specific, quantitative thresholds for assessing "substantially exceeds" and "major part" determinations, previous FASB guidance can serve as a reasonable approach to determining whether these thresholds are met.

For the **N** criteria, 90 percent or more of the fair value of the underlying asset would reasonably be considered "substantial." For the **E** criteria, a "major part" of the remaining economic life of the asset would reasonably be considered 75 percent or more.

In addition, for the purposes of determining whether a lease commences at or near the end of the underlying asset's economic life, a theoretically reasonable approach would be to use a threshold of 25 percent or less of the underlying asset's total economic life.

Illustration 2   Finance Lease Criteria

An entity leases equipment with a fair value of $3,500. Lease payments of $1,000 per year are due annually on December 31. The lease term is four years and the asset life is 10 years. The entity's incremental borrowing rate is 10 percent. The lease does not transfer ownership, there is no purchase option, and the asset is not specialized.

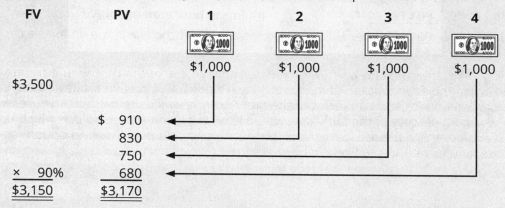

FV	PV	1	2	3	4
		$1,000	$1,000	$1,000	$1,000
$3,500					
	$ 910				
	830				
	750				
× 90%	680				
$3,150	$3,170				

This lease is accounted for as a finance lease because the present value of the minimum lease payments ($3,170) is greater than 90 percent of the fair value ($3,500 × 90% = $3,150) of the leased equipment.

Pass Key

Assuming that a lease is greater than 12 months in duration, the determination of how a lessee accounts for a lease is based on the **OWNES** criteria.

- **Finance Lease:** At least one of the **OWNES** criteria is met.
- **Operating Lease:** None of the **OWNES** criteria are met.

Example 2	Lease Classification

Facts: Landen leases furniture with an economic life of nine years to Haley Inc. for seven years, beginning July 1, Year 1. The present value of the lease payments and residual value are approximately 80 percent of the fair value of the asset. Ownership does not transfer to Haley at the end of the lease and there is no option for Haley to purchase the furniture after the period of seven years ends.

Required: Determine whether Haley will likely account for the lease as a finance lease or an operating lease.

Solution: A seven-year lease on furniture with a nine-year economic life would equate to 78 percent of the economic life of the asset, which would likely result in Haley classifying the lease as a finance lease. In terms of the other criteria which are not met, the present value, worth 80 percent of the fair value, would likely fall below a threshold at which Haley would consider this a finance lease. Also, there is no ownership transfer, no option to purchase, and furniture is unlikely to be specialized.

4 Calculating Leases

4.1 Lease Term

The "commencement date" for a lease is the date for which the lessor makes the underlying asset available to the lessee for use. The lease term begins on this date and extends to the end of the noncancelable period (the period in which the lessee's right is enforceable) for which the lessee has the right to use the underlying asset. A lease that can be terminated by both parties with only minor penalties results in a non-enforceable lease.

An option to terminate exists when one or the other (but not both) has the right to terminate. The lease term will also need to account for any options to extend or terminate the lease as follows:

- Periods covered by an option to extend the lease are included if the lessee is reasonably certain to exercise that option.

- Periods covered by an option to terminate the lease are included if the lessee is reasonably certain not to exercise that option.

- Periods covered by an option to either extend (or not to terminate) the lease are included if the exercise is controlled by the lessor.

Lessees must recognize right-of-use (ROU) assets and lease liabilities for all leases that are not considered short term. In order to qualify as short term, the lease will have a term of 12 months or less and there cannot be an option for the lessee to purchase the underlying asset which the lessee is reasonably certain to exercise. These short-term leases will qualify as operating leases and the lessee will recognize payments over the lease term on a straight-line basis.

4.2 Lease Payments

In the calculation of the lease payments, the lessee will *include* all of the following.

- **Required contractual fixed payments** (which will include any variable payments that are "in-substance" fixed payments) less any lease incentives paid or payable to the lessee.

- **Exercise option reasonably assured:** the exercise price of an option, which gives the lessee the right to purchase the underlying asset (if it is "reasonably certain" that the lessee will exercise this option).

- **Purchase price at the end of lease:** the stated purchase price of the underlying asset at the end of the lease term (when the lessor has the option to require the lessee to purchase the underlying asset).

- **Only indexed or rate variable payments:** No increase or decrease to future lease payments should be assumed based on increases or decreases in the index or rate. Instead, any difference in the payments due to changes in the index or rate are expensed in the period incurred.

- **Residual guarantees likely to be owed:** The lessee includes the full amount of the residual value guarantee at the end of the lease term in the present value test. The lessee does not consider unguaranteed residual value as part of the present value test.

- **Termination penalties reasonably assured:** Any penalty due from the lessee upon lease termination (the lease term must reflect the lessee exercising an option to terminate the lease).

Lessee lease payments *may or may not* include the following (at the lessee's option):

- **Nonlease** components: amounts allocated to nonlease components of a contract.

Lessee lease payments will specifically *exclude* the following.

- **Guarantees of lessor debt by lessee**

- **Other variable lease payments:** other than those noted above.

Illustration 3   Lease Payments (Included Payments)

Sterling is a lessee for a piece of moveable equipment with a useful life of eight years. Along with the equipment, the lessor is providing scheduled maintenance and upkeep that is accounted for separately from the lease. The terms of the lease include the following: a three-year lease with monthly fixed payments of $3,450 (with the first four months free to the lessee); an option to purchase the asset for $12,500 at the end of the lease, which Sterling is unlikely to exercise; and $8,000 allocated to the maintenance and upkeep component of the agreement.

Lease payments will include the $3,450 in monthly fixed payments for 32 total months (36-month lease with the first four months free). The option to purchase for $12,500 is not included because Sterling is unlikely to exercise the option. The $8,000 allocated to the maintenance and upkeep portion of the contract is also not included in the lease payments.

Illustration 4	Lease Payments (Excluded Payments)

Bowden Corp. is the lessee for two separate lease arrangements. Lease A involves monthly payments that are based on changes in the consumer price index (CPI). Lease B involves monthly lease payments that are based entirely on Bowden's use of the leased asset.

For Bowden, the calculation of the lease payment for Lease A will include the variable monthly payments because they are based on an index/rate. For Lease B, the payments will be recognized as expenses in the period incurred and not included in the lease payments calculation because they are contingent on asset usage, which can fluctuate significantly each period.

4.3 Discount Rate

When calculating the present value of the minimum lease payments, the lessor will use the rate implicit in the lease. The lessee uses either:

- the rate implicit in the lease (if known) or, if this rate is not readily determinable,
- the incremental borrowing rate of the lessee (the rate the lessee would be charged for a collateralized loan with equal payments and a similar lease term to the lease).

4.4 Initial Direct Costs

Initial direct costs will be included in the valuation of the ROU asset. These costs are only incurred as a result of the execution of the lease. Any costs incurred prior to signing the lease, which can include lease term negotiations, document preparation, credit checks, etc., are not included in the accounting for direct costs.

5 Lessee Accounting

As noted previously, when a lease commences, the lessee must evaluate the contract to determine whether a lease should be classified as a finance lease or an operating lease.

5.1 Operating Leases

If the lease is an operating lease, the balance sheet will reflect a right-of-use (ROU) asset and lease liability and both will be amortized over the life of the lease using the effective interest method. The ROU asset and lease liability amounts are calculated using the present value of the lease payments, using the appropriate discount rate. On the income statement, lease expense will be recognized each year over the lease term using the straight-line method for expense measurement. Instead of reporting interest expense on the income statement, the lessee will report the interest as part of lease expense.

Pass Key

When calculating the present value of the lease payments for the purpose of calculating the ROU asset and lease liability, keep in mind the following:

Periodic payment

- Beginning of period = PV of an annuity due
- End of period = PV of an annuity *(in arrears/ordinary)*

Purchase option

Or:

Guaranteed residual

- PV of $1

Note: Although leases generally require payment at the beginning of the period (first payment at lease inception), some CPA Exam questions state that the lease payments are made at the end of each period. Read each question carefully to determine whether you are dealing with an annuity due (payment at the beginning of each period) or an ordinary annuity (payment at the end of each period) and be sure to use the correct present value factors.

Initial Entry:

DR	ROU asset	$XXX	
CR	Lease liability		$XXX

Subsequent Entries:

DR	Lease expense	$XXX	
CR	Cash/lease liability		$XXX

DR	Lease liability	$XXX	
CR	Accumulated amortization—ROU asset		$XXX

Example 3   Reporting an Operating Lease: Lessee's Books

Facts: On January 1, Year 2, a lessee enters into a three-year asset operating (capital) lease with annual payments of $18,000 per year. The first payment will be made December 31 and the interest rate implicit in the lease is 5.75 percent. (The present value of an ordinary annuity for three years at 5.75% = 2.685424.)

Required: Prepare the journal entries for the lessee at the commencement date, the end of Year 2, the end of Year 3, and the end of Year 4.

Solution:

January 1, Year 2, journal entry:

The present value of $18,000 for three years (first payment made at the end of Year 1) at a rate of 5.75 percent per year is equal to $48,338.

DR	ROU asset	$48,338	
CR	Lease liability		$48,338

Date	Lease Liability	Lease Expense	Interest Expense	Reduction in ROU Asset	Carrying Value of ROU Asset
	$48,338				$48,338
12/31/Year 2	$33,117	$18,000	$2,779	$15,221	$33,117
12/31/Year 3	$17,021	$18,000	$1,904	$16,096	$17,021
12/31/Year 4	–	$18,000	$ 979	$17,021	–

Note: Because this is an operating lease, interest expense is not separately recorded on the income statement. Rather, interest expense is included in the total "lease expense" recorded in the income statement on the lessee's books.

December 31, Year 2, journal entry:

The lease payment of $18,000 comprises interest expense and the amortization of the ROU asset, as calculated in the table above.

DR	Lease expense	$18,000	
DR	Lease liability	15,221	
CR	Cash		$18,000
CR	Accumulated amortization—ROU asset		15,221

(continued)

(continued)

December 31, Year 3, journal entry:

DR	Lease expense	$18,000	
DR	Lease liability	16,096	
CR	Cash		$18,000
CR	Accumulated amortization—ROU asset		16,096

December 31, Year 4, journal entry:

DR	Lease expense	$18,000	
DR	Lease liability	17,021	
CR	Cash		$18,000
CR	Accumulated amortization—ROU asset		17,021

Once the final entry has been recorded, the ROU asset is fully amortized.

5.2 Finance Leases

If the lease is a finance lease, the lessee will recognize both an ROU asset and a corresponding liability on its balance sheet. The liability will equal the present value of lease payments owed. The ROU asset will include initial direct costs (such as commissions paid, legal and consulting fees, etc.) that were incurred as a result of the lease execution, as well as any lease payments made by the lessee to the lessor at or before lease commencement. Any incentives received by the lessee from the lessor will reduce the value of the asset.

Initial Entry:

DR	ROU asset	$XXX	
CR	Lease liability		$XXX

Subsequent Entries:

DR	Interest expense	$XXX	
DR	Lease liability	XXX	
CR	Cash/lease payable		$XXX

DR	Amortization expense	$XXX	
CR	Accumulated amortization—ROU asset		$XXX

Unlike with operating (capital) leases, the amortization of the ROU asset for a finance lease will be expensed based on how the entity recognizes amortization expense on similar assets.

Example 4   Reporting a Finance Lease: Lessee's Books

Facts: On January 1, Year 2, a lessee enters into a three-year asset lease with annual payments of $18,000 per year. The first payment will be made December 31 and the interest rate implicit in the lease is 5.75 percent. The lease qualifies as a finance lease.

Required: Assuming straight-line amortization, prepare the journal entries for the lessee at the commencement date, the end of Year 2, the end of Year 3, and the end of Year 4.

Solution:

January 1, Year 2, journal entry:

The present value of $18,000 for three years (first payment made at the end of Year 1) at a rate of 5.75 percent per year is equal to $48,338.

DR	ROU asset	$48,338	
CR	Lease liability		$48,338

Date	Lease Liability	Total Lease Expense	Interest Expense*	Amortization Expense	Carrying Value of ROU Asset
	$48,338				$48,338
12/31/Year 2	$33,117	$18,892	$2,779	$16,113	$32,225
12/31/Year 3	$17,021	$18,017	$1,904	$16,113	$16,112
12/31/Year 4	–	$17,091	$ 979	$16,112	–

*5.75% on liability.

Total lease expense is the sum of interest expense and amortization expense recorded through the journal entries below.

December 31, Year 2, journal entries:

The lease payment of $18,000 comprises interest expense and the reduction of the lease liability as calculated in the table above. The ROU asset will be amortized at $48,338 over three years, or 16,113 per year.

DR	Interest expense	$ 2,779	
DR	Lease liability	15,221	
CR	Cash		$18,000

DR	Amortization expense	16,113	
CR	Accumulated amortization—ROU asset		16,113

(continued)

(continued)

December 31, Year 3, journal entries:

DR	Interest expense	$ 1,904	
DR	Lease liability	16,096	
CR	Cash		$18,000
DR	Amortization expense	16,113	
CR	Accumulated amortization—ROU asset		16,113

December 31, Year 4, journal entries:

DR	Interest expense	$ 979	
DR	Lease liability	17,021	
CR	Cash		$18,000
DR	Amortization expense	16,112	
CR	Accumulated amortization—ROU asset		16,112

Once the final entry has been recorded, the ROU asset is fully amortized.

Example 5 — Reporting a Lease: Combining Contracts

Facts: On January 1, Year 5, a lessee enters into an eight-year asset finance lease with an option to extend for four years, which the lessee is unlikely to exercise. Initial lease payments are $35,000 per year for the first eight years (with payments on January 1 each year, beginning in Year 5) and then $40,000 per year if the lease is extended. Initial direct costs incurred by the lessee are $12,000. The interest rate implicit in the lease is 4.5 percent, and the lessee's incremental borrowing rate is 5.0 percent.

Required: Prepare the journal entry for the lessee at the commencement date.

Solution: Cash payouts of $35,000 for the first lease payment and $12,000 for the initial direct costs are recorded, as well as the present value of the seven remaining lease payments. The lease liability is equal to the present value of $35,000 per year for the next seven years at an interest rate of 4.5 percent (the rate implicit in the lease should be chosen as the discount rate, if known). Because the company is unlikely to extend the lease, the four years are not considered in the calculation amount. Seven payments of $35,000 at a rate of 4.5 percent equals a present value of $206,245. The ROU asset will be the combination of these three items.

DR	ROU asset	$253,245	
CR	Lease liability		$206,245
CR	Cash		47,000*

*$35,000 initial payment plus $12,000 initial direct costs.

Example 6   Reporting a Finance Lease: Amortization

Facts: On January 1, Year 5, a lessee enters into an eight-year asset finance lease with an option to extend for four years, which the lessee is unlikely to exercise. Initial lease payments are $35,000 per year for the first eight years (with payments on January 1 each year, beginning in Year 5) and then $40,000 if the lease is extended. Initial direct costs incurred by the lessee are $12,000. The interest rate implicit in the lease is 4.5 percent, and the lessee's incremental borrowing rate is 5.0 percent.

Required: Calculate interest expense, the amortization of the liability, the amortization of the asset (assuming straight-line), and total lease expense for Year 6. (When the first lease payment of $35,000 is made January 1, Year 5, the lease liability is immediately reduced from $241,245 to $206,245.)

Solution:

Date	Lease Payment	Interest (4.5% on Liability)	Reduction of Lease Liability	Lease Liability
1/1/Year 5	$35,000	$ 0	$35,000	$206,245
1/1/Year 6	$35,000	$9,281	$25,719	$180,526
1/1/Year 7	$35,000	$8,124	$26,876	$153,650
1/1/Year 8	$35,000	$6,914	$28,086	$125,564
1/1/Year 9	$35,000	$5,650	$29,350	$ 96,214
1/1/Year 10	$35,000	$4,330	$30,670	$ 65,544
1/1/Year 11	$35,000	$2,949	$32,051	$ 33,493
1/1/Year 12	$35,000	$1,507	$33,493	$ (0)

The payment made on January 1, Year 7, represents interest expense accrued during Year 6. Year 6 interest expense of $8,124 is equal to the lease liability balance as of 1/1/Year 6 ($180,526) multiplied by the interest rate of 4.5 percent. The reduction of the liability of $26,876 attributable to Year 6 is equal to the difference between the lease payment of $35,000 and the interest expense of $8,124. The asset, worth $253,245 on the lessee's books, will be depreciated over eight years at $31,656 per year. Total lease expense for Year 6 will be equal to $39,780 ($8,124 + $31,656).

In the early years of a finance lease, expense recognition is front-loaded as interest expense, plus asset amortization expense will create a higher total expense than under an operating (capital) lease. In later years, a finance lease will reflect a lower total expense than an operating lease. The overall expense total across the entire lease will be the same under both lease types.

5.3   Accounting Policy Election

Lessees can make an accounting policy election and choose to not recognize ROU assets and lease liabilities for leases with terms of 12 months or less. If this election is made, it must be done by the class of the underlying asset and cannot include purchase options for the asset the lessee is reasonably certain to exercise.

6   Financial Statement Presentation

6.1   Balance Sheet

ROU assets and associated lease liabilities may either be recognized as separate line items on the balance sheet (in their respective sections) or included with other assets/liabilities and disclosed separately in the notes to the financial statements (indicating which line items in the balance sheet include them). The portion of lease liabilities due within a year or the operating cycle, whichever is longer, should be reported in the current section and the remainder in the long-term section. Finance and operating lease ROU assets and lease liabilities cannot be presented together. The ROU asset will be amortized, and the lease liability will be paid down over the life of the lease.

The ROU asset will be amortized beginning on the commencement date using a straight-line basis (unless another methodology better reflects usage and consumption).

■ Criteria for determining amortization:

- Amortize over the underlying asset's useful life if **ownership** or **written option** criteria are met.

- Amortize over shorter of the lease term or the useful life of the asset if **net present value**, **economic life**, or **specialized asset** criteria are met.

Illustration 5   Finance Lease: Amortization

Cooper Industries leases a boat for five years from Kirkland Inc. There is no ownership transfer at the end of the lease, and Cooper has not been given an option to purchase the boat. The present value of the lease payments is equivalent to the boat's fair value, and the boat has an accounting useful life of seven years. On Cooper's books, this will qualify as a finance lease because of the equivalence of the present value of the lease payments to the boat's fair value (the **N** criteria is met). The ROU asset will be amortized over five years because this is the lesser of the useful life of the asset (seven years) and the lease term (five years).

6.2   Income Statement

For operating leases, lease expense will be included in income from continuing operations on the lessee's income statement. For finance leases, the income statement will include the amortization of the ROU asset and the portion of the lease expense related to interest on the lease liability.

6.3   Cash Flow Statement

For operating leases, lease payments (which include all variable lease payments) are classified as cash flow from operations. Payments for short-term leases are also included in cash flow from operations. Any payments needed to bring the asset to a condition and location in preparation for its intended use are considered investing activities.

For finance leases, the principal portion of the lease payment is a cash flow from financing, the interest portion of the lease payment is a cash flow from operations, and any variable lease payments and short-term lease payments not included in the lease liability are classified as cash flows from operations.

CFO	CFI	CFF
Operating Leases		
Lease payments	Preparing asset for intended use	
Variable lease payments		
Short-term lease payments		
Finance Leases		
Interest payments		Principal payments
Variable and short-term lease payments not included in the lease liability		

7   Lessee Disclosures

7.1   Lessee Disclosures

A lessee will have to disclose several qualitative pieces of information, including:

- information about the nature of the leases, including any restrictions or covenants;
- basis for determination of variable lease payments;
- options to extend or terminate (existence, terms, conditions);
- residual value guarantees (existence, terms, conditions);
- information on leases that have not commenced but create significant obligations and/or rights for the lessee;
- significant assumptions and judgments made in application (including determination of whether a contract contains a lease, allocation of consideration between lease and nonlease components, discount rate determination, etc.);
- sale-leaseback terms and conditions; and
- the entity's accounting policy related to short-term leases and practical expedients used to combine lease and nonlease components.

Quantitative disclosures will include:

- finance lease costs (separated between the amortization of ROU assets and interest on lease liabilities);
- operating lease costs;
- short-term lease costs;
- variable lease costs;
- cash payments for lease liabilities segregated between operating and financing cash flows;
- supplemental noncash information on lease liabilities due to obtaining ROU assets;
- the weighted average remaining lease term and discount rate; and
- separate maturity analyses for operating and finance lease liabilities for five years.

NOTES

FAR

5

Investments, Statement of Cash Flows, and Income Taxes

Module

1 Financial Instruments Overview

1.1 Financial Assets and Financial Liabilities

Financial instruments include financial assets and financial liabilities.

1.1.1 Financial Assets

The following are financial assets:

- Cash (e.g., demand deposits and foreign currencies)

- Evidence of an ownership interest in an entity (e.g., stock certificates, partnership interests, and LLC interests)

- A contract that conveys to one entity a right to:

    - receive cash or another financial instrument from a second entity (e.g., bond investments, notes receivable); or

    - exchange other financial instruments on potentially favorable terms with the second entity (e.g., stock options, futures/forward contracts, and other derivatives).

1.1.2 Financial Liabilities

A financial liability is a contract that imposes on one entity an obligation to:

- deliver cash or another financial instrument to a second entity (e.g., bond obligations, notes payable); or

- exchange other financial instruments on potentially unfavorable terms with the second entity (e.g., stock options, futures/forward contracts, and other derivatives).

1.2 Fair Value Option

On specified election dates, entities may choose to measure at fair value eligible financial instruments that are not typically measured at fair value. Under the fair value option, unrealized gains and losses are reported in earnings. The fair value option is irrevocable and is applied to individual financial instruments.

1.2.1 Eligible Financial Instruments

Entities may elect the fair value option for recognized financial assets and financial liabilities. For example, an entity can choose to measure at fair value a debt investment that would otherwise be classified as available-for-sale, with unrealized gains and losses recorded in earnings rather than in OCI. Or an entity can choose to measure at fair value an equity investment that would otherwise be accounted for using the equity method.

Financial instruments not eligible for the fair value option include investments in subsidiaries or VIEs that an entity is required to consolidate, pension benefit assets or liabilities, financial assets or liabilities recognized under leases, deposit liabilities of financial institutions, and financial instruments classified as equity.

1.2.2 Fair Value Changes Attributable to Instrument-Specific Credit Risk

For financial liabilities other than derivative liabilities that are designated under the fair value option, the portion of the change in fair value that relates to a change in instrument-specific credit risk is recognized in other comprehensive income. Derivative liabilities recognize these changes in net income. Once the financial liability is derecognized, any accumulated gains or losses in other comprehensive income are recognized in earnings.

1.2.3 Election Dates

The fair value option may only be applied on certain dates, including the date that an entity first recognizes an eligible financial instrument, the date that an investment becomes subject to equity method accounting, or the date that an entity ceases to consolidate an investment in a subsidiary or VIE.

2 Investments in Debt Securities

2.1 Debt Securities

A debt security is any security representing a creditor relationship with an entity.

- Debt securities include:
  - Corporate bonds
  - Redeemable preferred stock
  - Government securities
  - Convertible debt
  - Commercial paper
- Debt securities do not include:
  - Option, futures, or forward contracts
  - Lease contracts
  - Accounts and notes receivable

2.2 Classification

Debt securities should be classified into one of three categories, based on the intent of the company.

2.2.1 Trading Securities

Trading securities are debt securities that are bought and held principally for the purpose of selling them in the near term. Trading securities generally reflect active and frequent buying and selling with the objective of generating profits on short-term differences in price. Debt securities classified as trading securities are generally reported as current assets, although they can be reported as non-current, if appropriate.

2.2.2 Available-for-Sale Debt Securities

Available-for-sale debt securities are those not meeting the definitions of the other two classifications (trading or held-to-maturity). Debt securities classified as available-for-sale securities are reported as either current assets or non-current assets, depending on the intent of the corporation.

2.2.3   Held-to-Maturity Debt Securities

Investments in debt securities are classified as held-to-maturity only if the corporation has the positive intent and ability to hold these securities to maturity. If the intent is to hold the security for an indefinite period of time, but not necessarily to maturity, then the security is classified as available-for-sale. If a security can be paid or otherwise settled in a manner that the holder may not recover substantially all of its investment, the held-to-maturity classification may not be used. Securities classified as held-to-maturity are reported as current or non-current assets, based on their time to maturity.

2.3   Valuation

2.3.1   Debt Securities Reported at Fair Value

Debt securities classified as trading and available-for-sale must be reported at fair value. Fair value is the market price of the security or what a willing buyer and seller would pay and accept to exchange the security. Changes in the fair value of trading and available-for-sale debt securities result in unrealized holdings gains or losses. The reporting of these gains or losses in the financial statements depends on the classification of the securities. Although two general ledger accounts are normally maintained (i.e., one for the original cost of the security and the other for the valuation account), the presentation on the balance sheet is one *net* amount.

- **Unrealized Gains and Losses (Trading Securities):** Unrealized holding gains and losses on debt securities classified as trading securities are included in earnings. Therefore, the unrealized gain or loss on trading securities is recognized in net income.

  Journal entry to record loss in net income:

DR	Unrealized loss on trading securities	$XXX	
CR	Valuation account (fair value adjustment)		$XXX

- **Unrealized Gains and Losses (Available-for-Sale Debt Securities):** Unrealized holding gains and losses on available-for-sale securities are recognized in other comprehensive income.

  Journal entry to record unrealized loss in other comprehensive income:

DR	Unrealized loss on available-for-sale securities	$XXX	
CR	Valuation account (fair value adjustment)		$XXX

- **Realized Gains and Losses:** Realized gains or losses are recognized when a debt security is sold and when an available-for-sale debt security is deemed to be impaired. All realized gains or losses are recognized in net income.

2.3.2   Financial Assets Reported at Amortized Cost

Held-to-maturity debt securities are reported at amortized cost. Unrealized gains and losses on held-to-maturity securities are not recognized in the financial statements, as held-to-maturity securities are not marked-to-market at period end.

Classification	Balance Sheet	Reported	Unrealized Gain/Loss	Cash Flow
Trading	Current or non-current	Fair value	Net income	Operating or investing*
Available-for-sale	Current or non-current	Fair value	Other comprehensive income	Investing
Held-to-maturity	Current or non-current	Amortized cost	None	Investing

* Under U.S. GAAP, trading debt security transactions are classified in operating cash flows or investing cash flows based on the nature and purpose for which the securities were acquired. If trading debt securities are classified as non-current on the balance sheet, then trading debt security transactions will be reported as investing cash flows. If trading debt securities are classified as current on the balance sheet, then trading debt security transactions will be reported as operating cash flows.

2.4   Reclassification

Transfers between categories should occur only when justified. Transfers from the held-to-maturity category should be rare and should only be made when there is a change in the entity's intent to hold a specific security to maturity that does not call into question the entity's intent to hold other debt securities to maturity. Transfers to and from the trading category should also be rare.

Any transfer of a particular security from one group (trading, available-for-sale, or held-to-maturity) to another group (trading, available-for-sale, or held-to-maturity) is accounted for at fair value. Any unrealized holding gain or loss on that security is accounted for as follows:

- **From Trading Category:** The unrealized holding gain or loss at the date of transfer is already recognized in earnings and shall not be reversed.

- **To Trading Category:** The unrealized holding gain or loss at the date of transfer shall be recognized in earnings immediately.

- **Held-to-Maturity Transferred to Available-for-Sale:** The unrealized holding gain or loss at the date of transfer shall be reported in other comprehensive income. Remember that this debt security was valued at amortized cost as a held-to-maturity security and is being transferred to a category valued at fair value.

- **Available-for-Sale Transferred to Held-to-Maturity:** The unrealized holding gain or loss at the date of transfer is already reported in other comprehensive income. The unrealized holding gain or loss shall be amortized over the remaining life of the security as an adjustment of yield in a manner consistent with the amortization of any premium or discount.

Summary of Transfers Between Categories			
From	*To*	*Transfer Acct. For*	*Unrealized Holding Gain/Loss*
Trading	Any other	FV	It has already been recognized in income so no adjustment is necessary
Any other	Trading	FV	Recognized in current earnings
Held-to-maturity	Available-for-sale	FV	Record in other comprehensive income
Available-for-sale	Held-to-maturity	FV	Amortize gain or loss from other comprehensive income with any bond premium/discount amortization

2.5   Income From Investments in Debt Securities

Interest income from an investment in debt securities classified as trading or available-for-sale is recorded on the income statement.

Journal entry to record interest income:

DR	Cash	$XXX	
CR	Interest income		$XXX

2.6   Impairment of Debt Securities

Under the current expected credit losses (CECL) model, available-for-sale debt securities and held-to-maturity debt securities should be reported at the net amount expected to be collected using an allowance for expected credit losses. Expected credit losses are determined based on current conditions, past experience, and future expectations. A credit loss is recognized as a current period expense on the income statement and as an offsetting allowance on the balance sheet. Increases and decreases in expected credit losses are reflected on the income statement in the period incurred when the estimate of expected credit losses changes.

2.6.1   Impairment of Held-to-Maturity Securities

If it is determined that all amounts due (principal and interest) will not be collected on a debt investment reported at amortized cost, the investment should be reported at the present value of the principal and interest that is expected to be collected. The credit loss is the difference between the present value and the amortized cost.

Example 1	Held-to-Maturity Security Impairment

Facts: On January 2, Year 3, TGPO Co. purchased a $500,000, four-year bond at par with annual interest at 4.25 percent paid on December 31 each year. TGPO classified the investment as held-to-maturity. At the end of Year 3, TGPO received the full interest payment of $21,250, but determined that it would only collect $11,500 each year in interest for the remaining three years (along with the face value of $500,000 at maturity).

Present value of $1 at 4.25 percent for three periods = 0.88262

Present value of an ordinary annuity of 1 at 4.25 percent for three periods = 2.76198

Required: Prepare the entry that TGPO will record at the end of Year 3 to recognize the impairment.

(continued)

(continued)

Solution:

The first step is to calculate the present value as of December 31, Year 3.

Present value:

Interest payments: $11,500 × 2.76198 = $31,763

Principal payment: $500,000 × 0.88262 = $441,310

Total present value = $473,073

The credit loss is calculated as: Present value − Amortized cost = $473,073 − $500,000 = ($26,927)

The journal entry will be as follows:

DR	Credit loss	$26,927	
CR	Allowance for credit losses		$26,927

2.6.2 Impairment of Available-for-Sale Debt Securities

Impairment on available-for-sale securities is accounted for differently from impairment on held-to-maturity securities, because the investor has the option to sell an available-for-sale security if the loss on the sale will be less than the expected credit loss. As a result, the credit loss reported in net income on an available-for-sale security is limited to the amount by which fair value is below amortized cost. Any additional loss is reported as an unrealized loss in other comprehensive income.

Example 2	Available-for-Sale Security Impairment

Facts: The same facts as in Example 1, except the investment is an available-for-sale debt security.

Required: Determine the expected credit loss and/or unrealized holding gain/loss to be recognized on December 31, Year 3, for each of the following fair-value scenarios, and prepare the journal entry for each scenario.

Scenario 1: $510,000 fair value

Scenario 2: $480,000 fair value

Scenario 3: $450,000 fair value

(continued)

(continued)

Solution:

	Scenario 1	Scenario 2	Scenario 3
Amortized cost, 1/2/Year 3	$500,000	$500,000	$500,000
Fair value, 12/31/Year 3	$510,000	$480,000	$450,000
Expected credit loss*	$26,927	$26,927	$26,927
Expected credit loss (net income)	0	$20,000	$26,927
Unrealized gain (OCI)	$10,000	0	0
Unrealized loss (OCI)	0	0	$23,073

* The expected credit loss is the difference between present value and amortized cost, calculated as shown in Example 1 for the held-to-maturity debt security.

For Scenario 1, the journal entry would be:

DR	Valuation account (fair value adjustment)	$10,000	
CR	Unrealized gain on available-for-sale security		$10,000

For Scenario 2, the journal entry would be:

DR	Credit loss	$20,000	
CR	Allowance for credit losses		$20,000

For Scenario 3, the journal entry would be:

DR	Credit loss	$26,927	
DR	Unrealized loss on available-for-sale security	23,073	
CR	Allowance for credit losses		$26,927
CR	Valuation account (fair value adjustment)		23,073

2.7 Sale of Debt Securities

A sale of a debt security from any category results in a realized gain or loss and is recognized in net income for the period. The valuation account, if used, also would have to be removed on the sale of a security.

- **Trading Securities:** The realized gain or loss reported when a trading debt security is sold is the difference between the adjusted cost (original cost plus or minus unrealized gains and losses previously recognized in net income) and the selling price.

Trading securities:

DR	Cash	$XXX	
CR	Trading security		$XXX
CR	Realized gain on trading security		XXX

- **Available-for-Sale Securities:** The realized gain or loss reported when an available-for-sale debt security is sold is the difference between the selling price and the original cost of the security. Any unrealized gains or losses in accumulated other comprehensive income must be reversed at the time the security is sold.

Available-for-sale securities:

DR	Cash	$XXX	
DR	Unrealized gain on available-for-sale security	XXX	
CR	Available-for-sale security		$XXX
CR	Realized gain on available-for-sale security		XXX

3 Investments in Equity Securities

3.1 Equity Securities

An equity security is a security that represents an ownership interest in an enterprise or the right to acquire or dispose of an ownership interest in an enterprise at fixed or determinable prices.

- Equity securities include:
  - ownership shares (common, preferred, and other forms of capital stock);
  - rights to acquire ownership shares (stock warrants, rights, and call options); and
  - rights to dispose of ownership shares (put options).
- Equity securities do *not* include:
  - preferred stock redeemable at the option of the investor or stock that must be redeemed by the issuer;
  - treasury stock (the company's own stock repurchased and held); and
  - convertible bonds.

3.2 Classification

3.2.1 Fair Value Through Net Income (FVTNI)

Equity securities are generally carried at fair value through net income (FVTNI). This requirement does not apply to investments accounted for under the equity method, consolidated investees, or when the practicability exception is applied.

3.2.2 Practicability Exception

The practicability exception allows an entity to measure an equity investment at cost less impairment, plus/minus observable price changes (in orderly transactions) of identical or similar investments from the same issuer. This exception is applicable for equity investments that do not have a readily determinable fair value. Reporting entities that are broker-dealers in securities, investment companies, or postretirement benefit plans cannot use this exception.

3.3 Valuation

Equity securities are generally reported at fair value through net income (FVTNI). Unrealized holding gains and losses on equity securities are included in earnings as they occur.

Journal entry to record loss in net income:

DR	Unrealized loss on equity security	$XXX	
CR	Valuation account (fair value adjustment)		$XXX

3.4 Income From Investments in Equity Securities

Dividend income from an equity security investment is recognized in net income, unless the dividend is a liquidating dividend.

- **Normal (Nonliquidating) Dividend**

  Journal entry to record normal dividend income:

DR	Cash	$XXX	
CR	Dividend income		$XXX

- **Liquidating Dividend:** A liquidating dividend is a distribution that exceeds the investor's share of the investee's retained earnings. A liquidating dividend is a return of capital that decreases the investor's basis in the investment.

  Journal entry to record liquidating dividend:

DR	Cash	$XXX	
CR	Investment in investee		$XXX

Example 3   Liquidating Dividend

Facts: ABC Corporation owns a 10 percent interest in XYZ Corporation. During the current year, XYZ Corp. paid a dividend of $10,000,000. XYZ had retained earnings of $8,000,000 when the dividend was declared. ABC will receive a dividend of $1,000,000 ($10,000,000 × 10%) from XYZ and will record dividend income of $800,000 for its share of XYZ's retained earnings ($8,000,000 × 10%). The $200,000 difference reduces ABC's investment in XYZ.

Required: Prepare the journal entry that ABC will record for this liquidating dividend.

Solution:

Journal entry to record $1,000,000 ($10,000,000 × 10%) dividend received from XYZ Corporation:

DR	Cash	$1,000,000	
CR	Dividend income ($8,000,000 × 10%)		$800,000
CR	Investment in XYZ Corporation		200,000

3.5 Impairment

Equity investments that do not have readily determinable fair values are measured at cost minus impairment (the practicability exception). An entity should consider the following qualitative indicators in order to determine whether an equity investment with no readily determinable fair value is impaired:

- Heightened concerns regarding the ability of an investee to continue as a going concern due to factors such as noncompliance with capital or debt requirements, deficiencies in working capital, or negative operating cash flows.

- Significant and adverse changes in the industry, geographic area, technology, or regulatory or economic environment of the investee.

- A significant decline in earnings, business prospects, asset quality, or credit rating of the investee.

- Offers to buy from the investee (and willingness to sell on the part of the investee) the same or a similar investment for less than the investor's carrying value.

When a qualitative assessment indicates that impairment exists, the cost basis of the security is written down to fair value and the amount of the write-down is accounted for as a realized loss and included in earnings.

3.6 Sale of Security

The sale of an equity security does not give rise to a gain or loss if all changes in the equity's fair value have been reported in earnings as unrealized gains or losses as they occurred.

Journal entry for sale with no gain or loss:

DR	Cash	$XXX	
CR	Equity security*		$XXX

If an entity has not recorded an equity security's change in fair value up to the point of sale, a gain or loss is recorded at the time of the sale equal to the difference between adjusted cost (original cost plus or minus unrealized gains and losses previously recognized in earnings) and the selling price.

The journal entry for sale of equity security with a gain:

DR	Cash	$XXX	
CR	Equity security*		$XXX
CR	Gain on equity security		XXX

* Note that any valuation account would also have to be removed when the security is sold.

4   Required Disclosures

4.1   Disclosures for Investments in Debt Securities

The following information concerning securities classified as available-for-sale and separately for held-to-maturity securities must be disclosed in the financial statements or appropriate notes thereto:

- Aggregate fair value;
- Gross unrealized holding gains and losses;
- Amortized cost basis by major security type; and
- Information about the contractual maturities of debt securities.

4.2   Disclosures for Investments in Equity Securities

Entities should disclose the portion of unrealized gains and losses for the period that relates to equity securities still held at the end of the reporting period. This amount is calculated as follows:

Net gains and losses recognized during the period on equity securities
− **Net gains and losses recognized during the period on equity securities sold during the period**
Unrealized gains and losses recognized during the reporting period on equity securities still held at the reporting date

4.3   Fair Value

All public and private entities must disclose on the balance sheet or in the notes to the financial statements all financial assets and liabilities, grouped by measurement category (fair value through net income, other comprehensive income, or amortized cost), and, if a financial asset, the form of that asset.

Public business entities (PBEs) must provide fair value information regarding the classification level in the measurement hierarchy (Levels 1, 2, or 3). For assets and liabilities measured at amortized cost, fair value should be disclosed in accordance with the exit price. Exceptions are for payables and receivables due within one year, deposit liabilities with no defined maturities, and equity investments reported under the practicability exception.

For entities that have elected the practicability exception, the following must be disclosed:

- The carrying amount of all investments without readily determinable fair values.
- Any impairment charges incurred during the reporting period.
- The amount of the upward or downward adjustment made to the carrying amount due to any observable price changes, with the intent of the adjustments designed to reflect the fair value of the security.

4.4 Concentrations of Credit Risk

Entities must disclose all significant concentrations of credit risk arising from all financial instruments, whether from a single party or a group of parties engaged in similar activities and that have similar economic characteristics.

Credit risk is the possibility of loss from the failure of another party to perform according to the terms of a contract. A concentration of credit risk occurs when an entity has contracts of material value with one or more parties in the same industry or region or having similar economic characteristics (e.g., a group of highly leveraged entities).

Under U.S. GAAP, these disclosures apply to all entities (except nonpublic entities that have total assets less than $100 million and have no instruments that are accounted for as derivatives).

4.5 Market Risk

Market risk is the possibility of loss from changes in market value (not necessarily due to the failure of another party, but due to changes in economic circumstances).

Under U.S. GAAP, all entities are encouraged, but not required, to disclose quantitative information about the market risk of financial instruments that is consistent with the way it manages or adjusts those risks.

Example 4	Investments in Debt and Equity Securities

Facts: The following information pertains to Fox Inc.'s portfolio of marketable investments for the year ended December 31, Year 2:

	Cost	Fair value at 12/31/Year 1	Year 2 activity Purchases	Year 2 activity Sales	Fair value at 12/31/Year 2
Held-to-maturity debt securities					
Security ABC			$100,000		$ 95,000
Available-for-sale debt securities					
Security GHI	190,000	165,000		$175,000	
Security JKL	170,000	175,000			160,000
Equity Securities					
Security DEF	$150,000	$160,000			155,000

Security ABC was purchased at par. There are no expected credit losses on Fox's portfolio of debt investments.

Required:

1. Calculate the carrying amount of each security on the balance sheet at December 31, Year 2.

2. Calculate any realized gain or loss recognized in Year 2 net income.

3. Calculate any unrealized gain or loss recognized in Year 2 net income.

4. Calculate any unrealized gain or loss to be recognized in Year 2 other comprehensive income.

(continued)

(continued)

Solution:

1. **Carrying amount of each security at December 31, Year 2**

   Security ABC $100,000

   At year-end, the held-to-maturity debt investment is reported at amortized cost, because there is no expected credit loss. The amortized cost of security ABC is the purchase price of $100,000.

   Security DEF $155,000

   The year-end carrying amount of the equity investment is the fair value at year-end. Fair value of security DEF is $155,000.

   Security GHI was sold

   Security JKL $160,000

   The year-end carrying amount of available-for-sale debt investments is the fair value at year-end because there are no expected credit losses. Fair value of security JKL is $160,000.

2. **Realized gain or loss in net income**

   Security GHI   ($15,000)

   The $175,000 sales proceeds less the $190,000 cost yields a realized loss of $15,000. The sale of security GHI will be recorded with the following journal entry:

DR	Cash	$175,000	
DR	Realized loss	15,000	
CR	Security GHI		$165,000
CR	Unrealized loss (OCI)		25,000

3. **Unrealized gain or loss in net income**

   Security DEF   ($5,000)

   The unrealized loss on the equity investment is reported in net income. The $160,000 carrying value of security DEF must be reduced to the $155,000 fair value and an unrealized loss of $5,000 is recognized in net income.

4. **Unrealized gain or loss (current year change):** Other comprehensive income

   Security GHI & JKL (net) $10,000

	12/31/Year 1 Accumulated OCI Gain (Loss)	Year 2 OCI Gain (Loss)	12/31/Year 2 Accumulated OCI Gain (Loss)
Security GHI	($25,000)[1]	$25,000	–0–
Security JKL	5,000[2]	(15,000)	(10,000)
	($20,000)	$10,000	($10,000)

   [1] Security GHI – Loss in 12/31/Yr 1 AOCI = $165,000 fair value – $190,000 cost = ($25,000)

   [2] Security JKL – Gain in 12/31/Yr 1 AOCI = $175,000 fair value – $170,000 cost = $5,000

NOTES

1 When to Use the Equity Method

The equity method is used to account for investments if significant influence can be exercised by the investor over the investee. Consolidated statements should be presented when ownership is greater than 50 percent and there is control over the investee.

A parent company that does not consolidate a subsidiary that is more than 50 percent owned must use the equity method when presenting the investment in that subsidiary in consolidated financial statements. Such a situation could result, for example, when there is lack of control because a company is controlled by a bankruptcy trustee or a subsidiary is likely to be a temporary investment.

1.1 Significant Influence

A company that owns 20 percent to 50 percent of voting stock of another "investee" company is presumed to be able to exercise significant influence over the operating and financial policies of that investee and, therefore, must use the equity method when presenting the investment in that investee in:

- consolidated financial statements that include other consolidated entities, but not that investee; or

- unconsolidated parent company financial statements.

Pass Key

The CPA Examination frequently presents questions in which the ownership percentage is below 20 percent, but the "ability to exercise significant influence" exists. The *equity method* is the correct method of accounting for these investments.

1.2 Equity Method Not Appropriate

In the following situations, the equity method is not appropriate, even if an investor owns 20 percent to 50 percent of subsidiary:

- Bankruptcy of subsidiary.
- Investment in subsidiary is temporary.
- A lawsuit or complaint is filed.
- A "standstill agreement" is signed (under which the investor surrenders significant rights as a shareholder).
- Another small group has majority ownership and operates the company without regard to the investor.
- The investor cannot obtain the financial information necessary to apply the equity method.
- The investor cannot obtain representation on the board of directors in order to exercise significant influence.

2 Equity Method Accounting

Under the equity method the investment is originally recorded at the price paid to acquire the investment. The investment account is subsequently adjusted as the net assets of the investee change through the earning of income and payment of dividends. The investment account increases by the investor's share of the investee's net income with a corresponding credit to the investor's income statement account, Equity in Subsidiary/Investee Income. The distribution of dividends by the investee reduces the investment balance. Continuing losses by an investee may result in a decrease of the investment account to a zero balance.

2.1 Journal Entries

Three main journal entries are used to account for an equity method investment:

Journal entry to record investment at cost (FV of consideration plus legal fees):

DR	Investment in investee	$XXX	
CR	Cash		$XXX

Journal entry to record increase in the investment by the investor's share of the earnings of the investee:

DR	Investment in investee	$XXX	
CR	Equity in earnings/investee income*		$XXX

* Equity in earnings is reported as income on the income statement.

Journal entry to record decrease in the investment by the investor's share of the cash dividends from the investee:

DR	Cash	$XXX	
CR	Investment in investee		$XXX

Pass Key

An easy way to remember the GAAP accounting rules for the equity method is to think of it as a **bank account** and use your **BASE** account analysis:

Beginning balance

Add: Investor's share of investee's earning (like bank interest; it is income when earned, not when taken out).

Subtract: Investor's share of investee's dividends (like bank withdrawals; and it is not income)

Ending balance

Example 1   Equity Method

Facts: On January 1, Year 1, Big Corporation acquired a 40 percent interest in Small Company for $300,000. At the date of acquisition, Small Co.'s equity (net assets) had a book value of $750,000. Therefore, there was no difference between the purchase price and the book value of the net assets acquired ($300,000 = 40% × $750,000). During Year 1, Small Co. had net income of $90,000 and paid a $40,000 dividend.

Required:

1. Prepare the journal entries required in Year 1 to account for the investment in Small Co.

2. Determine the investment-related amounts to be reported at year-end on Big's balance sheet and income statement.

Solution:

1. *Journal entry to record the initial investment of 40 percent:*

DR	Investment in Small Co.	$300,000	
CR	Cash		$300,000

Journal entry to recognize the investee's net income (40% × $90,000):

DR	Investment in Small Co.	$36,000	
CR	Equity in investee income		$36,000

Journal entry to recognize the dividend paid by the investee (40% × $40,000):

DR	Cash	$16,000	
CR	Investment in Small Co.		$16,000

2. On December 31, Year 1, the investment account on the balance sheet would show $320,000 ($300,000 + $36,000 − $16,000), and the income statement would show $36,000 as Big's equity in subsidiary income.

2.2 Investments in Investee Common Stock and Preferred Stock

If an investor company owns both common and preferred stock of an investee company:

- The "significant influence" test is generally met by the amount of common stock owned (which is usually the only voting stock).

- The calculation of the income from subsidiary (or investee) to be reported on the income statement includes:

  - Preferred stock dividends

  - Share of earnings available to common shareholders (net income reduced by preferred dividends)

2.3 Differences Between the Purchase Price and Book Value (NBV) of the Investee's Net Assets

Additional adjustments to the investment account under the equity method result from differences between the price paid for the investment and the book value of the investee's net assets. This difference is attributable to:

1. **Asset Fair Value Differences:** Differences between the book value and fair value of the net assets acquired.

2. **Goodwill:** Any remaining difference is goodwill.

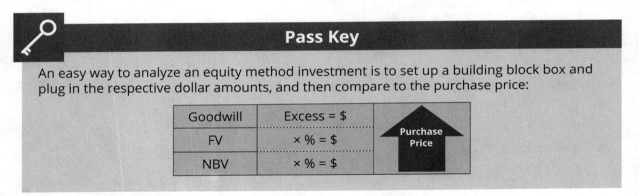

The following diagram illustrates the relationships between the purchase price of the equity method investment and the fair value and book value of the equity interest acquired:

Equity Method

2.3.1 Accounting for Asset Fair Value Differences

The excess of an asset's fair value over its book value is amortized over the life of the asset (excess caused by land is not amortized). This additional amortization causes the investor's share of the investee's net income to decrease.

DR	Equity in investee income	$XXX	
CR	Investment in investee		$XXX

Pass Key

To better understand the journal entry and its impact, think of the amortization of excess purchase price (premium) as a bank service charge. The *equity method*, which we treat like a bank account, will have the account balance (balance sheet asset) reduced by this *bank service charge* and also will have the net earnings from the account reduced by this (service) charge.

2.3.2 Accounting for Equity Method Goodwill

The fair value excess attributable to goodwill is not amortized and is not subject to a separate impairment test. However, the total equity method investment (including goodwill) must be analyzed at least annually for impairment.

Example 2   Equity Method With Fair Value Difference and Goodwill

Facts: On January 1, Year 1, Big Corporation acquired a 40 percent interest in Small Company for $300,000. At the date of acquisition, Small Co.'s equity (net assets) had a book value of $550,000 and a fair value of $600,000. The difference between the book value and fair value relates to equipment being depreciated over a remaining useful life of 10 years. During Year 1, Small Co. had net income of $90,000 and paid a $40,000 dividend.

Required:

1. Prepare the journal entries required in Year 1 to account for the investment in Small Co.

2. Compute the asset fair value difference and goodwill.

3. Record the journal entry to depreciate the fair value difference.

4. Determine the investment-related amounts to be reported at year-end on Big's balance sheet and income statement.

(continued)

(continued)

Solution:

1. **Investment and subsidiary activity**

   Journal entry to record the initial investment of 40 percent:

DR	Investment in Small Co.	$300,000	
CR	Cash		$300,000

   Journal entry to recognize the investee's net income (40% × $90,000):

DR	Investment in Small Co.	$36,000	
CR	Equity in investee income		$36,000

   Journal entry to recognize the dividend paid by the investee (40% × $40,000):

DR	Cash	$16,000	
CR	Investment in Small Co.		$16,000

2. **Asset adjustment and depreciation**

Goodwill	Excess = $60,000	$300,000
FV	$600,000 × 40% = $240,000	Purchase Price
NBV	$550,000 × 40% = $220,000	

   Asset Adjustment: The difference between the book value and fair value of net assets acquired:

FV of net assets acquired	$240,000
Less BV of net assets acquired	(220,000)
Asset adjustment	$ 20,000

   Goodwill: The excess of the purchase price over the fair value of net assets:

Purchase price of the investment in Small Co.	$300,000
Less: Fair value of Big Corp.'s equity in net assets of Small Co. (40% × 600,000)	(240,000)
Goodwill	$ 60,000

3. *Journal entry to record depreciation on undervalued equipment ($20,000 ÷ 10 years):*

DR	Equity in investee income	$2,000	
CR	Investment in Small Co.		$2,000

4. On December 31, Year 1, Big Corp.'s investment in Small Co.'s account would show a balance of $318,000 ($300,000 + $36,000 − $16,000 − $2,000), and the income statement would show $34,000 ($36,000 − $2,000) equity in investee income.

2.4   Equity Method Impairment

An impairment loss on an equity method investment is recognized when the following two conditions occur:

1.   The fair value of the investment falls below the carrying value of the investment.

2.   The entity believes the decline in value is other than temporary.

If both conditions are met, the entity reports the impairment loss on the income statement and the carrying value of the investment is reduced to the lower fair value on the balance sheet.

Under U.S. GAAP, the impairment loss is not permitted to be reversed if the fair value of the investment increases in subsequent periods.

Example 3   Impairment

Facts: Precious Metals Co. owns a 25 percent investment in Gems Inc. Precious Metals accounts for the investment using the equity method. On the December 31, Year 1, balance sheet, the investment was reported at a carrying value of $5,000,000.

During Year 2, Gems reported a net loss of $80,000 and paid no dividends. At the end of Year 2, Precious Metals' management estimated the fair value of its Gems Inc. investment at $4,000,000 due to the permanent closure of two factories and corresponding loss of sales. This decrease in fair value is considered to be other than temporary.

Required: Calculate the impairment loss to be reported on the Year 2 income statement of Precious Metals.

Solution: Before considering the effects of impairment, the investment in Gems would have a carrying value of $4,980,000 on the balance sheet of Precious Metals:

Year 2, beginning balance	$5,000,000	
+ (Share of Year 2 earnings)	(20,000)	[($80,000) × 25%]
− Share of Year 2 dividends	0	
Year 2, ending balance	$4,980,000	
− Fair value at end of Year 2	(4,000,000)	
Impairment loss	$ 980,000	

Precious Metals would recognize an impairment loss of $980,000 on its Year 2 income statement.

---

3   Comparison of Fair Value and Equity Methods

Do Not Consolidate

Fair Value
No significant influence
< 20%

Equity
Significant influence
20%–50%

Purchase Price
DR	Investment	
CR		Cash

Purchase Price
DR	Investment in investee	
CR		Cash

+ Investee Income
DR	Investment in investee	
CR		Equity in earnings

– Amortized FV > NBV
DR	Equity in earnings	
CR		Investment in investee

– Investee Dividends
DR	Cash	
CR		Investment in investee

Financial Asset at Fair Value Accounting
Report investment at fair value with gains and losses reported in net income (trading securities).

Balance Sheet
"Investment Account"

Liquidating Dividends
DR	Cash	
CR		Investment
CR		Dividend income

Nonliquidating Dividends
DR	Cash	
CR		Dividend income

Income Statement
"Reportable Income"

Investee Income
DR	Investment in investee	
CR		Equity in earnings

- Amortized FV > NBV
DR	Equity in earnings	
CR		Investment in investee

Goodwill
(*equity method only*)

- Not amortized
- Not impaired

4   Transition to the Equity Method

When significant influence is acquired, it is necessary to record a change from the fair value method to the equity method by doing the following on the date the investment qualifies for the equity method:

1. Add the cost of acquiring the additional interest in the investee to the carrying value of the previously held investment.

2. Adopt the equity method as of that date and going forward. Retroactive adjustments are not required.

Example 4	Transition to Equity Method

Facts: On January 1, Year 1, Big Co. paid $15,000 for a 15 percent interest in Small Co. Big did not have significant influence over Small. On January 1, Year 2, Big Co. increased its ownership in Small Co. to 45 percent, paying $60,000.

Required: Prepare the journal entry to be recorded on January 1, Year 2, to account for the transition to the use of the equity method for the investment in Small Co.

Solution:

Journal entry to record the acquisition of the additional interest in Small Co. on January 1, Year 2:

DR	Investment in Small Co.	$60,000	
CR	Cash		$60,000

For equity securities without readily determinable fair values, if transitioning to the equity method due to an observable transaction, the investment must be remeasured immediately *before* the transition. If transitioning from the equity method, the investment must be remeasured immediately *after* the transition.

NOTES

1 Basic Consolidation Concepts

1.1 Control (Over 50 Percent Ownership)

Under the voting interest model, consolidated financial statements are prepared when a parent-subsidiary relationship has been formed. An investor is considered to have parent status when control over an investee is established or more than 50 percent of the voting stock of the investee has been acquired.

Under U.S. GAAP, all majority-owned subsidiaries (domestic and foreign) must be consolidated except when significant doubt exists regarding the parent's ability to control the subsidiary, such as when:

1. the subsidiary is in legal reorganization; or

2. bankruptcy and/or the subsidiary operates under severe foreign restrictions.

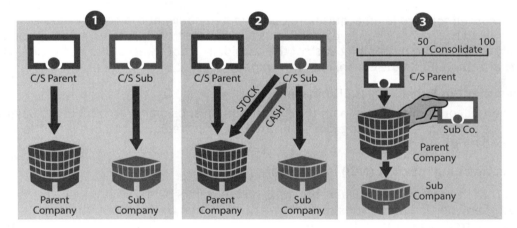

1.2 Controlling Interest and Noncontrolling Interest (NCI)

Business combinations that do not establish 100 percent ownership of a subsidiary by a parent company result in a portion of the subsidiary's equity (net assets) being attributable to noncontrolling shareholders.

1.2.1 Controlling Interest

An investor owning more than 50 percent of a subsidiary has a controlling interest in that subsidiary.

1.2.2 Noncontrolling Interest

Noncontrolling interest is the portion of the equity (net assets) of a subsidiary that is not attributable to the parent. Noncontrolling interest is reported at fair value in the equity section of the consolidated balance sheet, separately from the parent's equity.

2 Acquisition Method

The acquisition method, which is used to account for business combinations in which the investor/parent establishes control over the investee/subsidiary, has two distinct accounting characteristics: (1) 100 percent of the net assets acquired (regardless of ownership percentage) are recorded at fair value with any unallocated balance creating goodwill; and (2) when the companies are consolidated, the subsidiary's entire equity (including its common stock, APIC, and retained earnings) is eliminated (not reported).

Pass Key

The parent's basis is the acquisition price. The easy-to-remember formula is:

Fair value = Acquisition price = Investment in subsidiary

2.1 Consolidation Adjustments

An acquiring corporation should adjust the following items during consolidation:

1. Common Stock, APIC, and Retained Earnings of Subsidiary Are Eliminated

The pre-acquisition equity (common stock, APIC, and retained earnings) of the subsidiary is not carried forward in an acquisition. Consolidated equity at the time of acquisition will be equal to the parent's equity balance (plus any noncontrolling interest). The subsidiary's equity is eliminated by debiting each of the subsidiary's equity accounts in the eliminating journal entry (EJE) on the consolidating workpapers.

2. Investment in Subsidiary Is Eliminated

The parent company will eliminate the "investment in subsidiary" account on its balance sheet as part of the eliminating journal entry (EJE). This credit will be posted on the consolidating workpapers.

3. Noncontrolling Interest (NCI) Is Created

As part of the eliminating journal entry (EJE) on the consolidating workpapers, the fair value of any portion of the subsidiary that is not acquired by the parent must be reported as noncontrolling interest in the equity section of the consolidated financial statements, separately from the parent's equity.

4. Balance Sheet of Subsidiary Is Adjusted to Fair Value

All of the subsidiary's balance sheet accounts are to be adjusted to fair value on the acquisition date. This is accomplished as part of the eliminating journal entry (EJE) on the consolidating workpapers. This adjustment is done, regardless of the amount paid to acquire the subsidiary. The adjustment is for the full (100 percent) fair value of the subsidiary's assets and liabilities, even if the parent acquires less than 100 percent of the subsidiary.

5. Identifiable Intangible Assets of the Subsidiary Are Recorded at Their Fair Value

As part of the eliminating journal entry (EJE) on the consolidating workpapers, it is required that the parent record the fair value of all identifiable intangible assets of the subsidiary. This is done even if no amount was incurred to acquire these items in the acquisition.

6. Goodwill (or Gain) Is Required

If there is an excess of the fair value of the subsidiary (acquisition cost plus any noncontrolling interest) over the fair value of the subsidiary's net assets, then the remaining/ excess is debited to create goodwill. If there is a deficiency in the acquisition cost compared with the subsidiary's fair value, then the shortage/negative amount is recorded as a gain.

2.2 Consolidated Workpaper Eliminating Journal Entry

The year-end consolidating journal entry known as the consolidating workpaper eliminating journal entry (JE) is:

DR	Common stock—subsidiary	$XXX	
DR	APIC—subsidiary	XXX	
DR	Retained earnings—subsidiary	XXX	
CR	Investment in subsidiary		$XXX
CR	Noncontrolling interest		XXX
DR	Balance sheet adjustments to FV	XXX	
DR	Identifiable Intangible assets to FV	XXX	
DR	Goodwill	XXX	

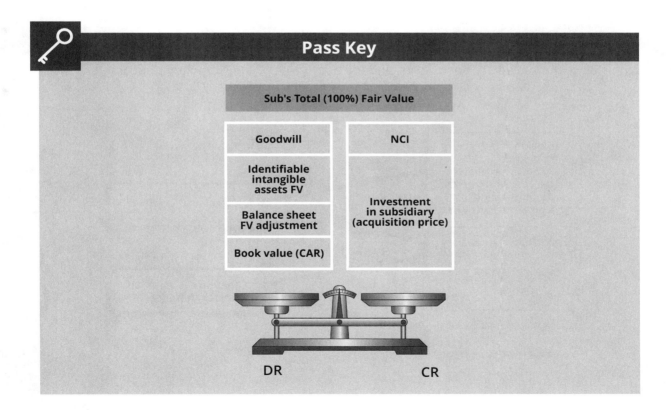

Pass Key

Sub's Total (100%) Fair Value

Goodwill	NCI
Identifiable intangible assets FV	
Balance sheet FV adjustment	Investment in subsidiary (acquisition price)
Book value (CAR)	

DR   CR

Journal Entry Flow Chart—Acquisition Date Calculation

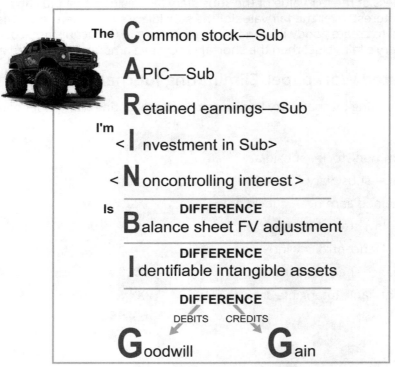

The **C**ommon stock—Sub

APIC—Sub

Retained earnings—Sub

I'm <**I**nvestment in Sub>

<**N**oncontrolling interest>

Is **DIFFERENCE** **B**alance sheet FV adjustment

DIFFERENCE **I**dentifiable intangible assets

DIFFERENCE

DEBITS   CREDITS

Goodwill   **G**ain

The following diagram illustrates the relationships between the fair value of the subsidiary, the fair value of the subsidiary's net assets, and the book value of the subsidiary's net assets.

Acquisition Method

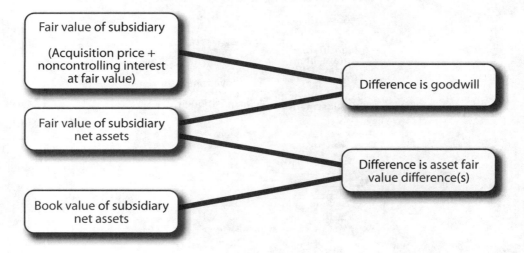

Fair value of subsidiary

(Acquisition price + noncontrolling interest at fair value)

Fair value of subsidiary net assets

Book value of subsidiary net assets

Difference is goodwill

Difference is asset fair value difference(s)

3   Intercompany Transactions

3.1   Eliminating Intercompany Transactions

When consolidating, 100 percent of intercompany transactions must be eliminated, even when the parent owns less than 100 percent of the subsidiary. Intercompany transactions must be eliminated because they lack the criteria of being "arm's length."

3.1.1   Simple Balance Sheet Eliminations

Eliminate 100 percent of all intercompany payables and receivables.

DR	Accounts payable	$XXX	
CR	Accounts receivable		$XXX

DR	Bonds payable (intercompany portion only)	$XXX	
CR	Bonds investment (in affiliate)		$XXX

DR	Accrued bond interest payable	$XXX	
CR	Accrued bond interest receivable		$XXX

DR	Dividends payable (affiliate portion only)	$XXX	
CR	Dividends receivable (from affiliate)		$XXX

3.1.2   Simple Income Statement Eliminations

- Interest expense / Interest income (bonds)
- Gain on sale / Depreciation expense (intercompany fixed asset sales)
- Sales / Cost of goods sold (intercompany inventory transactions)

3.2   Commonly Tested Intercompany Transactions

3.2.1   Intercompany Inventory / Merchandise Transactions

It is common for affiliated companies to sell inventory/merchandise to one another. Often this inventory/merchandise is sold at a profit. The total amount of this intercompany sale and cost of goods sold should be eliminated prior to preparing consolidated financial statements. In addition, the intercompany profit must be eliminated from the ending inventory and the cost of goods sold of the purchasing affiliate. 100 percent of the profit should be eliminated even if the parent's ownership interest is less than 100 percent. The intercompany profit in beginning inventory that was recognized by the selling affiliate in the previous year must be eliminated by an adjustment (debit) to retained earnings.

Workpaper Elimination: Intercompany Merchandise Transactions

DR	Intercompany sales	$XXX	
DR	Retained earnings (profit in beginning inventory)	XXX	
CR	Intercompany cost of goods sold		$XXX
CR	Cost of goods sold (intercompany profit included in COGS of the purchasing affiliate)		XXX
CR	Ending inventory (intercompany profit in the inventory remaining)		XXX

Pass Key

When inventory has been sold intercompany and the CPA Examination requires you to correct the accounts, remember to reverse the original intercompany transaction (sale and cost of goods sold, internally) and:

Inventory sold to outsiders ⟶ Correct cost of goods sold

Inventory still on hand ⟶ Correct ending inventory

Example 1   Intercompany Profit in Inventories

Facts: Gearty Corporation owns 100 percent of the common stock of Olinto Corporation. Gearty sold inventory with a cost of $1,000,000 to Olinto for $1,100,000 during Year 1. The Year 1 ending inventory of Olinto included goods purchased from Gearty for $660,000. Olinto had a remaining account payable balance to Gearty of $200,000 on December 31, Year 1. The following journal entries were prepared by Gearty and Olinto to record this intercompany inventory transaction:

Journal entry to record the sale by Gearty:

DR	Accounts receivable	$1,100,000	
CR	Intercompany sales		$1,100,000
DR	Intercompany cost of goods sold	1,000,000	
CR	Inventory		1,000,000

Journal entry to record the purchase by Olinto:

DR	Inventory	$1,100,000	
CR	Accounts payable		$1,100,000

(continued)

(continued)

Required: Prepare the entry to eliminate the intercompany inventory transaction.

Solution: The intercompany sales and intercompany cost of goods sold must be eliminated from Gearty's books and the intercompany profit on the sale of inventory must be eliminated from Olinto's books. The intercompany accounts payable and accounts receivable must also be eliminated.

Step 1: Calculate intercompany profit on sale of inventory:
Intercompany profit on sale of inventory = $1,100,000 sales price − $1,000,000 cost
= $100,000

Step 2: Allocate intercompany profit between purchaser's ending inventory and cost of goods sold:

Beginning inventory	$ 0
Purchases	1,100,000
Cost of goods available	1,100,000
Ending inventory	660,000 60%
Cost of goods sold	440,000 40%
Intercompany profit in Olinto's cost of goods sold ($100,000 × 40%)	$ 40,000 [1]
Intercompany profit in Olinto's ending inventory ($100,000 × 60%)	$ 60,000 [2]

DR	Intercompany sales—Gearty	$1,100,000	
CR	Intercompany cost of goods sold—Gearty		$1,000,000
CR	Cost of goods sold—Olinto		40,000 [1]
CR	Inventory—Olinto		60,000 [2]
DR	Accounts payable	200,000	
CR	Accounts receivable		200,000

3.2.2 Intercompany Bond Transactions

If one member of the consolidated group acquires an affiliate's debt from an outsider, the debt is considered to be retired and a gain/loss is recognized on the consolidated income statement. This gain/loss on extinguishment of debt is calculated as the difference between the price paid to acquire the debt and the book value of the debt. This gain/loss is not reported on either company's books, but is recorded through an elimination entry. All intercompany account balances are also eliminated.

Example 2	Intercompany Bond Transactions

Facts: On December 31, Year 1, Gearty Corporation issued bonds with a carrying value of $300,000 and a face value of $250,000. The premium on bonds payable was recorded as $50,000. Gearty recorded the following journal entry when the bonds were issued:

Journal entry to record the sale of the bonds on Gearty's books:

DR	Cash	$300,000	
CR	Bonds payable		$250,000
CR	Premium on bonds payable		50,000

On December 31, Year 1, before any portion of the premium was amortized, Olinto Corporation acquired all the outstanding bonds from the original purchasers at a price of $275,000 and recorded the following journal entry:

Journal entry to record the purchase of the bonds on Olinto's books:

DR	Investment in Gearty bonds	$275,000	
CR	Cash		$275,000

Required: Prepare the entry to eliminate the intercompany bond transaction.

Solution: *Workpaper elimination entry*—Eliminate the intercompany balances and recognize the gain on extinguishment of debt.

DR	Bonds payable	$250,000	
DR	Premium	50,000	
CR	Investment in Gearty bonds		$275,000
CR	Gain on extinguishment of bonds		25,000

- **Intercompany Interest:** Eliminate intercompany accounts such as interest expense, interest income, interest payable, and interest receivable.

- **Amortization of Discount or Premium:** Eliminate amortization of the discount or premium, which serves as an increase or decrease in the amount of interest expense/revenue that is recorded. The unamortized discount or premium on the intercompany bond is eliminated.

- **Subsequent Years:** The elimination for realized but unrecorded gain/loss on extinguishment of bonds in subsequent years would be adjusted to retained earnings. Noncontrolling interest would be adjusted if the bonds were originally issued by the subsidiary.

3.2.3 Intercompany Sale of Land

The intercompany gain/loss on the sale of land remains unrealized until the land is sold to an outsider. A workpaper elimination entry in the period of sale eliminates the intercompany gain/loss and adjusts the land to its original cost.

Example 3   **Intercompany Sale of Land**

Facts: On July 1, Year 1, Gearty Corporation sold land to Olinto Corporation for $200,000. The initial cost of the land to Gearty was $175,000. Gearty and Olinto recorded the following journal entries on the transaction date:

Journal entry to record the sale on Gearty's books:

DR	Cash	$200,000	
CR	Land		$175,000
CR	Intercompany gain on sale of land		25,000

Journal entry to record the purchase on Olinto's books:

DR	Land	$200,000	
CR	Cash		$200,000

Required: Prepare the entry required to eliminate the intercompany sale of land.

Solution: *Workpaper elimination entry*—Elimination of the intercompany gain and adjustment of land to its original cost:

DR	Intercompany gain on sale of land	$25,000	
CR	Land ($200,000 − $175,000)		$25,000

In the subsequent year and every year thereafter until the land is sold to a third party, retained earnings (Gearty) would be debited and land would be credited to eliminate the intercompany profit. Retained earnings are debited in subsequent years because the gain would have been closed to this account. Because Gearty (parent) was the seller of the land and Olinto (subsidiary) was the purchaser, there is no need to divide the intercompany gain between retained earnings and noncontrolling interest.

3.2.4 Intercompany Profit on Sale of Depreciable Fixed Assets

The gain or loss on the intercompany sale of a depreciable asset is unrealized from a consolidated financial statement perspective until the asset is sold to an outsider. A working paper elimination entry in the period of sale eliminates the intercompany gain/loss and adjusts the asset and accumulated depreciation to their original balance on the date of sale.

Example 4   Intercompany Sale of Fixed Assets

Facts: Olinto Corporation (subsidiary) sold equipment on January 1, Year 1, to Gearty Corporation (parent) for $100,000. The equipment had a net book value of $70,000 (cost of $90,000 and accumulated depreciation of $20,000), and a remaining life of 10 years. Gearty and Olinto prepared the following journal entries on the date of the transaction:

January 1, Year 1, journal entry to record the sale on Olinto's books:

DR	Cash	$100,000	
DR	Accumulated depreciation	20,000	
CR	Machinery (original cost)		$90,000
CR	Intercompany gain on sale of machinery		30,000

January 1, Year 1, journal entry to record the purchase on Gearty's books:

DR	Machinery	$100,000	
CR	Cash		$100,000

At year-end, Gearty recorded the following journal entry: December 31, Year 1, journal entry to record the depreciation on Gearty's books:

DR	Depreciation expense ($100,000 ÷ 10)	$10,000	
CR	Accumulated depreciation		$10,000

Required: Prepare the journal entries to eliminate the intercompany equipment sale and the excess depreciation.

Solution: December 31, Year 1, *workpaper elimination entry*—Elimination of intercompany gain and adjustment of the machine and accumulated depreciation accounts to their original balance:

DR	Intercompany gain on sale of machinery	$30,000	
CR	Machinery ($100,000 − $90,000)		$10,000
CR	Accumulated depreciation		20,000

The depreciation expense recorded by Gearty is overstated by the intercompany profit included in the cost of the machinery.

	GAAP Original	Non-GAAP Intercompany	Difference
NBV	$70,000	$100,000	$30,000
Depreciation years	÷ 10 Yrs	÷ 10 Yrs	÷ 10 Yrs
Depreciation	$ 7,000	$ 10,000	$ 3,000

Workpaper elimination entry—Elimination of excess depreciation:

DR	Accumulated depreciation	$3,000	
CR	Depreciation expense		$3,000

Illustration 1   Subsequent Year Workpaper Elimination Journal Entry

In the subsequent years, the intercompany gain/loss on the sale of the asset and the excess depreciation has been closed to retained earnings. The elimination entries in subsequent years therefore adjust retained earnings and, if appropriate, noncontrolling interest for the original gain or loss less the excess depreciation previously recorded (unrealized gain/loss at the beginning of the year). Continuing with the previous example, in Year 2 the workpaper elimination entries would be:

Journal entry to adjust fixed assets:

DR	Retained earnings	$27,000*	
CR	Machinery		$10,000
CR	Accumulated depreciation		17,000**

Journal entry to adjust depreciation:

DR	Accumulated depreciation	$3,000	
CR	Depreciation expense		$3,000

* Original gain: Excess depreciation previously recorded = Unrealized gain at the beginning of the year. $30,000 − $3,000 = $27,000.

** Original accumulated depreciation difference of $20,000 less excess depreciation of $3,000 previously recorded.

---

4   Preparing Consolidated Financial Statements

Example 5   Exercise: Consolidation Eliminating Journal Entries

Facts:

On January 1, Year 1, Gearty Corporation (parent) acquired 100 percent of Olinto Corporation. Gearty Corp. issued 100,000 shares of its $10 par common stock, with a market price of $25 on the date the acquisition was completed, for all of Olinto Corp.'s common stock.

On that date, the fair value of Olinto Corp.'s assets and liabilities equaled their respective carrying amounts except for land, which had a fair value that exceeded its book value by $200,000.

The fair value of Olinto Corp.'s identifiable intangibles (in process R&D) is $100,000. The in-process R&D will be amortized over a useful life of eight years.

For the year ending December 31, Year 1, Olinto reported net income of $350,000 and paid cash dividends of $150,000.

(continued)

(continued)

The stockholders' equity section of each company's balance sheet as of December 31, Year 1, was:

	Gearty	Olinto
Common stock	$5,000,000	$1,000,000
Additional paid-in capital	1,000,000	400,000
Retained earnings	3,000,000	500,000
	$9,000,000	$1,900,000

Required: Prepare the acquisition date and year-end consolidation workpaper eliminating journal entries.

Solution: Acquisition date calculation:

Common stock—subsidiary	$1,000,000
APIC—subsidiary	400,000
Retained earnings—subsidiary (at purchase date)	300,000

Beginning	$300,000
Add: income	350,000
Subtract: dividends	(150,000)
Ending	$500,000

Net book value	1,700,000
Investment (100,000 shares × $25 FV)	2,500,000
Difference	800,000
Noncontrolling interest	-0-
Difference	800,000
Balance sheet adjustment to asset land	200,000
Difference	600,000
Identifiable intangible assets	100,000
Goodwill	$ 500,000

Acquisition Date: Subsidiary's Total (100%) Fair Value $2,500,000			
Goodwill	$500,000	-0-	NCI
Identifiable intangible assets FV	$100,000		
Balance sheet FV adjustment	$200,000	$2,500,000	Investment in subsidiary
Book value (CAR)	$1,700,000		

(continued)

(continued)

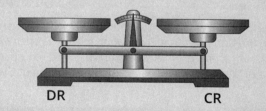

DR   CR

Acquisition Date Eliminating Journal Entry			
DR	Common stock—subsidiary	$1,000,000	
DR	APIC—subsidiary	400,000	
DR	Retained earnings—subsidiary	300,000	
CR	Investment in subsidiary		$2,500,000
CR	Noncontrolling interest		-0-
DR	Balance sheet adjustment fair value	200,000	
DR	Identifiable intangible assets fair value	100,000	
DR	Goodwill	500,000	

Assuming that Gearty accounts for its investment in Olinto using the equity method for internal accounting purposes, Gearty would report an investment in subsidiary of $2,700,000 at year-end:

Beginning investment in sub	$2,500,000
+ Share of subsidiary income	350,000
− Share of subsidiary dividends	(150,000)
Ending investment in sub	$2,700,000

Year-End Eliminating Journal Entry			
DR	Common stock—subsidiary	$1,000,000	
DR	APIC—subsidiary	400,000	
DR	Retained earnings—subsidiary	500,000	
CR	Investment in subsidiary		$2,700,000
CR	Noncontrolling interest		-0-
DR	Balance sheet adjustment fair value	200,000	
DR	Identifiable intangible assets fair value	100,000	
DR	Goodwill	500,000	

Example 6   Preparing Consolidated Financial Statements

Required: Prepare the December 31, Year 1, consolidated financial statements of Gearty Corporation and Olinto Corporation using the Consolidation Eliminating Journal Entries example on the previous pages and the intercompany transaction examples from Topic 3 Intercompany Transactions (the footnotes refer to the list of explanations of consolidated adjustments, which follows).

Solution:

	Gearty Dr(Cr)	Olinto Dr(Cr)	Elimination Debits	Elimination Credits	Adjusted Balance
Income Statement					
Sales	$(18,400,000)	$(6,000,000)	$1,100,000[1]		$(23,300,000)
Cost of goods sold	11,480,000	4,210,000		1,000,000[1] 40,000[1]	14,650,000
Operating expenses	5,505,000	1,330,000	12,500[2]	3,000[3]	6,844,500
Equity in earnings	(350,000)	0	350,000[4]		0
Investment income	(100,000)	0			(100,000)
Interest expense	80,000	140,000			220,000
Gain on fixed asset sales	(25,000)	(30,000)	25,000[5] 30,000[6]		0
Gain on debt	0	0		25,000[7]	(25,000)
Net income	$(1,810,000)	$(350,000)	$1,517,500	$1,068,000	$(1,710,500)
Statement of Retained Earnings					
RE, 1/1/Year 1	$(1,190,000)	$(300,000)	$300,000[4]		$(1,190,000)
Net income	(1,810,000)	(350,000)	1,517,500	$1,068,000	(1,710,500)
Dividends	0	150,000		150,000[4]	0
RE, 12/31/Year 1	$(3,000,000)	$(500,000)	$1,817,500	$1,218,000	$(2,900,500)
Balance Sheet					
Cash	$1,120,000	$ 520,000			$1,640,000
AR	2,075,000	1,605,000		$200,000[8]	3,480,000
Inventory	2,000,000	1,000,000		60,000[1]	2,940,000
Marketable securities	1,225,000	275,000		275,000[7]	1,225,000
Fixed Assets (net)	3,470,000	1,500,000	200,000[4] 3,000[3]	25,000[5] 10,000[6] 20,000[6]	5,118,000
In-process R&D	0	0	100,000[4]	12,500[2]	87,500
Goodwill	0	0	500,000[4]		500,000
Investment in Sub	2,700,000	0		2,700,000[4]	0
Total Assets	$12,590,000	$4,900,000	$803,000	$3,302,500	$14,990,500
AP	$(2,290,000)	$(1,250,000)	$200,000[8]		$(3,340,000)
Bonds payable (net)	(1,300,000)	(1,750,000)	250,000[7] 50,000[7]		(2,750,000)
Common stock	(5,000,000)	(1,000,000)	1,000,000[4]		(5,000,000)
APIC	(1,000,000)	(400,000)	400,000[4]		(1,000,000)
RE	(3,000,000)	(500,000)	1,817,500	$1,218,000	(2,900,500)
Liabilities and Equity	$(12,590,000)	$(4,900,000)	$3,717,500	$1,218,000	$(14,990,500)

(continued)

Explanation of consolidation adjustments:

1. Elimination of the intercompany sale of inventory:

DR	Intercompany sales—Gearty	$1,100,000	
CR	Intercompany cost of goods sold—Gearty		$1,000,000
CR	Cost of goods sold—Olinto		40,000
CR	Inventory—Olinto		60,000

2. Amortization of in-process R&D over 8 years ($100,000/8 = $12,500):

DR	Amortization expense	$12,500	
CR	In-process R&D		$12,500

3. Elimination of excess depreciation resulting from the intercompany sale of machinery:

DR	Amortization depreciation	$3,000	
CR	Depreciation expense		$3,000

4. Elimination of Olinto's equity and Gearty's investment in Olinto and the recognition of the land fair-value adjustment, in-process R&D, and goodwill on December 31, Year 1:

DR	Common stock—subsidiary	$1,000,000	
DR	APIC—subsidiary	400,000	
DR	Retained earnings—subsidiary	500,000	
CR	Investment in subsidiary		$2,700,000
CR	Noncontrolling interest		-0-
DR	Balance sheet adjustment FV	$200,000	
DR	Identifiable intangible assets FV	100,000	
DR	Goodwill	500,000	

5. Elimination of intercompany land transaction:

DR	Intercompany gain on sale of land	$25,000	
CR	Land		$25,000

6. Elimination of intercompany sales of equipment:

DR	Intercompany gain on sale of machinery	$30,000	
CR	Machinery ($100,000 − $90,000)		$10,000
CR	Accumulated depreciation		20,000

(continued)

(continued)

7. Record the retirement of intercompany bonds:

DR	Bonds payable	$250,000	
DR	Premium (Gearty's records)	50,000	
CR	Investment in Gearty bonds (Olinto's records)		$275,000
CR	Gain on extinguishment of bonds		25,000

8. Elimination of intercompany AR and AP resulting from intercompany sale of inventory:

DR	Accounts payable	$200,000	
CR	Accounts receivable		$200,000

5 Illustrative Consolidated Financial Statements

The following are samples of a comparative consolidated balance sheet, a consolidated income statement, a statement of consolidated comprehensive income, and a consolidated statement of changes in equity.

5.1 Sample: Consolidated Balance Sheet

The consolidated balance sheet includes 100 percent of the parent's and subsidiary's assets and liabilities (after eliminating intercompany transactions), but does not include the subsidiary's equity. Noncontrolling interest is presented as part of equity, separately from the equity of the parent company.

Consolidated Businesses Inc. (CBI) Consolidated Balance Sheet as of December 31		
Assets	**Year 4**	**Year 3**
Cash	$ 250,000	$ 195,000
Accounts receivable	125,000	140,000
Available-for-sale debt securities	320,000	315,000
Plant and equipment	675,000	590,000
Total assets	$1,370,000	$1,240,000
Liabilities		
Accounts payable	$ 207,000	$ 135,000
Accrued expenses	75,000	80,000
Long-term notes payable	400,000	400,000
Total liabilities	$ 682,000	$ 615,000

(continued)

(continued)

Equity

CBI shareholders' equity:

Common stock, $1 par	$ 275,000	$ 275,000
Additional paid-in capital	130,000	130,000
Retained earnings	220,000	165,000
Accumulated other comprehensive income	23,000	19,000
Total CBI shareholders' equity	$ 648,000	$ 589,000
Noncontrolling interest	40,000	36,000
Total equity	688,000	625,000
Total liabilities and equity	$1,370,000	$1,240,000

5.2 Sample: Consolidated Statement of Income

The consolidated income statement includes 100 percent of the parent's revenues and expenses and all of the subsidiary's revenues and expenses after the date of acquisition. The subsidiary's pre-acquisition revenues and expenses are not included in the consolidated income statement.

The consolidated income statement should show, separately, consolidated net income, net income attributable to noncontrolling interests, and net income attributable to the parent company.

Consolidated Businesses Inc. (CBI) Consolidated Statement of Income for the Year Ended December 31			
	Year 4	**Year 3**	**Year 2**
Sales	$620,000	$570,000	$595,000
Cost of goods sold	(280,000)	(255,000)	(265,000)
Gross profit	340,000	315,000	330,000
Selling, general, and administrative expenses	(224,000)	(190,000)	(226,000)
Operating income	116,000	125,000	104,000
Net interest expense	(12,000)	(8,000)	(6,000)
Income before tax	104,000	117,000	98,000
Income tax expense	(36,000)	(40,000)	(44,000)
Net income	68,000	77,000	54,000
Less: Noncontrolling interest in net income	(3,000)	(7,000)	(2,000)
Net income attributable to CBI	$ 65,000	$ 70,000	$ 52,000

5.3   Sample: Statement of Consolidated Comprehensive Income

The statement of comprehensive income should show, separately, consolidated comprehensive income, comprehensive income attributable to the noncontrolling interest, and comprehensive income attributable to the parent company.

Consolidated Businesses Inc. (CBI) Statement of Consolidated Comprehensive Income for the Year Ended December 31			
	Year 4	Year 3	Year 2
Net income	$68,000	$77,000	$54,000
Other comprehensive income, net of tax:			
Unrealized holding gain on available-for-sale debt securities, net of tax	5,000	6,000	4,500
Total other comprehensive income, net of tax	5,000	6,000	4,500
Comprehensive income	73,000	83,000	58,500
Comprehensive income attributable to noncontrolling interest	(4,000)	(8,500)	(3,000)
Comprehensive income attributable to CBI	$69,000	$74,500	$55,500

5.4   Sample: Consolidated Statement of Changes in Equity

Because noncontrolling interest is part of the equity of the consolidated group, it is presented in the statement of changes in equity. The consolidated statement of changes in equity should present a reconciliation of the beginning-of-period and end-of-period carrying amount of total equity, equity attributable to the parent, and equity attributable to the noncontrolling interest.

Consolidated Businesses Inc. (CBI) Consolidated Statement of Changes in Equity for the Year Ended December 31, Year 1							
		CBI Shareholders					
	Total	Comprehensive Income	Retained Earnings	AOCI	Common Stock	APIC	NCI
Beginning balance	$625,000		$165,000	$19,000	$275,000	$130,000	$36,000
Comprehensive income:							
Net income	68,000	$68,000	65,000				3,000
OCI, net of tax:							
Unrealized gain on securities	5,000	5,000		4,000			1,000
Comprehensive income	73,000						
Dividends on common stock	(10,000)		(10,000)	—	—	—	—
Ending balance	$688,000	$73,000	$220,000	$23,000	$275,000	$130,000	$40,000

5.5   Sample: Consolidated Statement of Cash Flows

5.5.1   Period of Acquisition

The preparation of the consolidated statement of cash flows in the period of acquisition is complicated by the fact that the prior year financial statements reflect parent-only balances while the year-end financial statements reflect consolidated balances. The following steps are necessary in order to prepare a consolidated statement of cash flows in the period of acquisition:

1. The net cash spent or received in the acquisition must be reported in the investing section of the statement of cash flows.

Illustration 2   Cash Outflow for Acquisition

If the parent company spent $2,500,000 to acquire a subsidiary that had $800,000 cash, the net decrease in cash of $1,700,000 would be shown as an investing outflow on the statement of cash flows as follows:

Payment for acquisition of subsidiary, net of cash acquired = $1,700,000

---

2. The assets and liabilities of the subsidiary on the acquisition date must be added to the parent's assets and liabilities at the beginning of the year in order to determine the change in cash due to operating, investing, and financing activities during the period.

Example 7   Consolidated Cash Flow From Notes Payable

Facts: A parent company that reported notes payable of $600,000 on January 1 acquired a subsidiary on May 1 that reported notes payable of $250,000 on the acquisition date. The December 31 consolidated balance sheet reported notes payable of $750,000.

Required: Determine the cash inflow or outflow from long-term debt.

Solution:

Beginning parent notes payable	$600,000
+ Acquisition date subsidiary notes payable	250,000
– Ending consolidated notes payable	750,000
Cash outflow	$100,000

5.5.2 Subsequent Periods

In subsequent periods, the preparation of the consolidated statement of cash flows is simplified by the fact that consolidated financial statements are available for the beginning and end of the period. The consolidated statement of cash flows should present the cash inflows and outflows of the consolidated entity, excluding cash flows between the parent and subsidiary.

The preparation of the consolidated statement of cash flows should be similar to the preparation of a statement of cash flows for a nonconsolidated entity, except for the following considerations:

1. When reconciling net income to net cash provided by operating activities, total consolidated net income (including net income attributable to both the parent and the noncontrolling interest) should be used.

2. The financing section should report dividends paid by the subsidiary to noncontrolling shareholders. Dividends paid by the subsidiary to the parent company should not be reported.

3. The investing section may report the acquisition of additional subsidiary shares by the parent if the acquisition was an open-market purchase.

1 Admission of a Partner

A new partner may be admitted by the purchase of an existing partnership interest or by investing additional capital into the partnership.

1.1 By Purchase or Sale of Existing Partnership Interest

A partner, with the consent of all partners, may sell his partnership interest to a new partner. Payment for the partnership interest by the new partner would go directly to the selling partner. The retiring partner could sell his interest in the same manner to the remaining partners.

- **No Journal Entry**

  No entries are made on the partnership books, except for the change of name on the capital account. Transactions of this type do not affect the assets, liabilities, or total capital of the partnership.

1.2 Formation of a Partnership

Contributions to a partnership are recorded as follows:

1. Assets are valued at fair value.

2. Liabilities assumed are recorded at their present value.

3. Partner's capital account therefore equals the difference between the fair value of the contributed assets less the present value of liabilities assumed.

Pass Key

It is important to distinguish the tax and GAAP rules relating to the formation of a partnership:

- GAAP Rule = Use FV of asset contributed
- Tax Rule = Use NBV of assets contributed

1.3 Creation of a New Partnership Interest With Investment of Additional Capital

When a new partnership interest is created by the investment of additional capital into the partnership, the total capital of the partnership does change, and the purchase price can be equal to, more than, or less than book value.

1.3.1 Exact Method—Equal to Book Value

When the purchase price is equal to the book value of the capital account purchased, no goodwill or bonuses are recorded.

- **Rules—Problem-Solving Steps**

    1. Determine the exact amount a new partner will have to pay to get his capital account in the exact proportional interest to the new net assets of the partnership.

    2. There is no goodwill or bonus.

    3. Old partners' capital account "dollars" stay the same.

    4. Old partners' "% ownership" changes, but that change is generally not a requirement on the CPA Exam.

Pass Key

Problems that deal with the exact method will always ask, "How much should the new partner contribute in order to have an x% interest in the new partnership?" and will not include references to goodwill or bonuses in the transaction.

Example 1 — New Partner Pays Book Value

Facts: A, B, and C are partners in a three-person partnership. They have capital accounts of $20,000, $30,000, and $50,000, respectively. A, B, and C decide to admit D as a new partner with a 25 percent interest in the new partnership.

Required: If D pays book value, how much should D contribute in order to have a 25 percent interest in the partnership?

Solution:

Equity of new partnership = $20,000 + $30,000 + $50,000 + D's contribution

Since D will contribute an amount equal to 25 percent of the total book value of the new partnership, D's contribution can be shown as 25 percent of total new equity.

Total new equity = $100,000 + 0.25 Total new equity

$100,000 = 0.75 Total new equity; $\dfrac{\$100,000}{0.75}$ = Total new equity

Total new equity = $133,333

0.25 total new equity = $33,333

Thus, D should pay $33,333 for a 25 percent interest.

1.3.2 Bonus Method—Recognize Intercapital Transfer

When the purchase price is more or less than the book value of the capital account purchased, bonuses are adjusted between the old and new partners' capital accounts and do not affect partnership assets.

- **Rules—Problem-Solving Steps**

    1. Determine total capital and the interest to the new partner.

    2. If interest less than amount contributed, bonus to old partner(s).

    3. If interest greater than amount contributed, bonus to new partner.

Pass Key

B = **B**onus = **B**alance in total capital accounts controls the capital account allocation.

Pass Key

Under the bonus method, the bonus will be credited to the following partner:

- Existing partners—when new partner pays more than NBV
- New partner—when new partner pays less than NBV

Illustration 1   Bonus to Existing Partners

A and B share profits and losses 60:40, and have capital accounts of $30,000 and $10,000, respectively. C has agreed to invest $35,000 for a one-third interest in the new ABC partnership. Since the partnership has decided not to recognize goodwill, the total capital of the resulting partnership is $75,000 ($30,000 + $10,000 + $35,000). C has purchased a one-third interest, so the balance in C's capital account should equal one-third of $75,000 or $25,000. The extra $10,000 paid by C is recorded as a bonus to the old partners and is shared according to their profit and loss ratio.

Journal entry to record the admission of C into the partnership and recognize the bonus to existing partners:

DR	Cash	$35,000	
CR	A, Capital ($10,000 × 60%)		$ 6,000
CR	B, Capital ($10,000 × 40%)		4,000
CR	C, Capital (30,000 + 10,000 + 35,000 = 75,000 × 1/3)		25,000

Illustration 2   Bonus to New Partners

It is possible for the existing partners to credit a bonus to a new partner. In the example above, if C had invested $14,000 for a one-third interest in the resulting partnership, C would have received a bonus from A and B, because the one-third interest in the partnership is $18,000 [1/3 ($30,000 + $10,000 + $14,000)] and exceeds C's contribution of $14,000. The $4,000 ($18,000 – $14,000) is a bonus credited to C by A and B, and is charged to A's and B's capital accounts according to their profit and loss ratio (60:40).

Journal entry to record the partnership and recognize the bonus to new partners:

DR	Cash	$14,000	
DR	A, Capital ($4,000 × 60%)	2,400	
DR	B, Capital ($4,000 × 40%)	1,600	
CR	C, Capital (30,000 + 10,000 + 14,000 = 54,000 × 1/3)		$18,000

1.3.3   Goodwill Method—Recognized Intangible Asset

Goodwill is recognized based upon the total value of the partnership implied by the new partner's contribution.

■ **Rules—Problem-Solving Steps**

1. Compute new "net assets before GW" (before goodwill) after admitting new (or paying old) partner.

2. Memo: Compute new "capitalized" net assets (= total net worth) and compare "Capitalized Net Assets" with "Net Assets before Goodwill;" and

3. The "Difference" is "Goodwill" to be allocated to the old partners according to their old partnership profit ratios.

Pass Key

G = **G**oodwill = **G**oing in investment (dollars) controls capital account allocation and goodwill calculation.

Illustration 3   Goodwill Credited to Capital Accounts of Existing Partners

A and B share profits and losses 60:40, and have capital accounts of $30,000 and $10,000, respectively. On the basis of A and B's present total capital, C has agreed to invest $35,000 for a one-third interest in the new ABC partnership. The partnership decides to recognize goodwill.

C pays $35,000 for a one-third interest in the partnership; goodwill is recognized as the difference between the implied value of the business and the total of the tangible net assets represented by the partners' capital account.

Implied value ($35,000 × 3 = $105,000)	$105,000
Total partner's capital accounts ($35,000 + $10,000 + $30,000 = $75,000)	(75,000)
Goodwill	$ 30,000

Journal entry to record the admission of C into the partnership and recognize goodwill:

DR	Cash	$35,000	
DR	Goodwill	30,000	
CR	A, Capital (60% × $30,000)		$18,000
CR	B, Capital (40% × $30,000)		12,000
CR	C, Capital (equals amount contributed by C)		35,000

Pass Key

The following summary will help you remember the differences among the above approaches:

Exact Method

- The incoming partner's capital account is their actual contribution. (You must calculate.)
- No adjustment to the existing partner's capital accounts is required.

Bonus Method

- Balance in total capital accounts controls the computation.
- The incoming partner's capital account is their percentage of the partnership total NBV (after their contribution).
- Adjust the existing partner's capital accounts to balance.

Goodwill Method

- Going in investment (dollars) controls the computation.
- The incoming partner's capital account is their actual contribution.
- Goodwill (implied) is determined based upon the incoming partner's contribution, and shared by the existing partners.

2 Profit and Loss Distribution

Income or loss is distributed among the partners in accordance with their agreement, and in the absence of an agreement all partners share equally irrespective of what their capital accounts reflect or the amount of time each partner spends on partnership affairs.

Unless the partnership agreement provides otherwise, all payments for interest on capital, salaries, and bonuses are deducted prior to any distribution in the profit and loss ratio. Such payments are provided for in full, even in a loss situation.

Pass Key

Partnership accounts may be different from their respective profit and loss ratios. The reason for this is that distributions/withdrawals will be at different times and for different reasons.

Example 2 Profit and Loss Distribution

Facts: A, B, and C, copartners, had capital balances at the end of the year (but before profit distribution) of $30,000, $60,000, and $90,000, respectively. The partnership's profit for the year, excluding any payments to partners, was $200,000. The partnership agreement provided for interest of 8 percent on ending capital balances, a salary to A of $10,000, and a bonus to C of 15 percent of partnership profits before any distribution to partners. The profit and loss ratios were 20 percent to A, 30 percent to B, and 50 percent to C.

Required: On the basis of this data, what was the total distribution to each partner?

Solution:

	Total	A	B	C
Total profit	$200,000			
15% guaranteed bonus to C	(30,000)			$ 30,000
Interest on ending capital balances (8% × capital balance)	(14,400)	$ 2,400	$ 4,800	7,200
Salary to A	(10,000)	10,000		
Balances	145,600	12,400	4,800	37,200
Distribution of balance in P&L ratio 20%; 30%; 50%	(145,600)	29,120	43,680	72,800
Total distribution of P&L	$ 0	$41,520	$48,480	$110,000

Note: All interest, salaries, and bonuses are deducted from total profit to arrive at the amount of profit and loss distributed in the profit and loss ratio. If these items exceed the amount of profit, then the resulting loss is distributed in the profit and loss ratio.

3 Withdrawal of a Partner

3.1 Bonus Method

The difference between the balance of the withdrawing partner's capital account and the amount that person is paid is the amount of the "bonus." The "bonus" is allocated among the remaining partners' capital accounts in accordance with their remaining profit and loss ratios. Although the partnership's identifiable assets may be revalued to their fair value at the date of withdrawal, any goodwill implied by the excess payment to the retiring partner is *not* recorded.

Step 1: Journal entry to revalue the assets to reflect fair value:

DR	Asset adjustment	$XXX	
CR	A, Capital (%)		$XXX
CR	B, Capital (%)		XXX
CR	X, Capital (%)		XXX

Step 2: Journal entry to pay off withdrawing partner:

DR	A, Capital (%)	$XXX	
DR	B, Capital (%)	XXX	
DR	X, Capital (100%)	XXX	
CR	Cash		$XXX

3.2 Goodwill Method

The partners may elect to record the implied goodwill in the partnership based on the payment to the withdrawing partner. The amount of the implied goodwill is allocated to *all* of the partners in accordance with their profit and loss ratios. After the allocation of the implied goodwill of the partnership, the balance in the withdrawing partner's capital account should equal the amount that person is to receive in the final settlement of his or her interest.

Step 1: Journal entry to revalue the assets to reflect fair value:

DR	Asset adjustment	$XXX	
CR	A, Capital (%)		$XXX
CR	B, Capital (%)		XXX
CR	X, Capital (%)		XXX

Step 2: Journal entry to record goodwill to make withdrawing partner's capital account equal payoff:

DR	Goodwill	$XXX	
CR	A, Capital (%)		$XXX
CR	B, Capital (%)		XXX
CR	X, Capital (%)		XXX

Step 3: Journal entry to pay off withdrawing partner:

DR	X, Capital (100%)	$XXX	
CR	Cash		$XXX

4 Liquidation of a Partnership

The process of winding up the affairs of a partnership after dissolution is generally referred to as liquidation. Liquidation involves the realization of cash from the disposal of partnership assets. Creditors or partners may agree to accept specific partnership assets in full or partial satisfaction of their claims against the partnership.

4.1 Order of Preference Regarding Distribution of Assets

Where a solvent partnership is dissolved and its assets are reduced to cash, the cash must be used to pay the partnership's liabilities in the following order:

4.1.1 Creditors

Creditors, including partners who are creditors, must be paid before the noncreditor partners receive any payments.

4.1.2 Partners' Capital

Right of offset between a partner's loans to and from the partnership and that person's capital balances generally exists in liquidation.

4.2 Losses Considered in Liquidation

1. All possible losses must be provided for in a liquidation before any distribution is made to the partners. The rule to follow is not to distribute any cash until maximum potential losses have been taken into consideration.

2. Losses in liquidating a partnership are charged to the partners in accordance with the partnership agreement; in the absence of such an agreement, the losses are shared equally.

4.3 Convert Noncash Assets

The general procedure in a liquidation is that all noncash assets are converted into cash, all liabilities are paid, and the remainder, if any, is distributed to the partners.

4.4 Gain or Loss on Realization

The liquidation of partnership assets may result in:

1. A gain on realization;

2. A loss on realization; or

3. A loss on realization resulting in a capital deficiency.

4.5 Capital Deficiency

A capital deficiency is a debit balance in a partner's capital account and indicates that the partnership has a claim against the partner for the amount of the deficiency.

4.5.1 Right of Offset

If a partner with a capital deficiency has a loan account (the partnership has payable to the partner), the partnership has a legal right to offset and may use the loan account to satisfy the capital deficiency.

4.5.2 Remaining Partners Charged

If a deficiency still exists, the remaining partners must absorb the deficiency according to their respective (remaining) profit and loss ratios.

4.6 Partnership Liquidation Schedule

The objective of the schedule is to distribute cash, as it becomes available, to the partners.

It is important that no partner is either overpaid or underpaid as the result of any cash distributed by the liquidator because that person could be personally liable for overpayments made to a partner that were not repaid.

Pass Key

Generally, the "poor" partners do not have any money to repay their shortage; so (generally), the "richest" partners are paid first.

Many multiple-choice exam questions ask for ending partners' balances after liquidation of a partner or the partnership; some questions merely ask for amount of "cash" to be paid upon liquidation. If all "other" assets and all liabilities are liquidated, the answer will be the same: Cash = Partners' balances.

Illustration 4   Partnership Liquidation Schedule

After discontinuing the regular business operations and closing the books, A, B, and C decide to liquidate their partnership. The partnership agreement provides for income or loss to be divided 50 percent to A, 30 percent to B, and 20 percent to C. The following is an adjusted trial balance before commencing liquidation:

Cash	$20,000	
Noncash assets	75,000	
Liabilities, creditors		$25,000
Partner advance, A		15,000
Partner advance, C		5,000
Partner's capital, A		10,000
Partner's capital, B		20,000
Partner's capital, C		20,000
	$95,000	$95,000

Illustration 5	A, B, C Partnership—Statement of Liquidation and Realization Date

Assumption 1: Gain on realization (noncash assets sold for $125,000)	Cash	Noncash Assets	Liabilities Outside Creditors	Liabilities Partner's Advance		Partner's Capital		
				A	C	A 50%*	B 30%*	C 20%*
Balances—before realization	20,000	75,000	25,000	15,000	5,000	10,000	20,000	20,000
Sale of *noncash* assets & division of gain	125,000	(75,000)				25,000	15,000	10,000
Balances after realization	145,000	0	25,000	15,000	5,000	35,000	35,000	30,000
Payment of liabilities	(25,000)		(25,000)					
Balances	120,000		0	15,000	5,000	35,000	35,000	30,000
Payment of partners' advances	(20,000)			(15,000)	(5,000)			
Balances	100,000			0	0	35,000	35,000	30,000
Distribution of cash	(100,000)					(35,000)	(35,000)	(30,000)

Assumption 2: Loss on realization (noncash assets sold for $65,000)	Cash	Noncash Assets	Liabilities Outside Creditors	Liabilities Partner's Advance		Partner's Capital		
				A	C	A	B	C
Balances—before realization	20,000	75,000	25,000	15,000	5,000	10,000	20,000	20,000
Sale of noncash assets & division of loss	65,000	(75,000)				(5,000)	(3,000)	(2,000)
Balances—after realization	85,000	0	25,000	15,000	5,000	5,000	17,000	18,000
Payment of liabilities	(25,000)		(25,000)					
Balances	60,000		0	15,000	5,000	5,000	17,000	18,000
Payment of partners' advances	(20,000)			(15,000)	(5,000)			
Balances	40,000			0	0	5,000	17,000	18,000
Distribution of cash	(40,000)					(5,000)	(17,000)	(18,000)

Assumption 3: (see the notes that follow) Loss on realization—capital deficiency (noncash assets sold for $15,000)	Cash	Noncash Assets	Liabilities Outside Creditors	Liabilities Partner's Advance		Partner's Capital		
				A	C	A	B	C
Balances—before realization	20,000	75,000	25,000	15,000	5,000	10,000	20,000	20,000
Sale of noncash assets & division of loss	15,000	(75,000)				(30,000)	(18,000)	(12,000)
Balances—after realization	35,000	0	25,000	15,000	5,000	(20,000)	2,000	8,000
Payment of liabilities	(25,000)		(25,000)					
Balances	10,000		0	15,000	5,000	(20,000)	2,000	8,000
Transfer of A—advance account				(15,000)		15,000		
Balances	10,000			0	5,000	(5,000)	2,000	8,000
Division of "A's" deficiency						5,000	(3,000)	(2,000)
Balances	10,000				5,000	0	(1,000)	6,000
Division of "B's" deficiency							1,000	(1,000)
Balances	10,000				5,000		0	5,000
Distribution of cash	(10,000)				(5,000)			(5,000)

*Profit and loss ratio

Notes to Assumption 3:

1. It is important to remember that a partnership has a claim against any partner with a capital deficiency. In this example the $15,000 credit balance in A's advance account constitutes a preferred claim once A's capital balance is in a deficiency position. A's advance account is transferred to A's capital account to offset part of the $20,000 capital deficiency balance.

2. All possible losses must be charged to the partners' capital accounts in their income and loss ratios before any distribution is made. A still has a $5,000 capital deficiency that B and C must absorb in their respective income and loss ratios before any cash distribution is made. B and C will have a claim of $3,000 and $2,000, respectively, against A for absorbing the $5,000 capital deficiency that is calculated as follows:

    (B) 3/5 x $5,000 = $3,000
    (C) 2/5 x $5,000 = $2,000

3. Any partner may pay a capital deficiency in cash directly to the partnership.

4. A partnership is not completely liquidated and their affairs wound up until all claims, including those of partners, are settled.

5 Statement of Cash Flows

1 Overview

A statement of cash flows is a required part of a full set of financial statements for all business enterprises. The purpose of the statement of cash flows is to provide information about the sources of cash and cash equivalents (i.e., cash receipts) and the uses of cash and cash equivalents (i.e., cash disbursements), including:

- **Operating Cash Flows:** Cash receipts and disbursements from transactions reported on the income statement and current assets and current liabilities (excluding current notes payable and the current portion of long-term debt, which are reported in financing cash flows).

- **Investing Cash Flows:** Cash receipts and disbursements from non-current assets.

- **Financing Cash Flows:** Cash receipts and disbursements from debt (including non-current liabilities) and equity.

The statement also presents information about material noncash events. Cash flow amounts per share are *not* disclosed under U.S. GAAP.

2 Cash and Cash Equivalents

The statement of cash flows reconciles the cash and cash equivalents amount presented on the beginning balance sheet to the cash and cash equivalents amount presented on the ending balance sheet (i.e., the change in cash for the period).

2.1 Definitions

- Cash is defined as actual cash (i.e., currency and demand deposits).

- Cash equivalents are defined as short-term, liquid investments that are:

    - quickly convertible into specific amounts of cash *and*

    - so near maturity (i.e., the original maturity date to the investor was within three months of the purchase date) that the risk of changes in the value because of interest rate changes is insignificant.

2.2   Purpose

The cash concept is used because investors, creditors, and other interested parties need information about the entity's available cash and cash needs (i.e., ability to pay obligations, dividends, etc.).

Illustration 1   Summarized Statement Format

X Company
Statement of Cash Flows
For the Year Ended December 31, Year 1

Net cash provided by (used in) operating activities	$XXX	
Net cash provided by (used in) investing activities	XXX	
Net cash provided by (used in) financing activities	$XXX	
Net increase (decrease) in cash		$XXX
Cash and cash equivalents at beginning of year		XXX
Cash and cash equivalents at end of year		$XXX

---

3   Methods of Presenting the Statement of Cash Flows

There are two ways to prepare the operating section of a statement of cash flows—the *direct method* and the *indirect method*. Only the indirect method is testable on the CPA exam. Regardless of the method used, the presentation of investing and financing activities is the same. Only the sections that present operating activities and certain required disclosures are different.

3.1   Indirect Method

Companies report net cash flows from operating activities (CFO) indirectly, by adjusting net income to reconcile it to net cash flows from operating activities, as follows:

Cash flows from operating activities (CFO)	=	Net income	+	Noncash expenses/ losses	−	Noncash income/ gains	+	Increases (decreases) in operating liabilities/ (assets)	−	Increases (decreases) in operating assets/ (liabilities)

4 Sections of the Statement of Cash Flows

The following balance sheet and income statement for Cox Retail Company are to be used for the examples in this section.

Cox Retail Company **Balance Sheet** For the Years Ended December 31, Year 4 and Year 3 (in thousands)		
	Dec. 31, Year 4	*Dec. 31, Year 3*
ASSETS		
Current assets		
Cash and cash equivalents	$ 4,040	$ 2,705
Accounts receivable, net	2,520	2,305
Prepaid expenses	1,540	1,515
Inventory	2,715	2,920
Non-current assets		
Property, plant, and equipment (gross)	11,795	11,315
Accumulated depreciation	(1,245)	(800)
Marketable securities	5,500	4,750
Note receivable (long-term)	150	–
Other assets	3,360	3,360
Total assets	**$30,375**	**$28,070**
LIABILITIES AND EQUITY		
Current liabilities		
Wages payable	490	565
Unearned revenue	1,200	950
Accounts payable	1,235	1,560
Interest payable	345	300
Taxes payable	950	800
Notes payable (short-term)	300	–
Non-current liabilities		
Bonds payable	6,400	6,000
Other non-current liabilities	1,200	1,200
Total liabilities	**12,120**	**11,375**
Common stock	8,665	8,465
Retained earnings	6,200	5,140
Additional paid-in capital	3,390	3,090
Total equity	**18,255**	**16,695**
Total liabilities and equity	**$30,375**	**$28,070**

Notes (referenced dollar amounts in thousands):
The company received $600 in proceeds upon the sale of a facility.
The company paid $200 in dividends during Year 4.

Cox Retail Company **Income Statement** For the Year Ended December 31, Year 4 (in thousands)	
Net sales	$13,815
Cost of goods sold	8,290
Gross profit	5,525
Salaries and wages	3,120
Depreciation and amortization	445
Other selling, general, and admin. expense	245
TOTAL OPERATING INCOME	**1,715**
NONOPERATING INCOME AND EXPENSES	
Gain on sale of PP&E	80
Interest income	55
Interest expense	(125)
Other nonoperating income/expenses	(150)
TOTAL NONOPERATING INCOME, NET	**(140)**
Income before taxes	1,575
Income tax expense	315
NET INCOME	**$ 1,260**

Notes (referenced dollar amounts in thousands):
Other nonoperating income/expenses includes:

Insurance proceeds received	15
Cash paid to settle lawsuit	30
Dividends received from investments	20
Other nonoperating expenses	155

Other SG&A includes:

Provision for losses on AR	200
Marketing and advertising materials	45

Assume a tax rate of 20 percent

4.1 Operating Activities

Operating activities involve producing goods and delivering services to customers. All transactions not categorized as investing or financing activities (discussed below) are categorized as operating activities. Crypto assets received as noncash consideration in the ordinary course of business and converted nearly immediately (within a few days) into cash are classified as operating activities.

Under the indirect method, net income is adjusted to arrive at net cash flows from operating activities. In addition, supplemental disclosure of cash paid for interest and income taxes is required.

- **Adjustment to Net Income:** The adjustment to net income is performed by removing the effects on net income of the following items:

  - All *deferrals* of past operating cash receipts and disbursements (e.g., subtracting increases in inventory and prepaid expenses);

  - All *accruals* of expected future operating cash receipts and disbursements (e.g., subtracting increases in accounts receivable and adding increases in accounts payable and accrued expenses);

  - All items that are included in net income that *do not affect operating cash receipts and disbursements* (e.g., those that should be omitted altogether or categorized as investing or financing activities, such as adding depreciation and amortization and subtracting gains on sales of productive assets).

- **Determination of Effect on Cash Flow:** The effect on cash flows for comparative balance sheet changes in asset, liability, and equity accounts can be easily determined (these rules apply to all changes in balance sheet items, including those in the investing and financing activities sections), as follows:

  - An increase to an asset or a "debit balance" account (e.g., accounts receivable) will have the effect on the statement of cash flows as a decrease to cash (indirect effect).

  - A decrease to an asset of a "debit balance" account (e.g., inventory) will have the effect on the statement of cash flows as an increase to cash (indirect effect).

  - An increase in a liability, an equity, or a "credit balance" account (e.g., accounts payable) will have the effect on the statement of cash flows as an increase to cash (direct effect).

  - A decrease in a liability, an equity, or a "credit balance" account (e.g., allowance for doubtful accounts) will have the effect on the statement of cash flows as a decrease to cash (direct effect).

- **Shortcut Cash Flow Effects**

  - Changes in debit balance accounts will have the opposite effect on cash flows (because cash is a debit balance account).

  - Changes in credit balance accounts will have the same effect on cash flows.

- **Gains and Losses**

  - *Gains* are adjusted out of the operating activities section and (generally) into the investing activities section by *subtracting* their effects from net income.

  - *Losses* are adjusted out of the operating activities section and (generally) into the investing activities section by *adding* their effects to net income.

Pass Key

You will be able to easily remember approximately 85 percent of the adjustments made to the operating activities section under the indirect method by remembering the mnemonic **CLAD**.

- **C**urrent assets and liabilities
- **L**osses and gains
- **A**mortization and depreciation
- **D**eferred items

Example 1   Cash Flows From Operating Activities (Indirect Method)

Facts: Cox Retail Company balance sheet and income statement.

Required: Using the information in Cox's financial statements, calculate the company's cash flow from operating activities using the indirect method.

Solution:

Cash Flows From Operating Activities (000s)

Net income	$1,260 [1]
Adjustments to reconcile net income to net cash provided by operating activities	
Depreciation and amortization	445 [2]
Provision for losses on AR	200 [3]
Gain on the sale of PP&E	(80) [4]
Change in current assets and current liabilities	
Increase in accounts receivable	(415) [5]
Increase in unearned revenue	250 [6]
Decrease in inventory	205 [7]
Decrease in accounts payable	(325) [8]
Decrease in wages payable	(75) [9]
Increase in prepaid expenses	(25) [10]
Increase in interest payable	45 [11]
Increase in income taxes payable	150 [12]
Net cash provided by operating activities	$1,635

[1] Net income line on the income statement.
[2] From income statement.
[3] From notes section of the income statement.
[4] From gain on sale of PP&E on the income statement.
[5] See calculation below.
[6] Increase on the balance sheet from $950 to $1,200.
[7] Decrease on the balance sheet from $2,920 to $2,715.
[8] Decrease on the balance sheet from $1,560 to $1,235.
[9] Decrease on the balance sheet from $565 to $490.
[10] Increase on the balance sheet from $1,515 to $1,540.
[11] Increase in interest payable from $300 to $345.
[12] Increase in taxes payable from $800 to $950.

Accounts receivable increased from $2,305 in Year 3 to $2,520 in Year 4, an increase of $215. A $200 provision for losses on AR in the notes to the income statement must also be subtracted.

4.2   Investing Activities

Investing activities include cash flows from the purchase or sale of *non-current assets:*

- Making loans to other entities (cash outflow);

- Purchasing (cash outflow) or disposing of (cash inflow) trading securities (if classified as non-current), available-for-sale securities, and held-to-maturity investment securities of other entities (debt or equity);

- Acquiring (cash outflow) or disposing of (cash inflow) property, plant, and equipment (productive assets); and

- Acquiring another entity under the acquisition method using cash (cash outflow). The payment for the acquisition is shown net of the cash acquired.

Example 2   Cash Flows From Investing Activities

Facts: Cox Retail Company balance sheet and income statement.

Required: Using the information in Cox's financial statements, calculate the company's cash flow from investing activities.

Solution:

Cash Flows From Investing Activities

Capital expenditures	$(1,000) [1]
Proceeds from sale of facility	600 [2]
Loan made to outside entity	(150) [3]
Purchase of marketable securities	(750) [1]
Net cash used in investing activities	$(1,300)

[1] See calculation below.
[2] Notes to the balance sheet.
[3] Long-term note receivable 150 in Year 4.

Capital expenditures

Increase in gross PP&E	$ 480	PP&E increased from $11,315 to $11,795.
+ Proceeds from sale of facility	600	See notes to balance sheet.
− Gain on sale of PP&E	(80)	See income statement.
Capital expenditures	$1,000	

Purchase of marketable securities

Increase in marketable securities	$ 750	Increase from $4,750 to $5,500.

4.3   Financing Activities

Financing activities include cash flows from *non-current liability* (creditor-oriented) and *equity* (owner-oriented) activities.

4.3.1   Equity (Owner-Oriented) Activities

- Obtaining resources from owners, such as issuing stock (cash inflow).
- Providing owners with a return on their investment, such as paying cash dividends or repurchasing stock (cash outflow).

4.3.2   Non-current Liability (Creditor-Oriented) Activities

- Obtaining resources from creditors, such as issuing bonds, notes, and other borrowings (cash inflow).
- Payments of principal (not interest, which is part of the operating activities section) on amount borrowed (cash outflow).

Example 3   Cash Flows From Financing Activities

Facts: Cox Retail Company balance sheet and income statement.

Required: Using the information in Cox's financial statements, calculate the company's cash flow from financing activities.

Solution:

Cash Flows From Financing Activities

Net borrowings under line of credit arrangement	$ 300 [1]
Proceeds from issuance of long-term debt	400 [2]
Proceeds from issuance of common stock	500 [3]
Dividends paid	(200) [4]
Net cash provided by financing activities	$1,000

[1] Notes payable increased from $0 to $300.
[2] Bonds payable from $6,000 to $6,400.
[3] Increase in common stock ($8,465 to $8,665) and APIC ($3,090 to $3,390).
[4] From the notes to the balance sheet.

4.4   Noncash Investing and Financing Activities

Information about material noncash financing and investing activities (those that do not result in cash receipts or payments) should be provided separately in a supplemental disclosure. Of course, any part of the transaction that does involve cash would be included in the statement of cash flows. Examples include:

- A purchase of fixed assets by issuance of stock, which is not a cash transaction, but would likely be a material transaction for the entity.
- The conversion of bonds to equity, which generally does not involve cash.
- Acquiring assets through the incurrence of a capital lease obligation.
- The exchange of one noncash asset for another noncash asset.

4.5   Summary of Cash Flow Classifications of Individual Transactions

The following table summarizes the statement of cash flow classifications of individual transactions under U.S. GAAP:

Transaction	Operating Cash Flow (CFO)	Investing Cash Flow (CFI)	Financing Cash Flow (CFF)	No Net Cash Flow
Selling products/collecting receivables	✓			
Purchasing inventory/paying vendors	✓			
Purchasing supplies and services/paying vendors	✓			
Paying taxes	✓			
Purchasing/selling trading securities (general rule)	✓			
Purchasing long-term assets or long-term investments for cash		✓		
Recording depreciation, amortization, or depletion				✓
Collecting interest on an investment	✓			
Collecting dividends on an investment	✓			
Recording income of equity method affiliates				✓
Selling long-term assets or investments (noncash equivalents and nontrading securities): cash proceeds		✓		
Borrowing funds (e.g., bank loans, issuing debt)			✓	
Paying interest on debt	✓			
Paying principal on debt			✓	
Issuing common or preferred stock			✓	
Paying dividends on common or preferred stock			✓	
Repurchasing stock (e.g., treasury shares)			✓	
Prepaying debt or paying debt extinguishment costs			✓	
Crypto assets received as noncash consideration (and converted to cash within a few days)	✓			

Note: The statement of cash flows should include amounts generally described as restricted cash or restricted cash equivalents in its reconciliation of beginning-of-period and end-of-period total amounts. U.S. GAAP does not currently provide a definition of restricted cash or restricted cash equivalents. An entity should disclose the nature of any restrictions, if applicable.

5 Statement of Cash Flows: Indirect Method Presentation

Cox Retail Company
Consolidated Statement of Cash Flows
For the Year Ended December 31, Year 4
Increase (Decrease) in Cash and Cash Equivalents (in thousands)

CASH FLOWS FROM OPERATING ACTIVITIES

Net income		$ 1,260
Adjustments to reconcile net income to net cash provided by operating activities		
Depreciation and amortization	$ 445	
Provision for losses on accounts receivable	200	
Gain on sale of PP&E	(80)	
Change in current assets and liabilities:		
Increase in accounts receivable (gross)	(415)	
Increase in unearned revenue	250	
Decrease in inventory	205	
Decrease in accounts payable	(325)	
Decrease in wages payable	(75)	
Increase in prepaid expenses	(25)	
Increase in interest payable	45	
Increase in income taxes payable	150	
Total adjustments		375
Net cash provided by operating activities		**$ 1,635**
CASH FLOWS FROM INVESTING ACTIVITIES		
Capital expenditures	$(1,000)	
Proceeds from sale of facility	600	
Loan made to outside entity	(150)	
Purchase of marketable securities	(750)	
Net cash used in investing activities		**$(1,300)**
CASH FLOWS FROM FINANCING ACTIVITIES		
Net borrowings under line-of-credit agreement	300	
Proceeds from issuance of long-term debt	400	
Proceeds from issuance of common stock	500	
Dividends paid	(200)	
Net cash provided by financing activities		**1,000**
NET INCREASE IN CASH AND CASH EQUIVALENTS		1,335
Cash and cash equivalents at beginning of year		2,705
Cash and cash equivalents at end of year		**$ 4,040**

DISCLOSURE OF ACCOUNTING POLICY

For purposes of the statement of cash flows, Cox Retail Company considers all highly liquid debt instruments purchased with an original maturity of three months or less to be cash equivalents.

Summary of Statement of Cash Flows

Operating Activities:

1. Record net income.

2. Adjust net income for noncash items such as depreciation and the impairment of goodwill.

3. Reverse the income statement gain or loss shown on the sale of any asset.

4. Adjust for changes in current assets and current liabilities except for cash and current interest bearing debt (recorded in financing activities):

   Current assets increase: subtract

   Current assets decrease: add

   Current liabilities increase: add

   Current liabilities decrease: subtract

Investing Activities:

1. All sums lent and/or repaid (principal only).

2. Purchase and/or sale of non-current assets (including fixed assets, intangible assets, and marketable securities).

Financing Activities:

1. All sums borrowed and/or repaid (principal amount only).

2. Issuance and/or repurchase of own company stock.

3. Dividends paid (not received).

NOTES

6 Income Taxes: Part 1

1 Overview

Accounting for income taxes involves both intraperiod and interperiod tax allocation. Intraperiod allocation matches a portion of the provision for income tax to the applicable components of net income and retained earnings.

Income for federal tax purposes and financial accounting income frequently differ. Obviously, income for federal tax purposes is computed in accordance with the prevailing tax laws, whereas financial accounting income is determined in accordance with GAAP. Therefore, a company's income tax expense and income taxes payable may differ. The incongruity is caused by temporary differences in taxable and/or deductible amounts and requires interperiod tax allocation.

1.1 Intraperiod Tax Allocation

Intraperiod tax allocation involves apportioning the total tax provision for financial accounting purposes in a period between the income or loss from:

- **Income** from continuing operations,
- **Discontinued** operations
- **Accounting** principle change (retrospective)
- Other comprehensive income
  - **Pension** funded status change
  - **Unrealized** gain/loss on available-for-sale debt security and hedges
  - **Foreign** translation adjustment
  - **Instrument**-specific credit risk
- Components of stockholders' equity
  - Retained earnings for prior period adjustments and accounting principle changes (retrospective); and
  - Items of accumulated (other) comprehensive income

Any amount not allocated to continuing operations is allocated to other income statement items, other comprehensive income, or to shareholders' equity in proportion to their individual effects on income tax or benefit for the year. Such items (e.g., discontinued operations) are shown net of their related tax effects.

The amount of income tax expense (or benefit) allocated to continuing operations is the tax effect of pretax income or loss from continuing operations plus or minus the tax effects of changes in:

1. Tax laws or rates.

2. Expected realization of a deferred tax asset.

3. Tax status of the entity.

1.2   Comprehensive Interperiod Tax Allocation

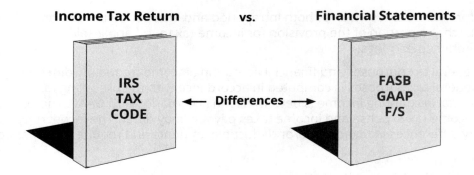

1.2.1   Objective

The objective of interperiod tax allocation is to recognize through the matching principle the amount of current and future tax related to events that have been recognized in financial accounting income.

■ **Current Year Taxes:** Payable (liability) or refundable (asset)

Or:

■ **Future Year Taxes:** Deferred tax asset or deferred tax liability

1.2.2   Differences

There are two types of differences between pretax GAAP financial income and taxable income. All differences are either permanent differences or temporary differences.

1.   Permanent Differences

- Permanent differences are items of revenue and expense that either:

  —enter into pretax GAAP financial income, but never enter into taxable income (e.g., interest income on state or municipal obligations); or

  —enter into taxable income, but never enter into pretax GAAP financial income (e.g., dividends-received deduction).

- Permanent differences do not affect the deferred tax computation. They only affect the current tax computation. These differences affect only the period in which they occur. They do not affect future financial or taxable income.

2.   Temporary Differences

- Temporary differences are items of revenue and expense that may:

  —enter into pretax GAAP financial income in a period *before* they enter into taxable income.

  —enter into pretax GAAP financial income in a period *after* they enter into taxable income.

- Temporary differences affect the deferred tax computation.

- Items that are first recognized for tax purposes will eventually be recognized for GAAP purposes (or vice versa); therefore, the differences are temporary and will eventually "turn around."

- These temporary differences affect future period(s) and require:

    —a liability (for future taxable amounts); or

    —an asset (for future deductible amounts).

- These should be recognized in the financial statement until the difference turns around completely.

1.2.3 Comprehensive Allocation

The asset and liability method (sometimes referred to as the balance sheet approach) is required by GAAP for comprehensive allocation. Under comprehensive allocation, interperiod tax allocation is applied to all temporary differences. The asset and liability method requires that either income taxes payable or a deferred tax liability (asset) be recorded for all tax consequences of the current period.

1.2.4 Accounting for Interperiod Tax Allocation

- Total income tax expense (GAAP income tax expense) or benefit for the year is the sum of:

    - current income tax expense/benefit, and

    - deferred income tax expense/benefit.

- Current income tax expense/benefit is equal to the income taxes payable or refundable for the current year, as determined on the corporate tax return (Form 1120) for the current year.

- Deferred income tax expense/benefit is equal to the change in deferred tax liability or asset account on the balance sheet from the beginning of the current year to the end of the current year (called the "balance sheet approach").

- Thus, total income tax expense/benefit can be depicted as follows:

| Current income tax payable or refundable as determined on the corporate tax return | ± | Change in the deferred income tax asset or liability from the beginning to the end of the reporting period | = | Total income tax expense or benefit |

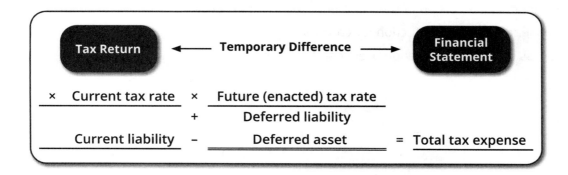

Pass Key

Total tax expense for financial statements is the combination of current tax plus or minus deferred taxes.

The CPA examiners frequently provide an incorrect calculation of financial statement income times the current tax rate. This is an incorrect method to determine the total expense for the following reasons:

- Use of financial statement income (which has permanent differences) is incorrect.

- Use of the current tax rate ignores future changes to the enacted rate.

2 Permanent Differences

A permanent difference is a transaction that affects only income per books or taxable income, but not both. Income tax expense for a period is calculated only on taxable items. For example, tax-exempt interest (municipal and state bonds) is included in financial income, but is excluded in computing income tax expense.

In effect, permanent differences create a discrepancy between taxable income and financial accounting income that will never reverse.

2.1 No Deferred Taxes

Because they do not reverse themselves, no interperiod tax allocation is necessary for permanent differences. The income tax provision for financial accounting purposes is computed on the basis of pretax book income adjusted for all permanent differences.

2.2 Examples

Permanent differences are either (a) nontaxable, (b) nondeductible, or (c) special tax allowances. Examples are:

- Tax-exempt interest (municipal, state)

- Life insurance proceeds on officer's key person policy

- Life insurance premiums when corporation is beneficiary

- Certain penalties, fines, bribes, kickbacks, etc.

- Nondeductible portion of meal and entertainment expense

- Dividends-received deduction for corporations

- Excess percentage depletion over cost depletion

Pass Key

The deduction for business interest expense is limited to the sum of business interest income plus 30 percent of the adjusted taxable income.

Example 1   Permanent Differences

Facts: ABC Company reported $200,000 of pretax financial income. Included in this income was $10,000 of life insurance premiums for policies on which the corporation is the beneficiary and interest income on municipal bonds of $50,000.

Required: Calculate and record the tax expense for ABC Company, assuming a 21 percent tax rate.

Solution:

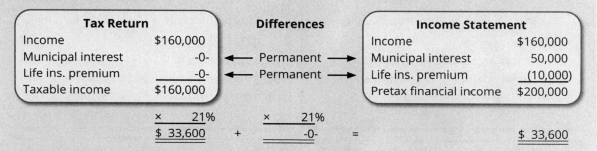

Tax Return		Differences	Income Statement	
Income	$160,000		Income	$160,000
Municipal interest	-0-	← Permanent →	Municipal interest	50,000
Life ins. premium	-0-	← Permanent →	Life ins. premium	(10,000)
Taxable income	$160,000		Pretax financial income	$200,000
	× 21%	× 21%		
	$ 33,600	+ -0- =		$ 33,600

Note that there are no deferred taxes resulting from temporary differences, and that the income tax expense and the income tax liability are the same.

Journal entry to record income tax expense and income tax liability:

DR	Income tax expense	$33,600	
CR	Income tax payable		$33,600

3 Temporary Differences

3.1 Transactions That Cause Temporary Differences

When revenues (or gains) are included in financial statement income before taxable income and/or when expenses (or losses) are deducted from taxable income before financial statement income, the result is a deferred tax liability (DTL) because more will be owed in taxes later when differences reverse. When revenues (or gains) are included in taxable income before financial statement income and/or when expenses (or losses) are deducted from financial statement income before taxable income, the result is a deferred tax asset (DTA) because less will be owed in taxes later when differences reverse.

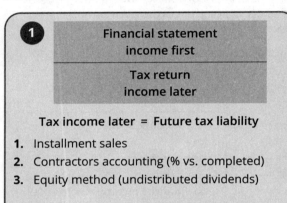

1

| Financial statement income first |
| Tax return income later |

Tax income later = Future tax liability

1. Installment sales
2. Contractors accounting (% vs. completed)
3. Equity method (undistributed dividends)

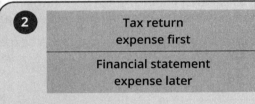

2

| Tax return expense first |
| Financial statement expense later |

Tax deduct first = Future tax liability

1. Depreciation expense
2. Amortization of franchise
3. Prepaid expenses (cash basis for tax)

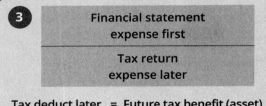

3

| Financial statement expense first |
| Tax return expense later |

Tax deduct later = Future tax benefit (asset)

1. Bad debt expense (allowance vs. direct w/o)
2. Est. liability/warranty expense
3. Start-up expenses

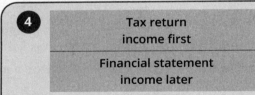

4

| Tax return income first |
| Financial statement income later |

Tax income first = Future tax benefit (asset)

1. Prepaid rent*
2. Prepaid interest*
3. Prepaid royalties*
* — The IRC uses the term "prepaid," GAAP uses the term "unearned"

The conditions in boxes 1 and 2 result in deferred tax liabilities. The conditions in boxes 3 and 4 result in deferred tax assets. Additional causes of temporary differences are:

- Differences between the financial reporting and tax basis of assets and liabilities arising in a business combination accounted for as an acquisition.

- Differences in the tax basis of assets due to indexing, whenever the local currency is the functional currency.

3.2 Deferred Tax Liabilities and Assets Recognition

Pass Key

- DTL ⟶ Future tax accounting income > Future financial accounting income
- DTA ⟶ Future tax accounting income < Future financial accounting income

3.2.1 Deferred Tax Liabilities

Deferred tax liabilities are anticipated future tax liabilities derived from situations in which future taxable income will be greater than future financial accounting income due to temporary differences. All deferred tax liabilities are recognized on the balance sheet.

Example 2	Deferred Tax Liability

Facts: Stone Co. began operations in Year 1 and reported $225,000 in financial income for the year. Stone Co.'s Year 1 tax depreciation exceeded its book depreciation by $25,000. Stone's tax rate for Year 1 and years thereafter was 21 percent. In Year 2, book depreciation exceeded tax depreciation by $25,000. This is a reversal of the temporary difference between GAAP and tax accounting and results in the reversal of the deferred tax liability in Year 2.

Required: Prepare the tax journal entries for Year 1 and Year 2.

Solution:

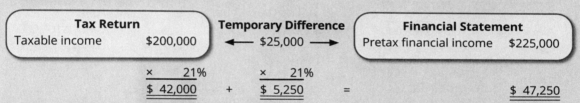

The excess depreciation on the tax return results in a future liability, a financial accounting expense in future years that will not be deductible in future years because it was deducted in Year 1. The deferred tax liability reflects the fact that less depreciation will be deducted on the tax return in future years, compared with the financial statements. This yields a future taxable income which will be greater than the future financial accounting income.

Journal entry to record the taxes in Year 1:

DR	Income tax expense—current	$42,000	
DR	Income tax expense—deferred	5,250	
CR	Deferred tax liability		$ 5,250
CR	Income tax payable		42,000

Journal entry to record the Year 2 reversal of the deferred tax liability:

DR	Deferred tax liability	$5,250	
CR	Income tax expense—deferred		$5,250

3.2.2 Deferred Tax Assets

Deferred tax assets arise when the amount of taxes paid in the current period exceeds the amount of income tax expense in the current period. They are anticipated future benefits derived from situations in which future taxable income will be less than future financial accounting income due to temporary differences.

3.2.3 Valuation Allowance (Contra-Account)

If it is more likely than not (a likelihood of more than 50 percent) that part or all of the deferred tax asset will not be realized, a valuation allowance is recognized. The net deferred tax asset should equal that portion of the deferred tax asset which, based on available evidence, is more likely than not to be realized.

Example 3   Deferred Tax Asset

Facts: Black Co., organized on January 2, Year 1, had pretax accounting income of $500,000 and taxable income of $800,000 for the year ended December 31, Year 1. The enacted tax rate for all years is 21 percent. The only temporary difference is accrued product warranty costs, which are expenses to be paid as follows:

Year 2, $100,000; Year 3, $100,000; Year 4, $100,000

Required: Prepare the tax journal entries for Year 1 and Year 2.

Solution:

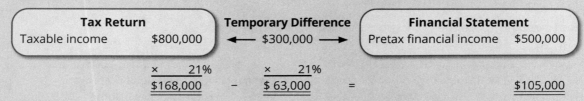

Tax Return		Temporary Difference		Financial Statement	
Taxable income	$800,000	← $300,000 →		Pretax financial income	$500,000
×	21%	×	21%		
	$168,000	−	$ 63,000	=	$105,000

Journal entry to record the Year 1 taxes:

DR	Deferred tax asset	$ 63,000	
DR	Income tax expense—current	168,000	
CR	Income tax payable		$168,000
CR	Income tax benefit—deferred		63,000

When the company pays the warranty costs of $100,000 in Year 2, the company will take a $21,000 ($100,000 × 21%) tax deduction related to the warranty costs and will reverse out the related deferred tax asset.

Journal entry to record reversal of a portion of the deferred tax asset for warranty costs paid and deducted in Year 2.

DR	Income tax expense—deferred	$21,000	
CR	Deferred tax asset		$21,000

Example 4   Valuation Allowance

Facts: Black expects to have taxable income of $100,000 in Year 2, but no taxable income after Year 2.

Required: Prepare the journal entry to record the deferred tax asset and valuation allowance in Year 1.

Solution: The deferred tax asset would be limited to the amount to be realized in Year 2 ($21,000 = $100,000 × 21%). A deferred tax asset of $63,000 would be recognized, but a valuation account of $42,000 would result in a net deferred tax asset of $21,000.

Journal entry:

DR	Deferred tax asset	$ 63,000	
DR	Income tax expense—current	168,000	
CR	Deferred tax asset valuation allowance		$ 42,000
CR	Income tax benefit—deferred		21,000
CR	Income tax payable		168,000

Example 5   Permanent and Temporary Differences

Facts: Foxy Inc.'s financial statement and taxable income for Year 1 follows (income before the effect of tax-related differences was $140,000):

Financial statement pretax income		$115,000
Differences: municipal interest income		(12,000)
Penalty expense		7,000
Tax depreciation	$40,000	
Book depreciation	(30,000)	
Excess tax depreciation		(10,000)
Income tax return		$100,000

The enacted tax rate is 21 percent for this year and future years.

Required: Prepare the tax journal entry for Year 1.

(continued)

(continued)

Solution:

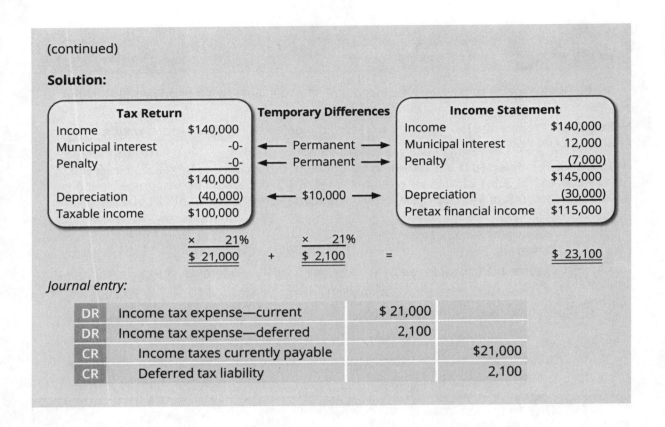

Tax Return		Temporary Differences	Income Statement	
Income	$140,000		Income	$140,000
Municipal interest	-0-	◄— Permanent —►	Municipal interest	12,000
Penalty	-0-	◄— Permanent —►	Penalty	(7,000)
	$140,000			$145,000
Depreciation	(40,000)	◄— $10,000 —►	Depreciation	(30,000)
Taxable income	$100,000		Pretax financial income	$115,000

	× 21%	× 21%		
	$ 21,000	+ $ 2,100	=	$ 23,100

Journal entry:

DR	Income tax expense—current	$ 21,000	
DR	Income tax expense—deferred	2,100	
CR	Income taxes currently payable		$21,000
CR	Deferred tax liability		2,100

7

Income Taxes: Part 2

1 Uncertain Tax Positions

An uncertain tax position is defined as some level of uncertainty of the sustainability of a particular tax position taken by a company. U.S. GAAP requires a more-likely-than-not level of confidence before reflecting a tax benefit in an entity's financial statements.

1.1 Scope

A tax position is a filing position that an enterprise has taken or expects to take on its tax return, including:

- A tax deduction (the most common type of tax position).

- A decision to not file a tax return.

- An allocation or shift of income between jurisdictions.

- The characterization of income, or a decision to exclude reporting taxable income, in a tax return.

- A decision to classify a transaction, entity, or other position in a tax return as tax exempt.

1.2 Two-Step Approach

1.2.1 Step 1: Recognition of the Tax Benefit

- **Test "More-Likely-Than-Not"**

  The "more-likely-than-not" threshold must be met before a tax benefit can be recognized in the financial statements.

  - The assessment is based on the expected outcome if the dispute with the taxing authority were taken to the court of last resort.

- **Threshold Considerations**

  - The threshold is based on the technical merits of the position.

  - Presume that the relevant taxing authority will examine the tax position and has full knowledge of all relevant information.

  - Each tax position should be evaluated separately.

- **Test Failed**

  - The tax benefit is not recognized in the financial statements if it fails to meet the "more-likely-than-not" test; and

  - Financial statement tax expense is increased.

1.2.2 Step 2: Measurement of the Tax Benefit

■ **Recorded Amount**

- Recognize the largest amount of tax benefit that has a greater than 50 percent likelihood of being realized upon ultimate settlement with the taxing authority.

- If the tax position is based on clear and unambiguous tax law, recognize the full benefit in the financial statements.

Pass Key

Step 1: The evaluation is based on the expected outcome in the court of last resort.

Step 2: The evaluation is based on the expected outcome in a settlement with the taxing authority.

Illustration 1   Uncertain Tax Position

Foxy Inc. prepared its Year 1 tax return. Foxy Inc. has taken a tax deduction for $2,000 that results in a $420 tax savings (21 percent tax rate). Foxy believes that there is a greater than 50 percent chance that, if audited, the tax deduction would be sustained as filed (the tax deduction meets the "more-likely-than-not" test). However, Foxy concludes that if challenged, it would negotiate a settlement. The following is Foxy's assessment of outcomes:

Potential Outcomes	Probability	Cumulative Probability
$420 savings	26%	26
$300 savings	25%	51 > 50%
$200 savings	21%	72
$100 savings	18%	90
$0 savings	10%	100

Result:

- Based on Foxy Inc.'s assessment of possible outcomes, Foxy should recognize a tax savings/benefit of $300.

- This amount represents the largest benefit that has a greater than 50 percent likelihood of being realized.

- Accordingly, Foxy must record a $120 income tax liability.

2 Enacted Tax Rate

Measurement of deferred taxes is based on the applicable tax rate. This requires using the enacted tax rate expected to apply to taxable items (temporary differences) in the periods the taxable item is expected to be paid (liability) or realized (asset).

Example 1 — Choice of Tax Rate

Facts: Stone Co. began operations in Year 1 and reported $225,000 in income before income taxes for the year. Stone's Year 1 tax depreciation exceeded its book depreciation by $25,000. Stone's tax rate for Year 1 was 30 percent, and the enacted rate for years after is 21 percent.

Required: Prepare the tax journal entry for Year 1.

Solution:

Tax Return		Temporary Difference	Financial Statement	
Taxable income	$200,000	← $25,000 →	Pretax financial income	$225,000

	× 30%		× 21%			
	$ 60,000	+	$ 5,250	=		$ 65,250

		Debit	Credit
DR	Income tax expense—current	$60,000	
DR	Income tax expense—deferred	5,250	
CR	Deferred tax liability		$ 5,250
CR	Income tax payable		60,000

Pass Key

Use the tax rate in effect when the temporary difference reverses itself. Do not allow the CPA examiners to trick you into using the following tax rates:

- Anticipated
- Proposed
- Unsigned

3   Treatment of and Adjustment for Changes

3.1   Changes in Tax Laws or Rates

The liability method requires that the deferred tax account balance (asset or liability) be adjusted when the tax rates change. Thus if future tax rates have been enacted, not just proposed or estimated, the deferred tax liability and asset accounts will be calculated using the appropriate enacted future effective tax rate.

Changes in tax laws or rates are recognized in the period of change (enactment).

- The amount of the adjustment is measured by the change in applicable laws/rates applied to the remaining cumulative temporary differences.

- The adjustment enters into income tax expense for that period as a component of income from continuing operations.

- An entity must reflect the impact of the enacted change in the annual effective tax rate computation in the interim period that includes the enactment date.

3.2   Change in the Valuation Allowance

A change in circumstances that causes a change in judgment about the ability to realize the related deferred tax asset in future years should be recognized in income from continuing operations in the period of the change.

3.3   Change in the Tax Status of an Enterprise

- An entity's tax status may change from taxable to nontaxable (e.g., corporation to partnership) or from nontaxable to taxable (S corporation to C corporation).

- At the date a nontaxable entity becomes a taxable entity, a deferred tax liability or asset should be recognized for any temporary differences.

- At the date a taxable entity becomes a nontaxable entity, any existing deferred tax liability or asset should be eliminated (written off).

- The effect of recognizing or eliminating a deferred tax liability or deferred tax asset should be included in income from continuing operations in the period of the change.

3.4   Net Temporary Adjustment (From Beginning Balance)

The deferred tax account is adjusted for the change in deferred taxes (asset or liability), due to the current year's events. The *income tax expense/benefit – deferred* is the difference between the beginning balance in the deferred tax account and the properly computed ending balance in the account.

Example 2   Change in Tax Rate

Facts: Julie Co. had previously recorded temporary differences of $10,000. The enacted rate in the year the temporary differences originated was 20 percent. The deferred tax liability has a beginning balance of $2,000 ($10,000 × 20%). For the current year, taxable income is $100,000 and financial statement income is $120,000. The $20,000 difference is a temporary difference caused by depreciation. The newly enacted rate for the current and future periods is 21 percent. The previously recorded temporary differences have not yet reversed.

Required: Prepare the current year tax journal entry.

Solution:

	Temporary Difference	
Tax Return	$10,000 (Beg)	**Financial Statement**
Taxable income $100,000	← $20,000 →	Pretax financial income $120,000
	$30,000	
× 21%	× 21%	
	6,300	
	(2,000) (Beg)	
$ 21,000 +	$ 4,300 =	$ 25,300

Journal entry to record the taxes:

DR	Income tax expense—current	$21,000	
DR	Income tax expense—deferred	4,300	
CR	Deferred tax liability		$ 4,300
CR	Income tax payable		21,000

4   Balance Sheet Presentation

Under U.S. GAAP, deferred tax liabilities and assets should be classified and reported as a non-current amount on the balance sheet. All deferred tax liabilities and assets must be offset (netted) and presented as one amount (a net non-current asset or a net non-current liability), unless the deferred tax liabilities and assets are attributable to different tax-paying components of the entity or to different tax jurisdictions.

5 Operating Losses

A net operating loss (NOL) generated before 2018 can be carried forward for up to 20 years to offset 100 percent of taxable income in future years. An NOL that is generated starting in 2018 or later can be carried forward indefinitely.

NOLs arising in 2018 or later and that are carried forward to taxable years beginning in 2021 or later are limited to 80 percent of the future year's taxable income before the NOL deduction. Taxable income and financial accounting income will differ for the years in which the loss is incurred and carried forward.

5.1 Operating Loss Carryforwards

If an operating loss is carried forward, the tax effects are recognized to the extent that the tax benefit is more likely than not to be realized. Tax carryforwards should be recognized as deferred tax assets (because they represent future tax savings) in the period in which they occur.

■ Net operating loss (NOL) carryforwards should be "valued" using the enacted (future) tax rate for the period(s) they are expected to be used.

■ Tax credit carryforwards should be "valued" at the amount of tax payable to be offset in the future. A current net operating loss of $100,000 is carried forward to be used in a period for which the current enacted tax rate is 21 percent.

Journal entry to record the deferred tax benefit:

DR	Deferred tax asset	$21,000	
CR	Tax benefit *		$21,000

*This is a reduction of the book loss (not a contra-expense).

■ The deferred tax asset (DR) will reduce tax payable in a future period.

■ The tax benefit (CR) would reduce the net operating loss of the current period.

Example 3	Net Operating Losses

Facts: The pretax financial accounting income and taxable income of ABC Company were the same for each of the following years. No temporary or permanent differences exist. Assume that it is more likely than not that there will be no taxable earnings after 2026.

	Income	Enacted Rates
2025 (current year)	(60,000)	21%
2026 (expected)	10,000	21%
2027 and forward	-0-	21%

Required: Prepare the journal entry to record the 2025 income taxes.

Solution:

2025 net operating loss (NOL) carryforward		$60,000
Deferred tax asset (NOL carryforward benefit):		
2026 and future years ($60,000 × 21%)		$12,600
Deferred tax asset valuation allowance:		
NOL carryforward from 2025	$60,000	
Less: 80% of 2026 income	(8,000)	
Carryforward that will not be used	$52,000	
Tax rate (enacted)	× 21%	
Less: deferred tax asset valuation allowance		(10,920)
Net realizable deferred tax asset		$ 1,680

Journal entry to record income taxes for 2025:

DR	Deferred tax asset	$12,600	
CR	Deferred tax asset valuation allowance		$10,920
CR	Income tax benefit		1,680

6 Investee's Undistributed Earnings

6.1 Income Tax Return

Taxable income is the dividends received. Under U.S. tax law, there is a dividends-received deduction (exclusion) based on the percentage of ownership in the stock of the other corporation:

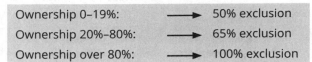

Ownership 0–19%:	→	50% exclusion
Ownership 20%–80%:	→	65% exclusion
Ownership over 80%:	→	100% exclusion

6.2 GAAP Financial Statement

Report percentage of investee's income using the equity method for an investment between 20 and 50 percent.

6.3 Temporary Difference

It should be presumed that all undistributed earnings will ultimately be distributed to the investor/parent at some future time. Financial statement income of the investee claimed by the investor/parent as earnings is greater than actual dividends received from the investee that are claimed on the tax return.

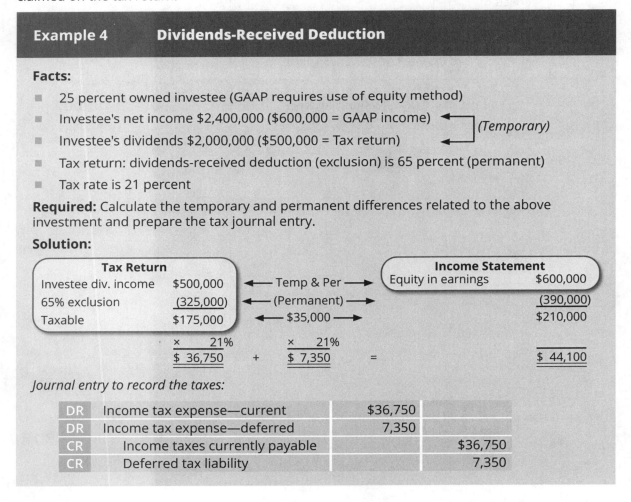

Example 4   Dividends-Received Deduction

Facts:

- 25 percent owned investee (GAAP requires use of equity method)
- Investee's net income $2,400,000 ($600,000 = GAAP income) *(Temporary)*
- Investee's dividends $2,000,000 ($500,000 = Tax return)
- Tax return: dividends-received deduction (exclusion) is 65 percent (permanent)
- Tax rate is 21 percent

Required: Calculate the temporary and permanent differences related to the above investment and prepare the tax journal entry.

Solution:

Tax Return				Income Statement	
Investee div. income	$500,000	← Temp & Per →		Equity in earnings	$600,000
65% exclusion	(325,000)	← (Permanent) →			(390,000)
Taxable	$175,000	← $35,000 →			$210,000
	× 21%	× 21%			
	$ 36,750	+ $ 7,350	=		$ 44,100

Journal entry to record the taxes:

DR	Income tax expense—current	$36,750	
DR	Income tax expense—deferred	7,350	
CR	Income taxes currently payable		$36,750
CR	Deferred tax liability		7,350

7   Income Tax Disclosures

7.1   Balance Sheet Disclosures

- The components of a net deferred tax liability or asset should be disclosed, including the total of:

    - All deferred tax liabilities

    - All deferred tax assets

    - The valuation allowance for deferred tax assets

- Other balance sheet disclosures include:

    - The net change during the year in the total valuation allowance.

    - The tax effect of each type of temporary difference and carryforward that is significant to the deferred tax liability or asset.

7.2   Income Statement Disclosures

The amount of income tax expense (or benefit) allocated to continuing operations and the amount(s) separately allocated to other item(s) must be disclosed.

- The significant components of income tax expense attributable to continuing operations must be disclosed. These include:

    - Current tax expense or benefit

    - Deferred tax expense or benefit

    - Investment tax credits

    - Government grants (that cause a reduction of income tax expense)

    - Benefits of NOL carryforwards

    - Tax expense allocated to shareholders' equity items

    - Adjustments of deferred taxes from changes in tax laws or rates

    - Adjustments of the beginning-of-the-year deferred tax asset valuation due to changes in expectations

- The tax benefit of an operating loss carryforward should be reported in the same manner (income statement location) as the current year source of income or loss that gave rise to the benefit recognition.

- A recognition (in either percentages or dollar amounts) of income tax expense attributable to continuing operations and the amount of income tax expense that would have resulted from applying the statutory rate to pretax income from continuing operations should be presented.

- Income (or loss) from continuing operations before income tax expense (or benefit) disaggregated between domestic and foreign must be disclosed.

- Income tax expense (or benefit) from continuing operations disaggregated by federal, state, and foreign must be disclosed. Income taxes imposed by a jurisdiction shall be included in the jurisdiction imposing the tax.

7.3   Statement of Cash Flows Disclosures

All entities must disclose income taxes paid (net of refunds received):

- Disaggregated by federal, state, and foreign.

- To each jurisdiction, if the amount of income taxes paid in a jurisdiction is equal to or greater than 5 percent of the total income taxes paid net of refunds.

7.4   Other Disclosures

The income tax expense (or benefit) reported may differ from what is otherwise expected based on statutory tax rates.

Disclosure requirements include a reconciliation between the reported income tax expense (or benefit) from continuing operations and the amount computed by multiplying the income (or loss) from continuing operations before income taxes by the applicable statutory federal or national income tax rate of the jurisdiction or country.

8 Corporation Tax Summary

Corporation Tax Summary	GAAP: Financial Statements	IRC: Tax Return	Temp.	Perm.	None
Gross Income					
Gross sales	Income	Income			✓
Installment sales	Income	Income when received	✓		
Rents and royalties in advance	Income when earned	Income when received	✓		
State tax refund	Income	Income			✓
Dividends: equity method 100/65/50% exclusion	Income is subsidiary's earnings No exclusion	Income is dividends-received Excluded forever	✓	✓	
Items Not Includable in "Taxable Income"					
State and municipal bond interest	Income	Not taxable income		✓	
Life insurance proceeds	Income	Generally not taxable income		✓	
Gain/loss on treasury stock	Not reported	Not reported			✓
Ordinary Expenses					
Cost of goods sold	Currently expensed	Uniform capitalization rules			✓
Officers' compensation (top)	Expense	$1,000,000 limit			✓
Bad debt	Allowance (estimated)	Direct write-off	✓		
Estimated liability for contingency (e.g., warranty)	Expense (accrue estimated)	No deduction until paid	✓		
Interest expense: business loan	Expense	Deduct (up to limit)	✓		✓
Tax-free investment	Expense	Not deductible		✓	
Charitable contributions	All expensed	Limited to 10% of adjusted taxable income	✓	✓	✓
Loss on abandonment/casualty	Expense	Deduct			✓
Loss on worthless securities	Expense	Deduct			✓
Depreciation: MACRS vs. straight-line	Slow depreciation	Fast depreciation	✓		
Section 179 expense deduction	Not allowed (must depreciate)	$1,250,000 (2025)	✓		
Different basis of asset-	Use GAAP basis	Use tax basis		✓	
Amortization: start-up/organizational expenses	Expense	$5,000 maximum/amortize excess over 15 years	✓		
Franchise	Amortize	Amortize over 15 years	✓		
Goodwill	Impairment test	Amortize over 15 years	✓		
Depletion: percentage vs. straight-line (cost)	Cost over years	Percentage of sales	✓		
Percentage in excess of cost	Not allowed	Percentage of sales		✓	
Profit sharing and pension expense	Expense accrued	No deduction until paid	✓		
Accrued expense (50% owner/family)	Expense accrued	No deduction until paid	✓		
State taxes (paid)	Expense	Deduct			✓
Meals	Expense	Generally 50% deductible		✓	
GAAP Expense Items That Are Not Tax Deductions					
Life insurance expense (corporation)	Expense	Not deductible		✓	
Penalties	Expense	Not deductible		✓	
Entertainment	Expense	Not deductible		✓	
Lobbying/political expense	Expense	Not deductible		✓	
Federal income taxes	Expense	Not deductible		✓	
Special Items					
Net capital gain (NCG)	Income	Income			✓
Net capital loss (NCL)	Report as loss	Not deductible	✓		
Carryback/carryover (3 years back/5 years forward)	Not applicable	Offset NCGs in other years	✓		
Related shareholder	Report as a loss	Not deductible		✓	
Net operating loss	Report as a loss	Carryover indefinitely	✓		
Research and development	Expense	Expense/amortize/capitalize	✓	✓	✓

NOTES

FAR

6

NFP Accounting and Governmental Accounting

Module

1 Not-for-Profit Financial Reporting: Part 1

1 Introduction to Not-for-Profit Accounting

1.1 Characteristics of Not-for-Profit Organizations

Not-for-profit entities are defined by the FASB as entities that have the following characteristics:

1. Their revenues come from contributions.

2. Their operating purpose does not include profit, although there is nothing to preclude the generation of a profit.

3. Their ownership interests are unlike business enterprises.

1.2 Industries That Use Not-for-Profit Accounting

Not-for-profit entities are generally divided into four separate categories related to various industries:

- **Health Care Organizations**
  - Hospitals
  - Nursing homes
  - Hospices

- **Educational Institutions**
  - Colleges and universities
  - Other schools

- **Voluntary Health and Welfare Organizations**
  - United Way
  - American Red Cross
  - March of Dimes

- **Other Private (Not Governmental) Not-for-Profit Organizations**
  - Cemetery organizations
  - Fraternal organizations
  - Labor unions
  - Museums, libraries, and performing arts organizations
  - Professional organizations (e.g., the AICPA)

1.3   Users of Not-for-Profit Financial Statements

Users of not-for-profit financial statements include donors, members, creditors, and others who provide resources to the not-for-profit entity (e.g., the government via grants, etc.).

1.3.1   Needs of Users

Users of not-for-profit financial statements have common needs. These common needs include the ability to assess:

- The services the organization provides.

- The organization's ability to continue to provide those services.

- The method the organization's managers use to discharge their stewardship responsibility.

1.3.2   Financial Statement Information

The following information should be provided in not-for-profit organization financial statements in order to meet these common needs:

- The amount and nature of an organization's assets, liabilities, and net assets (Statement of Financial Position).

- The effects of events and circumstances that change the amount and nature of net assets (Statement of Activities).

- The amount and kinds of inflows and outflows of economic resources occurring within a period (Statement of Activities).

- The relationship between the inflows and outflows (Statement of Activities).

- How an organization obtains and spends cash (Statement of Cash Flows).

- The service efforts of an organization (Statement of Activities or Notes to Financial Statements).

1.4   Full Accrual Basis of Accounting

Generally accepted accounting principles require that not-for-profit organizations report using the full accrual basis of accounting.

The primary reporting emphasis is placed on disclosing the sources of the institution's resources and how they were expended, rather than on the periodic determination of net income. The overall emphasis for not-for-profit financial statements is on basic information for the organization as a whole.

Pass Key

The external financial statements of not-for-profit entities do not present funds. The focus of the financial statements is on the basic information of the organization taken as a whole.

2 Not-for-Profit Financial Reporting Standards

2.1 FASB ASC

The external financial reporting standards for not-for-profit organizations are outlined in the FASB Accounting Standards Codification (ASC). General principles of not-for-profit financial reporting include the following:

- All types of private, not-for-profit organizations are required to have consistent external reporting, making it easier to compare the performance of different not-for-profit organizations.

- Fund accounting is not used for external financial reporting, although separate funds may be maintained for internal purposes.

- External financial statements must focus on the basic information for the organization as a whole.

- Governmental not-for-profits (for example, a state university) are governed by the Government Accounting Standards Board (GASB), not the FASB.

2.2 Required Financial Statements

A complete set of general purpose, external financial statements for a not-for-profit entity include the following:

- Statement of Financial Position (equivalent to a commercial Balance Sheet)

- Statement of Activities (equivalent to a commercial Income Statement and Statement of Changes in Retained Earnings)

- Statement of Cash Flows (equivalent to a commercial Statement of Cash Flows using either the direct or indirect method)

2.3 Reporting Expenses by Nature and Function

All not-for-profit organizations must report information about the relationships between functional classifications and natural classifications of expenses in one location. Not-for-profits have the latitude to report in one of three ways:

- On the face of the Statement of Activities

- As a schedule in the notes to the financial statements

- In a separate financial statement (no specific title provided by the FASB)

Pass Key

Functional classifications of expenses categorize costs by major classes of program and support services. Program services relate to the purpose and mission of the not-for-profit organization; support services relate to such activities as management and general, fundraising, and membership development.

Natural classifications of expenses include such descriptions as salaries, rent, utilities, interest expense, supplies, etc., similar to general ledger titles for expense.

3 Statement of Financial Position

3.1 Components of the Statement of Financial Position

The not-for-profit *statement of financial position* is divided into three major components:

- Assets
- Liabilities
- Net assets (equity)

3.2 Sequence of Account Display for Assets and Liabilities

Assets and liabilities should be presented based on the following principles:

- Assets and liabilities should be classified as current or non-current;
- Assets should be sequenced by nearness to cash, and liabilities sequenced by nearness to maturity; and
- Assets restricted or designated for non-current purposes (e.g., debt liquidation, acquisition of long lived assets, etc.) should be displayed as non-current.

3.3 Net Assets (With and Without Donor Restrictions)

The components of net assets of not-for-profit organizations may include one or both of the following two classifications: *with* donor restrictions or *without* donor restrictions. Classifications are based on the existence or absence of *donor*-imposed restrictions.

3.3.1 Net Assets Without Donor Restrictions

Net assets without donor restrictions are available to finance general operations of a not-for-profit organization and may be expended at the discretion of the governing board.

- Net assets without donor restrictions are not otherwise restricted by external donor-imposed restrictions.
- Internal board-designated funds are classified as net assets without donor restrictions and may include:
  - Board-designated endowment funds
  - Board-designated net assets (for future expenditure)

3.3.2 Net Assets With Donor Restrictions

Net assets with donor restrictions are subject to specific, externally imposed limitations made by a donor. Information regarding the nature and amounts of different types of donor-imposed restrictions should be either reported within the financial statement classification of net assets with donor restrictions or in the notes to the financial statements. Examples of various types of donor-imposed restrictions include:

- Support of particular operating activity
- Investment for a specified term
- Use in specified period
- Acquisition of long-lived assets

- Assets that are to be used for a specified purpose and not sold
- Donor-restricted endowments that are perpetual in nature (assets donated with a stipulation that they be invested to provide a permanent source of income)

Pass Key

Internal board-designated funds are classified as net assets without donor restrictions. The examiners sometimes try to trick candidates with incorrect answer options that suggest board-designated endowment funds created by self-imposed limits should be reported as net assets with donor restrictions

3.4   Statement of Financial Position Disclosures

Not-for-profit entities must disclose relevant information about the liquidity or maturity of assets and liabilities including restrictions and self-imposed limits on the use of particular items.

Not-for-profit organizations are also required to measure crypto assets at fair value in the statement of financial position and recognize changes from remeasurement in the statement of activities. In addition, there are required disclosures so that users of the financial statements can analyze and assess the exposure and risk of significant individual crypto asset holdings.

In addition to information displayed on the face of the statement of financial position, not-for-profit organizations must disclose in the notes of the financial statements:

- Qualitative information useful in assessing liquidity, including how the organization manages its liquid resources to meet cash needs for general expenditures within one year of the statement of financial position date. Additional qualitative disclosures include:
  - A description of the type of asset whose use is limited
  - Nature and amount of limits
  - Contractual limits
  - How and when resources can be used
- Quantitative information that displays or discloses the availability of its liquid resources as affected by:
  - The nature of the resources
  - External limits imposed by donors
  - Internal limits imposed by governing boards

3.4.1 Supplemental Disclosures, Net Assets With Donor Restrictions

Not-for-Profit Organization
Notes to Financial Statements
Net Assets With Donor Restrictions
As of December 31, Year 2
(in thousands)

Net assets with donor restrictions are restricted for the following purposes or periods:

Subject to expenditure for specified purpose

Program Alpha activities		
Purchase of equipment	$ 3,060	
Research and seminars	1,190	
Program Beta activities		
Disaster relief	1,025	
Program Gamma activities		
Building and equipment	2,150	
Research	3,025	
Subtotal		$ 10,450

Subject to the passage of time

For periods after Year 2		3,140

Subject to Not-for-Profit spending policy and appropriations

Investment in perpetuity, which once appropriated is expendable to support:		
Program Alpha activities	$ 33,300	
Program Beta activities	15,820	
Program Gamma activities	16,480	
Any activities of the organization	109,100	
Subtotal		174,700

Subject to appropriation and expenditure when a specified event occurs

Endowment requiring income to be added to original gift until the fund's value is $2,500	$ 2,120	
Paid-up life insurance policy that will provide proceeds upon the death of insured for an endowment to support general activities	80	
Subtotal		2,200

Not subject to appropriation or expenditure

Land required to be used for a recreational area		3,000
Total net assets with donor restrictions		**$193,490**

3.4.2 Supplemental Disclosures, Net Assets Without Donor Restrictions

Not-for-Profit Organization
Notes to Financial Statements
Net Assets Without Donor Restrictions
As of December 31, Year 2
(in thousands)

Not-for-Profit Organization's governing board has designated, from net assets without donor restrictions of $92,600, net assets for the following purpose as of December 31, Year 2.

Quasi-endowment	$36,600
Liquidity reserve	1,300
Total	$37,900

Not-for-Profit Organization
Statement of Financial Position
As of December 31, Year 2 and Year 1
(in thousands)

	Year 2	Year 1
Assets:		
Cash and cash equivalents	$ 4,575	$ 4,960
Accounts and interest receivable	2,130	1,670
Inventories and prepaid expenses	610	1,000
Contributions receivable	3,025	2,700
Short-term investments	1,400	1,000
Assets restricted to investment in land, buildings, and equipment	5,210	4,560
Land, buildings, and equipment	61,700	63,590
Long-term investments	218,160	203,500
Total assets	$296,720	$282,980
Liabilities and net assets:		
Liabilities:		
Accounts payable	$ 2,570	$ 1,050
Refundable advance	–	650
Grants payable	875	1,300
Notes payable	–	1,140
Annuities obligations	1,685	1,700
Long-term debt	5,500	6,500
Total liabilities	10,630	12,340
Net assets:		
Without donor restrictions	92,600	84,570
With donor restrictions	193,490	186,070
Total net assets	286,090	270,640
Total liabilities and net assets	$296,720	$282,980

4 Statement of Activities

4.1 Elements of the Statement of Activities

The not-for-profit statement of activities reports revenues and expenses (shown gross), gains and losses (often shown net), and reclassification between classes of net assets (for example, from net assets with donor restrictions to net assets without donor restrictions, once restrictions have been satisfied).

4.1.1 Required Elements

Three required elements are presented in the statement of activities:

1. Change in total net assets.

2. Change in net assets without donor restrictions.

3. Change in net assets with donor restrictions.

4.1.2 Format

Preparers have latitude in presentation formats that sequence data in any number of orders, including:

- Revenues, expenses, gains and losses, and reclassification of assets shown last.

- Certain revenues less directly related to expenses, followed by a subtotal, then other revenues and other expenses, gains and losses, and reclassification of net assets.

- Expenses followed by revenues, gains and losses, and the reclassification of net assets.

Other formatting issues to consider include:

- Presentation of intermediate totals such as operating income should be disclosed in the notes to the financial statements.

- Prior period adjustments and changes in accounting principle are reported as adjustments to beginning net assets.

- Items classified as other comprehensive income in commercial accounting are presented in the statement of activities after operating income.

4.2 Classification of Revenue, Gains, and Other Support

Revenues are classified into one of two categories, according to the existence or absence of donor-imposed restrictions.

4.2.1 Net Assets Without Donor Restrictions

Revenues are classified as net assets without donor restrictions unless the use of the assets received is limited by donor-imposed restrictions. Examples of revenues received without donor restrictions include:

- Fees from rendering services.

- Contributions that have no explicit donor stipulation restricting use.

- Gains and losses recognized on investment that are not accompanied with explicit donor restrictions (investment returns are displayed net of related expenses).

4.2.2 Net Assets With Donor Restrictions

Revenues are classified as net assets with donor restrictions (donor-restricted support) if the use of the asset received is limited by donor-imposed restrictions. All restricted revenue is included in the same classification regardless of whether the restriction is perpetual or if the restriction can be satisfied by the recipient. Classification grouping does not, however, preclude the not-for-profit organization from itemizing the character of restrictions on either the face of the financial statements or the notes. Examples of revenues received with donor restrictions include:

- Contributions subject to expenditure for a specified purpose (e.g. programs or capital projects).

- Contributions subject to the passage of time.

- Contributions associated with restrictions that are otherwise temporary in nature.

- Contributions requiring investment in perpetuity with returns eligible for appropriation (e.g., donor-restricted endowment funds).

4.3 Reclassification of Restrictions

Contributions with donor-imposed restrictions are recognized as donor-restricted support in the period in which they are received and recognized as an increase to net assets with donor restrictions.

When a donor restriction is satisfied, a reclassification is reported on the statement of activities. Reclassifications are items that simultaneously increase one net asset class and decrease another.

- Donor-imposed restrictions that are met in the same period they are received may be recorded as an increase to net assets without donor restrictions (contribution revenue), provided that the organization discloses and consistently applies this accounting policy.

- Support that results in perpetually restricted net assets ordinarily are not reclassified, because the donor restrictions never expire.

- Revenue, gains, and other support that result in an increase to net assets without donor restrictions ordinarily do not become restricted.

Illustration 1 Reclassification

A not-for-profit clinic receives operating subsidies for indigent care under a state contract. The contract represents a donor-restricted contribution to the clinic; however, the clinic routinely spends adequate amounts on the state-funded services to reclassify the funding from net assets with donor restrictions to net assets without donor restrictions in the year received. Assuming consistent application of its accounting policies, the clinic has the option of immediately reporting the subsidies received under the state contract as an increase to net assets without donor restrictions.

4.4 Expense Classification in the Statement of Activities

All expenses (other than investment expenses) are reported as decreases in net assets without donor restrictions. Investment expense is netted against investment returns and classified according to the requirements of the investment revenue. Details of functional classifications and their relationship to natural expense classifications must be presented on the face of the financial statements or the notes. Examples of functional expense classifications are as follows:

4.4.1   Program Services

Program services (expenses) are the activities for which the organization is chartered. Examples are:

- **Universities:** Education and research
- **Hospitals:** Patient care and education
- **Union:** Labor negotiations and training
- **Day Care:** Child care

4.4.2   Support Services

Supporting services include everything not classified as a program service. Examples are:

- Fundraising
- Management and general (administrative expenses)
- Membership development

4.4.3   Combined Costs

Not-for-profit organizations that combine fundraising efforts with educational (or program) services should allocate the combined cost between functions.

Not-for-Profit Organization **Statement of Activities** For the Year Ended December 31, Year 2 *(in thousands)*			
	Without Donor Restrictions	**With Donor Restrictions**	**Total**
Revenues, gains, and other support:			
Contributions of cash and other financial assets	$ 6,790	$ 7,430	$ 14,220
Contributions of nonfinancial assets	1,850	960	2,810
Fees	5,200	–	5,200
Investment return, net	6,650	18,300	24,950
Gain on sale of equipment	200	–	200
Other	150	–	150
Net assets released from restrictions			
Satisfaction of program restrictions	8,990	(8,990)	–
Satisfaction of equipment acquisition restrictions	1,500	(1,500)	–
Expiration of time restrictions	1,250	(1,250)	–

Appropriation from donor endowment and
    subsequent satisfaction of any related
    donor restrictions
	7,500	(7,500)	–

Total net assets released from restrictions	19,240	(19,240)	–
Total revenues, gains, and other support	40,080	7,450	47,530

(continued)

(continued)

Expenses and losses:

Program Alpha	13,296	–	13,296
Program Beta	8,649	–	8,649
Program Gamma	5,837	–	5,837
Management and general	2,038	–	2,038
Fundraising	2,150	–	2,150
Total expenses	31,970	–	31,970
Fire loss	80	–	80
Actuarial loss on annuity obligations	–	30	30
Total expenses and losses	32,050	30	32,080
Changes in net assets	8,030	7,420	15,450
Net assets at beginning of year	84,570	186,070	270,640
Net assets at end of year	$92,600	$193,490	$286,090

4.4.4   Reporting Expenses by Nature and Function

Expense information should include the relationships between functional classifications and natural classifications.

- Functional expenses should be classified as:
    - Major classes of program services; or
    - Supporting activities
- Natural expense components of each functional expense must be presented, including such classifications as:
    - Salaries
    - Rent
    - Electricity
    - Supplies
    - Interest expense
    - Depreciation
    - Awards and grants
    - Professional fees
- Gains and losses and external and direct internal investment expenses that have been netted against the investment return should not be included in the functional expense analysis.

Not-for-Profit Organization
Notes to Financial Statements
Expenses Classification
For the Year Ended December 31, Year 2
(in thousands)

The table below presents expenses by both their nature and function.

	Program Activities				Supporting Activities			
	Alpha	**Beta**	**Gamma**	**Programs Subtotal**	**Management and General**	**Fund-raising**	**Supporting Subtotal**	**Total Expenses**
Salaries and benefits	$ 7,400	$3,900	$1,725	$13,025	$1,130	$ 960	$2,090	$15,115
Grants to other organizations	2,075	750	1,925	4,750	–	–	–	4,750
Supplies and travel	890	1,013	499	2,402	213	540	753	3,155
Services and professional fees	160	1,490	600	2,250	200	390	590	2,840
Office and occupancy	1,160	600	450	2,210	218	100	318	2,528
Depreciation	1,440	800	570	2,810	250	140	390	3,200
Interest	171	96	68	335	27	20	47	382
Total expenses	$13,296	$8,649	$5,837	$27,782	$2,038	$2,150	$4,188	$31,970

The financial statements report certain categories of expenses that are attributable to more than one program or supporting function. Therefore, these expenses require allocation on a reasonable basis that is consistently applied. The expenses that are allocated include depreciation, interest, and office and occupancy, which are allocated on a square footage basis, as well as salaries and benefits, which are allocated on the basis of estimated time and effort.

1 Statement of Cash Flows

A statement of cash flows is required for all not-for-profit organizations. FASB ASC 230 is applicable to not-for-profit organizations, to the extent that it does not conflict with industry guidance. Identical to commercial standards, the primary purpose of the statement of cash flows is to provide relevant information about the cash receipts and cash payments of the not-for-profit organization during a period. The statement classifies cash receipts and cash payments as operating, investing, and financing activities, and either the direct or the indirect method may be used. The use of the direct method, however, does not require presentation of the reconciliation of net income to cash flows from operations.

1.1 Classification of Sources and Uses of Cash

1.1.1 Operating Activities

Sources and uses of cash classified by a not-for-profit organization as operating activities include receipts and payments that do not stem from transactions defined as investing or financing, such as:

- Receipts or payments for the settlement of lawsuits.
- Proceeds from insurance settlements (other than those specifically associated with investing activities such as the destruction of a building).
- Refunds from suppliers or refunds to customers.
- Charitable contributions (and disbursements) made by the not-for-profit.

Specifically identified transactions to be classified as cash flows from operations also include:

- Reported activity by major class of gross receipts (when the direct method is used), including contributions, program income, and interest or dividend income.
- Receipts of unrestricted resources designated by the governing body to be used for long-lived assets.
- Proceeds from the sale of financial assets not restricted for long-term purposes.
- Cash payments to suppliers and employees.
- Cash payments for interest.
- Cash activity associated with agency transactions.
- Crypto assets received as a noncash contribution and converted nearly immediately (within a few days) into cash are classified as operating activities.

Pass Key

Contributions of unrestricted revenue later earmarked (board designated) for construction or purchase of long-lived assets is classified as cash flows from operating activities.

1.1.2 Investing Activities

Sources and uses of cash classified by a not-for-profit organization as investing activities include receipts and payments for such items as:

■ Investments in property, plant, and equipment.

■ Proceeds from the sale of works of art or disbursements for purchases of works of art.

■ Proceeds from the sale of assets that were received in the prior period and whose sale proceeds were restricted to investment in equipment.

1.1.3 Financing Activities

Sources and uses of cash classified by a not-for-profit organization as financing activities include receipts and payments for such items as:

■ Proceeds from issuing bonds, mortgages, notes, and other short- or long-term borrowing.

■ Repayment of amounts borrowed.

■ Receipts from contributions restricted for the purpose of acquiring, constructing, or improving property, plant, and equipment or other long-lived assets.

■ Receipts from contributions restricted for the purpose of establishing or increasing a donor-restricted endowment fund.

■ Receipts of crypto assets with donor-imposed restrictions for long-term or capital use that are nearly immediately (within a few days) liquidated.

Pass Key

Cash flows from financing activities not only include the cash transactions related to borrowing that are typically found in a commercial statement of cash flows, but also include cash transactions related to certain restricted contributions. Cash flows from financial activities may be segregated on the face of the financial statements as follows:

• Proceeds from Donor-Restricted Contributions (for long-lived assets)

• Other Financing Activities

1.1.4   Cash and Cash Equivalents

The statement of cash flows will explain the change during the period of total cash and cash equivalents and amounts generally described as restricted consistent with commercial accounting. Transfers among cash, cash equivalents, and amounts generally described as restricted are not reported as cash flow activities in the statement of cash flows.

Pass Key

Note that in not-for-profit reporting, the statement of cash flows has the three typical commercial classifications: operating activities, financing activities, and investing activities.

1.1.5   Noncash Transactions

Noncash transactions that should be disclosed in the statement of cash flows include:

- Contributed securities.

- Construction in progress and other fixed asset purchases included in accounts payable.

- Contributions of beneficial interests (unconditional promises to receive specified cash flows from a charitable trust or other identifiable pool of assets).

- Noncash debt refinancing transactions (e.g., changes in interest rates or other terms, etc.).

1.1.6   Direct Method (Supplemental Reconciliation of Cash Flow From Operations Not Required)

Not-for-profits that use the direct method of reporting net cash flows from operations *are not* required to provide a reconciliation of change in net assets to net cash flows from operating activity. This is in contrast to an entity other than a not-for-profit organization (a commercial entity), which is required to provide the reconciliation in a separate schedule.

Not-for-Profit Organization **Statement of Cash Flows** For the Year Ended December 31, Year 2 *(in thousands)*		
Cash flows from operating activities:		
Change in net assets	$15,450	
Adjustments to reconcile change in net assets to net cash used by operating activities:		
Depreciation	3,200	
Fire loss	80	
Actuarial loss on annuity obligations	30	
Gain on sale of equipment	(200)	
Increase in accounts and interest receivable	(460)	
Decrease in inventories and prepaid expenses	390	
Increase in contributions receivable	(325)	
Increase in accounts payable	1,520	
Decrease in refundable advance	(650)	
Decrease in grants payable	(425)	
Contributions restricted for long-term investment	(2,740)	
Interest and dividends restricted for reinvestment	(300)	
Realized and unrealized gains on investments	(15,800)	
Net cash used by operating activities		$(230)
Cash flows from investing activities:		
Proceeds on sale of equipment	200	
Insurance proceeds from fire loss on building	250	
Purchase of equipment	(1,500)	
Proceeds from sale of investments	76,100	
Purchase of investments	(75,000)	
Net cash used by investing activities		50
Cash flows from financing activities:		
Proceeds from contributions restricted for:		
Investment in perpetual endowment	$ 200	
Investment in term endowment	70	
Investment in land, buildings, and equipment	1,210	
Investment subject to annuity agreements	200	
	1,680	
Other financing activities:		
Interest and dividends restricted for reinvestment	300	
Payments of annuity obligations	(145)	
Payments on notes payable	(1,140)	
Payments on long-term debt	(1,000)	
	(1,985)	
Net cash used by financing activities		(305)
Net decrease in cash, cash equivalents, and restricted cash		(485)
Cash, cash equivalents, and restricted cash at beginning of year		5120
Cash, cash equivalents, and restricted cash at end of year		$4,635

Note H

The following table provides a reconciliation of cash, cash equivalents, and restricted cash reported within the statement of financial position that sum to the total of the same such amounts shown in the statement of cash flows:

	12/31/Yr 2
Cash and cash equivalents	$4,575
Restricted cash included in assets restricted to investment in land, buildings, and equipment	60
Total cash, cash equivalents, and restricted cash shown in the statement of cash flows	$4,635

Assets restricted to investment in land, buildings, and equipment on the statement of financial position include restricted cash received with a donor-imposed restriction that limits use of that cash to long-term purposes.

NOTES

3 Not-for-Profit Revenue Recognition

1 Revenue From Exchange Transactions

An exchange transaction is one in which the not-for-profit organization earns resources in exchange for a service performed. Revenues from not-for-profit exchange transactions are recognized when realized or realizable and earned.

Revenues from exchange transactions are classified as increases to net assets without donor restrictions.

The following are examples of revenues earned by not-for-profits in exchange transactions:

- Student tuition and fees earned by not-for-profit educational institutions.

- Patient service revenue earned by not-for-profit health care organizations.

- Membership fees earned by not-for-profit membership organizations.

2 Contributions Received

A *contribution* is defined as an unconditional transfer of cash or assets (collection is certain) to a new owner (title passes) in a manner which is voluntary (the donor is under no obligation to donate) and is nonreciprocal (the donor gets nothing in exchange). Contributions may include cash, services, and other assets.

2.1 Recognition

Unconditional contributions are recognized as revenues or gains and reported as either an increase to net assets without donor restrictions or donor-restricted support in the period received and as assets, decreases of liabilities, or expenses, depending on the form of the benefits received. A contribution is classified as revenue if it is part of the ongoing major or central activities of the not-for-profit organization. A contribution is classified as a gain if the transaction is incidental to the purpose of the not-for-profit organization. Conditional contributions are not recognized. Conditions are indicated by the existence of both barriers and the right of the donor to demand return of the contribution.

2.1.1 Barriers That Indicate a Conditional Contribution

The existence of measurable performance-related barriers or other barriers that may indicate a condition include:

- Specified levels of service (e.g., the provision of a specific number of meals at a facility).

- Specific outputs or outcomes (e.g., the construction of a building to an exact architectural design, the achievement of specific program objectives, or the conditioning of revenue on incurring specific eligible expenses).

- Matching (e.g., revenue conditioned on the collection or accumulation of community match).

- Outside event (e.g., the satisfaction of a contingency outside the control of the not-for-profit receiving the contribution).

2.1.2 Right of Return

The donor has the right to require return of the donation from the recipient not-for-profit organization.

2.2 Cash Contributions

Cash contributions should be recognized as revenues or gains and reported as contributions that increase net assets without donor restrictions or donor-restricted support in the period in which they are received, and they should be measured at their fair value at the date of the gift.

2.3 Promises to Give (Pledges)

2.3.1 Unconditional Promises

An unconditional promise to give (also known as a pledge) is a contribution and is recorded at its fair value when the promise is made. An unconditional promise may be written or verbal. However, verbal pledges should be documented by the organization internally and may be more difficult to collect.

2.3.2 Conditional Promises

A conditional promise to give (or pledge) is a transaction that depends on an occurrence of a future and uncertain event. Recognition does not occur until the conditions are substantially met (or when it can be determined that the chances of not meeting the conditions are remote) and the promise becomes unconditional.

Good faith deposits that accompany a conditional promise are accounted for as a refundable advance in the liability section of the statement of financial position.

To recognize a good faith deposit received before the conditions of a conditional promise are met by the not-for-profit:

DR	Cash		$XXX	
CR	Refundable advance			$XXX

Pass Key

Conditions are *not* synonymous with donor restriction. Donor restrictions are satisfied by the not-for-profit organization by use of the donated resources consistent with restrictions. Conditions are satisfied by the resolution of barriers used to condition the contribution by the donor.

2.3.3 Multiyear Pledges

Multiyear pledges are recorded at the net present value at the date the pledge is made. Future collections are considered donor-restricted revenues and net assets (time-restricted). The difference between the previously recorded present value and the current amount collected is recognized as contribution revenue, not interest income.

2.3.4 Placed-in-Service Approach

In the absence of specific donor restrictions, not-for-profits must use the placed-in-service approach to report the expiration of restrictions on contributions associated with long-lived assets.

Illustration 1	Placed-in-Service Approach

Community Not-for-Profit Inc. receives a building from Gerry Generous at the beginning of the year and immediately begins to use it in a manner consistent with its mission. Gerry places no restrictions on the building. The building has a value of $200,000 and it has a 20-year life. Community Not-for-Profit Inc. would recognize the entire $200,000 donation as a contribution without donor restriction using the placed-in-service approach.

Community Not-for-Profit Inc. also receives a building from the River City. The building is also valued at $200,000 with a 20-year life. The City stipulates that the building must be used for specific community programs and, if it is not used for that purpose, the building's ownership will revert to the City. Community Not-for-Profit Inc. would record the building as an asset and donor-restricted support of $200,000. Each year that Community Not-for-Profit met its restrictions, it would record depreciation expense of $10,000 and would reclassify $10,000 from net assets with restrictions to net assets without restrictions.

2.3.5 Allowance for Uncollectible Pledges

An allowance for uncollectible pledges should be recorded in accordance with commercial accounting principles for accounts receivable in order to present the pledge at its net realizable value. However, in contrast to commercial accounting principles, there is no credit loss (or bad contribution) expense recognized at any point. Instead, both the pledge and related contribution revenue are reported net of any allowance.

2.4 Split-Interest Agreements

Split-interest agreements represent donor contributions of trusts or other arrangements under which the not-for-profit organization receives benefits that are shared with other beneficiaries.

- Examples include:
  - Charitable lead trust
  - Perpetual trust held by a third party
  - Charitable remainder trust
  - Charitable gift annuity
  - Pooled life income fund
- During the term of the agreement, changes in the value of split-interest agreements should be recognized for:
  - Amortization of discounts
  - Revaluations
- Assets and liabilities recognized under split-interest agreements should be disclosed separately from other assets and liabilities in the statement of financial position.
- Contributions and changes in the value of split-interest agreements should be disclosed as separate line items in the statement of activities (or the related notes).
- Split-interest contributions should be:
  - measured at their fair values at the date of acquisition;
  - estimated based on the present value of the estimated future distributions; and
  - displayed as donor-restricted.

Pass Key

Do not confuse the net asset classification concept of with versus without donor restrictions with the revenue recognition concept of conditional versus unconditional. Unconditional pledges are assured of collection and may be recognized as either with or without donor restrictions. Conditional pledges are still subject to important contingencies and are not recorded.

2.5 Donated Services

Donated services received by a not-for-profit organization are generally not recorded because of the difficulty in placing a monetary value on donated services (and the absence of control over them). However, donated services should be recorded as a contribution and expense at fair value if the services meet one of the following criteria:

- They create or enhance a nonfinancial asset (e.g., land, building, inventory, etc.); or

- They require specialized skills that the provider possesses and would otherwise have been purchased by the organization (e.g., attorney, accountant, and doctor services, etc.).

Pass Key

Contributions of services that do not enhance nonfinancial assets are recognized only **SOME** of the time:

- **Specialized** skills are required and possessed by the donor

- **Otherwise** needed by the organization

- **Measurable**

- **Easily** (at fair value)

Donated services that qualify for recognition are displayed as nonoperating.

The following journal entry is used to record contributed services that meet the criteria for recognition:

DR	Expense or asset	$XXX	
CR	Contributions—without donor restrictions		$XXX

2.5.1 Examples

- An attorney provides general counsel services to a not-for-profit organization. Services would be recognized at an appropriate market rate.

- A doctor provides services to a clinic for a vastly reduced fee. The difference between the market rate of the service and the amount paid would be recognized as a contribution.

- An individual volunteers to fill a budgeted position doing general office work. The time will be recognized as a contribution at an appropriate rate. Another individual offers to volunteer to do general office work, but there is no budget for the work performed. The unbudgeted time will not be recognized as a contribution.

Illustration 2　　Donated Services

A storm damaged the roof of a new building owned by K-9 Shelters, a not-for-profit organization. A supporter of K-9, a professional roofer, repaired the roof at no charge. The value of the repairs was $10,000.

In K-9's statement of activities, the repair of the roof should be reported as an increase to expenses and contributions using the following journal entry:

DR	Expense	$10,000	
CR	Contribution without donor restrictions		$10,000

2.5.2　Volunteer Recruitment

Costs of soliciting contributed services are considered fundraising expenses regardless of whether services meet recognition criteria.

2.6　Donated Collection Items

Donated collection items are contributed works of art or historical treasures. They are not required to be recorded by the recipient not-for-profit organization if all of the following requirements are met:

1. The item is part of a collection, which is held for public viewing, exhibition, education, or research (and not for investment or financial gain);

2. The collection is cared for, preserved, and protected by the organization; and

3. The organization has a policy that requires any proceeds from the sale of donated items to be reinvested in other collection items or used to support the direct care of existing collections.

Note: If the preceding requirements are not met, the donation must be recorded as revenue and capitalized as an asset, which is generally depreciated over its estimated useful life. The policy may not be selectively applied and must be used for all assets.

2.6.1　Extraordinary Long-Lived Items

If an individual work of art or historical treasure has an extraordinarily long estimated useful life and its economic benefit or service potential is used up very slowly, it may not need to be depreciated. This exception applies if:

■ the asset has cultural, aesthetic, or historical value that is worth preserving perpetually; and

■ there is verifiable evidence that the owner has the ability and intent to protect and preserve the asset's service potential essentially undiminished.

2.7   Donated Materials

If significant in amount, donated materials should be recorded at their fair value on the date of receipt if the fair value can be objectively determined.

DR	Asset	$XXX	
CR	Contribution—support		$XXX

Donated materials that merely pass through the organization to an ultimate beneficiary, such as used clothing, should not be recorded, unless the amounts involved are substantial.

Assuming that donated materials are substantial, they should be recorded as a contribution with an offsetting entry to expenses and appropriately disclosed in the financial statements.

DR	Expense	$XXX	
CR	Contributions—supplies		$XXX

When donated items are sold at greater than fair value, the amount received in excess of fair value is considered an additional contribution.

2.8   Gifts-in-Kind

Nonfinancial contributions are called gifts-in-kind. Examples of gifts-in-kind include land, buildings, materials, supplies, intangible assets, services, or use of facilities or utilities. A gift-in-kind is recognized as a contribution at fair value at the date of donation.

Gifts-in-kind that are donated as part of a fundraising appeal are valued at fair value when received and revalued upon their sale as part of the fundraising appeal. The difference between the fair value at the time of donation and the value at the time of sale is accounted for as an additional contribution.

2.9   Presentation and Disclosure of Nonfinancial Assets

Contributed nonfinancial assets are displayed as a separate line item on the statement of activities, apart from contributions of cash or other financial assets.

The notes should disclose the amount of contributed nonfinancial assets recognized by category. For each category of nonfinancial assets recognized, the notes should state whether contributed assets will be sold (monetized), what donor-imposed restrictions may be associated with the donation, and the manner in which the donation is valued.

3   Accounting for Promises to Contribute and Other Support Transactions

3.1   Contributions Without Donor Restrictions

Unconditional promises to contribute in the future are reported as donor-restricted support (implied time restriction), at the present value of the estimated future cash flows using a discount rate commensurate with the risks involved. If the unconditional promises are expected to be collected or paid in less than one year, they may be measured at net realizable value since that amount is a reasonable estimate of fair value.

Pledges without donor restriction (with implied time restriction and thus initially recognized as donor-restricted):

DR	Pledge receivable—with donor restriction	$XXX	
CR	Allowance for doubtful accounts		$XXX
CR	Contributions—with donor restriction		XXX

Later, when collected, assets with donor restrictions are adjusted:

DR	Cash—with donor restriction	$XXX	
CR	Pledge receivable—with donor restriction		$XXX
DR	Satisfaction of time restriction—with donor restriction	XXX	
CR	Cash—with donor restriction		XXX

Assets without donor restrictions:

DR	Cash—without donor restriction	$XXX	
CR	Satisfaction of time restriction—without donor restriction		$XXX

Collection of the pledge satisfies the time restriction and results in a reclassification.

Example 1   Accounting for Pledges Receivable

Facts: The League, a not-for-profit organization, received the following pledges:

Without donor restrictions	$200,000
Donor-restricted for capital additions	150,000

All pledges are legally enforceable; however, the League's experience indicates that 10 percent of all pledges prove to be uncollectible.

Required: Determine the amount the League should report as pledges receivable, net of any required allowance account.

Solution: Net pledges receivable are gross pledges receivable ($350,000) less allowance for uncollectible (10% × $350,000), or $315,000.

3.2 Donor-Restricted Support (Contributions With Donor Restrictions)

A contribution may be restricted by the donor. Donor-imposed restrictions limit the use of contributed assets. They are recognized as revenues, gains, and other support in the period received and as assets, decreases of liabilities, or expenses, depending on the form of the benefits received.

Increases to net assets with donor restrictions:

DR	Pledge receivable—with donor restrictions	$XXX	
CR	Allowance for doubtful accounts		$XXX
CR	Donor-restricted support		XXX

Later, after receivable is collected and when money is spent on restricted purpose, net assets with donor restrictions will be reduced:

DR	Reclassification—satisfaction of donor restriction	$XXX	
CR	Cash—with donor restrictions		$XXX

Net assets without donor restrictions are simultaneously increased and decreased:

DR	Cash—without donor restrictions	$XXX	
CR	Reclassification—satisfaction of donor restriction		$XXX
DR	Operating expense	XXX	
CR	Cash—without donor restrictions		XXX

4 Fundraising

When a not-for-profit offers premiums (e.g., calendars, coffee mugs, tote bags, etc.) to donors as part of a fundraising campaign, the cost of the premiums is classified as a fundraising expense.

The cost of premiums given to acknowledge donations is also classified as a fundraising expense.

Generally, the difference between the contribution made by the donor and the fair value of any premiums transferred is classified as contribution revenue.

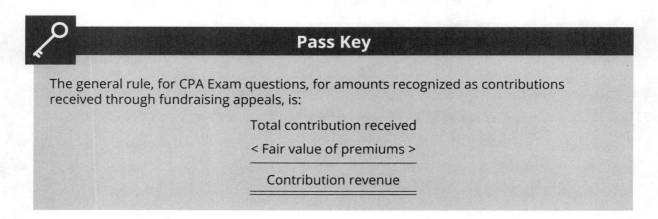

Pass Key

The general rule, for CPA Exam questions, for amounts recognized as contributions received through fundraising appeals, is:

Total contribution received

< Fair value of premiums >

Contribution revenue

5   Industry-Specific Revenue Recognition

5.1   Educational Institutions

5.1.1   Revenues

Revenues consist of all increases in net assets without donor restrictions and *all donor-restricted* resources that were actually *expended* during the period, such as:

- Student tuition and fees (includes amounts paid by the student and amounts granted as scholarships).

- Government aid, grants, and contracts.

- Gifts and private grants.

- Endowment income.

- Sales and services of educational departments, such as publications and testing services.

- Revenues of auxiliary enterprises, such as food service, residence halls, campus store, and athletics.

Pass Key

Student tuition and fees (including amounts paid by students and scholarships granted by the university) are reported at the gross amount as total tuition revenue. Many prior CPA Exam questions have required students to compute gross revenue from tuition and fees:

Assessed student tuition and fees
(including scholarships)

< Refunds for canceled classes >
_____

Gross revenue from tuition and fees
_____

Scholarships are considered as financial aid that covers tuition fees but does not directly reduce the gross revenue calculation. Scholarships, tuition waivers, and similar reductions may be presented separately either as expenses or allowances, depending on the institution's reporting practices. Tuition revenue is always recognized in its gross amount regardless of the manner in which scholarships are identified.

5.1.2   Gains and Losses

Gains and losses on investments and other assets, classified as with or without donor restrictions, are reported in the statement of activities.

5.2   Revenue Recognition in Health Care Organizations

5.2.1   Patient Service Revenue

Patient service revenue should be accounted for on the accrual basis at established standard rates (usual and customary fees), even if the full amount is not expected to be collected. Although patient service revenue is recorded on a gross basis, deductions are made from gross revenue to recognize patient service revenue net of deductions. Central transactions include medical services such as doctors, surgery, recovery room, and room and board.

■ **Charity Care**

Charity care is defined as health care services that are provided but never expected to result in cash flows to the hospital.

- Management's policy for providing charity care (as well as the level of charity care provided) should be disclosed in the financial statements.

- Charity care is not recognized as a receivable or as revenue.

- Charity care is not recognized as a credit loss expense.

■ **Deductions**

Deductions from patient service revenue to arrive at "net patient service revenue" include the following for uncompensated services:

- Contractual adjustments for third-party payments.

- Policy discounts.

- Administrative adjustments.

- Credit losses associated with services billed prior to the organization's assessment of the patient's ability to pay (e.g., emergency room services provided and billed at full cost before the likelihood of collection can be determined).

Pass Key

Credit losses may be afforded one of two treatments, depending on the character of the loss.

1. Operating expense: Credit loss expense resulting from failure to collect revenues that the health care organization anticipated earning (e.g., a self-pay patient screened for ability to pay is billed and does not pay).

2. Deduction from revenue: Credit losses resulting from inability to collect large volumes of revenue that the health care organization never assessed for quality or collectibility.

■ **Premium Revenue for Capitation Agreements**

Capitation revenues are the fixed amount per individual that is paid periodically, usually monthly, to a provider as compensation for providing health care services for that period.

Pass Key

Prior CPA Exam questions have required candidates to compute "Patient Service Revenue"; use this formula to answer these questions correctly:

Gross patient service revenue

< Charitable services >
_____

Patient service revenue
═══════════════════════════

5.2.2 Other Operating Revenue

Other operating revenue of a health care organization may include:

- Tuition from schools
- Revenue from educational programs
- Donated supplies and equipment
- Specific purpose grants
- Revenue from auxiliary activities
- Cafeteria revenue
- Parking fees
- Gift shop revenue
- Medical transcription fees

5.2.3 Nonoperating Revenue and Support Gains and Losses

Nonoperating revenue and gains and losses of a health care organization may include the following transactions that are recognized without donor restrictions:

- Interest and dividend income from investment activities
- Gifts and bequests
- Grants
- Income from endowment funds
- Income from board-designated funds
- Donated services

Pass Key

Many prior CPA Exam questions have required candidates to identify which of the three categories of revenue a particular item of income is to be reported in:

1. Patient service revenue
2. Other operating revenue (includes donated supplies)
3. Nonoperating revenue (includes donated services)

NOTES

1 Transfers of Assets to a Not-for-Profit Organization or Charitable Trust That Raises or Holds Contributions for Others

An important issue in not-for-profit accounting is the accounting for asset transfers to other not-for-profit organizations, such as foundations, and the circumstances under which those transfers should be accounted for as (1) a contribution, (2) a liability, or (3) a change in interest in net assets.

1.1 Financially Interrelated Organizations

Financially interrelated organizations are defined as organizations related by both of the following characteristics:

1. One organization has the ability to influence the operating and financial decisions of the other; and

2. One organization has an ongoing economic interest in the net assets of the other.

1.2 Recipient Accounting

A not-for-profit is a recipient entity when it accepts assets from a resource provider and agrees to use the assets on behalf of, or transfer the assets (and/or the return on the assets) to, a specified beneficiary. The accounting by the recipient entity depends on whether the recipient has variance power and whether the recipient and the beneficiary are financially interrelated.

1.2.1 Not Financially Interrelated: Without Variance Power

An organization that accepts assets from a resource provider and agrees to use or manage them on behalf of a specified beneficiary *without variance power* and *without any financial interrelationship* accounts for assets received as follows:

- Assets are valued at fair value.

- The recipient recognizes a *liability* to the beneficiary.

DR	Asset	$XXX	
CR	Refundable advance liability		$XXX

- Assets transferred to recipient organizations are not contributions and are accounted for as liabilities when *any one* of the following conditions are met:

  - The resource provider can change the beneficiary.

  - The resource provider's asset transfer is conditional or otherwise revocable or repayable.

  - The resource provider controls the recipient organization and specifies an unaffiliated beneficiary.

  - The resource provider specifies itself or its affiliate as the beneficiary and does not qualify for equity accounting.

1.2.2   Not Financially Interrelated: With Variance Power

When there is no financial interrelationship between the recipient and the beneficiary, an organization that accepts assets from a resource provider and agrees to use or manage them on behalf of a beneficiary follows donee accounting *if it is granted variance power*, the unilateral authority to redirect assets to another beneficiary.

- Assets are valued at fair value.
- Assets are recognized as a contribution when received and expensed when distributed to the beneficiary.

DR	Asset	$XXX	
CR	Contribution		$XXX

1.2.3   Financially Interrelated: With or Without Variance Power

An organization *financially interrelated* with a beneficiary that accepts assets from a resource provider and agrees to use or manage them on behalf of a beneficiary follows donee accounting. Regardless of whether variance power is granted:

- Assets are valued at fair value.
- Assets are recognized as a contribution when received and expensed when distributed to the beneficiary.

DR	Asset	$XXX	
CR	Contribution		$XXX

1.3   Beneficiary Accounting

Specified beneficiaries recognize their rights to assets held by the recipient unless the recipient is explicitly granted variance power. Rights, when recognized, will be recorded as a receivable and contribution, a beneficial interest, or a change in interest in the net assets of the recipient.

1.3.1   Receivable and Contribution

In cases that do not involve financial interrelationship or beneficial interests, the beneficiary recognizes a receivable and a contribution consistent with treatment of all other unconditional promises to give.

DR	Receivable	$XXX	
CR	Contribution		$XXX

1.3.2   Not Financially Interrelated: Beneficial Interest

Beneficiaries recognize a beneficial interest in an unconditional right to receive specified cash flows from a pool of assets as contribution revenue, or when donations held by the recipient are nonfinancial.

DR	Beneficial interest	$XXX	
CR	Contribution		$XXX

1.3.3   Financially Interrelated: Interest in the Net Assets of the Recipient

Beneficiaries recognize a change in their interest in the net assets of the recipient when the organizations are financially interrelated.

DR	Interest in recipient net assets	$XXX	
CR	Change in interest in recipient net assets		$XXX

Example 1   Financially Interrelated Recipient and Beneficiary

Facts: Farleigh State University, a private not-for-profit institute of higher learning, established the Farleigh State Foundation Inc. (FSF), a not-for-profit corporation, to raise funds for the university and to account for and manage the investments of the university. The university and the foundation are financially interrelated. During the current year, an alumnus donated investments with a fair value of $25,000,000 to the foundation and specified that the earnings from the investments must be used to fund scholarships at Farleigh State University.

Required: Determine how the university and the foundation should account for this donation.

Solution:

Farleigh State Foundation

The foundation is the recipient of the donation and does not have variance power because the donation must be used to fund university scholarships. *The foundation will record the following journal entry because it is financially interrelated with the university:*

DR	Investments	$25,000,000	
CR	Contribution		$25,000,000

Farleigh State University

The university is the beneficiary and will recognize an interest in the change in net assets of the foundation because it is financially interrelated with the foundation:

DR	Interest in FSF net assets	$25,000,000	
CR	Change in interest in FSF net assets		$25,000,000

---

2   Other Accounting Issues

2.1   Financial Instruments

2.1.1   Fair Value

All debt securities and those equity securities that have readily determinable fair values are measured at fair value in the statement of financial position.

2.1.2 Gains and Losses

Realized and unrealized gains and losses on investments are reported in the statement of activities as increases or decreases in net assets without donor restrictions unless the use of the investment is donor-restricted, either temporarily or in perpetuity, by explicit donor stipulations or by law. Gains and losses that are limited to specific uses by donor stipulations may be reported as increases in net assets without donor restrictions if the stipulations are met in the same reporting period as the gains and income are recognized.

2.1.3 Derivatives

A not-for-profit organization should recognize the change in fair value of all derivatives in the period of the change. Not-for-profits are not permitted to use special hedge accounting rules.

2.1.4 Dividends, Interest, and Other Investment Income

Investment income (e.g., dividends and interest) is reported in the period earned as increases in unrestricted net assets unless the use of the investment is restricted by explicit donor stipulations or by law. Investment returns are reported net of any related investment expense.

2.2 Endowment Funds

Endowment funds are used to account for assets established to provide income for the maintenance of a not-for-profit entity and may be classified as either net assets without donor restrictions or net assets with donor restrictions. Issues surrounding endowment funds typically relate to their duration, the source of any restriction on them (internal or external), and the accounting issues related to the treatment of changes in value.

2.2.1 Duration

Endowment funds may be established in perpetuity or for a specified period of time (sometimes referred to as a term endowment).

2.2.2 Source of Restriction

Although endowment funds may be established by a governing board from resources without donor restrictions, they are generally established by a donor-restricted gift. Types of endowment funds include:

- **Board-Designated Endowment Funds**
  - Board-designated endowment funds are created by a not-for profit entity's governing board by designating a portion of its net assets without donor restrictions to provide income for a long but not necessarily specified period of time.
  - Alternative names include funds functioning as endowment or quasi-endowment funds.
- **Donor-Restricted Endowment Funds (Most Common)**
  - An endowment fund created by a donor stipulation requiring investment of the donor's gift in perpetuity or for a specified term.

2.2.3 Accounting and Reporting for Endowment Funds

A not-for-profit organization would report an endowment fund in the statement of financial position in one of the following two classes of net assets based on the existence or absence of donor-imposed restrictions:

1. **Net Assets With Donor Restrictions**

   Donor-restricted endowments would be accounted for under net assets with donor restrictions.

Illustration 1   Donor-Restricted Endowment Fund

Ben Benefactor gives $10,000,000 to his alma mater, Private University, a private not-for-profit university, with the stipulation that the principal would not be spent and that earnings from the donation would be used to fund an accounting professor's salary and accounting research. Benefactor's donation would be accounted for as an increase to net assets with donor restrictions and would represent a donor-restricted endowment fund established in perpetuity.

---

2. **Net Assets Without Donor Restrictions**

   Board-designated endowment funds resulting from an internal designation of net assets without donor restrictions would be classified as net assets without donor restrictions.

Illustration 2   Board-Designated Endowment Fund

The governing board of Private University, a private not-for-profit university, sets aside $8,000,000 from its net assets without donor restrictions to be invested for the next 20 years with related income to be used for a finance professor's salary. The act of the governing board would be accounted for within net assets without donor restrictions and would represent a board-designated endowment established for a specified period of time.

2.2.4   Specific Issues Regarding Changes in Value of Donor-Restricted Endowments

■ **Inception**

- The original gifted amount and (generally) related returns shall be initially classified as net assets with donor restrictions.

- Unless a purpose or other donor restriction exists on the use of the income, investment income is deemed available for spending and is classified as net assets without donor restrictions.

■ **Returns on the Endowment Assets Subject to Donor Restriction**

- Investment returns subject to restriction by donor or by law shall be reported within net assets with donor restriction until appropriated for expenditure.

- Investment returns are commonly restricted by either time (until appropriated for use) or purpose (until appropriated and expended on the specified purpose described by the donor).

- Upon approval for expenditure (meeting the requirements of the donor restriction), the funds are deemed to have been appropriated for expenditure.

■ **Underwater Endowments**

- An underwater endowment is a donor-restricted endowment fund for which the fair value of the fund at the reporting date is less than either the original gift amount or the amount required to be maintained by the donor *or* by a law that extends donor restrictions.

- Underwater endowment funds will report accumulated losses together with the endowment fund in net assets with donor restrictions.
- Underwater endowments require the following disclosures in total:
  —The fair value of the underwater endowment;
  —The original endowment gift amount or level required to be maintained by donor stipulations or law; and
  —The amount of the deficiencies of the underwater endowment fund.

Pass Key

Underwater endowments must disclose how hard it will be for their intended beneficiaries to be **FED**:

- **Fair** value of the underwater endowment
- **Endowment** gift's original amount
- **Deficiency**

Illustration 3   Underwater Endowment

Ben Benefactor gives a $10,000,000 endowment to Private University, a private not-for-profit entity. The endowment is properly accounted for as an increase in net assets with donor restrictions. At year-end, the endowment had a fair value of $9,750,000. Private University would need to disclose:

Fair value of Ben Benefactor's original gift	$ 9,750,000
Ben Benefactor's original gift	10,000,000
Deficiency	$ (250,000)

2.2.5 Required Disclosures for All Endowment Funds

- The governing board's interpretation of the requirements that underlie the net asset classification of the endowment and the ability to spend from underwater endowment funds.
- Policies for the appropriation of endowment assets.
- Investment policies.
- Composition of the not-for-profit endowment by net asset class.
- A reconciliation of the beginning and ending balance of the not-for-profit's endowments by net asset class.

2.3 Basis of Assets

Purchased fixed assets are carried at cost, as required by GAAP. Donated fixed assets are recorded at fair value at the date of the gift. Depreciation is recorded in accordance with GAAP for nongovernmental not-for-profit organizations. However, works of art and historical treasures are not depreciated.

5 Governmental Accounting Overview

1 Governmental Accounting and Reporting Concepts

1.1 Objectives of Governmental Reporting

Governmental financial reporting is designed to demonstrate the accountability of each organization for the stewardship of the resources in their care. Although the accountability for privately owned enterprises may be clearly measured in either the net income of the entity or the increased wealth of its shareholders, governmental organizations are focused on providing efficient and effective delivery of services with public resources in compliance with applicable laws. Identifying and displaying the accountability objectives of governmental organizations is integral to related accounting.

1.2 Objectives of Fund Accounting and Reporting

Foundational to governmental accounting is the concept of fund accounting. Fund accounting enables service and mission-driven organizations to easily monitor and report compliance with spending purposes (fund restrictions), spending limits (budget), and other fiscal accountability objectives. Governments use fund accounting to demonstrate fiscal accountability in their external reporting and use funds for internal accounting.

2 Industries That Use Governmental Accounting and Reporting Principles

Governmental, not-for-profit, and commercial accounting are applied to entities consistent with their basis of organization and their funding sources, not their industries.

Illustration 1 Basis of Organization
Hospitals could be governmentally funded and accounted for using an enterprise fund, could be organized as a not-for-profit organization, or could be organized as private businesses that report income and profitability to their shareholders. Although this can be confusing in practice, the CPA Exam is generally very clear as to the manner in which an entity is organized and the applicable accounting principles.

The following industries commonly have the organizational characteristics and funding streams that lend themselves to the accountability objectives met by governmental reporting models.

2.1   Governmental Units

Governmental units include federal, state, county, municipal, and a variety of local governmental units (e.g., townships, villages, and special districts) and entities (e.g., hospitals and universities) that are run by governments and use governmental accounting and reporting principles.

2.2   Colleges and Universities

Colleges and universities may be governmental entities or nongovernmental entities, depending on whether they are financially accountable to a primary government. In addition, some colleges and universities are organizations operated to earn a profit (i.e., "for-profit" entities); thus, they follow FASB standards for commercial entities rather than the standards developed for governmental entities or not-for-profit entities.

2.3   Health Care Organizations

Organizations that provide health care services to individuals include hospitals, nursing care facilities, home health agencies, and clinics. Health care providers can be organized as governmental, not-for-profit, or commercial entities. If the health care entity is financially accountable to a primary government, it could be classified as a component unit of the government. If a health care entity is organized as a not-for-profit or commercial organization, it follows applicable FASB standards rather than the standards developed for governmental entities.

Pass Key

Not-for-profit organizations not run by governments (e.g., hospitals, universities, voluntary health and welfare organizations, and research organizations) do *not* use governmental accounting and reporting principles.

3   Generally Accepted Accounting Principles for Governmental Entities

3.1   Governmental Accounting Principles and Standards

The Governmental Accounting Standards Board (GASB), which is the governmental counterpart of the FASB, establishes accounting and reporting standards for governments. The hierarchy of GAAP as it relates to governments was established by GASB 76 as follows:

■   GASB Accounting Standards Board Statements (most authoritative—category A)

■   GASB Technical Bulletins, GASB Implementation Guides, and literature of the AICPA cleared by the GASB (category B)

Governmental entities should consult guidance in category B documents in the event treatment for a transaction is not specified by a pronouncement in category A.

3.2   GASB Conceptual Framework

The GASB has outlined its conceptual framework for governmental financial reporting in GASB Concept Statements Nos. 1–6. These concept statements establish the objectives and concepts that underlie governmental financial reporting but do not establish standards for governmental financial reporting.

According to the conceptual framework, governmental financial reporting communicates financial information to users and fulfills a government's duty to be publicly accountable.

3.2.1   Information Used by Financial Report Users

Financial statements are a part of the overall financial reporting done by governments. The information needs of users of governmental financial reports include all of the following:

All Information Used to Assess Accountability				
All Financial Reporting				
General Purpose External Financial Reporting				
GASB 34 Reporting Requirements				
Basic financial statements (including notes)	Required supplementary information	Annual comprehensive financial report	Budgets and other special purpose reports (e.g., to grantor agencies)	Other information (e.g., economic indicators)

- Financial reporting objectives identified by the framework pertain to *general purpose external financial reporting*, which includes the basic financial statements and required supplementary information, as well as the annual comprehensive financial report (ACFR).

- Financial reporting objectives identified by the framework may not fully address budgets, other special purpose reporting or other information (such as stand-alone budget documents or reports to grantor agencies).

3.2.2   Governmental-Type and Business-Type Activities

Government entities engage in both governmental-type and business-type activities. Each type of activity requires accounting and reporting standards that address their individual characteristics and user needs. Governmental-type activities are typically supported by taxes and business-type activities are supported by user fees.

3.2.3   Users of Governmental Financial Reports

The three groups of primary users of governmental financial reports are:

1.   Citizens, including taxpayers, voters, recipients of services, the media, researchers, etc.

2.   Legislative and oversight bodies, including state legislators, county and city commissioners, and executives with oversight authority.

3.   Investors and creditors, including institutional investors, bond rating agencies, bond insurers, financial institutions, etc.

3.2.4 Uses of Financial Reports

Governmental financial reports are used to make economic, social, and political decisions and to assess accountability by:

- Comparing actual financial results to budget

- Assessing financial condition and results of operations

- Assisting in determining compliance with finance-related laws, rules, and regulations

- Assisting in evaluating operating efficiency and effectiveness

3.2.5 Accountability and Interperiod Equity

Accountability is the cornerstone of governmental financial reporting. Interperiod equity, or the concept of balancing the budget on an annual basis, is a significant part of accountability.

- **Accountability**

  - Governments provide financial information to the citizenry to justify the raising of resources and demonstrate the purposes for which they are used.

  - Financial reporting plays a major role in fulfilling a government's duty to be publicly accountable.

  - Minimum disclosure includes whether the government operated within the legal constraints imposed by the citizens.

- **Interperiod Equity**

  - Balanced budgets contribute to interperiod equity by enabling a government to meet its commitment to live within its means.

  - Financial reporting should help users assess whether current year revenues are sufficient to pay for the services provided that year and whether future taxpayers will be required to assume burdens for services previously provided.

3.2.6 Characteristics of Information in Governmental Financial Reports

Financial information included in governmental financial reports should have the following characteristics:

- **Understandability**

  Information in financial reports should be expressed as simply as possible so the reports can be understood by individuals who may not have detailed knowledge of accounting principles.

- **Reliability**

  Reports should be verifiable and free from bias and should faithfully represent the subject matter. Reliability does not imply precision or certainty.

- **Relevance**

  Information provided should have a close logical relationship to the purpose for which it is needed. Relevance implies reported information will make a difference to users.

- **Timeliness**

  Reported information should be issued in time to have an effect on decisions. Timeliness may supersede absolute precision or detail.

■ **Consistency**

The accounting principles used to prepare financial reports should not change year over year. Accounting principles relate to such issues as transaction valuation, basis of accounting, and the determination of the financial reporting entity.

■ **Comparability**

Financial reports should be comparable. Differences between financial reports should be due to substantive differences in underlying transactions or government structure rather than the selection of methods.

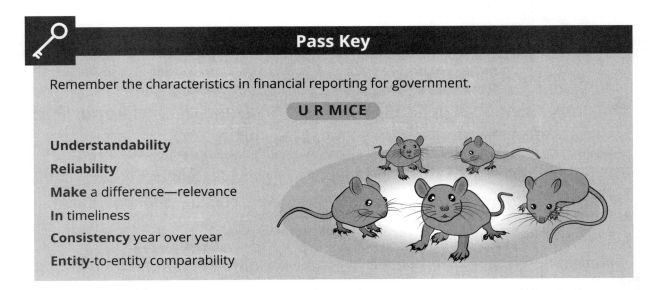

Pass Key

Remember the characteristics in financial reporting for government.

U R MICE

Understandability

Reliability

Make a difference—relevance

In timeliness

Consistency year over year

Entity-to-entity comparability

3.2.7 Limitations on Governmental Financial Reporting

There are some limitations on the information that governmental financial reporting can provide, such as:

■ Financial reports use approximate measures that are often based on judgments or estimates.

■ Financial reporting is only one source of information for users and might be more useful when used in combination with other pertinent data.

■ Financial reports may not meet the diverse needs of all users.

■ Cost-benefit relationships must be considered.

3.2.8 Financial Reporting Objectives

Accountability is the primary objective of governmental financial reporting and is implicit in the following main objectives of governmental financial reporting:

■ Financial reporting should assist in fulfilling a government's duty to be publicly accountable and should enable users to assess that accountability by:

• Demonstrating whether current year revenues were sufficient to pay for current year services.

• Demonstrating budgetary and legal or contractual compliance.

• Providing information that allows users to assess service efforts, costs, and accomplishments of the governmental entity.

- Financial reporting should assist users in evaluating the operating results of the governmental entity for the year by providing information about:
  - Sources and uses of financial resources
  - How the governmental entity financed its activities and met its cash requirements
  - Whether financial position has improved or deteriorated
- Financial reporting should assist users in assessing the level of services that can be provided by the governmental entity and its ability to meet obligations as they come due by providing information about:
  - The financial position and condition of the governmental entity
  - Noncurrent physical assets available to the government and their service potential for future periods
  - Legal or contractual restrictions on resources and risks of potential loss of resources

4 Key Concepts in Governmental Accounting and Reporting

Governmental accounting generally revolves around three themes that differentiate it from commercial and not-for-profit accounting:

1. Fund structure
2. Fund accounting
3. External reporting

Pass Key

A fund is a sum of money or other resource segregated for the purpose of carrying on a specific activity or attaining certain objectives in accordance with specific regulations, restrictions, or limitations, constituting an independent fiscal and accounting entity. Each fund is a self-balancing set of accounts.

4.1 Fund Structure

GASB 34 defines a fund structure for governments. Eleven fund types are classified in the following three generic categories:

1. Governmental funds
2. Proprietary funds
3. Fiduciary funds

Fund financial statements should be separately presented for governmental, proprietary, and fiduciary funds to report additional and detailed information about the primary government. A government will establish the minimum number of funds consistent with legal requirements and sound financial administration. A government is not required to have a specific number of funds.

4.2   Fund Accounting

Fund classifications within the fund structure defined by the GASB affect the basis of accounting (when revenues and expenditures/expenses are recognized) and the measurement focus (how transactions are recognized; either assuming flow of funds or net income determination) principles associated with each fund category. The application of different accounting principles to the funds in each generic fund grouping described below provides financial data consistent with the reporting accountability objectives of each fund. This feature of governmental accounting is a frequent source of exam questions.

4.3   External Reporting

GASB 34 (as amended) establishes minimum reporting requirements to be in compliance with GAAP. Reporting requirements include both fund-based and government-wide financial statement presentations supported by notes to the financial statements and a variety of required supplementary information.

Presentation of a reconciliation of fund financial statements to government-wide financial statements is also required.

NOTES

1 Fund Structure

A governmental entity, although a single entity, consists of a number of separate funds. Funds are generally classified into three generic categories:

- Governmental funds
- Proprietary funds
- Fiduciary funds

1.1 Governmental Funds

1.1.1 Fund Accounting

Governmental funds are accounted for using the:

- Modified accrual basis of accounting
- Current financial resources measurement focus

The source, use, and balance of the government's current financial resources and the related current liabilities are accounted for through the use of governmental funds. Governmental funds often have a budgetary focus, and seek to measure financial position and the changes therein. The focus of financial reporting is on the *statement of revenues, expenditures, and changes in fund balance*, which is used to demonstrate the use of resources in compliance with laws, rules, and regulations. Accounts are of a "current" nature; thus, the *balance sheet* of governmental funds contains no fixed asset or long-term debt accounts.

1.1.2 Fund Types

Governmental fund types include the following:

- **General Fund:** The *general fund* is set up to account for the ordinary operations of a governmental unit that is financed from taxes and other general revenues. All transactions not accounted for in other funds are accounted for here.

- **Special Revenue Funds:** *Special revenue funds* are set up to account for revenues from specific taxes or other earmarked sources that (by law) are restricted or committed to finance particular activities of government.

- **Debt Service Funds:** *Debt service funds* are set up to account for the accumulation of resources and the payment of interest and principal on all "general obligation debt," other than that serviced by enterprise funds or by special assessments in another fund. Resources of the fund are restricted, committed, or assigned to debt service expenditures.

- **Capital Projects Funds:** *Capital projects funds* are set up to account for resources restricted, committed, or assigned for the acquisition or construction of major capital assets by a governmental unit, except those projects financed by an enterprise fund.

- **Permanent Fund:** *Permanent funds* are used to report resources that are legally restricted to the extent that income, and not principal, may be used for purposes supporting the reporting government's programs (i.e., for the benefit of the public).

Balance Sheet
Current assets + Deferred outflows
Current liabilities + Deferred inflows of resources + Fund balance
Total current liabilities, deferred inflows of resources, and fund balances

Statement of Revenues, Expenditures, and Changes in Fund Balance
Revenues
< Expenditures >
Other financing sources < uses >
Net change in fund balance

1.2   Proprietary Funds

1.2.1   Fund Accounting

Proprietary funds account for business-type activities, and their accounting is similar to commercial accounting. Proprietary funds should be accounted for using the:

- Full accrual basis of accounting
- Economic resources measurement focus

1.2.2   Fund Types

Proprietary funds include:

- **Internal Service Funds:** *Internal service funds* are set up to account for goods and services provided by designated departments on a cost-reimbursement fee basis to other departments and agencies within a single governmental unit or to other governmental units. Customers of the internal service fund are primarily internal.

Illustration 1   Internal Service Funds
A central motor pool or building maintenance department may be accounted for with an internal service fund.

- **Enterprise Funds:** *Enterprise funds* are set up to account for the acquisition and operation of governmental facilities and services that are intended to be primarily (more than 50 percent) self-supported by user charges. Customers of the enterprise fund are primarily external.

Illustration 2   Enterprise Funds
Enterprise funds are often used for utilities (water and sewer), airports, and transit systems.

Enterprise funds are required when any one of three criteria is met:

- The activity of the fund is financed by debt secured by a pledge of fee revenue;
- Laws require collection fees adequate to recover costs; or
- Pricing policies are established to produce fees to recover costs.

Statement of Net Position	Statement of Revenues, Expenses, and Changes in Fund Net Position
All assets + Deferred outflows of resources	Operating revenue
< All liabilities + Deferred inflows of resources >	< Operating expenses >
Net position	Nonoperating revenue < expenses >
	Change in net position

1.3 Fiduciary (Trust) Funds

1.3.1 Fund Accounting

Fiduciary funds account for assets controlled by a government in the capacity of a trust on behalf of beneficiaries with whom a beneficiary relationship exists. Financial statements of fiduciary funds should generally be accounted for using the:

▪ Full accrual basis of accounting

▪ Economic resources measurement focus.

1.3.2 Fund Types

Fiduciary funds include:

▪ **Custodial Funds**

Custodial funds usually account for resources in temporary custody of the governmental unit (e.g., taxes collected for another governmental entity) and any fiduciary activities that are not required to be reported in other fiduciary fund classifications.

▪ **Investment Trust Funds**

Investment trust funds account for external investment pools.

▪ **Private Purpose Trust Funds**

Private purpose trust funds are used for activities not properly accounted for either as pension or investment trust funds, in which assets are dedicated to providing benefits to recipients in accordance with benefit terms and assets are legally protected from creditors of the government.

▪ **Pension (and Other Employee Benefit) Trust Funds**

Pension trust funds account for resources of defined benefit plans, defined contribution plans, post-employment benefit plans, and other long-term employee benefit plans.

Statement of Fiduciary Net Position	Statement of Changes in Fiduciary Net Position
All assets + Deferred outflows of resources	Additions
< All liabilities + Deferred inflows of resources >	< Deductions >
Net position	Change in net position

2 Fund Accounting

The measurement focus and basis of accounting used in government-wide and fund financial presentations facilitate the reporting of accountability objectives unique to each fund and to the government-wide presentation. The measurement focus of a fund is complemented by the basis of accounting used.

- The modified accrual basis of accounting is used with the current financial resources measurement focus.

- The accrual basis of accounting is used with the economic resources measurement focus.

2.1 Measurement Focus

Measurement focus determines the items to be reported on the balance sheet.

2.1.1 Current Financial Resources (GRaSPP)

Under the current financial resources measurement focus, fund balance is a measure of available, spendable, or appropriable resources. Only current assets and current liabilities are included on the balance sheet.

- No fixed assets are reported.

- No non-current liabilities are reported.

Pass Key

Adding fixed assets excluded from governmental fund financial statements and subtracting non-current liabilities (also excluded) are two of the most significant reconciling items between governmental funds and government-wide financial statements.

2.1.2 Economic Resources (SE-CIPPOE and Government-wide)

Under the economic resources measurement focus, financial reporting centers on the costs of services and the efficiency and effectiveness with which invested capital has been used. All assets and all liabilities (current or non-current) are included on the balance sheet, including certain transactions classified as deferred outflows/inflows of resources. Net position is analyzed and reported in three components: net investment in capital assets, restricted (distinguishing between major categories of external restrictions), and unrestricted.

- Fixed assets are reported.

- Non-current liabilities are reported.

2.2 Basis of Accounting

The basis of accounting determines when revenues and expenditures or expenses are recognized and reported in the financial statements.

2.2.1 Modified Accrual (GRaSPP)

The modified accrual basis of accounting is used with the current financial resources measurement focus. It is a blend of accrual and cash basis accounting concepts.

- Revenue is recognized when measurable and available to finance the expenditures of the current period. The only difference between the timing of revenue recognition under the modified accrual and full accrual basis of accounting is the manner in which each basis defines the word *available*.

    - Available, under modified accrual, means collectible within the current period or soon enough thereafter to be used to pay liabilities in the current period (generally within 60 days after year-end).

    - Measurable means quantifiable in monetary terms.

- Expenditures are generally recorded when the related fund liability is incurred, with some exceptions. Most notably, debt service expenditures (both principal and interest) are not recognized until either due or paid. Incurred but unpaid debt service expenditures are not accrued.

Pass Key

Addition of accrual basis revenues in excess of modified accrual revenues along with subtraction of accrued interest expenses not recognized in governmental financial statements are frequent reconciling items between the governmental fund financial statements and the government-wide financial statements.

2.2.2 Full Accrual (SE-CIPPOE and Government-wide)

The *full accrual* basis of accounting is used with the economic resources measurement focus. It is identical to the accrual basis used in commercial enterprises.

- Revenue is recognized when earned.

- Expenses are recognized when incurred.

2.3   Fund Accounting Summary

2.3.1 Modified Accrual Basis of Accounting and Current Financial Resources Measurement Focus

Modified accrual basis of accounting and current financial resources measurement focus are used in connection with the governmental funds (**GRaSPP**).

- **General**
- Special **Revenue**

and

- Debt **Service**
- Capital **Projects**
- **Permanent**

2.3.2   Economic Resources Measurement Focus and Full Accrual Basis of Accounting

The economic resources measurement focus and full accrual basis of accounting is used for both the government-wide financial statements as well as the fund presentations of the fiduciary and proprietary funds (**SE-CIPPOE**).

- **Service** (internal)
- **Enterprise**
- **Custodial**
- **Investment** trust
- **Private** purpose trust
- **Pension** (and **Other Employee** benefit) trust

Pass Key

To help remember the differences in focus and accounting, use the following:

Governmental funds are **MAC-GRaSPP**	Proprietary and fiduciary funds **SCARE**
Modified	**SE**
Accrual accounting	**CIPPOE**
Current financial resources measurement focus	**Accrual** accounting
GRaSPP	**Record** non-current assets and liabilities
	Economic resources measurement focus
